T0305415

Business Rhetoric in German Novels

Studies in German Literature, Linguistics, and Culture

Business Rhetoric in German Novels

From *Buddenbrooks* to the Global Corporation

Ernest Schonfield

CAMDEN HOUSE

Rochester, New York

First published 2018
by Camden House

Camden House is an imprint of Boydell & Brewer Inc.
668 Mt. Hope Avenue, Rochester, NY 14620, USA
www.camden-house.com
and of Boydell & Brewer Limited
PO Box 9, Woodbridge, Suffolk IP12 3DF, UK
www.boydellandbrewer.com

ISBN-13: 978-1-57113-983-2
ISBN-10: 1-57113-983-4

Library of Congress Cataloging-in-Publication Data

CIP data is available from the Library of Congress.

This publication is printed on acid-free paper.
Printed in the United States of America.

To my parents, Susan and Victor Schonfield

Contents

Acknowledgments

T HE PUBLICATION SUBSIDY for this book was generously provided by the Royal Society of Edinburgh (RSE), funded by the Scottish government, through an Arts & Humanities Network Award (Network for Oratory and Politics, 2015–17). I should add that the opinions expressed in this book are solely my own; they do not purport to reflect in any way the views of the RSE or the Scottish government. I am very grateful to my colleagues in the School of Modern Languages and Cultures in Glasgow for their support. I am grateful also to my colleagues in the Network for Oratory and Politics for some stimulating interdisciplinary discussions, particularly Henriette van der Blom, Gesine Manuwald, and Rob Goodman. Earlier versions of chapter 4 appeared as "The Rhetoric of Business in Brecht's *Dreigroschenroman*" in *German Life and Letters* 69, no. 2 (2016): 173–91, and as "Sprachgebrauch als Waffe und Tarnung im 'Dreigroschenroman'" in *Über Brechts Romane*, edited by Christian Hippe (Berlin: Verbrecher Verlag, 2015), 107–20; many thanks to the editors and publishers of these volumes for giving permission to include a revised version here. For their invaluable and perceptive comments on the manuscript, I would particularly like to thank Jim Walker, Elizabeth Boa, and the two anonymous referees for Camden House. I am also very grateful to Martin Swales, who read chapters 1 and 2; Astrid Köhler, who read chapter 6; Ray Stokes, who read chapter 7; and Daniel Steuer, who read chapter 9. Thanks are also due to Phil Dematteis at Camden House for his careful copyediting. Any mistakes are, of course, my own. Thanks also to my partner, Anne-Marie, and our daughters, Nina and Milly, for their patience, support, and sense of humor.

Abbreviations

B   Thomas Mann. *Buddenbrooks: Verfall einer Familie*. Große kommentierte Frankfurter Ausgabe, vol. 1.1. Edited by Eckhard Heftrich. Frankfurt am Main: S. Fischer, 2002.

BFA   Bertolt Brecht. *Werke: Große kommentierte Berliner und Frankfurter Ausgabe*. Edited by Werner Hecht, Jan Knopf, Werner Mittenzwei, and Klaus-Detlef Müller. 31 vols. Berlin: Suhrkamp, 1989–98.

Bu   Thomas Mann. *Buddenbrooks: The Decline of a Family*. Translated by John E. Woods. New York: Everyman's Library/Alfred A. Knopf, 1994.

D   Bertolt Brecht. *Dreigroschenroman*. Frankfurt am Main: Suhrkamp, 1991.

DI   Hermann Kant. *Das Impressum* [1972]. Berlin: Rütten & Loening, 1975.

DS   Philipp Schönthaler. *Das Schiff das singend zieht auf seiner Bahn*. Berlin: Matthes & Seitz, 2013.

GuI   Ingeborg Bachmann. *Wir müssen wahre Sätze finden: Gespräche und Interviews*. Edited by Christine Koschel and Inge von Weidenbaum. Munich: Piper, 1991.

Kb   Gabriele Tergit. *Käsebier erobert den Kurfürstendamm*. Edited by Nicole Henneberg. Frankfurt am Main: Schöffling, 2016.

KS   Ingeborg Bachmann. *Kritische Schriften*. Edited by Monika Albrecht and Dirk Göttsche. Munich: Piper, 2005.

LS   Heinrich Mann. *The Loyal Subject*. Edited by Helmut Peitsch. Translated by Ernest Boyd and Daniel Theisen. New York: Continuum, 2006.

M   Ingeborg Bachmann. *Malina*. Frankfurt am Main: Suhrkamp, 1980.

Ma   Ingeborg Bachmann. *Malina*. Translated by Philip Boehm. New York: Holmes & Meier, 1990.

TN   Bertolt Brecht. *Threepenny Novel*. Translated by Desmond I. Vesey. Harmondsworth, UK: Penguin, 1961.

TP   Ingeborg Bachmann. *"Todesarten"-Projekt: Kritische Ausgabe*. Edited by Monika Albrecht and Dirk Göttsche. 4 vols. Munich: Piper, 2005.

U   Heinrich Mann. *Der Untertan*. Edited by Peter-Paul Schneider. Studienausgabe in Einzelbänden. Frankfurt am Main: Fischer, 2001.

USW Friedrich Christian Delius. *Wir Unternehmer. Unsere Siemens-Welt. Einige Argumente zur Verteidigung der Gemüseesser. Satiren. Werkausgabe in Einzelbänden.* Reinbek bei Hamburg: Rowohlt, 2014.

WNS Kathrin Röggla. *We Never Sleep.* Translated by Rebecca Thomas. Studies in Austrian Literature, Culture and Thought. Riverside, CA: Ariadne Press, 2009.

wsn Kathrin Röggla. *wir schlafen nicht.* Frankfurt am Main: Fischer, 2004.

Introduction

parler, c'est agir
[to speak is to act]
—Abbé d'Aubignac,
La Pratique du théâtre

SINCE THE TURN of the millennium, there has been extensive research on the representation of economic processes in German-language literature.[1] The interdisciplinary dialogue between literary studies and economics was pioneered in the 1980s by the economic historian Deirdre N. McCloskey, who argued that economic science has a "literary character" and that literary criticism can offer economists "a model for self-understanding."[2] For McCloskey, seeing economics as "rhetorical" does not mean "abandoning mathematics"; it means advocating "the study of how economists actually persuade each other and the world."[3] Adopting a similar position, Arjo Klamer describes the market as a conversation and views the entrepreneur as a "rhetor"—a person whose business it is to persuade or convince.[4] Such interdisciplinary approaches are sometimes known as "New Economic Criticism," after two conferences held in the 1990s in the USA.[5] Sometimes research on literature and economics is framed in terms of a particular literary genre, e.g., the Bildungsroman, sometimes in terms of a particular economic category, such as labor, the gift, or inflation.[6] Occasionally, research focuses on the literary marketplace itself.[7] Richard T. Gray's study *Money Matters* (2008) argues that German literature is deeply implicated in the economic discourse of its time.[8] Gray focuses on the period around 1800, however, and his emphasis on concepts of value and exchange means that he has little to say about performative aspects of business, which is the focus of interest here. The only recent study to consider performance in novels about business is by Christian Kremer, who draws on Judith Butler.[9] Kremer recognizes that doing business is a kind of performance, but he does not connect this notion with classical oratory and rhetoric, which have informed business practice and legal practice for over two thousand years. This is where this present study comes in.

This book explores the representation of business rhetoric in nine German-language novels published between 1901 and 2013. The novels have been chosen for their literary quality and because they are particularly attentive both to the rhetorical function of language in business and to the performative aspects of business itself. The language of business, broadly understood, features in most of the novels examined, which are nearly all about businesspeople, journalists, ghostwriters, and/or management consultants. The fundamental reference point for this book is the classical tradition of rhetoric, because this tradition enables speech acts to be understood as performative interventions in general debates (political, economic) and in actual business practices. The focus here is not on economic theory or history in literature but on the literary representation of rhetoric and persuasion as essential aspects of any business activity. Modern business, like ancient oratory, relies on the ability to persuade people to do deals. Rhetoric aims at agreement and consensus, which are also the requirements for any business transaction. People only sign contracts if they are persuaded that it is in their interest to do so. While contexts and communications media have changed radically over the last two thousand years, the fundamental techniques of persuasion have remained remarkably consistent since they were first formulated in antiquity by Aristotle and Cicero. These writers regarded the persuasive use of language as closely connected to the exercise of political and economic control. In other words, what sets this book apart from other studies is its focus on the persuasive and performative aspects of literary depictions of economic activity.

Human beings use words performatively to persuade their audiences, and, in doing so, reshape and renegotiate the audiences' lived "reality." Instead of regarding language as something separate from "reality," this book considers language as an essential component of it. Instead of focusing on the "facts" of business, it explores literary texts that reveal how so-called facts are framed and selected in order to pursue specific interests. It argues that there is an agenda behind every statement of "fact" (usually, a business agenda). If the idea of an interdisciplinary dialogue between literature and economics is to be taken seriously, then this has consequences for both sides. Our understanding of each should be revised in the light of the other. As McCloskey points out: "Economists have begun to see that their talk is rhetorical . . . in the Aristotelian sense of honest argument directed at an audience."[10] For example, *value* is a central term in both economics and the humanities: objects have moral, aesthetic, and cultural value as well as monetary value. Economic values always exist in relation to other modes of cultural valuation.[11]

The arts and humanities can shed light on actual economic practices, too. While economic theory focuses on concepts and categories such as prices and production, supply and demand, and imports and exports, economic practice often relies heavily on communication and publicity. If training in classical rhetoric is obligatory for lawyers, and recommended for politicians, then its relevance for business is obvious. Indeed, Aristotle's theory of rhetoric is often cited in contemporary textbooks of public relations and business communication.[12] Modern sales pitches often rely on classical techniques, including *captatio benevolentiae* (capturing the good-will of the audience) and *dissimulatio artis* (concealing the art).[13]

Rhetoric and Oratory: The Classical Tradition

What do literature, politics, and economic activity all have in common? Rhetoric, the use of language to persuade. Rhetoric has been a required field of study for poets, politicians, lawyers, priests, merchants, and administrators from Greek and Roman antiquity until today. Aristotle's *Rhetoric* defines rhetoric as "the faculty of observing in any given case the available means of persuasion."[14] In other words, rhetoric teaches you how to persuade people to do what you want. According to Aristotle, there are three "modes of persuasion": the character of the speaker (which he calls *ethos*), the emotions of the audience (*pathos*), and, finally, the logical content of the words (*logos*).[15] Thus for Aristotle, rational argument (*logos*) is only the third aspect of persuasion; the most powerful form of persuasion is the personality (*ethos*) projected by the speaker. Note that when Aristotle uses the word *ethos*, he is not referring to the speaker's "guiding beliefs" but to the audience's *perception* of the speaker's character. This perception can be affected by vocal delivery, gestures, and the style of performance, and so these are essential aspects of persuasion. Understanding this alerts us to the performative dimension of persuasion. Aristotle also divides rhetoric into three genres: deliberative (political), forensic (legal), and epideictic (ceremonial oratory of display).[16] Political speech is about making decisions; it "urges us either to do or not to do something."[17] This type of rhetoric applies to economic decisions, as well. Aristotle subordinates economic activity to political activity; for him, "the human being by nature is a political animal" (*zoōn politikon*).[18] As Joseph Vogl has shown, however, Aristotle's attempt to separate politics and economics is unsuccessful; as a result, his discussion of *chrematistics* (the art of getting rich) in the first book of his *Politics* is ambivalent.[19] Aristotle himself preferred knowledge to wealth. In the second book of *Rhetoric* he observes: "In a word, the type of character produced by wealth is that of a prosperous fool."[20] Even so, Aristotle's *Rhetoric* does not distinguish clearly between politics and economics—for example, when he states: "The main matters on which all men deliberate and on which political speakers make speeches are some five in number: ways and means, war and peace, national defense, imports and exports, and legislation."[21] If politics, for Aristotle, includes "ways and means" and "imports and exports," then this suggests that he understands politics and economics as interrelated activities. Rhetoric is just as essential to economic activity as it is to politics. This view is confirmed by the Roman politician and lawyer Marcus Tullius Cicero (106–43 BC), who admits that merchants often conceal the flaws in the merchandise they are trying to sell. While Cicero recognizes the element of performance in business, however, he also calls for dishonest business practices to be punished by law: in this way he seeks to distinguish between permissible exaggeration and fraud.[22] Throughout the Middle Ages and the early modern period, rhetoric and oratory were grounded in the classical tradition. For many centuries, textbooks of rhetoric such as Quintilian's *Institutio Oratoria* (95 AD; *Institutes of Oratory*) were used primarily as "handbooks of ruling-class power"; as Terry Eagleton puts it, these manuals were not objects for aesthetic contemplation but "ideological weapons whose practical deployment was to be learnt."[23]

The Enlightenment Critique of Rhetoric

For seventeenth-century authors such as the French classical tragedian Racine and the baroque German dramatists Gryphius and Lohenstein, with their concept of *homo eloquens*, the world was a stage upon which every human being had to play a speaking part.[24] Renaissance humanists based their idea of *scientia civilis* (civil science) on Cicero's argument at the beginning of *De inventione* (*On Invention*) that "many cities have been established . . . by deliberate wisdom much assisted and facilitated by eloquence."[25] Here, Cicero implies that rhetorical training in eloquence is needed in order to complement *ratio* (wisdom, reason). The primacy of rhetoric in humanist education was, however, overthrown by the founders of modern political science, Thomas Hobbes, John Locke, and Jean-Jacques Rousseau. In *The Elements of Law Natural and Politic* (1640) Hobbes said that rhetoric has no part to play in any type of science.[26] Another decisive step toward the exclusion of rhetoric from modern economics was taken when the French philosopher Claude Adrien Helvétius (1715–71) published *De l'esprit* (1758; "On the Mind"), claiming that pleasure and pain are the sole basic determinants of human motivation.[27] Although Adam Smith gave some lectures on rhetoric in the early 1750s, his intellectual interests lay elsewhere. Like Helvétius, Smith's *Theory of Moral Sentiments* (1759) presents people as driven by self-interest, but with the caveat that this can be moderated by sympathy and compassion. Smith extended this theory in *An Inquiry into the Nature and Causes of the Wealth of Nations* (1776). The works of Smith and Helvétius inaugurated the concept of a new, "realistic" type of human being: the *homo economicus*.[28] For Smith, the chief mode of social intercourse was no longer discursive and rhetorical but financial. While rhetoric was still widely taught in the late eighteenth century, as evidenced by Hugh Blair's best-selling *Lectures on Rhetoric and Belles Lettres* (1783) and Thomas Sheridan's *Lectures on Elocution* (1762), its prestige was starting to wane. Immanuel Kant dismissed rhetoric in *Kritik der Urtheilskraft* (1790; *Critique of Judgment*), and by the nineteenth century the status of rhetoric suffered because it was an art as opposed to a science and, worse still, an art of persuasion.[29] The positivism of the nineteenth century was hostile to rhetoric, and this attitude was exemplified by Theodor Mommsen's character assassination of Cicero himself in his three-volume *Römische Geschichte* (1854–56; *The History of Rome*). Although classical rhetoric declined in status throughout the nineteenth century, it continued to inform parliamentary oratory in Britain, France, and the US. Rhetoric also remained on the syllabi of many universities, particularly in Germany, France, and the USA, although it tended to exist on the intellectual margins. Despite the relegation of rhetoric to a relatively marginal status, its fortunes gradually began to revive in the late nineteenth century, assisted by the reception of Jacob Burckhardt and Friedrich Nietzsche.[30]

Modernism and *Sprachkritik*

The modernist revival of classical rhetoric owes much to Friedrich Nietzsche, who was a classical scholar.[31] Nietzsche's discussions of rhetoric formed the basis of the modernist tradition of *Sprachkritik* (language criticism), which was inaugurated by Fritz Mauthner in his *Beiträge zur Kritik der Sprache* (1901–2; *Contributions to the Critique of Language*).[32] The language criticism of Nietzsche, Mauthner, and Karl Kraus serves as an important point of reference for several authors in this present study, particularly Bertolt Brecht, Ingeborg Bachmann, Friedrich Christian Delius, and Kathrin Röggla. In the famous essay "Ueber Wahrheit und Lüge im aussermoralischen Sinne" (written 1873, published 1903; "On Truth and Lies in a Nonmoral Sense") Nietzsche states that truth is "ein bewegliches Heer von Metaphern" (a mobile army of metaphors) and other rhetorical devices.[33] Nietzsche's conception of language as a martial implement, loaded with the intent to persuade, owes much to classical theorists of rhetoric such as Cicero and Quintilian.[34] For example, in *Jenseits von Gut und Böse* (1886; *Beyond Good and Evil*) Nietzsche criticizes German authors for their ignorance of the classical view of language as something that should be spoken aloud and performed.[35] Many authors associated with Sprachkritik are Austrian—e.g., the critic Karl Kraus—and, perhaps in consequence, contributions by German authors (Brecht, Delius) have often gone unnoticed. German explorations of business rhetoric around 1930 include Walter Benjamin's radio play about how to ask your boss for a raise[36] and Ernst Bloch's analysis of Latin business terms such as "*Substanz*" (substance) and "*Bonität*" (credit rating).[37]

The Reappraisal of Rhetoric in
the Late Twentieth Century

By the mid-twentieth century, the relevance of rhetoric and oratory for advertising and political propaganda was increasingly obvious. Modern communications media such as the newspaper and the radio had extended the reach of political oratory, with both impressive and catastrophic results. Modern demagogues provoked a new interest in the arts of persuasion and propaganda. Kenneth Burke's "The Rhetoric of Hitler's 'Battle'" (1939) argued that Adolf Hitler provided "a noneconomic interpretation of economic ills," deflecting the attention of his audience away from economic factors, for example, "by attacking 'Jew finance' instead of *finance*."[38] The American psychologist Carl I. Hovland (1912–61) used Aristotelian rhetoric as a starting point for his own studies of the role of personality in persuasion.[39] In 1951 Marshall McLuhan delivered an incisive analysis of modern advertising, observing that "Today it is not the classroom nor the classics which are the repositories of models of eloquence, but the ad agencies."[40] Rhetoric does not consider linguistic formulation alone, however. Under the heading of oratory, rhetoric also addresses how public speakers present themselves to the audience, paying close attention to their gestures and their vocal delivery. These performative and theatrical aspects of oratory and rhetoric are particularly relevant for the works of the American sociologist Erving Goffman (1922–82), who observed the performance of character in the modern world in *The Presentation of Self in Everyday Life* (1956; revised edition, 1959) and *Stigma* (1963).[41] Goffman's account of how our lives are performed and managed with reference to behavioral norms anticipated Judith Butler's theory of performativity by several decades. Goffman's analysis is particularly relevant for this book because he sheds light on the performative aspect of doing business. Goffman's work reminds us that rhetoric (and particularly business rhetoric) is not just about using the right words; it is also about projecting the correct persona, making the proper gestures, and adopting the right tone of voice. Goffman describes numerous roles that are often encountered in business life, including the "go-between" who mediates between different groups, the "colleague" who has to put on the same kind of performance as his or her peers, and the "service specialist" who is an expert "in the construction, repair, and maintenance of the show their clients maintain before other people."[42] For Goffman, the category of the service specialist includes a wide range of professions: dentists and hairdressers who "deal with personal front," architects and interior designers who "specialize in settings," and "staff economists, accountants, lawyers and researchers" who "formulate the factual element of a client's verbal display, that is, his team's argument-line or intellectual position."[43] In this way, Goffman delivers a groundbreaking analysis of the importance of image maintenance in modern business.

Although Goffman does not reference Aristotle explicitly, his discussion of "impression management" has close affinities with Aristotle's discussion of the need for the speaker to project the correct character (*ethos*).[44] In this way, Goffman's work suggests the relevance of classical rhetoric to a modern business context, showing that persuasion is all about projecting the right image. Businesspeople have to operate within the expected boundaries of their roles: in order to be taken seriously, they have to present themselves in accordance with certain professional and social norms.

European philosophers also began to rediscover the socio-political significance of rhetoric. In France, Chaim Perelman and Lucie Olbrechts-Tyteca sought to ground argumentative practice in considerations of value in their *New Rhetoric* (1969). In doing so, they intended to encourage more informed debate in the fields of law, politics, ethics, and journalism.[45] In the seventies and eighties Louis Althusser examined the workings of ideological discourse in social institutions, which he regarded as instrumental in the formation of the subject. Michel Foucault built on this analysis, showing how discourses operate to obscure argument in the interests of domination. In West Germany, Jürgen Habermas developed his theory of communicative rationality, which aims at consensual agreement between well-informed dialogue partners. Habermas's view of dialogue has affinities with the rhetorical tradition, although his emphasis on consensus makes it hard for his model to accommodate difference, as George Myerson has shown.[46] These European authors had little to say about rhetoric in a commercial context, but they affirmed the wider political significance of rhetoric for modern societies in general.

The importance of rhetoric for liberal democracy is also stressed by the West German philosopher Hans Blumenberg (1920–96), a key figure in the revival of the study of rhetoric in the late twentieth century. It is worth summarizing some of his arguments here. Blumenberg argues that metaphysics is so concerned with first causes and final ends that it neglects the question of means.[47] In contrast to metaphysics, rhetoric sees "consensus" as the basis for a concept of what is "real."[48] For Blumenberg, the great virtue of rhetoric is that it is always provisional: it operates in the absence of conclusive evidence.[49] He argues that human beings have learned to survive by relating to reality through metaphors.[50] Rhetoric is practically useful because it changes and modifies human practice: it guides new forms of action by replacing one traditional practice with another.[51] Like Goffman, Blumenberg emphasizes the constitutive element of performance in social roles, arguing that "Lebenkönnen und Sich-eine-Rolle-definieren sind identisch" (being able to live and defining a role for oneself are identical).[52] He conceives rhetoric as a system for soliciting mandates for action and for effecting and defending a specific conception of the self.[53] Rhetoric comes into play when we are compelled to act; it does not deal with facts but with expectations.[54]

Blumenberg admits that people are susceptible to being influenced by rhetoric, but he argues that "The theory of rhetoric has always exposed people's
intentions of taking advantage of these 'weaknesses of men,' at the same
time that it has served them."[55] Thus, while Blumenberg concedes the dangerous potential of rhetoric, he sees rhetoric as a constitutive element of
human self-understanding: we all live by metaphors, whether we like it or
not. Blumenberg's insights into the cognitive function of metaphor have
been developed by George Lakoff and Mark Johnson in *Metaphors We Live
By* (1980).[56] More recently, Katrin Kohl has also considered how metaphor
structures our communication and thought.[57] If we live by metaphors, then
it makes sense to study rhetoric so that we can make more informed decisions about which metaphors we choose to live by.

The work of Habermas and Blumenberg initiated a turn toward a
discursive model of the social sciences. This approach has been exemplified
in Britain by social psychologist Michael Billig, a founder of the Discourse
and Rhetoric Group (DARG) at Loughborough University, which examines the role of language in society. Billig explains that our understanding
of social interaction is dominated by two metaphors in particular: the
metaphor of "life as theater" and the metaphor of "life as a game."[58] Billig,
however, criticizes both of these metaphors. He argues that the theatrical
metaphor "underestimates the argumentative aspects of social life"[59] and
that the game metaphor ignores the fundamental role of argument in shaping and changing the rules of the game.[60] For Billig, then, argument is the
constitutive element in social interaction and in human thought itself,
which, for him, proceeds like an "internal argument."[61] He points out that
while Lakoff and Johnson focus on metaphor, it is also important to consider the function of metonymy in human cognition.[62] Billig's approach to
rhetoric is particularly relevant for the methodology of this book because
he emphasizes that rhetoric is, above all, about argumentation. Political
and economic rhetoric is shaped by the fact that there are conflicts of interest at stake. In a situation characterized by opposing positions, rhetoric
aims at consensus either by mediating between conflicting positions or by
obscuring them and denying that they exist. In this book the literary analysis is informed by an awareness of Blumenberg's and Billig's work on the
social function of rhetoric and, in particular, on rhetoric's potential either
to restrict debate or to open it up.

Modern Economic Rhetoric

So far, this introduction has focused on the discipline of rhetoric, while
suggesting its relevance for political and business practice because it foregrounds persuasion and performance. Before we discuss business rhetoric
in a specifically German context, however, it seems appropriate to make

some brief observations about modern economic theory in general and its relationship to rhetoric. Ha-Joon Chang's *Economics: The User's Guide* (2014) contains an inserted booklet titled "The Little Blue Book: Five things they don't tell you about economics." The five points are as follows:

1. 95% of economics is common sense
2. Economics is not a science
3. Economics is politics
4. Never trust an economist
5. Economics is too important to be left to the experts[63]

For the purposes of this present study, the third point is particularly relevant. If economics is a form of politics, however, then any attempt to separate economics and politics is itself a political move. This viewpoint is shared by Ulrich Beck, who observes that the project of a market economy has always been political.[64] It follows that if economics is a form of political process, it must also involve the practice of rhetoric. This line of thought has been developed by the economic historian Keith Tribe, who argues that the history of economics must include the history of the word "economics" itself and the rhetorical uses to which it has been put. Tribe therefore begins with an investigation of the word "economy" and how its meaning has shifted from antiquity to the later twentieth century.[65] He then proceeds to analyze some foundational texts of modern economics in rhetorical terms, focusing on Adam Smith's account of international trade. A close reading of books 3 and 4 of the *Wealth of Nations* suggests that Smith's understanding of free trade is linked to "the consideration of the disposition of capital and labor in the domestic economy."[66] According to Tribe's interpretation, Smith does not promote free trade as an absolute principle in order to generate wealth but as a means to rearrange capital and labor within the domestic economy, suggesting that individual accumulation of profit should be balanced by the needs of the domestic economy. For Tribe, the nineteenth-century reception of Smith's work has "effaced" the complexities of Smith's thought on the advantages and disadvantages of international trade.[67] Tribe's approach places emphasis upon the analysis of economic language as a philological enterprise. In order to guard against a reductive approach to economic thought, Tribe asks us to use philological techniques and to regard an economic treatise as a nuanced, structured, sequential performance.

An analysis of modern economic theory along rhetorical lines would go well beyond the scope of this book.[68] As the outline of Tribe's analysis indicates, however, economic discussions need a sense of historicity as well as a sense of close textual detail. When weighing up the advantages and disadvantages of an economic theory, it is advisable to read the small print. Nowadays, much economic debate is seen in terms of a clash between the theories of Friedrich Hayek and John Maynard Keynes, who represent two different versions of liberalism.[69] While Keynes defends the expansion of government and infrastructure in order to safeguard individual initiative, Hayek opposes the idea that the state should impose any form of "social justice," arguing that the idea of social justice is a mirage, "a quasi-religious superstition."[70] The conventional opposition between Keynes and Hayek ignores the contribution of the Hungarian-American economist Karl Polanyi (1886–1964). In *The Great Transformation* (1944) Polanyi argues that the transition to a modern free-market economy is a dogma that was planned and implemented ideologically, a utopian experiment. He points out that, historically, markets and their regulation developed side by side: the idea that a market could be self-regulating was radically new and a reversal of previous developments.[71] Until the nineteenth century the sale of land and the organization of labor were closely regulated by the feudal system and the guilds. For Polanyi, labor, land, and money are not commodities, because they are not produced for sale. Labor is "only another name for a human activity that goes with life itself"; land is "only another name for nature, which is not produced by man"; and money is "merely a token of purchasing power."[72] Because labor, land, and money comprise the means of social production, Polanyi thinks that their exchange should be regulated. According to Polanyi, if wages, rent, and interest rates are not regulated, then they will fluctuate so wildly that the social fabric will be disrupted.[73]

While Hayek regards social justice as a mirage, for Polanyi it is the idea of a "self-regulating market" that is a mirage. Polanyi's view of neoliberalism as a "utopian experiment" turns the tables on the liberal critique of socialism, which is often described in precisely these terms. A similar approach is taken by James Arnt Aune, who argues that the same criticisms that are usually applied to communism can also be applied to libertarianism. Aune's main points are as follows:

1. There is a problem with the "rationalist" desire to radically transform traditional institutions and human nature on the basis of an intellectual plan.
2. There is a need to maintain a strong commitment to "mediating institutions" that stand between the individual and the market.
3. Human motivation cannot be reduced solely to economic terms.
4. Those who revolt so intensely against the real world as to scorn such accomplishments and well-established institutions as representative democracy, unions, welfare, and public education are mentally at odds with themselves and the real world.[74]

Free-market rhetoric has been persuasive because of its skillful use of a "realist style" that denies its own discursiveness.[75] This denial is a fundamental move of contemporary neoliberalism, which, presenting itself as a science, represses its own political and ideological foundations. Much the same can be said about Marxism,[76] however, although Catherine Chaput and Joshua S. Hanan argue that Marxist rhetoric has always focused on the concept of economic justice. They see the bedrock of Marx's rhetorical project as "the attempt to establish human agency as society's future potential."[77] In this way, the contemporary clash of economic theories can also be interpreted as a clash between different rhetorical conceptions of justice as something desirable in purely individual terms (Hayek) or in terms of society as a whole (Marx, Polanyi). These debates provide an ideological context for the literary analysis that follows, because many of the novels discussed in this book adopt or interrogate such positions. With this in mind, we can now turn to Germany itself.

German Business and Economics

German identity has, for many centuries, been connected with economic activity. For example, the north German trading cities of the Hanseatic League (Bremen, Hamburg, Lübeck) and the medieval trading centers of Leipzig and Nuremberg have always been proud of their mercantile traditions. For centuries there has been a belief that German manufacturing is of high quality, and this belief is reflected in the unique concept of *Wertarbeit* (quality work). At the turn of the twentieth century this concept was updated by institutions such as the Deutscher Werkbund (German Association of Craftsmen), which were inspired by the British arts and crafts movement, in an attempt to challenge Britain's export monopoly. By the early twentieth century the trademark "Made in Germany" had already acquired considerable prestige.[78] The West German industrial design of the fifties sought to consolidate this reputation, giving form to the economic prosperity of the West German *Wirtschaftswunder* (economic miracle).[79] In the twenty-first century, too, Germany's identity is linked to its reputation as a producer and exporter of high-quality goods—it is ranked third in the list of exporting countries after China and the USA. As the German author Zafer Şenocak puts it: "Deutschland ist . . . das Land, in dem die besten Maschinen gebaut werden" (Germany is . . . the country in which the best machines are made).[80] This is less an analysis than an article of faith, or at least a statement of a widely held stereotype. While the image certainly has a solid basis in reality and is reflected in the strength of German exports, it is also a cultural construct.[81] Behind the stereotype is over a century of state investment in German manufacturing: for example, through state funding of the Fraunhofer Gesellschaft, "Europe's largest application-oriented research organization."[82] More than 70 percent of its research budget of over two billion euros comes from contracts with industry and from publicly financed research projects.[83] This organization exemplifies the extent to which the German economy relies on partnerships between the state and private companies. Indeed, research foundations themselves have an ambivalent status as institutions situated halfway between the state and the market.[84] The prestige of the German manufacturing sector is also suggested by the fact that economic debate in Germany tends to avoid the term "postindustrial society," in contrast to its popularity in the US, Britain, and France.[85] Even so, in the twenty-first century the German service sector is certainly expanding, and many German manufacturers deliver product services in addition to the products themselves.[86]

Any investigation of Germany's current economic success must go back at least as far as the nineteenth century. The liberal German economist Friedrich List (1789–1846) argued that German "infant industries" required a degree of protectionism under a strong (Prussian) state.[87] In Germany state authority has traditionally been strong. From 1949 onward West Germany embraced a political system known as a "social market economy" or "ordoliberalism," in which free-market competition is encouraged but only to the extent that it does not endanger the social order. Ordoliberalism, as theorized by Alexander Rüstow (1885–1963) and Franz Böhm (1895–1977) in the 1930s, has affinities with the *Nationalökonomie* of the Prussian economist Gustav von Schmoller (1838–1917). Schmoller, Rüstow, and John Maynard Keynes all argue in favor of state investment in industry and infrastructure.[88] Werner Abelshauser also stresses the continuity of economic institutions in Germany.[89] Another architect of West Germany's economic success was Heinrich Dinkelbach (1891–1967), who in 1946 presented the Allies with a "deconcentration plan" for German industry, which favored "smaller, economically efficient production units that oriented themselves to market signals."[90] His reorganization of West Germany's heavy industry, combined with his support for *Mitbestimmung* (codetermination between management and workers), laid the foundations for West Germany's institutional advantage.[91]

German Fiction and Business Rhetoric

Business and commerce have been major themes in German fiction ever since Goethe's *Wilhelm Meisters Lehrjahre* (1795–96; *Wilhelm Meister's Apprenticeship*), in which the protagonist joins a group of actors in an attempt to avoid becoming a merchant like his father. The figure of the bourgeois merchant is represented in the novel by Wilhelm's friend Werner, who is limited in outlook compared to the aristocratic members of the secret society Wilhelm joins at the end of the novel.[92] Bourgeois readers in search of a literary role model had to wait until Gustav

Freytag's best-selling novel *Soll und Haben* (1855; *Debit and Credit*), which has been described as "a liberal national manifesto."[93] In a famous passage of the novel, the hero, Anton Wohlfart, extols the moral beauty of business:

> Ich weiß mir gar nichts, was so interessant ist als das Geschäft. Wir leben mitten unter einem bunten Gewebe von zahllosen Fäden, die sich von einem Menschen zu dem anderen, über Land und Meer, aus einem Weltteil in den anderen spinnen. Sie hängen sich an jeden einzelnen und verbinden ihn mit der ganzen Welt.[94]

> [I know of nothing that interests me more than business. We live in the midst of a many-colored network composed of countless threads stretching from one person to another, over land and sea, from one part of the world to another. They are attached to each and every individual and they connect him with the entire world.]

Wohlfart thinks that business depends upon honesty and goodness. He even regards financial calculation and speculation as something honorable: "der ganze Handel ist doch so sehr auf die Redlichkeit anderer und auf die Güte der menschlichen Natur berechnet" (to a very great extent, all trade is calculated on the basis of the honesty of others and the goodness of human nature).[95] The bourgeois capitalist is presented as a hero precisely because he takes a well-intentioned gamble on human nature, based on the calculation that his business contacts will honor their commitments. This notion expresses the liberal ideology of the period, which relies heavily upon a conception of human nature as something fundamentally decent. As Benedict Schofield puts it, Freytag taps directly "into the hopes and aspirations of his middle-class readership."[96] Bourgeois optimism after German unification in 1871 was, however, dented by the Vienna stock market crash of 1873. Friedrich Spielhagen responded to this financial crisis in his novel *Sturmflut* (1877; *The Breaking of the Storm*),[97] while Wilhelm Raabe's novels tracked the implications of economic globalization for German culture.[98] At the end of the century Theodor Fontane's *Der Stechlin* (1897–98) registered the transition to a modern, industrialized Germany with considerable ambivalence.[99]

By the turn of the twentieth century the representation of business in German literature was becoming increasingly critical. German modernists, under the influence of Nietzsche and Marx, mocked the *Betulichkeit* (fussiness) of the German bourgeoisie. In Thomas Mann's *Buddenbrooks* (1901) the narrator directs his irony at both artists and bourgeois figures. Significantly, the fussy precision of the company secretary, Herr Marcus, is seen as embarrassing. The Expressionist dramas of Carl Sternheim and Georg Kaiser adopted an even bolder satirical approach to the entrepreneur. Alfred Döblin, in *Wadzeks Kampf mit der Dampfturbine* (1918; Wadzek's Struggle with the Steam Turbine), depicted business life as a ruthless existential struggle between rival entrepreneurs. The novel also set the scene for an exploration of the industrial and technological transformation of the economy and society; this theme was developed by a number of authors, including Ernst Toller, Franz Jung, Erik Reger, and Ernst Jünger.[100] Among modernist authors, it was in particular Thomas Mann, Heinrich Mann, Tergit, and Brecht who brought linguistic awareness to the depiction of business (see chapters 1–4 of this book).

During the Third Reich, German industry was depicted uncritically; for example, by Karl Aloys Schenzinger in his best-selling novel *Anilin* (1936; Aniline).[101] After 1945, it took a while for German authors to resume their critical depictions of business and economics. In East Germany, differentiated portrayals of economic activity only began to emerge in the sixties; for example, Erwin Strittmatter's *Ole Bienkopp* (1963) and Erik Neutsch's *Spur der Steine* (1964; Trace of Stones).[102] In West Germany, Wolfgang Koeppen, Heinrich Böll, and Martin Walser produced critical representations of the economic miracle from the early fifties onward.[103] Böll's short satire on modern business, "Es wird etwas geschehen: Eine handlungsstarke Geschichte" (1956; Something's Going to Happen: An Action-Packed Story), examines the rhetoric of business managers who keep promising to take decisive action but fail to do so. Böll indicates the emptiness of such rhetoric, but he also shows that such phrases are a conventional aspect of business life. Even if they are unaccompanied by deeds, they help to maintain an aura of professionalism. Böll also offers insights in his radio play *Zum Tee bei Dr. Borsig* (1955; Tea with Dr. Borsig), in which an industrialist offers Robert, an aspiring young author, a job in his public relations department. As Borsig explains to Robert: "wir leben im Zeitalter der Public relations" (we live in an age of public relations).[104] Creative writers are, therefore, economically useful because they can use their literary skills to produce good advertising copy, helping the market economy to function. Robert's talent enables him to join what Ralph Glasser has called "the new high priesthood" of marketing executives.[105]

This book includes an examination of three novels published in the early 1970s against a background of global political change (the Prague Spring of 1968; student movements in Western Europe and the USA). The early seventies were an economic high point before the Oil Crisis of 1973. The three novels have been selected to provide an international perspective on this crucial juncture in Cold War history: chapter 5 considers Bachmann's *Malina* (1971), which is set in neutral Austria; chapter 6 discusses Hermann Kant's novel *Das Impressum* (1972; The Imprint), which gives an insider's view of East German rhetoric; and chapter 7 examines Delius's *Unsere Siemens-Welt* (1972; Our Siemens World), a documentary satire of West German corporate rhetoric. While in the West the language of freedom was (and is) sometimes used to obscure conflicts of interests and to assert that a level playing field exists, in the Eastern bloc official rhetoric obscured social inequalities in other ways. Thus, on both sides of the Cold War divide there were discrepancies between rhetoric and social realities.

After the reunification of Germany in 1990, there was considerable debate in the media and among academics about the advantages and disadvantages of the "German model" or "Rhineland model" of business organization.[106] Ulrich Beck observed increasing structural change in the employment market in *Risikogesellschaft: Auf dem Weg in eine andere Moderne* (1986; *Risk Society: Towards a New Modernity*), and this uncertain climate was also expressed by the Swiss author Urs Widmer in his play *Top Dogs* (1997), which shows top managers struggling to cope with being laid off. At the turn of the millennium, as Germany appeared to be in an economic downturn, many English-speaking commentators delivered a pessimistic analysis of the German economy, exemplified by titles such as *The Future of the German Economy: An End to the Miracle?* (2000).[107] A more accurate prediction was, however, provided by Werner Meyer-Larsen in *Germany, Inc.: The New German Juggernaut and Its Challenge to World Business* (2000), which delivered case studies of nine blue-chip German companies in the process of breaking into the American market.[108] Meyer-Larsen's predictions about German economic expansion have proved to be correct, and by 2010 *The Economist* was running headlines acclaiming Germany as "Europe's Engine."[109] At the time of writing (December 1, 2017), the German economy is doing remarkably well.

As well as European integration, another aspect of German business shown in literature is the *Mittelstand* (midsized sector of the economy). Some of these midsize companies are now regarded as market leaders.[110] The Mittelstand has a totemic quality for postreunification Germany: a recent article in the *Frankfurter Allgemeine Zeitung* describes it as the "Rückgrat der deutschen Wirtschaft" (backbone of the German economy).[111] Although the German Mittelstand is shown in decline by Ernst-Wilhelm Händler in his novel *Wenn wir sterben* (2002; When We Die), the depiction of the Mittelstand is more optimistic in Burkhard Spinnen's *Der schwarze Grat* (2002; The Black Ridge), based on a series of interviews with Walter Lindenmaier, owner and director of a typical midsized car-component manufacturer. In an article published in 2002 Sandra Pott considers *Wenn wir sterben* and *Der schwarze Grat* as examples of the literary genre of the *Wirtschaftsroman* (business novel). She provides a useful typology of the genre, dividing it into lowbrow financial thrillers and more highbrow, reflexive fiction about business.[112] She puts *Der schwarze Grat* in the latter category because it has a reflective dimension in terms of the narrator, who reflects upon his own role within the literary marketplace.[113]

Der schwarze Grat, however, contains remarkably little reflection on the role of the business manager. The rugged mountain ridge of the book's title functions as a metaphor for the rugged entrepreneur who is the "backbone" of the German economy. He is a pioneer who steers the ship through rough waters and pilots planes over mountainous terrain. Although Spinnen includes himself in the narrative, his main function is to provide hero worship. *Der schwarze Grat* is a ripping yarn, but hardly challenging as literature. Instead, the twenty-first century is represented here by two novels that are much more revealing about German business rhetoric: Röggla's *wir schlafen nicht* (2004; *We Never Sleep*) and Schönthaler's *Das Schiff das singend zieht auf seiner Bahn* (2013; The Ship that Goes Singing on Its Way).

This present study deliberately avoids the restrictions of genre fiction, e.g., its recourse to stock figures. Defining novels about business activities in narrow generic and typographical terms excludes many important works that are too complex and challenging to conform to such definitions. The novels discussed in this book have been selected in spite of the fact that they do not conform to Pott's narrow definition of the Wirtschaftsroman. For example, Thomas Mann's *Buddenbrooks* is generally considered to be a *Familienroman* (family novel); Heinrich Mann's *Der Untertan* (1918; *The Loyal Subject*) is usually regarded as a *Zeitroman* (a novel about the period) or as a political satire; Gabriele Tergit's *Käsebier erobert den Kurfürstendamm* (1931; Käsebier Conquers the Kurfürstendamm) is typically seen as a media satire; Ingeborg Bachmann's *Malina* is unique in terms of genre but could perhaps be termed a psychological novel; Hermann Kant's *Das Impressum* is a "state-of-the-nation" novel; and Friedrich Christian Delius's *Unsere Siemens-Welt* is a work of documentary fiction. Arguably, these works are all the richer precisely because they do not conform to the genre of the Wirtschaftsroman. In this study, questions of genre are secondary; what matters is attention to the persuasive functions of language itself, and particularly in a business context.

Literary Criticism: Learning to Judge Business Rhetoric

Literary criticism helps us to judge language in use and to regard language as a mode of social action, as an intervention that is intended to produce practical results. It is a form of training that helps us "to judge political propaganda and commercial rhetoric."[114] Education can help people to weigh up the arguments of politicians and salespeople before they "buy." In focusing on nine German-language novels published between 1901 and 2013, this book does not seek to provide a general historical overview.

Instead, it presents a series of soundings at key points in German literary history. The selection of texts has been based on their literary quality and on their depiction of persuasive uses of language.[115]

Chapter 1, "Managing Appearances in Thomas Mann's *Buddenbrooks*, 1901," deals with what is unarguably the most canonical German novel about business ever written. This chapter considers the performative dimension of *Buddenbrooks*: specifically, the characters' determination to "keep up appearances." It observes the disjunction between business rhetoric and business practice in the novel, and it concludes with a parallel between classical (Ciceronian) rhetoric and Mann's use of rhetorical questions as a structuring device.

Chapter 2, "Oratory and Publicity in Heinrich Mann's *Der Untertan*, 1914/18," explores the business career of the owner of a paper factory in "Netzig," a provincial town in northern Germany. As the name "Netzig" implies, networking and publicity are shown to be the keys to success. The chapter demonstrates that montage is central to the novel, as the political oratory of Kaiser Wilhelm II is adopted in order to facilitate the protagonist's rise to power. It analyzes the protagonist's use of oratory and publicity to establish his credibility and demolish the credibility of his opponents.

Chapter 3, "Organizing Speech in Gabriele Tergit's *Käsebier erobert den Kurfürstendamm*, 1931," looks at a novel that is usually regarded as a critique of the media. Although acknowledging the importance of literary journalism, the chapter examines *Käsebier* in terms of its business context, focusing on the depictions of property deals and the banking collapse. The chapter foregrounds the narrator's protest against the decline of liberal values and the corruption of the business world.

Chapter 4, "Seeing through the Rhetoric in Bertolt Brecht's *Dreigroschenroman* [*Threepenny Novel*], 1934," explores the novel's presentation of language as an instrument of persuasion. The protagonist, Macheath, transforms himself from a small-time crook into the owner of a retail empire. Macheath is portrayed as a manipulator who uses noneconomic arguments to persuade his employees to accept their exploitation. It concludes by arguing that the novel exemplifies the Brechtian method of "blunt thinking" as a means to resist ideological manipulation.

Chapter 5, "Giving an Account of the Self in Ingeborg Bachmann's *Malina*, 1971," considers the role of economic discourse in the novel, which has largely been unnoticed in the secondary literature. *Malina* hinges on the tension between the female first-person narrator, known only as "Ich" (I), and her male counterpart, Malina. The chapter approaches this central dichotomy in a number of different ways. Interpreted in Max Weber's terms, Malina stands for disenchantment, Ich for enchantment. Reading the text in terms of Marx and of Elaine Scarry's work on the relation between pain, labor, and creativity, Malina represents an economy of restraint, while Ich represents the extremes of hurting and imagining. In Brechtian terms, Malina stands for the entrepreneur, Ich for the dupe in need of "rationalization." The chapter concludes with an analysis of the text's rhetorical dimension, which stresses the importance of open-ended argumentation.

Chapter 6, "Negotiating Bureaucracy in Hermann Kant's *Das Impressum*, 1972," considers the role of business and political negotiation in a planned socialist economy. It considers the aesthetic form of the novel—its use of circumlocution—as a strategy of "talking around corners" in order to address taboo subjects in permissible ways. It also discusses the novel's strategic use of rhetorical commonplaces.

Chapter 7, "Corporate Discourse in Friedrich Christian Delius's *Unsere Siemens-Welt*, 1972," reads this satirical text as a dissection of corporate image-making and public relations, observing Delius's use of the genre of epideictic rhetoric, which enables him to censure under the cover of praise. The chapter sets out the historical context of Delius's intervention. It starts with the shaping of the corporation's image by the brand manager Hans Domizlaff (1892–1971) and then considers how Siemens coped with the revelation of its involvement in the forced-labor program during the Third Reich. It concludes with a look at the rhetoric of cooperation and the corporation's aim to encourage the outsourcing of government functions to the private sector.

Chapter 8, "Producing Ethos in Kathrin Röggla's *wir schlafen nicht*, 2004," investigates the world of investment banks and global consultancy firms such as McKinsey. Röggla's novel derives from interviews conducted with German-speaking investment bankers and management consultants based in New York. The chapter examines the ways in which Röggla's management consultants display skills associated with classical oratory, such as the projection of *ethos* and the switching of perspective in order to make more effective sales pitches. It concludes that the "new" economy of the twenty-first century relies on business practices that are remarkably similar to the "old" economies of earlier periods.

Chapter 9, "Communicative Contests in Philipp Schönthaler's *Das Schiff das singend zieht auf seiner Bahn*, 2013," focuses on the novel's depiction of human-resource managers, showing how it embraces corporate jargon in order to subvert it. The key locations here are the assessment center and the presentation room. The novel reveals how corporate discourse relies on sporting and gaming metaphors, as personified in the figure of the corporate athlete. The chapter examines how business experts are currently rediscovering Aristotelian rhetoric and its principles, e.g., the importance of nonverbal factors such as voice and body language. It concludes with a close reading of the rhetoric used in the corporate award ceremony, showing how this affirms the corporate regime of athletic self-discipline.

The conclusion argues that these novels not only share a common theme—the ability to interpret rhetoric—but also cultivate this ability, challenging their readers to refine their interpretive skills and their critical judgement. In this way, the novels encourage readers to make better-informed decisions in the future, whether economic or otherwise.

1: Managing Appearances in Thomas Mann's *Buddenbrooks*, 1901

> *er . . . ließ seine Künste spielen und*
> *machte ein unglaubliches Geld*
> [he . . . put all his arts to work, and
> made an incredible profit]
> —Thomas Mann, *Buddenbrooks*

Introduction: The Art of Doing Business

MOST SCHOLARSHIP ON *Buddenbrooks* has tended to focus on the theme of decline and on what the Germans call *Innerlichkeit*: the interiority or inner life of the characters.[1] Sometimes the characters' inwardness is interpreted in terms of economic change: Anna Kinder and Michael Cowan argue that the nervousness of the Buddenbrooks increases in direct response to the economic uncertainty of capitalist modernity.[2] Unfortunately, this tendency to focus on the characters' "interiority," even when it is connected to the wider economic framework, distracts attention from the actual business practices depicted in the novel. It also runs the risk of ignoring something the characters themselves take very seriously: external appearances (*Äußerlichkeiten*). If Thomas Mann (1875–1955) learned one thing from Theodor Fontane, it is that only by paying close attention to so-called casual appearances is it possible to gain an understanding of society.[3] Few scholars have seriously considered appearances and externalities in *Buddenbrooks*. Notable exceptions are Martin Swales, who observes the portrayal of a family that consciously works very hard to sustain its public role,[4] and Elizabeth Boa, who considers the ways in which the Buddenbrooks seek to regulate sensual pleasure.[5] Reading *Buddenbrooks*, we find that appearances, far from being casual, are careful constructs to which the family members themselves attach huge importance. Many valuable studies of *Buddenbrooks* that investigate the character and ethos of the family in terms of a sociohistorical perspective[6] miss the point, noted in the introduction to this book, that classical authors consider ethos to be a performative construct. Referring to classical oratory helps us to comprehend the Buddenbrooks as *actors* in both senses of the word: as participants in economic (and political) processes, and as theatrical performers. In this sense, the *Bürger* (citizen) is also, simultaneously, a performing *Künstler* (artist). There is a constant social performance that is required of the Buddenbrooks precisely because of their social position. Social convention means that they are always both citizens and artists, in the sense of the daily social performance they must enact. It took Thomas Mann many years to realize that the Bürger is very often a Künstler as well, and that everyone can benefit from having a sense of *Lebenskunst* (the art of life).[7]

A significant step toward recognizing the affinities between business-people and artists is taken in Mann's early story "Der Bajazzo" (1897; "The Joker"), when the father understands that the son's talent for performing and clowning around could be an asset to the family business:

> Er . . . versteht es, mit den Leuten umzugehen, sie zu amüsieren, ihnen zu schmeicheln, er hat das Bedürfnis, ihnen zu gefallen und Erfolge zu erzielen; mit derartiger Veranlagung hat bereits mancher sein Glück gemacht, und mit ihr ist er angesichts seiner sonstigen Indifferenz zum Handelsmann größeren Stils relativ geeignet.[8]

> [He . . . understands how to get along with people, how to amuse and flatter them, he has a need to please people and to achieve success. Many have already made their fortune with this kind of disposition, and, considering that he is otherwise indifferent to commerce, this makes him relatively well equipped to become a merchant in the grand style.]

A crowd-pleasing performance is not only a matter for artists; it can also help to close an important business deal. Merchants must be able to perform in public if they want to convince people to buy their goods. What Bürger and Künstler have in common is the need to persuade their respective audiences. This implies that oratory and rhetoric are not only a pursuit for artists, lawyers, or politicians; they are also relevant for commerce. In the context of oratory, it is also highly significant that Thomas and Hanno suffer from serious dental problems, since these impede oral communication. As Stephen Joy points out, the mouth is a "privileged figure" for the discursive field of speech.[9] Speech impediments are particularly unsettling because they disrupt normal economic activity, and this theme also appears in novels by Bachmann, Röggla, and Schönthaler (see chapters 5, 8, and 9 in this book).

Approaching *Buddenbrooks* from the perspective of classical oratory enables us to interpret it in a quite different light. If the patrician families of the Hanseatic League model themselves on Renaissance merchants, then this suggests a much closer relationship between Bürger and Künstler than has previously been assumed. For the merchants of Renaissance Florence were trained in classical oratory, and their sons would learn entire sections of Aristotle and Cicero.[10] The fact that Christian Buddenbrook studies Cicero is no accident: learning to make speeches and polish his phrases is an essential aspect of his business training. Renaissance merchants often patronized the arts to enhance their commercial prestige. As his play *Fiorenza* (1907) suggests, Mann knew a great deal about Renaissance Italy, with its connections between art, oratory, and commerce. Mann's awareness of Renaissance culture, which he gained from Burckhardt and Nietzsche, suggests that we need to rethink the relationship between Bürger and Künstler in Mann's early work. As noted above, the protagonists' artistic inclinations in "Der Bajazzo" are not necessarily a barrier to a business career; in a business context those same artistic inclinations could be an asset.

For Jacob Burckhardt, commerce and poetry are comparable because both are based on the principle of *agon* (competition)—the central feature of classical Greek culture, according to Burckhardt, which he sees as a sign of cultural excellence, whether manifested in athletic contests, poetry recitals, or even in the prestige of great merchant houses.[11] When Hoffstede recites his poem at the housewarming party at the beginning of *Buddenbrooks*, his performance recollects the *skolion* (banquet songs sung by invited guests) of ancient Greece. Hoffstede's occasional verse suggests that art is by no means an idle pursuit. Rather, the domain of art is an arena (or amphitheater) in which invited guests (poets) compete for glory and prestige. If we understand Hoffstede's verse as an instance of *skolion*, then this subverts the distinction between Bürger and Künstler in which so much Thomas Mann criticism is mired. If artworks are viewed as *skolion*, then Bürger and Künstler are united in their *agon*, i.e., in their competitive pursuit of glory and prestige. And the covert affinity between Bürger and Künstler is implied even more strongly when Hoffstede refers to his humble dwelling-place at the end of his poem: "Und behaltet wert und lieb / Den, der in geringer Klause / Heute diese Zeylen schrieb!" (*B* 38; "Always keep that man most dear, / Who in humbler quarters 'biding / Penned these stanzas offered here," *Bu* 30). The German word *Klause* means hermitage or cell; therefore, when Hoffstede compares his home to a monk's cell, he is invoking the artist as an ascetic figure who is bound by his calling to a life of *askesis* (severe self-discipline). But this ascetic persona is also the embodiment of the Protestant work ethic as formulated by Max Weber and discussed later in this chapter. Self-discipline is part and parcel of the Buddenbrooks' existence as well. The fact that Bürger and Künstler relish competition and enforce strict self-discipline on themselves suggests a close affinity between them.

Keeping Up Appearances

Just as actors or politicians have to stay within their roles, the Buddenbrooks invest considerable effort in "die dehors wahren" (*B* 291; "keeping up appearances," *Bu* 260; also *B* 343, *Bu* 309). The phrase occurs so often that it comes to seem like the family's guiding principle; indeed, for Consul Johann, the phrase is "erstes Gesetz" (*B* 343; "first law," *Bu* 309). The standard interpretation of "die dehors wahren" is that it is an attempt to conceal the family decline beneath a façade of prosperity and well-being.[12] But if we stop there, we miss an important aspect of the novel: its respect for social conventions. The Buddenbrooks' fellow citizens are also very careful to maintain the correct exterior, which is described as the "Weltanschauung [der] Mitbürger" (*B* 343; "the creed of [their] fellow citizens," *Bu* 309). This can be seen as the social pressure to conform, the "Gesellschafts-Etwas" (social something) that Mann's literary mentor Theodor Fontane writes about in *Effi Briest*.[13]

In *The Presentation of the Self in Everyday Life* Goffman argues that the presentation of the self is aided by the use of fixed props and settings such as houses, clothes, and institutions. He also observes the importance of staying within role: an "individual's initial projection commits him to what he is proposing to be."[14] Goffman's insights are particularly relevant for the rhetorical situation, in which the speaker makes a bid to be considered as legitimate. According to Hans Blumenberg, political and economic actors must perform in accordance with the audience's expectations in order to avoid encountering contradiction. Self-presentation is an essential aspect of self-preservation, and not only for the Buddenbrooks.[15] Even when a person encounters failure, it is important to "save face"; in other words, to behave in a manner that is consistent with his or her social role.

The need to stay within role also applies to sexual morality; for example, in the case of the lawyer Gieseke. Like Christian Buddenbrook and the other "Suitiers" (suitors), outside the office he has spent much of his time partying and enjoying casual sexual liaisons with actresses. But Gieseke knows how to put on a good show of respectability when he needs to:

> Aber, wie die übrigen behäbigen Lebemänner verstand er es, die richtige Miene dazu zu machen, Ärgernis zu vermeiden, und seinen politischen und beruflichen Grundsätzen den Ruf unanfechtbarer Solidität zu wahren. (*B* 343)

> [But, like the other pleasure-loving bon vivants, he understood how to put on the right face, to avoid public offense, and to maintain a reputation for absolute reliability in matters political and professional. (*Bu* 309)][16]

This show of respectability pays dividends, enabling Gieseke to become engaged to Fräulein Huneus, the daughter of one of the richest men in town. Christian's problem is not that he lives a life of sexual excess but that he is too naively open about it. Keeping up appearances is essential for anyone who wants to succeed.

This performativity necessitates what Thorstein Veblen, in *The Theory of the Leisure Class* (1899), calls "conspicuous consumption":[17] in other words, in order to maintain your social status, you have to spend money. Successful members of the bourgeoisie had a tendency to build large, ostentatious houses, and Thomas Buddenbrook is no exception. We see this when Hermann Hagenström seizes the opportunity to gain prestige by purchasing the Buddenbrooks house toward the end of the novel. We see it when Bendix Grünlich charms his way to a fortune by marrying Tony Buddenbrook. We also see it in Tony herself, who knows that one of her primary duties—apart from marrying appropriately and producing children—is to represent the family in public. Tony is a natural performer. She may be dignified, but the narrator comments that there is something childish and playful about her dignity: "diese ganze Würde [war] etwas unendlich Kindliches, Harmloses und Spielerisches" (*B* 223; "this great dignity was a childish, harmless game," *Bu* 202). She is so aware that she has to put on a good show for the benefit of the family that she even treats her father's funeral as an opportunity to show herself off to her best advantage:

> Tony legte den Kranz auf den in goldenen Buchstaben frisch in die Platte eingelassenen Namen des Vaters und kniete dann trotz des Schnees am Grabe nieder, um leise zu beten; der schwarze Schleier umspielte sie, und ihr weiter Kleiderrock lag ein wenig malerisch schwungvoll neben ihr ausgebreitet. Gott allein wußte, wieviel Schmerz und Religiosität, und andererseits wieviel Selbstgefälligkeit einer hübschen Frau in dieser hingegossenen Stellung lag. (*B* 283)

> [Tony laid the wreath over the golden letters of her father's name, which had only recently been added to the stone, and despite the snow she knelt down on the grave to pray softly; her black veil fluttered about her, and her broad skirt lay spread out beside her in soft, picturesque folds. God alone knew how much of this molded pose was grief and piety—and how much was the vanity of a pretty woman. (*Bu* 253)]

And Tony also carefully stage-manages the reading of her father's will, turning it into a family council meeting: "sie trug Sorge, dieser Zusammenkunft den Charakter einer Sitzung, eines Familienrates zu verleihen" (*B* 274; "she was anxious to give the meeting the character of a formal family council," *Bu* 246). In other words, Tony is an expert at behaving comme il faut, performing the class-based, gendered role into which she has been born. And should Tony ever forget the performance that is required of her, then her brother Thomas is on hand to remind her: "So, liebe Tony! Nun etwas mehr Haltung und Würde, wenn ich dich bitten darf!" (*B* 452; "All right, Tony—and now a little more self-control and dignity are in order, please," *Bu* 403).

In *Buddenbrooks* this performativity is perhaps most pronounced in the case of Thomas. Of all the characters, he is the one who is most concerned with how he presents himself. He knows very well that business is not merely a technical activity; it requires a good sense of public relations. And so he comes to perform the externalities of doing business almost lovingly, as he makes clear to his friend Kistenmaker:

> "Ein Geschäftsmann darf kein Bureaukrat sein! . . . Es gehört Persönlichkeit dazu, das ist *mein* Geschmack. Ich glaube nicht, daß ein großer Erfolg vom Comptoirbock aus zu erkämpfen ist. . . . Der Erfolg will nicht bloß am Pulte gerechnet sein. . . . Mein Großvater zum Beispiel . . . er kutschierte vierspännig nach Süd-Deutschland, der alte Herr mit seinem Puderkopf und seinen Escarpins, als preußischer Heereslieferant. Und dann charmierte er umher und ließ seine Künste spielen und machte ein unglaubliches Geld, Kistenmaker!" (*B* 293–94)

> ["A businessman cannot be a bureaucrat. . . . It takes personality, and that's *my* specialty. I don't think great things can ever be accomplished from behind a desk. . . . Calculations from behind a desk don't lead to success. . . . My grandfather, for instance, a fine old gentleman in a powdered wig and pumps, rode in a coach-and-four to southern Germany as a contractor for the Prussian army. And he turned his charm on everyone, put all his arts to work, and made an incredible profit, Kistenmaker." (*Bu* 262)]

Here Thomas shows a fleeting awareness that his grandfather, old Johann, was not only a Bürger but a Künstler. The truly talented businessman is both Bürger and Künstler at the same time. His grandfather was a businessman in the grand manner, an artist who could "seine Künste spielen lassen" ("put all his arts to work"). Thomas is still idealizing his grandfather to a certain extent here. He does not quite understand how ruthless old Johann has been, even to his own son Gotthold. Was this patrician way of life ever as "noble" as Thomas imagines it to be? Of course not. His problem is that he is caught between various conflicting ideas of what it means to be a Bürger. As Tony tells him: "Ja, Tom, wir fühlen uns als Adel und fühlen einen Abstand" (*B* 425; "Yes, Tom, we feel that we are aristocrats, and we're aware of that distance," *Bu* 376). Thomas never attempts to deny his bourgeois origins, however. Indeed, he proudly recalls an occasion when he won the respect of an aristocrat (*B* 504; *Bu* 451).[18] Even so, he shares an awareness that they both fulfill representative functions. To a certain extent, Thomas is trapped between his bourgeois ideals, his quasi-noble representative function, and the harsh reality of commerce. In cultivating his public image he neglects to expand the economic basis of the firm. To understand this public image more fully, it is worth considering Weber's formulation of Protestant ethics.

Protestant Rhetoric

Max Weber's *Die protestantische Ethik und der Geist des Kapitalismus* (1904–5; *The Protestant Ethic and the Spirit of Capitalism*) appeared a few years after *Buddenbrooks*. Mann later regarded Weber's study as a confirmation of his own insights into the psychology of the bourgeoisie.[19] Weber argues that the religious concept of *Beruf* (vocation, calling) facilitated the emergence of modern capitalism because it inspired and a devotion to labor for its own sake: "Labor must . . . be performed as if it were an absolute end in itself, a calling."[20] The bourgeois vocation consists in a devotion to making money for its own sake, and this goes hand in hand with "a certain ascetic tendency."[21] Weber characterizes the bourgeois way of life as "worldly asceticism": the bourgeois acquires worldly goods relentlessly but refrains from enjoying them and lives a sober, monklike existence. This ethical system enabled the bourgeois merchant to "follow his pecuniary interests" and at the same time "feel as if he was fulfilling a duty in doing so."[22] This sense of a calling is indeed central to the self-definition of the Buddenbrooks. For example, when Tony decides that she will marry Grünlich, the narrative slips into *erlebte Rede* (free indirect discourse) as she mentally affirms her own calling: "[Sie war] *berufen* [italics added], mit That und Entschluß an der Geschichte ihrer Familie mitzuarbeiten!" (*B* 173; "she was *called* [italics added] to help shape, by deeds and personal resolve, the history of her family," *Bu* 155). The most forceful expression of the Protestant work ethic in *Buddenbrooks* is the opening of part 2, when Consul Jean records the birth of his daughter Clara. He writes the record into the family chronicle, which is described as "Eine dicke Ledermappe, gefüllt mit Papieren" (*B* 55; "a heavy leather writing case filled with papers," *Bu* 49) containing "ein Heft mit gepreßten Umschlage und Goldschnitt" (*B* 55; "one gilt-edged notebook with an embossed cover," *Bu* 49). Consul Jean regards the acquisition of wealth as a form of moral duty that is pleasing to the Lord. This is evident when he writes: "Ich habe meiner jüngsten Tochter eine Police von 150 Courant-Thalern ausgeschrieben. Fuhre du sie, ach Herr! auf deinen Wegen" (*B* 57; "I have had a policy written for my youngest daughter in the amount of 150 *courant*-thalers. Lead her, O Lord, in thy ways," *Bu* 50). Writing in the family chronicle, too, appears as a form of religious devotion. When Consul Jean starts to think about putting the pen down, he forces himself to keep writing: "Wie aber! Wurde er es so bald müde, sich mit seinem Schöpfer und Erhalter zu bereden? Welch ein Raub an Ihm, dem Herrn, schon jetzt einzuhalten mit Schreiben" (*B* 57; "But how could he! Was he so quickly weary of communing with his Creator and Redeemer? To break off now would be as good as stealing from the Lord," *Bu* 51). John E. Woods translates "sich bereden" here as "communing," but the verb literally means "to discuss." The verb is cognate with *Beredsamkeit* (eloquence), and it can also mean "to persuade": understood in this way, this might suggest that Jean is trying to persuade himself, or persuade his God, about something. The use of the verb "sich bereden" is a subtle allusion to the tradition of Christian oratory. The early Christian church took over the forms of classical rhetoric, particularly the eulogy, and used them for devotional purposes. The Reformation brought about devolution of religious oratory. In Protestant sects, lay believers were encouraged to bear witness to the Lord. Consul Jean's devotional writing exercise is an intimate expression of his own mercantile ideology. It is essentially a form of self-affirmation. In affirming his devotion to the Lord he is simultaneously providing a moral justification for his own mercantile activities. This is another way in which the Buddenbrooks keep up appearances: their religious rhetoric reaffirms the solidity and respectability of their identity.

There is a contradiction here, however, and it is one of which the novel is well aware. Although Consul Jean tries hard to persuade himself that business is a moral calling or a kind of sacred duty, many of the events in *Buddenbrooks* demonstrate the opposite. Many modern capitalists accumulate wealth for its own sake, and not because of any religious sentiment. The conclusion of Weber's study emphasizes the ultimate tension between religion and capitalism. Weber quotes John Wesley, the founder of Methodism:

> I fear, wherever riches have increased, the essence of religion has decreased in the same proportion. Therefore I do not see how it is possible, in the nature of things, for any revival of true religion to continue long. For religion must necessarily produce both industry and frugality, and these cannot but produce riches.[23]

This is a succinct expression of the paradoxical relationship between Protestantism and capitalism. According to Weber, Protestantism encourages the acquisition of wealth and thus undermines itself by establishing the conditions of modern capitalism. In turn, modern capitalism detaches itself from the conditions of its emergence in the Protestant Reformation and becomes a purely rationalistic process of acquisition. The ambivalent relation between business and morality is crystallized in the Buddenbrook family motto: "Mein Sohn, sey mit Lust bey den Geschäften am Tage, aber mache nur solche, daß wir bey Nacht ruhig schlafen können!" (*B* 190; "My son, show zeal for each day's affairs of business, but only for such that make for a peaceful night's sleep," *Bu* 173). The motto has an ironic potential. It can be taken literally as an injunction to act morally when doing business. Read against the grain, however, it could mean that a good night's sleep is more important than moral scrutiny. Weber observes: "A good conscience simply became one of the means of enjoying a comfortable bourgeois life, as is well expressed in the German proverb about the soft pillow";[24] the proverb is "Ein gutes Gewissen ist das beste Kopfkissen" (A good conscience is the best pillow). Such facile say-ings hardly suggest an injunction to moral self-scrutiny as practiced by the early Protestants.

Concealing and Revealing Exploitation

In *The Communist Manifesto* (1848) Karl Marx and Friedrich Engels claim that "the bourgeoisie has torn away from the family its sentimental veil, and has reduced the family relation to a mere money relation."[25] In con-trast, Franco Moretti observes that the Victorian bourgeoisie continually shied away from admitting the implications of capitalism.[26] The first gen-eration of Buddenbrooks shows little sentiment: old Johann and Justus Kröger disinherit their sons without compunction. Subsequent genera-tions of Buddenbrooks become increasingly waylaid, however, by their own sentiments. Unlike old Johann, Consul Jean feels guilty about disin-heriting Gotthold. Jean's fondness for churchgoing and Protestant rheto-ric is in one sense a practical form of self-affirmation, but his extreme piety could also be interpreted a sign of his ineptitude for business, especially when one considers that his father enjoys mocking the catechism. When Jean's eyes linger on the motto engraved above the door, "Dominus providebit" (*B* 47; *Bu* 39), and he lowers his head, this suggests a fatalistic, even submissive response to religion that is absent in his father. Later, the novel highlights Jean's internal struggle between religious sentiment and business sense:

> wieder durchschauerte ihn die schwärmerische Ehrfurcht seiner Generation vor menschlichen Gefühlen, die stets mit seinem nüchternen und praktischen Geschäftssinn in Hader gelegen hatte. (*B* 247)

> [once again a shudder passed through him—like any man of his gen-eration, he felt a fanatical reverence for all human emotions that stood at odds with his sober and practical outlook as a man of business. (*Bu* 222)]

Two chapters later, Jean's religious tendencies are exacerbated by the onset of old age and infirmity (*B* 263–64; *Bu* 235), thus linking Christian piety with biological decline, as Nietzsche does. When Jean forces his daughter Tony to marry Grünlich, he seems to think that he is the realist and that Tony is the sentimental one. But he is mistaken. Tony's choice (the medi-cal student Morten Schwarzkopf) would have been much more economi-cally sound, and Jean is completely taken in by Grünlich. When Kesselmeyer finally reveals how he and Grünlich plotted to get Tony's dowry, Jean turns "totenblaß" (*B* 249; "pale as death," *Bu* 223) at the thought that he is trapped "mit einem Gauner und einem vor Bosheit tollen Affe" (*B* 249;

"with a swindler and a vicious ape gone mad," *Bu* 223). Jean is brought up, uncomfortably, against his own image here. These words are telling: "Gauner" (swindler) reminds us of his brother Christian's damning verdict that every businessmen is a "Gauner" (*B* 348; *Bu* 314), and "Affe" (ape) recalls Charles Darwin. In this scene, then, Jean is forced to encounter the brutal reality of business practices that he has sought to camouflage by means of Christian philanthropy. Just as nineteenth-century Christianity was shaken by Darwin's monkeys, so, too, Consul Jean is shaken by the revelation that his colleagues are apes. The apparently civilized bourgeois reveals his bestial ancestry. This recalls how Thomas is tormented by the presence of his brother Christian, because Christian represents a truth about himself that he has tried to repress. Jean tries to ward off the implication that he has ruined his daughter's life so thoughtlessly, claiming that he made "sichere Erkundigungen" (*B* 249; "serious enquiries," *Bu* 223) about Grünlich's finances among Hamburg merchants. Kesselmeyer shouts back that they were all in on the deal, because Grünlich owed them money. Jean has not only been fooled by Grünlich; he has been fooled by all the Hamburg companies that vouched for him, as well. This is a degree of infamy that Jean is unable to contemplate, and he does his best to deny the truth even when it is hurled in his face: "Er wandte sich, er *wollte* nichts mehr hören" (*B* 249; "Determined not to hear any more, he turned," *Bu* 223). He learns that he has been playing by one set of rules, while his fellow businessmen have been playing by another. He has been misled by his Protestant rhetoric (discussed in the previous section of this chapter); he has ignored the harsh reality of business such rhetoric conceals.

Something similar can be observed in the case of Thomas Buddenbrook, although he lacks the religious sentiment of his father. Thomas is a "verwirrter Bürger" (confused bourgeois)[27] who makes the error of believing his own rhetoric. His view of his own activity as a businessman is an idealized one. This is shown by his reflections after the death of his uncle Gotthold. Thomas addresses his dead uncle, who was disinherited for marrying a shopgirl, thus:

> Obwohl du trotzig warst und wohl glaubtest, dieser Trotz sei etwas Idealistisches, besaß dein Geist wenig Schwungkraft, wenig Phantasie, wenig von dem Idealismus, der Jemanden befähigt, mit einem stillen Enthusiasmus, süßer, beglückender, befriedigender als eine heimliche Liebe, irgend ein abstraktes Gut, einen alten Namen, ein Firmenschild zu hegen, zu pflegen, zu verteidigen, zu Ehren und Macht und Glanz zu bringen. Der Sinn für Poesie ging dir ab. (*B* 302)

> [You were stubborn, though, and probably thought that there was something idealistic in being stubborn. You had too little momentum and imagination, too little of the idealism that enables a man to cherish, to nurture, to defend something as abstract as a business with an old family name—and to bring it honor and power and glory. That

> requires a quiet enthusiasm that is sweeter and more pleasant, more
> gratifying than any secret love. You lost your sense of poetry.
> (*Bu* 269–70)]

But Thomas's later reactions show that he does not entirely believe in this
ethos of duty, honor, and decency that he has just elaborated.

Thomas's bad faith is revealed by his extreme reaction to Christian's
statement that businessmen are swindlers (*B* 348; *Bu* 314). He shouts,
"Du bist ein Auswuchs, eine ungesunde Stelle am Körper unserer Familie"
(*B* 352; "You're an abscess, an unhealthy growth on the body of our family," *Bu* 316–17), revealing a hysterical fear that Christian might "infect"
the family firm. He protests so loudly that there is a sense of tacit agreement with Christian. The incongruity between business rhetoric and business practice is also shown when the old postmaster comes to congratulate
Thomas on the firm's centenary and insists that he hasn't come simply to
collect his tip: "Es is nich *da*rum, Herr Senator, ick komm nich *da*rum!"
(*B* 536; "*That* ain't why I come by, Senator Buddenbrook, 'tain't it at all,"
Bu 478). This is a lie, of course: in fact, the mailman *has* come to get his
financial reward. Underneath the polite exteriors, people are out for what
they can get. Thomas tries to ignore this fact; he clings to the liberal ideal
of business as a moral, dignified pursuit. Gradually, though, he is forced to
confront the harsh reality of actual business practices.[28]

The Pöppenrade harvest in part 8 is a key episode in this respect. This
transaction highlights the ultimate incongruity between ethics and profits.
The Pöppenrade deal, buying the grain from Ralf von Maiboom "auf dem
Halm [literally: on the stalk]" (*B* 499; "The whole crop," *Bu* 446) before
it has ripened, is not only risky; it is also morally dubious: "Einen
Menschen brutal ausbeuten," *B* 499–500; "To brutally exploit a man," *Bu*
447). Tony tells Thomas that if he were a true businessman he would
abandon his scruples and seize the opportunity (*B* 500; *Bu* 448). Alone in
his study, Thomas reflects on Tony's words and admits to himself that she
is correct. He is the one who is at fault, and worse still, he is at fault precisely because of his own moral scruples. At this point, the narrative shifts
into free indirect speech to ask the key question: "War Thomas
Buddenbrook ein Geschäftsmann, ein Mann der unbefangenen That oder
ein skrupulöser Nachdenker?" (*B* 515; "Was Thomas Buddenbrook a businessman, a man of dispassionate deeds, or a brooder haunted by scruples?"
Bu 461). Thomas is caught on the horns of the double standard that he,
as a businessman, is required to practice. He senses the impossibility of
squaring ethics and profits. But this collision between opposite moral
codes anguishes and torments him. It is almost as if he is living a double
life, the life of an actor (*B* 677; *Bu* 597). Thomas finds that he cannot
square his liberal ideals about what business should be with the Darwinian
brutality of what actually goes on. In *Buddenbrooks* the sentimental veil

with which the bourgeoisie attempts to conceal the harsh truths of capitalism has been torn back. We have left the moral absolutes of nineteenth-century realism behind us and entered a more frightening, ambivalent zone.

Philosophical Rhetoric

The representation of business in *Buddenbrooks* is highly ambivalent precisely because it reflects Thomas Mann's reception of the works of Nietzsche, Arthur Schopenhauer, and Henrik Ibsen, the great nineteenth-century critics of bourgeois morality (and hypocrisy). Anyone who takes Schopenhauer and Nietzsche seriously will be inclined to perceive life in terms of a Darwinian struggle. The internal monologue of Thomas Buddenbrooks expresses this secular, postreligious, neoliberal view of economics:

> Das Leben war hart, und das Geschäftsleben war in seinem rücksicht-slosen und unsentimentalen Verlaufe ein Abbild des großen und ganzen Lebens. (*B* 515)

> [Life was hard, and business, as it took its ruthless, unsentimental course, was the epitome of life in general. (*Bu* 461)]

And Thomas shudders when he recalls another time when he lost a large sum of money, and all his business friends suddenly cold-shouldered him. Far from being sympathetic, they only treated him with mistrust: "er hatte zum ersten Male in vollem Umfange und am eigenen Leibe die grausame Brutalität des Geschäftslebens verspüren müssen" (*B* 516; "For the first time in his life he had been forced to experience personally and completely just how cruel and brutal business can be," *Bu* 461). At these moments we see how Thomas Buddenbrook is tormented by a contradiction in his own being. He is torn between two conflicting images of himself: Is he a righteous citizen and a pillar of the community, or a calculating opportunist? His problem is that his position requires him to be both.

It is only when Thomas starts to read Schopenhauer (in part 10, chapter 5) that he comes to realize the thin ice on which he has been standing, i.e., the fragility of his bourgeois ethics. He could have started with the Renaissance—with Machiavelli, for example.[29] For Machiavelli, a prince should appear to be good, but "his disposition should be such that, if he needs to be the opposite, he knows how."[30] This is Thomas's problem: he knows very well how to perform according to social conventions, but he does not know how to break those codes without hesitation when the occasion demands. He knows the cruelty of the world, but he tries hard to conceal it from himself. When he finally reads Schopenhauer's *Die Welt als Wille und Vorstellung* (1819; *The World as Will and Representation*), he is confronted with the abyss that has haunted him. Then he feels "die Genugthuung des Leidenden, der vor der Kälte und Härte des Lebens sein Leiden beständig schamvoll und bösen Gewissens versteckt hielt und plötzlich . . . die Berechtigung erhält, an der Welt zu leiden" (*B* 721; "the satisfaction of a sufferer who has always known only shame and the bite of conscience for hiding the suffering that cold, hard life brings, and who now, suddenly, . . . receives elemental, formal justification for having felt such suffering in this world," *Bu* 633). Only by reading Schopenhauer is he finally able to acknowledge the doubts that he had carefully repressed when performing his role as a merchant. Faced with this insight into the world's cruelty, different philosophers draw different conclusions. Machiavelli and Nietzsche offer reasons to ignore or even cause suffering; Schopenhauer offers a justification for suffering. Faced with such an alternative between sadism and masochism, Thomas Mann's characters tend to opt for an ethics of suffering.

Nietzsche's distinction between the Apollonian and Dionysian is relevant here. According to Franco Moretti, it is possible to divide the bourgeoisie of the nineteenth century into two ideal types. The first type is "the sober puritan" who is "modest in his aspirations," for example, "Robinson Crusoe's father, or Wilhelm Meister's."[31] The second type is the "hypnotic entrepreneur"[32] or "creative destroyer"[33] represented by Goethe's Faust or by Ibsen's John Gabriel Borkman. Moretti's two "types" recall Nietzsche's distinction between the Apollonian and the Dionysian, suggesting a Nietzschean dichotomy at the heart of bourgeois business practice. Seen in Apollonian terms, business is a measured and ethical activity; but seen from the Dionysian side it is a hypnotic struggle of wills. Given Thomas Mann's reception of Nietzsche, it is hardly surprising that we find this dichotomy in *Buddenbrooks*. In the novel the Apollonian type is represented by the *Prokurist* (company secretary), Herr Friedrich Wilhelm Marcus. He is cautious, honest, and sober. With his "peinliche Ordnungsliebe" (*B* 292; almost embarrassingly meticulous love of detail),[34] Marcus exerts a retarding influence on the activities of the firm. In contrast, the Dionysian types are old Johann and Hermann Hagenström. One thinks of old Johann in his prime, riding around southern Germany supplying grain to the Prussian army (*B* 294; *Bu* 262). When we first encounter him at the opening of the novel, he radiates health and well-being with his "rundes, rosig überhauchtes und wohlmeinendes Gesicht" (*B* 10; "round, pastel pink, good-humored face," *Bu* 4) and his broad double chin that rests "mit einem Ausdruck von Behaglichkeit auf dem weißen Spitzen-Jabot" (*B* 10; "comfortably on the wide lace jabot," *Bu* 4).[35] There is something superhuman about Hermann Hagenström. He is grotesquely overweight: "Er war so außerordentlich fett, daß nicht nur sein Kinn, sondern sein ganzes Untergesicht doppelt war" (*B* 662; "He was so extraordinarily fat that not only did he have a double-chin, but the whole lower half of his face was double as well," *Bu* 583). His mouth emits gentle chomping sounds that make Tony go pale as she recalls the time that he forced her to kiss him in exchange for a lemon roll: "Eine Vision von Citronensemmeln . . . suchte sie heim dabei" (*B* 662; "It called up visions of lemon buns," *Bu* 583), and her humiliation increases when Hagenström gets even closer to her and breathes in her face, making her feel "das Gezwungene und Unangenehme ihrer Lage" (*B* 665; "the unpleasant, constrained situation he had put her in," *Bu* 586). Hagenström, with his vast appetite and lemon rolls, certainly qualifies as a hypnotic predator.

Apollonian and Dionysian can be seen as opposing character types, but they also correspond to two different "faces" of the bourgeois, two attitudes required in bourgeois life. In this sense, they could be seen a structural feature of modern society, a consequence of the double standard the bourgeois is forced to apply. The implication is that within capitalist society the honest, decent, sentimental bourgeois *coexists* with the rule-breaking entrepreneur. These two types can even battle for supremacy within one single character. This is the tragedy of Thomas Buddenbrook. He would like to be an old Johann or a Hermann Hagenström, but despite his elegant airs he has a quality reminiscent of the crabbed, painstaking Friedrich Wilhelm Marcus. Thomas does not even know whether he is a decent pillar of society or a vicious, opportunistic profiteer. He fails to grasp that society requires him to perform in both of these ways, depending on the situation. Thomas's obsession with his *Lebensform* (way of life) means that he becomes a prisoner of his own social ideology, unable to handle double standards like his rival Hagenström.

Thomas certainly knows how to deceive: "Wirklich! Thomas Buddenbrooks Dasein war kein anderes mehr, als das eines Schauspielers" (*B* 677; "No doubt of it—Thomas Buddenbrook's existence was no different from that of an actor," *Bu* 597). His entire life becomes a kind of "Produktion" (*B* 677; "production," *Bu* 597). From a Machiavellian or a Nietzschean perspective, therefore, Thomas Buddenbrook's problem is not that he is an actor; his problem is that he is a mediocre one. He is a performer who lacks the killer instinct. Hanno sees through his father's performance. Under the smooth surface, Hanno observes how hard his father has to work to maintain his mask. When Thomas entertains his fellow merchants, this social interaction appears as something unnatural and forced (*B* 691; *Bu* 608).

Buddenbrooks, like Ibsen's dramas, depicts a "gray area" of shady, semilegal practices that attempt to exploit loopholes in the law, or bend the rules to the very utmost.[36] This gray zone is presented in the case of Hugo Weinschenk, who is sent to prison for insurance fraud. Thomas explains that Weinschenk is not an aberration, not an isolated case. On the contrary, he only did what most of his competitors were doing; the only difference is that he failed to cover his tracks adequately (*B* 578–79; *Bu* 513). It seems that getting caught red-handed and being sent to prison for white-collar crime is just one of the risks of the profession. When one of their colleagues is jailed for forging a note of exchange, the town merchants are not at all surprised:

> Man kam auf den letzten Skandal der Stadt, eine Wechselfälschung, auf Großkaufmann Kaßbaum, P. Philipp Kaßbaum & Co., der nun hinter Schloß und Riegel saß. Man ereiferte sich durchaus nicht; man nannte Herrn Kaßbaums That eine Dummheit, lachte kurz und zuckte die Achseln. (*B* 735–36)

> [They got around to the latest scandal: some checks had been forged, and now Kassbaum, a wholesale merchant with P. Philipp Kassbaum & Co., was sitting behind bars. They were not outraged at all; Herr Kassbaum had simply made a foolish mistake—they laughed and shrugged their shoulders. (*Bu* 644)]

At moments such as this, we see the gap that opens up between business theory and actual business practices.

Classical Rhetoric

Buddenbrooks demonstrates the power of classical oratory. Jean's title "Consul" recalls Cicero himself, who was elected consul in 64 BC, thus suggesting a parallel between Lübeck, with its proud civic tradition as an independent city-state, and the ancient Roman republic. The parallel becomes even stronger when we consider that both consuls make speeches that are instrumental in stopping a rebellion. Cicero's speeches against Lucius Sergus Catilina—Catiline in English—are celebrated examples of political oratory. Catiline conspired to have himself appointed consul, and Cicero exposed the plot in a series of speeches in 63 BC. Consul Jean Buddenbrook, too, shows himself to be an orator capable of disarming a rebellion by means of speech alone when he speaks to the people during the German Revolution of 1848. The scene shows the importance of *ethos* (character) for the orator.[37] Jean establishes his character by using Plattdeutsch, which signals his down-to-earth quality and his patrician status within the community. His opening gambit is: "Lüd, wat is dat nu bloß für dumm Tüg, wat Ji da anstellt!" (*B* 208; "Folks, what sort of foolishness are you up to now?" *Bu* 188). In this way, he uses the local dialect to establish his credentials as a man with the right to speak before the community. Then he reduces their spokesman, Corl Smolt, to a figure of ridicule by firing questions at him until it becomes obvious that Smolt cannot formulate his demands clearly enough. When Smolt calls for a republic, the consul demolishes him by pointing out that the republic has already been achieved—Smolt's comical response is to ask for another republic (*B* 209; *Bu* 189). In this way, the tension is defused as the crowd bursts into laughter. The consul triumphs over his opponent not only because he is more eloquent but also because he reduces his opponent to a figure of fun. The strategy accords fully with Cicero's advice in *De Oratore* (*On the Ideal Orator*) on the uses of laughter: "laughter crushes the opponent, makes light of him, discourages him, defeats him, . . . and laughter dismisses offensive matters that are not easily refuted by arguments."[38]

The letter Jean writes to his daughter Tony instructing her to marry Grünlich contains several effective rhetorical devices. The key sentence, "Wir sind . . . Glieder in einer Kette" (*B* 160; "We are . . . links in a chain," *Bu* 144) contains the slippery pronoun "we," which invites assent; the use of a strong metaphor intensifies the argument, reminding Tony of the duty she owes to the family as an institution that transcends the individual.[39] The sentence that precedes this masterstroke is also worth examining:

> Denn obgleich die mündliche Rede lebendiger und unmittelbarer wirken mag, so hat doch das geschriebene Wort den Vorzug, daß es mit Mühe gewählt und gesetzt werden konnte, daß es feststeht und in dieser vom Schreibenden wohl erwogenen und berechneten Form und Stellung wieder und wieder gelesen werden und gleichmäßig wirken kann. (*B* 160)

> [For, although the words we speak are more vivid and immediate, the written word has the advantage of having been chosen with great care and is fixed in a form that its author has weighed and considered, so that it may be read again and again to cumulative effect. (*Bu* 143– 44)]

This sentence has a threefold function: first, it demonstrates Jean's awareness of the rhetorical tradition and its debates about the primacy of the spoken over the written word; second, it proclaims the huge investment ("Mühe," care) of the writer himself, thus lending his words further weight; and third, it acts as an invitation to Tony to reflect "again and again" on her father's words. Faced with such a rhetorical barrage from her father, it is hardly surprising that Tony falls back into line.

Consul Jean's nemesis, Bendix Grünlich, is also a master of rhetoric. Grünlich exemplifies the young Thomas Mann's ambivalent attitude toward classical oratory, because he uses rhetorical eloquence for immoral purposes. Grünlich knows that language can be employed as a weapon to manipulate people. He succeeds in fooling Jean because he skillfully exploits the latter's weakness, excessive piety.[40] Grünlich is a highly effective manipulator of linguistic form, well trained in the classical discipline of oratory as formulated by Cicero. It is appropriate that when Grünlich first appears, Christian Buddenbrook is studying Cicero's second Catilinarian oration: "während Christian, ein wenig seitwärts, mit einem unglücklichen

Gesichtsausdruck Ciceros zweite Catilinarische Rede präparierte" (*B* 100; "sour-faced Christian was a little off to one side, memorizing Cicero's second oration against Catiline," *Bu* 91). Grünlich notices this at once and comments:

> Und Sie lesen, Herr Buddenbrook? Ah, Cicero! Eine schwierige Lektüre, die Werke dieses großen römischen Redners. Quousque tandem, Catilina . . . hä-ä-hm, ja, ich habe mein Latein gleichfalls noch nicht völlig vergessen! (*B* 105–6)
>
> [And what are you reading, Master Buddenbrook? Ah, Cicero! A difficult text, the work of a great Roman orator. *Quousque tandem, Catilina.* Huh-uh-hmmm, yes, I've not entirely forgotten my Latin, either. (*Bu* 95)]

Here he quotes the first Catilinarian oration, which comprises a devastating series of rhetorical questions, starting with: "How far, I ask you, Catiline, do you mean to stretch our patience?"[41] It is significant not only for its rhetorical skill but also because it hinges on the subject of decadence, denouncing Catiline's decadent, immoral character. At this point Grünlich is trying to impress Tony's parents by showing off his *Bildung*, his classical humanist education. But Consul Jean is not pleased. He sounds a note of warning: in contrast to old Johann, he dislikes the practice of exposing young men to the classics, especially when so many other important things are necessary. His Protestant faith makes him suspicious of classical oratory—despite the fact that he uses it himself. The consul's words evoke the tension between Bürger and Künstler that lurks beneath so much of the novel. In this instance, classical education falls onto the morally questionable, artistic side of the divide. The implication is that classical culture, being either pagan or associated with Roman Catholicism, is inappropriate for the moral education of a good Lutheran citizen. The Luther of cultural memory is, after all, a plain-speaking German who rejected the Latin of the Church, translating the Bible into the plain vernacular. From the traditional Lutheran perspective, eloquence is suspect because of its link with the papacy.[42] Seen in the context of the novel as a whole, Grünlich's allusion to Cicero's first Catilinarian oration is particularly threatening: first because it is about decadence, second because it is about homosexuality, and third because it is emblematic of the subversive, manipulative power of speech itself. Cicero uses speech as a weapon to enforce his own political agenda. He does not rely on the morality of his cause but on the skill of his tongue. As an orator he is essentially a public performer and, worse still, a kind of actor. Cicero's theatrics put him squarely on the immoral side of the Künstler, in opposition to Lutheran and North German values. Grünlich understands the reasons for Consul Jean's concern, and he immediately backtracks:

Sie sprechen meine Meinung aus, Herr Konsul . . . bevor ich ihr
Worte verleihen konnte! Eine schwierige und, wie ich hinzuzufügen
vergaß, *nicht unanfechtbare* Lektüre. Von allem abgesehen, erinnere
ich mich einiger direkt anstößiger Stellen in diesen Reden. . . .
(*B* 106)

[My opinion entirely, Herr Buddenbrook . . . you took the words
right out of my mouth. A difficult text, and as I failed to add, a *not
unexceptionable* one. Quite apart from anything else, I can recall several passages in those speeches that are blatantly offensive. (*Bu* 95)]

Grünlich alludes to the sections of the Catilinarian orations in which
Cicero expounds on Catiline's homosexual practices. Thomas Mann no
doubt enjoyed making a coded reference to homosexuality here. But
Cicero's speech also contains a warning that may apply directly to the
Buddenbrooks themselves:

The internal war is all that remains: the plots are within, the danger
is within, the enemy is within! Our struggle is against decadence,
against madness, against crime. . . .[43]

Cicero's denunciation of Catiline as an intolerable presence is remarkably
similar in tone to Thomas's outburst against Christian, when he says: "Du
bist vom Übel hier in dieser Stadt" (*B* 352; "You're a scandal to the whole
town," *Bu* 317). Woods's translation here is inadequate: "Übel" actually
means illness, evil, or misfortune. The implication is that Christian is a
human infection who threatens the body politic. Cicero was a conservative;
he belonged to the party of the Optimates, who opposed much-needed
political reforms,[44] and shows an affinity with the Buddenbrooks' resistance to change.

The cascade of rhetorical questions in Cicero's "In Catilinam I" provides a clue to the use of questions to propel the narrative in *Buddenbrooks*.
Cicero tells his students to practice *inventio* (the invention of arguments)
by asking a series of questions. Preparing a legal case, students should ask
themselves "why, and with what intention, and with what hopes and plans,
each thing was done."[45] Cicero's technique of asking rhetorical questions
may have served as an inspiration for the inner monologues of Thomas and
Hanno. Why is the rhetorical question so important to Thomas Mann?
Perhaps because the question issues a challenge to the reader; it opens up
a dialogue, a sense of ongoing debate. Like Mann's use of irony, his use of
questions leaves things open for the reader to decide. *Buddenbrooks* is a
novel of questions. It begins with a question: "Was ist das" [What is it] (*B*
9; "What does this mean," *Bu* 3). This opening sets the agenda for the
novel's incessant questioning, the relentless scrutiny of the family and its
way of life. This sense of constant self-questioning is most apparent when
the characters give in to Innerlichkeit and search their own souls. Two of

the most important scenes in *Buddenbrooks*, the "Schopenhauer" scene and the "Wagner" scene, are introduced by a series of questions. The fact that Thomas's reading of Schopenhauer is a decisive episode in the novel is signaled by the urgent series of questions Thomas asks himself:

> Was war dies? fragte er sich, während er ins Haus ging. . . . Was ist mir geschehen? Was habe ich vernommen? Was ist zu mir gesprochen worden, zu mir, Thomas Buddenbrook, Ratsherr dieser Stadt . . .? War dies für mich bestimmt? Kann ich es ertragen? (*B* 722)

> ["What was that?" he asked himself as he went into the house. . . . "What happened to me? What did I learn? What did it say to me—to me, Senator Thomas Buddenbrook . . .? Was it written for me? Can I bear what it says?" (*Bu* 634)]

And there is another series of questions during Hanno's fateful Wagnerian piano improvisations: "Was geschah? Was war in Vorbereitung? . . . Was geschah? Was wurde erlebt?" (*B* 825–26; What was happening? What was coming now? . . . What was happening? What was he feeling? *Bu* 720). Perhaps *Buddenbrooks* can best be understood in terms of these questions that recur throughout the narrative. It is arguably the incessant moral scrutiny of the family that drives the narrative forward. At these moments of questioning, the novel seems to take on the form of a Ciceronian forensic discourse. What is at stake is the status and value of the Buddenbrooks, their *ethos* (character) and entire way of life. Who and what are they, and what are we to think of them? Much of the novel's force derives from the fact that it asks these questions very urgently, but—unlike Cicero—the novel refuses to answer the questions in a definitive manner. The debate about the essence of the Buddenbrooks remains undecided, and this exemplifies the democratic, dialogic spirit of Thomas Mann's rhetoric.[46]

Conclusion: Stage-Managing Success

Public performance is an essential requirement for a Buddenbrook. This is why the sons of the merchant class are required to study Cicero's speeches as a preparation for business life. The centrality of oratory to the Buddenbrook ethos is underlined when Hanno recites Ludwig Uhland's poem "Schäfers Sonntagslied" (The Shepherd's Sunday Song) to his father. The narrative confirms that Thomas understands Hanno's poetic recital as a test of "Haltung und Widerstandskraft" (*B* 533; "composure and self-control," *Bu* 476). A good Bürger must also be a good orator.[47] The family's concern to keep up appearances becomes dangerous, however, in the cases of Consul Jean and Senator Thomas. Jean mistakes the show of religious sentiment for the genuine article in the case of Grünlich. Thomas invests so much in public relations that he neglects his profit-making instincts. He finds it hard to face the fact that in business, profits take priority over ethics.

In the fate of this merchant family we can sense the novel's profound ambivalence about business and economics, and indeed about the value of social forms themselves. And yet the novel also shows that the entrepreneurs must also be social performers. When Hermann Hagenström buys the Buddenbrook house in part 9, he does so because he values their image and their prestige; and he is willing to pay a great deal of money to acquire these attributes. This is because businesspeople need to develop a polished, carefully managed public image. And the ultimate test of Hanno's ability as a Bürger is, of all things, a poetic recital, a test of oratory. Therefore, the opposition between Bürger and Künstler is, to a certain extent, misleading. Thomas Mann became increasingly aware of this. The concern of the Buddenbrooks to "keep up appearances" and to be representative public figures is not simply symptomatic of weakness and decadence, although those issues do, of course, come into the novel. Rather, the Buddenbrooks' focus on aesthetic representation invites us to reflect on the inevitability of performance in institutional affairs, whether social, economic, mercantile, or familial. The aesthetics of the novel's form keep interlocking with the aesthetics of its theme. Which is perhaps why *Buddenbrooks* is one of the greatest realistic novels ever written: because it both delivers and reflects on its own realistic performance.

2: Oratory and Publicity in Heinrich Mann's *Der Untertan*, 1914/18

> *ein Redner ist er zwar nicht, aber ein*
> *Schreier und auch das genügt manchen.*
> [He is not an orator but a shouter—that
> is enough for some people.]
> —Franz Kafka

Introduction: The Media Kaiser; Business Networks

*D*ER UNTERTAN (*The Loyal Subject / The Man of Straw*), by Heinrich Mann (1871–1950), depicts the rise of Diederich Heßling, a paper manufacturer who builds an economic empire in the small town of Netzig. He is a charismatic businessman who continually invokes a sense of crisis in order to achieve his ends, acting as if he is "pflichtmäßiger Vollstrecker einer harten Notwendigkeit"[1] ("the conscientious instrument of dire necessity").[2] Set in the 1890s, it is a study of the German bourgeoisie in the age of global imperialism. The broad plotline bears comparison to Thomas Mann's *Buddenbrooks*: readers are presented with two rival business families, the Heßlings and the Bucks. The Buck family declines, and Diederich takes over. At the end of the novel Diederich even buys his rivals' family home (*U* 453; *LS* 330), just as Hagenström does in *Buddenbrooks*. The characters in both novels share an obsession with form. As Diederich's mentor Wiebel tells him, "Formen sind kein leerer Wahn" (*U* 35; "good form is not a vain illusion," *LS* 21). And yet Heinrich Mann comes to very different conclusions about the German middle classes than his younger brother. *Der Untertan* is overshadowed by the most prominent media personality of the age, Kaiser Wilhelm II.[3] The kaiser's prominence caused him to function as the mirror in which the entire period saw itself.[4] Walther Rathenau described the kaiser's many prominent media interventions as "elektro-journalistischer Cäsaropapismus" (electro-journalistic Caesaropapism).[5] The reign of Wilhelm II, the "media emperor," represents an important transitional stage between the ruling elites of the nineteenth century and their more media-conscious imitators in the twentieth century.[6] The new configuration between politics and media influenced German literary modernism, too. Cultural production in Imperial Germany occurred under the sign of Paragraph 95 of the *Reichsstrafgesetzbuch* (Imperial Criminal Law Code), detailing the crime of *Majestätsbeleidigung* (lèse-majesté), with a penal sentence of between two months and five years. Liberal journalists such as Maximilian Harden, the editor of the weekly magazine *Die Zukunft* (The Future), frequently served prison sentences for this crime.[7] Peter Sprengel suggests that Majestätsbeleidigung could even be seen as a programmatic procedure for German modernism.[8] In *Der Untertan*, the major turning point in Diederich's career is when his opponent Lauer is tried for Majestätsbeleidigung and sentenced to six months' imprisonment. Moreover, *Der Untertan* itself can be seen as an instance of Majestätsbeleidigung in which the kaiser and his views are reduced to miniature size.[9] Journalistic strategies also differed. Harden accused one of the kaiser's friends, the prince of Eulenburg, of homosexual conduct in 1906.[10] Karl Kraus, the editor of *Die Fackel* (The Torch), regarded the kaiser instead as personifying the corruption of language by the mass media.[11]

Der Untertan has always divided its readers along political lines. The conservative reception of the novel was inaugurated by Thomas Mann in *Betrachtungen eines Unpolitischen* (1918; *Reflections of an Unpolitical Man*), where he describes *Der Untertan* as "ein Unfug" (nonsense, mischief).[12] Werner Mahrholz took a similar line when the novel appeared in book form in 1918, describing it as a satirical pamphlet.[13] Satire is, of course, a low form of art and thus a key word for critics who would like to dismiss *Der Untertan* for political reasons.[14] Kurt Tucholsky refused to call *Der Untertan* a satire, describing it instead as a "modest photograph" of Wilhelmine Germany.[15] Any serious study of the novel has to show how it goes beyond satire. For example, it can be seen as a psychological study in the vein of Stendhal's *Le rouge et le noir* (1830; *The Red and the Black*). Instead of a young man who is obsessed with Napoleon, *Der Untertan* gives us a young man who is obsessed with Kaiser Wilhelm II.[16] Both novels thus depict the careerist's fascination with the public face of power. The protagonist rises through the ranks of the establishment only to become a defender of the political status quo. The other dominant approach to *Der Untertan* is to read it as an analysis of the "authoritarian personality."[17] As Helmut Peitsch points out, however, if *Der Untertan* were only a psychological Bildungsroman, then it could just as well end after chapter 2 (*LS* xiv).

The present chapter argues that *Der Untertan* is important, first, because it shows how the kaiser's speeches are deployed in the service of business interests, and second, because it depicts the networks that enable the protagonist's rise to power. The key feature of the German economic model of "korporative Marktwirtschaft" (corporate market economy) that developed around 1900 is "die hohe Verdichtung und Vernetzung des institutionellen Rahmens" (the high density of interconnected networks between the institutions).[18] The novel presents its fictional setting, Netzig, as a network, implying multiple interconnections among local and national politics, economics, and media. These are networks the protagonist skillfully exploits by campaigning simultaneously on a number of different fronts. Diederich Heßling uses politics as leverage to gain control of the paper factory in Gausenfeld. Politics here is a continuation of business by other means. Diederich understands that politics and business go hand in hand and that the best way to succeed in his career is to proceed not as a private individual but in a corporate manner.[19] Politically he is a conservative; his political mentor, Herr von Barnim, advocates the idea of a "people's parliament" formed of medieval estates (*ständische Volksvertretung*) in which each social order and craft guild would have its own representative. Diederich imagines himself as the representative of the paper manufacturers (*U* 56–57; *LS* 37).[20] Despite this fantasy, however, Diederich shows little solidarity with his own class. His rise is predicated on his ability to do deals with political forces who are hostile to the bourgeoisie: the aristocracy, represented by Herr von Wulckow, the chair of the Regional Council, and the Social Democrats (SPD), represented by Napoleon Fischer. In this way, he succeeds in overturning the liberal political orthodoxy in Netzig. Sensing that the political tide is turning toward nationalism, he exploits this tendency for his own ends. He thus typifies an era in which large sections of the German middle classes perceived that imperialism was more profitable than the pursuit of democratic reforms.

Diederich's career as a paper manufacturer is also significant because this period saw an exponential growth in newspaper circulation owing to population increase, expansion of literacy, and advances in print technology. At the end of the 1860s there were six newspapers with a print run higher than ten thousand. Three decades later, leading titles such as Ullstein's *Berliner Morgenpost* (Berlin Morning Post) had daily print runs of around a quarter of a million. In 1871 there were around 1,525 daily papers; in 1914 there were 4,200.[21] Hans-Ulrich Wehler notes that around this time journalists earned as much as lawyers.[22] It was also a good time to be a paper manufacturer. Diederich owes much of his success to his close relationship with Nothgroschen, the editor of the local *Netziger Zeitung* (Netzig Newspaper). He profits from newspapers both materially, since he supplies the paper on which they are printed, and in terms of his career, instigating scandals to disarm his opponents and persuading the newspaper to steer a more right-wing course.

Netzig is a microcosm of Imperial Germany, and its local politics parallel the major historical events of the Wilhelmine period.[23] The most important parallel occurs, however, on a textual level. The words people use and the thoughts they think are modeled on the German emperor's official public discourse. This is the linguistic network that knits business and politics together and overcomes the distance between imperial center and periphery, metropolis and region. Diederich Heßling and Kaiser Wilhelm II speak exactly the same language. Critics who regard Diederich as a mere caricature of the kaiser are missing the point. Diederich is not simply a caricature but a montage construction, a linguistic reproduction of the kaiser. The textual corpus of the kaiser's speeches forms the textual body of Diederich Heßling. This makes *Der Untertan* not a naturalist or an expressionist novel but a montage novel. By taking the kaiser's speeches out of context and inserting them into a different setting (the life of the bourgeoisie), the novel is able to reflect upon the practical uses of official discourse in everyday life and to explore the transmission of ideology as it occurs through the production and consumption of mass media. We will now consider the novel's montage technique in order to explore the function of political oratory in the work. This will then serve as a means to interpret the sociopolitical mechanisms Diederich exploits during his rise to economic preeminence.

Der Untertan as a Montage Novel

The scholar who discovered the principal source used by Heinrich Mann for *Der Untertan* was Hartmut Eggert in 1971.[24] Eggert found close textual parallels between *Der Untertan* and *Das Persönliche Regiment: Reden und sonstige öffentliche Aeußerungen Wilhelms II* (Personal Rule: Speeches and Other Public Statements of Wilhelm II).[25] This is a book-length collection of the kaiser's speeches edited by a Social Democrat, Wilhelm Schröder, and published in 1907, precisely when Mann was beginning to write his novel.[26] As a Social Democrat, Schröder was opposed to the kaiser, and his book deviates in several respects from the, chronological three-volume Reclam official edition of the kaiser's speeches: (1) Schröder prints the speeches in thematic groupings, not chronologically. (2) He does not reproduce the speeches in full, but only the most striking passages. (3) In the official versions of speeches printed the next day in establishment newspapers, phrases were often moderated and toned down. Schröder, in contrast, prints the more drastic versions of the kaiser's speeches, which he derived from other news reports. (4) Schröder includes telegrams sent by the kaiser, which were not included in the Reclam edition. (5) He prints the kaiser's most inflammatory phrases in boldface.[27] All of these features made the book suited for Heinrich Mann's purposes.[28] Indeed, Schröder states that he would like his book to be used as a political weapon against the kaiser: "Dies Buch soll dem Politiker als Handhabe dienen" (This book is intended to serve the politician as a tool).[29] This is underlined in the description of the kaiser's speeches as "Auslassungen" (remarks, outbursts).[30] Schröder recognizes the kaiser's stature as an orator, his talent

for coining "geflügelte Worte" (literally "winged words," i.e., sayings that
enter everyday usage), but he also stresses the shock value of these statements. His use of bold print magnifies their scandalous dimensions; e.g.,
when the kaiser tells army recruits that they may one day have to shoot
down their own brothers: "Es kann vorkommen, daß ihr eure eignen
Verwandten und Brüder niederschießen oder —stechen müßt" (it could
happen that you will have to **shoot** or cut down your own **relatives and
brothers**).[31]

Perhaps the most notorious speech included in Schröder's book is the
one given on February 24, 1892, at the Brandenburg Provincial Assembly.
It contains no less than three famous "sound bites," reproduced by
Schröder in bold type. All three phrases occur frequently throughout *Der
Untertan*: (1) those who are discontented and who complain ("Nörgler")
should "den **deutschen Staub von ihren Pantoffeln schütteln**" (**shake
off** the **German soil from their heels** [i.e., leave the country]; cf. *U* 184,
317, 320, 349). (2) "zu Großem sind wir noch bestimmt, und **herrlichen
Tagen** führe ich euch noch entgegen" (we are destined for greatness, and
I will lead you to **glorious days**; cf. *U* 106, 320, 432). (3) "**Mein Kurs
ist der richtige** und er wird weiter gesteuert" (**My course is the right one**
and it will be kept to; cf. *U* 106, 162, 380).[32] The textual borrowings from
the kaiser are woven into the text in various ways: sometimes they are
openly announced as quotations; at other times Diederich improvises on
them.[33]

Just as the kaiser functioned as a projection screen for many German
citizens, so Diederich articulates his business strategy using the kaiser's
discourse. The kaiser coined the phrase "der Platz an der Sonne" (place in
the sun) in a speech at a regatta on June 18, 1901, in which he claimed
that Germany's future would be decided at sea.[34] His ambition to rival
British naval supremacy is mirrored in Diederich's ambition to supplant
the factory owner Klüsing in Gausenfeld: "Der Fabrik war zu vergrößern.
. . . Man mußte konkurrenzfähig werden. Der Platz an der Sonne! Der alte
Klüsing . . . bildete sich wohl ein, er werde ewig das ganze Geschäft
machen?" (*U* 107; "The factory would have to be enlarged. . . . The operation would have to be made competitive. A place in the sun! Did old
Klüsing . . . imagine that he would go on forever getting all the business?"
LS 74). In this way, the novel sets up a parallel between imperialist foreign
policy and corporate takeovers, suggesting that they are two sides of the
same coin.

Diederich models his own domestic interventions closely on the kaiser's—for example, when a sentry shoots a worker whom Diederich had
fired earlier in the day. This episode alludes to an actual event that occurred
on April 2, 1892, when a sentry named Grenadier Lück shot a worker dead
in the street in Berlin. The newspapers reported that the kaiser had personally congratulated Lück on the shooting, promoted him to *Gefreiter* (pri-

vate first class), and presented him with a signed photograph.[35] In the fictional version Diederich Heßling invents a personal telegram from the kaiser informing the sentry of his promotion, which is later reported as fact by the newspapers. Diederich takes this acknowledgment of the rumor he has created as a sign of his profound affinity with the kaiser (*U* 172; *LS* 121). He imagines ermine robes around his shoulders. Later in the novel, when Diederich saves the kaiser from a demonstrator armed with tooth powder, Diederich's photo is published in a newspaper next to the kaiser's (*U* 370; *LS* 268–69). These are the moments in which Diederich's imitation of the kaiser reaches its apotheosis.

The novel's sustained use of montage sets up close parallels between bourgeois business circles and imperial politics. Diederich does not only represent the kaiser's political views in Netzig. He actually expresses himself using exactly the same words as the kaiser. In effect, he assumes the kaiser's voice and ventriloquizes him.[36] At one point the novel comments on its own artistic procedure:

> Er unterschrieb jedes Wort in jeder Rede des Kaisers, und zwar in der ersten, stärkeren Form, nicht in der abgeschwächten, die sie am Tage darauf annahmen. Alle diese Kernworte deutschen und zeitgemäßen Wesens—Diederich lebte und webte in ihnen, wie Ausstrahlungen seiner eignen Natur, sein Gedächtnis bewahrte sie, als habe er sie selbst gesprochen. Manchmal hatte er sie wirklich selbst gesprochen. Andere untermischte er bei öffentlichen Gelegenheiten seinen eigenen Erfindungen, und weder er noch ein anderer unterschied, was von ihm kam und was von einem Höheren. . . . (*U* 444)

> [He subscribed to every word in every speech of the Emperor's, and always in their first and strongest form, not in the toned-down version which appeared the next day. All these words so expressive of German character, so in tune with the times—Diederich lived and breathed in them, as if they had been manifestations of his own nature; they remained in his memory as if he himself had spoken them. Sometimes he really had spoken them. Others he mixed up on public occasions with his own remarks, and neither he nor anybody else could tell what came from him and what from one more exalted. . . . (*LS* 323)]

This is not just an imitation of the kaiser; it is an assumption of his personality. It is important to bear in mind, however, that Diederich's process of identification is not driven by genuine conviction but by ambition. Despite his professed loyalty, Diederich makes a deal with Napoleon Fischer, guaranteeing that Fischer will be elected as a Social Democrat. He sets up Major Kunze as a dummy candidate in the Reichstag election so that Fischer will win (*U* 383). Diederich has only acquired the kaiser's convictions (*Gesinnungen*) because he feels that doing so will benefit his career. His shocked response to the unorthodox ideas of his rival, Wolfgang Buck, is particularly revealing: "Dachte der Mensch mit solchen Gesinnungen Karriere zu machen?" (*U* 82; "Did the man actually hope to make a career for himself with opinions like that?" *LS* 56).[37] This does not mean, however, that Diederich has a secure self that consciously chooses to "play the game" while somehow remaining intact. On the contrary, his investment in his role means that his selfhood has been hollowed out. He becomes a living montage, the embodiment of what Jean-Paul Sartre would call *mauvaise foi* (bad faith). This makes him representative of an inauthentic era characterized by the performance of imperial ambition.[38] So pervasive is the emulation of the kaiser in Wilhelmine society that Wolfgang Buck decides that the most honest thing to do is to become an actor, because at least everyone knows that they speak borrowed lines (*U* 340; *LS* 246). The sense of performativity is foregrounded in *Der Untertan* through the figure of the orator.

Diederich as Orator

Heinrich Mann's interest in classical oratory derives from his reading of the naturalist journal *Die Gesellschaft* (Society), which he began in 1886 at the age of fifteen.[39] The journal introduced him to Conrad Alberti, whose dual activity as a novelist and public intellectual anticipates Mann's own career.[40] Like Mann, Alberti was an admirer of Émile Zola, an exponent of the naturalist novel who produced works combining social milieu and political critique. Although Alberti's literary fame was short-lived, he remains significant as an educator who raised public awareness about the importance of democratic debate and classical oratory. One of Alberti's essays for *Die Gesellschaft* even described Cicero and Darwin as the most influential figures of the modern age.[41] In 1890 Alberti edited a collection of great speechmakers, including Demosthenes, Girolamo Savonarola, Otto von Bismarck, and August Bebel, entitled *Die Schule des Redners* (The Orator's School).[42] Alberti's portrayal of Cicero in particular exerted a profound influence on Heinrich Mann, shaping the character of the humanist lawyer Belotti in the novel *Die kleine Stadt* (1910; *The Little Town*), as well as Wolfgang Buck in *Der Untertan*. Indeed, *Der Untertan* shows a particularly close affinity with Alberti: Alberti's novel *Die Alten und die Jungen* (1889; The Old and the Young) depicts an intergenerational conflict centering on an artist-hero who is inspired by Kaiser Wilhelm II.[43] The connection with Alberti is relevant here because it informs Mann's conception of his protagonist, Diederich Heßling, who constantly practices his skills as an orator, rehearsing the postures and received ideas he has absorbed from his idol. In particular, he adopts the kaiser's rhetoric of imperial expansion to give credence to his own business agenda.

The structure of *Der Untertan* revolves around a series of verbal clashes between two rival orators: Diederich Heßling and Wolfgang Buck. Their verbal exchanges embody the clash of conservative and liberal ideologies, so that Mann's novel starts to read like a courtroom drama. The protagonists embody two very different attitudes to oratory: Wolfgang is a highly conscious orator who admits that he uses the tricks of the orator's trade, while Diederich professes a scorn of rhetoric. Much like Bismarck, Diederich is an orator who claims not to be one, a speaker whose denial of rhetoric is itself a rhetorical tactic.[44] As an orator he adopts an authoritarian persona, insisting on order and hierarchy. In contrast, Wolfgang is an orator in the republican, Ciceronian tradition. He recalls the liberal politician Eduard von Simson, who modeled himself on Cicero.[45] Wolfgang's identification with Cicero is underlined in the trial scene by his deliberate use of pathos (*U* 239; *LS* 171) and by the fact that he is described as wearing a Roman toga (*U* 240; translated incorrectly as "gown," *LS* 171).

Orators and actors are both paid to convince people, and classical orators were often trained by actors.[46] Like actors, they delivered speeches that were written by others—by speechwriters. For example, the emperor Nero's debut oration in the senate was ghostwritten for him by his tutor, Seneca. Nero's "borrowed eloquence" caused a minor scandal because it drew attention to "the fragile boundary between the orator and the actor."[47] In *Der Untertan* Wolfgang creates a similar scandal when he invites a group of actors into the courtroom, drawing attention to the performativity of the judicial process itself. He is a kind of Brechtian performer who deliberately draws attention to his performance. In contrast, Diederich is a method actor who is determined to conceal his performance and uphold a feeling of authenticity. He immerses himself in his borrowed role and even practices it when nobody else is around (*U* 442–45; *LS* 321–24). Wolfgang, in contrast, keeps falling out of role. He regards the actor as the representative type of the era (*U* 206; *LS* 147) and understands that Diederich and the kaiser are both essentially performers.[48]

The turning point in the novel is the trial for Majestätsbeleidigung. As the chief witness for the prosecution, Diederich is a more powerful speaker than Wolfgang, the defense lawyer. As Diederich talks, Wolfgang leans forward in his seat and studies him closely:

> Wolfgang Buck aber: vorgebeugt auf seinem Stuhl, spähte er zu Diederich hinauf, gespannt, sachkundig und die Augen voll eines feindlichen Entzückens. Das war eine Volksrede! Ein Auftritt von bombensicherer Wirkung! Ein Schlager! (*U* 230)

> [Wolfgang Buck leaned forward in his chair and gazed up at Diederich, with the excited interest of an expert, his glance betraying a hostile joy. That was a mob oration! A sure hit! A winner! (*LS* 164)]

An orator must establish his or her ethos, i.e., his or her character and personal credibility as an individual that the audience can trust, which for Aristotle was "the most effective means of persuasion."[49] Diederich is extremely proud of his "männliche Gesinnung" (*U* 99; "manly noble sentiments," *LS* 69); *Gesinnung* can be translated as "sentiments" or "attitudes" but also as "ethos." While his obsession with Gesinnung may seem comical, it is arguably the hallmark of the orator and performer who, like Aristotle, recognizes that the appeal to character is the strongest proof. This explains Diederich's obsessive desire to appear as a *vir bonus*, a man of good moral character. Ethos is not simply a quality of the speaker; it expresses the audience's perception of the speaker.[50] At the same time, Diederich alleges that his opponent, Wolfgang, has a "schlappe Gesinnung" (*U* 317; "a flabby point of view," *LS* 229). This is not merely an attack on Buck's views, though, as the English translation would suggest. It is a direct attack on his ethos, his character. Diederich asserts that Wolfgang lacks character in order to destroy his credibility.

In this way, Diederich's continual emphasis on Gesinnung effectively implements Aristotelian rhetoric. If he can appear as a man of good character, then he will be credible, and so he presents himself as an unselfish man of the people: "Der uneigennützige Idealismus, meine Herren Richter, ist ein Vorrecht des Deutschen, er wird ihn unentwegt betätigen" (*U* 230; "Unselfish idealism, gentlemen, is the privilege of a German, and he will defend his ideals," *LS* 164). In summing up, he once again underlines his Germanic ethos:

> Sachlich sein heißt deutsch sein! Und ich meinerseits . . . bekenne mich zu meinen Handlungen, denn sie sind der Ausfluß eines tadellosen Lebenswandels, der auch im eigenen Hause auf Ehre hält und weder Lüge noch Sittenlosigkeit kennt! (*U* 231)[51]

> [To be impartial is to be German! I for my part . . . stand by my actions, for they spring from an exemplary life, which rests upon honor in the home and which knows neither untruth nor immorality! (*LS* 165)]

This is why Diederich's *Volksrede* (public speech) has the popular touch: because he continually affirms shared values and commonplaces that are familiar to his audience. Wolfgang Buck, in contrast, speaks without any regional accent, and this alienates much of his audience: "Den andern sprach Buck zu gewählt, und daß er an keinen Dialekt anklang, befremdete" (*U* 238; "For the others, Buck's language was too refined, and they were put off by his avoidance of dialect," *LS* 169–70). Wolfgang's lack of dialect and his eclecticism render his ethos suspect. As Aristotle puts it, an orator must "disguise his art and give the impression of speaking naturally and not artificially. Naturalness is persuasive, artificiality is the contrary; for our hearers are prejudiced and think we have some design against them, as if we were mixing their wines for them."[52] Wolfgang ignores Aristotle's recommendation and undermines his own arguments by the artificiality of his style. Ultimately, his speech fails because he gets too carried away by his own eloquence: "Aber Buck mißbrauchte seinen Erfolg, er ließ sich berauschen" (*U* 241; "But Buck spoiled his effect by allowing his excitement to carry him away," *LS* 172).[53] The public mood swings in Diederich's favor. Later, Wolfgang admits to Diederich that "Ihre Rolle vor Gericht hat mich mehr interessiert als meine eigene. Später, zu Hause vor meinem Spiegel, habe ich sie Ihnen nachgespielt" (*U* 313; "your role in court interested me much more than my own. Afterwards, when I got home, I imitated you in front of the mirror," *LS* 226). Wolfgang is fascinated by Diederich for aesthetic and technical reasons; he regards him as a fellow actor and performer. But just as Wolfgang has studied Diederich, so, too, has Diederich studied the kaiser. Diederich is a successful orator precisely because he has modeled himself so closely on the kaiser. Indeed, Diederich is at his most convincing when he invents phrases that could have come from the kaiser himself. When Diederich tells the veterans' association that the kaiser has threatened to dissolve parliament, this is not a quotation but an inspired guess. After the speech, Diederich no longer knows if these are his own words or the kaiser's (*U* 246; *LS* 175). At such moments, Diederich's identification with the kaiser appears complete.

Publicity and Charisma

Like Donald Trump, Kaiser Wilhelm II had a genius for publicity. Both are famous for their shock rhetoric and "rednerische Entgleisungen" (oratorical derailments).[54] Reflecting on the importance of publicity, Diederich quotes the kaiser: "Das Theater ist auch eine meiner Waffen" (*U* 354; "The theater is one of my weapons as well!" *LS* 256).[55] The new speed of print media around 1900 meant that government actions came under unprecedented public scrutiny. In consequence, the German state needed to develop new "strategies of acceptance" to steer its relationship with the public.[56] Wilhelm II courted celebrity because his position required him to do so.[57] The parallel with Trump's Twitter account is obvious.

Der Untertan considers the role models who shaped the kaiser's public persona: Napoleon I, Bismarck, and, of course, the kaiser's own father, Wilhelm I. In February 1892, when unemployed workers demonstrate in Berlin, Wilhelm II confronts them on horseback. A bystander comments: "Kennen wir. Napoleon in Moskau, sich solo unter der Bevölkerung mischend. . . . Theater, und nicht mal gut." (*U* 62; "Old stuff. Napoleon in Moscow fraternizing alone with the people. . . . Theatrics, and not even good ones at that," *LS* 40.) Wolfgang Buck makes a similar point as he contemplates the memorial to Kaiser Wilhelm I (*U* 455; *LS* 331). The kaiser's style also mimics Bismarck's charismatic rule. As Wolfgang exclaims to Diederich: "Erst jetzt, da ihr über ihn [Bismarck] hinaus sein solltet, hängt ihr euch an seinen kraftlosen Schatten!" (*U* 319; "But now, when you should have moved beyond him [Bismarck], you cling to his powerless shadow! *LS* 230). Wolfgang thinks that the age of great, world-historic individuals is over, and that any imitation of Bismarck will be fruitless. He states: "Zukunft hat nur die Masse. Einen Bismarck wird es nicht mehr geben und auch keinen Lassalle mehr" (*U* 81; the future belongs to the masses. There will be no more Bismarcks and no more Lassalles," *LS* 55). From today's perspective this comment seems absurdly naive, given that Bismarck and Ferdinand Lassalle were soon to be eclipsed by the dictators of the twentieth century. Nevertheless, the idea rings true that the kaiser's style of personal rule was—on one level, at least—a response to Bismarck's legacy.

Every political leader and business leader needs to cultivate a certain charisma, as defined by Max Weber in the essay "Die drei reinen Typen der legitimen Herrschaft" (1922; "The Three Types of Legitimate Rule").[58] The charismatic ruler gains legitimation primarily by overcoming a series of emergencies; he or she thrives on crisis.[59] The danger for the charismatic ruler is that, in the absence of any further crisis, his or her charisma will gradually dissipate. Therefore, the charismatic leader is often forced, or tempted, to engineer a crisis in order to reestablish his or her authority.[60] This theory explains Bismarck's technique of staging a crisis to secure his own political dominance. Under Bismarck, mobilization against internal and external enemies was used to brush aside internal political opposition.[61] Wilhelm II continued this policy, denouncing "the enemy within"—socialists, Jews, "Nörgler"—in order to crush internal opposition.[62] He also invoked the threat of French aggression, as personified at the time by General Georges Boulanger (nicknamed "Général Revanche," 1837–91). In *Der Untertan* Diederich makes a speech referring to Boulanger's call for revanche, and a heckler shouts out: "Wieviel hat er aus Berlin dafür bekommen?" (*U* 409; "How much is he getting for that from Berlin?" *LS* 297). The point for politicians and would-be business leaders is simple: invoke an external threat to keep people in line. Manufacture the opposition to serve your own purposes.

Diederich as Publicist

Diederich's rise to power depends on his skillful manipulation of public opinion.[63] He uses an astonishing variety of media and public forums to get his message across: not only print media but also the telegraph, the courtroom, the town hall, the beer cellar, the political rally, the high-society ball, and the civic ceremony. His public appearances are carefully managed in advance. And like a good performer he calculates the effect he is likely to produce and times his entrances. When he goes to the Harmony Ball in chapter 5 he takes care not to arrive too early, as this would spoil the effect: "Die ganze Wirkung der Persönlichkeit ging zum Teufel, wenn man zu früh da war" (*U* 269; "The impression one made went to the devil when one arrived too early," *LS* 192). Diederich's first great publicity coup is the court case in which Lauer is sentenced for lèse-majesté. Diederich is careful to gauge the mood in the courtroom. He takes his cue from the judge, Dr. Fritzsche. When he hears that Fritzsche is determined to be severe, he amends his statement and denounces Lauer. Like a good orator or public-relations expert, he studies his audience with precision before he acts.

The role of the media is represented here by the editor of the *Netziger Zeitung*, Nothgroschen. His name, which means "nest egg," is telling: it suggests that his main motivation is financial. Called to the witness stand, he responds to the judge's questions like a "Musterschüler" (*U* 221; "model pupil," *LS* 157). He has heard in the corridor how things are going and hastens to join the winning side. When the defense protests, Nothgroschen declares: "Wir sind ein liberales, also unparteiisches Blatt. Wir geben die Stimmung wieder. Da aber jetzt und hier die Stimmung dem Angeklagten ungünstig ist—" (*U* 221; "Ours is a liberal—that is, an impartial paper. We reflect public opinion. Since here and now opinion is unfavorable to the defendant—," *LS* 157). This shows the flexibility of the editorial line: the journalist is essentially a *Mitläufer* (follower, collaborator) who mirrors the dominant ideology. His claim that he merely reflects public opinion is a half-truth, however. Sometimes he listens to public opinion; more frequently, though, he manages and shapes it in tacit accordance with the authorities. In the course of the novel the *Netziger Zeitung* moves gradually to the right until it is entirely at Diederich's disposal (*U* 432; *LS* 314). While Hans-Ulrich Wehler describes the Wilhelmine press as critical and outspoken,[64] *Der Untertan* presents it as servile and supine.

The main technique Diederich Heßling uses to destroy his rivals is *Rufmord* (character assassination). Slander and "fake news" have been used as political methods from ancient times to the present day. Jacob Burckhardt devotes an entire chapter to "Spott und Witz" (ridicule and wit) in part 2, section 4 of his history of the Italian Renaissance, noting Machiavelli's prologue to his drama *La Mandragola* (1518; *The Mandrake*), in which he threatens his enemies "daß er sich auf Übelreden verstehe" (that he knows how to talk spitefully of people).[65] Burckhardt compares the Italian publicists of the Renaissance to modern Parisian journalists and gives special mention to Pietro Aretino (1492–1556), calling him "der größte Lästerer der modernen Zeit" (the greatest slanderer of the modern period), a specialist at using blackmail to achieve his ends.[66] Fake news requires skill in the art of "pikante Lügenhaftigkeit, [die] das So zum Anders und das Nichts zum Etwas verkünstelt" (suggestive falsehood, [which] turns black into white and everything into anything).[67] In early modern Venice malicious gossip was so powerful that court proceedings could be initiated on the basis of *vox et fama publica* (public opinion or hearsay).[68] In this sense, saying bad things about one's opponents is as old as humanity. In the twenty-first-century context the term for this technique is "opposition research": "Investigation into the dealings of political opponents, typically in order to discredit them publicly."[69] This strategy was widely used during the US presidential election campaign of 2016.[70]

Diederich Heßling is an expert at character assassination, rumor, slander, and scandal. He uses allegations of sexual misconduct against Wolfgang Buck and allegations of financial misconduct against Wolfgang's father, old Buck. These are classic tactics.[71] In order to cause a split between Wolfgang and Guste Daimchen, he resurrects some old gossip about Guste being born "too early," implying that she was conceived as a result of her mother's adulterous relationship with old Buck (*U* 263; *LS* 187). This could mean that Guste and Wolfgang have the same father; if so, their marriage would be incestuous. As readers, we never learn whether the gossip is true or not, but that is not the point. The point is that Diederich shapes public opinion into a powerful weapon. He is careful to spread the gossip all around town without appearing to do so. He relies on his mother, his sisters, and the seamstress Fräulein Gehritz to disseminate the tale (*U* 265; *LS* 189). The ploy succeeds, and before long the entire town is talking of nothing else but the shameful union of Guste and Wolfgang. Diederich is amazed: the phantom that he sent out into the world has taken on physical form (*U* 281; *LS* 201). As he observes: "über die Meinung seiner Mitmenschen setzt niemand sich ungestraft hinweg" (*U* 315; "nobody can defy public opinion with impunity," *LS* 227).

In Diederich's election campaign against old Buck, the key issue is how the city council will spend old Kühlemann's legacy. The liberals want a new home for foundlings to be built; the nationalists want a new memorial to Kaiser Wilhelm I. Diederich writes a polemical newspaper article against the foundlings' home, alleging that it will encourage vice (*U* 380; *LS* 275–76). He gathers loyal foot soldiers who will implement his campaign strategy: Gottlieb Hornung and the veterans' association, which functions as a base of operations (*U* 375; *LS* 272). Hornung canvasses building contractors who stand to benefit, ensuring that the nationalist campaign meeting is packed with Diederich's supporters. He orchestrates the entire event from behind a cloud of cigar smoke: if anyone fails to clap, he sends in the innkeeper and his daughter with more beer to ensure that the audience applauds (*U* 382; *LS* 277). Kunze and Hornung are the warm-up acts, and Diederich gives the closing speech, which is a rousing success. At the next election meeting he ensures once again that the audience has been carefully selected in advance: the memorial contractors and their employees are present to heckle the liberal speakers (*U* 406; *LS* 295). These are the loyal troops who mingle with the audience and support Diederich when he accuses the liberals of making a property deal that involves misappropriation of public funds (*U* 412; *LS* 300). Diederich himself is involved in a similar deal, but he has covered his tracks much better than his opponents. The scene is managed so well that public opinion turns against the liberals. The allegations against old Buck cannot be entirely disproved. Diederich has successfully masterminded a hostile smear campaign. *Der Untertan* is, among other things, a master class in successful media management.

Transforming Politics into Profits

Behind the scenes, Diederich has been making a series of political deals. The Wilhelmine state pursued *Sammlungspolitik* (bringing-together policy), fostering an alliance between big landowners and heavy industry in order to outflank German liberals. In 1879 the Nationalliberale Partei (National Liberal Party) fractured, with Heinrich von Treitschke leading the charge to the right.[72] The left liberals regrouped under Eugen Richter's Deutsche Freisinnige Partei (DFP, German Free-Minded Party).[73] Old Buck's defeat in *Der Untertan* is symptomatic of the electoral decline of Richter's brand of left liberalism. Diederich Heßling's deal with the aristocracy exemplifies the Sammlungspolitik of this period: as an industrialist, he makes his fortune by forming a secret alliance with the Junkers, Wulckow and Quitzin. He assists their property speculation, and in return they force Klüsing, the rival factory owner, to appoint Diederich as his successor. In order to seal the deal, Diederich accepts humiliating treatment from the aristocrats.[74] But he achieves his object and becomes the managing director of Gausenfeld. In this way, Diederich's political agitation is a mask for his opportunism, leverage to be used for personal advantage. His political engagement serves the cause of disinformation, as the most important deals are done in private.

This is also evident in his relations with the workers. In public, Diederich likes to bully his employees; but in private, he enters into a pact with their elected representative, Napoleon Fischer. This aspect of *Der Untertan* gives a damning verdict on the SPD.[75] Heinrich Mann had witnessed the transformation of the SPD in the Wilhelmine period from a revolutionary party to a moderate reform movement. This shift, known as revisionism, occurred under the aegis of Social Democratic leaders such as Georg Vollmar and Eduard Bernstein, as well as trade union leaders such as Carl Legien.[76] Mann's liberalism and idealism made him suspicious of materialism. In an essay of 1923 he commented that trade unionists and industrialists ultimately share the same views, namely, that human beings are determined by economics.[77] In *Der Untertan* the Bucks are defeated, but they retain a certain dignity. In contrast, Fischer, the Social Democrat, is portrayed as an unprincipled careerist. For example, when a fourteen-year-old worker is injured in an industrial accident, Diederich persuades Fischer not to ask for compensation and bribes him with the compromising story of the Bucks' personal affairs (*U* 266–69; *LS* 190–92); the injured girl is soon forgotten. Then Diederich and Fischer make a pact: each will help the other to get elected as a city councillor (*U* 324; *LS* 232). Fischer even says that he would rather do a deal with the Nationalists than with the Liberals: "Wir in unserer Partei haben gewissermaßen allerhand Achtung vor dem nationalen Rummel. Bessere Geschäfte sind allemal damit zu machen" (*U* 323; "In my party we have a certain respect for patriotic hullabaloo, [it makes it] easier to do business," *LS* 233). In real life this sort of cooperation culminated in the "Burgfrieden" (party truce) of August 1914, when the SPD approved military expenditures for the war. And Diederich does not forget to bribe the workers as well as their leaders: his housing projects for his workers are reported positively in the *Netziger Zeitung* (*U* 435–36; *LS* 317).

In *Der Untertan* politics is frequently represented as a cover for personal advancement. Most of the characters are careerists and opportunists. Napoleon Fischer sells out the socialist cause to advance his own career. Similarly, Jadassohn is a Jew who sells out the Jewish cause to advance *his* career. He makes anti-Semitic comments (*U* 157; *LS* 111) and prosecutes a man for saying that the royal family has been infiltrated by Jews because he regards this statement as an insult to the monarchy (*U* 147; *LS* 103). Later, he goes to Paris and has plastic surgery so that he can look less like a Jew (*U* 310–11, 423).[78]

Even the Liberals sell out their political cause. The promise of a colonial empire and a fleet wins the remaining Liberals to Diederich's way of thinking (*U* 448; *LS* 326–27). Before the trial, the two bourgeois parties—the Liberals and the Nationalists—sit at separate tables in the beer cellar; but after the approval of military spending, they sit at the same table.[79] The liberals in *Der Untertan*, Heuteufel and Cohn, are representative of an entire generation of liberals who approved the expansion of German militarism. The colonial empire was accepted as a compensation for semi-authoritarian rule.[80] From the late nineteenth century onward, the German economy was increasingly geared to the world export market.[81] The capitulation of the Liberals in *Der Untertan* is an indication that, for many, growth in German exports took precedence over democratic reform. Diederich's final speech provides a narrative in which Germany's ambitions for world-power status and its economic growth are closely coupled. Germany's entry into the world market is portrayed as a guarantee of future prosperity: "denn das Weltgeschäft ist heute das Hauptgeschäft!"

(*U* 466; "today, world commerce is our chief concern," *LS* 339). Diederich denounces the ideals of 1848 in favor of practical power politics:

> In der Politik dagegen war bekanntlich jede Ideologie vom Übel. Seinerzeit im Frankfurter Parlament hatten gewiß hochbedeutende Männer gesessen, aber es waren noch keine Realpolitiker gewesen, und darum hatten sie nichts als Unsinn gemacht (*U* 447)

> [In politics, on the other hand, the consensus was that every ideology was anathema. In its day, the Frankfurt Parliament could count among its ranks some truly illustrious men, granted, but there were no true *realpolitiker* [*sic*], and therefore their works amounted to nothing but rubbish (*LS* 326)]

Diederich accuses his opponents of ideology and claims to be a "realist" who is free from ideology. The irony here is that Diederich does have an ideology. He calls it "Realpolitik," and he understands it as the primacy of power and brute force.[82] In this respect, Max Weber's comment on "Realpolitik" speaks volumes:

> Im ganzen neigen die Menschen hinlänglich stark dazu, sich dem Erfolg oder dem jeweiligen Erfolg Versprechenden innerlich anzupassen, nicht nur . . . in den Mitteln oder in dem Maße, wie sie ihre letzten Ideale jeweils zu realisieren trachten, sondern in der Preisgabe dieser selbst. In Deutschland glaubt dies mit dem Namen "Realpolitik" schmücken zu dürfen.[83]

> [On the whole, people have this inclination to adapt strongly to those things that promise success or temporary success . . . not only in the means or the method by which they hope to achieve their final ideals, but even to the extent of giving up these very ideals. In Germany, people try to embellish such behavior with the slogan "Realpolitik."[84]]

Weber's warning against those who take realpolitik to mean abandoning one's principles certainly applies to the Liberals' capitulation in *Der Untertan*.

Conclusion: The Growth of the Corporation

At the end of the novel two rival factories are merged. Now Diederich is no longer the head of a family business but the director of an *Aktiengesellschaft* (AG), a corporation limited by share ownership. As managing director, Diederich surrounds himself with "gefügige Männer" (*U* 433; "docile men," *LS* 315) to give himself a free hand. The severing of the business from the family completes its transformation to a modern corporation. Diederich becomes a captain of industry recalling Carl Ferdinand von Stumm-Halberg (1836–1901), the conservative politician and industrialist. Like Stumm-Halberg, he calls for the introduction of eugenics and sterilization programs (*U* 385; *LS* 280).[85]

Readers of *Der Untertan* will recognize the prefiguration of fascist rhetoric, with its insistence on scapegoating "the enemy within." Throughout the twenties, Heinrich Mann continued to warn that the slavish mentality and authoritarianism of the Wilhelmine era still existed, but in new and more dangerous forms (military, judiciary, bureaucracy, cartels). The dominant figure of the age was no longer the kaiser, but money itself. In 1929 Mann wrote the preface to a new edition of *Der Untertan* in which he observed:

> Man kann auch in der Republik ein rechter Untertan sein. Dafür ist nicht nötig, daß man Herrscher verehrt und nachäfft. Dafür genügt, daß man irgendeine ander Macht gewähren läßt, vielleicht die Geldmacht. (*U* 618)

> [Even in a republic you can still be a proper "subject." In order to qualify as a subject it is not necessary to worship and mimic your rulers. To qualify as a subject it is enough to let another power prevail, for example the power of money.]

While the face of power changes, the mechanisms of persuasion as studied in classical oratory continue to be valid. Orators still need to construct their own ethos by building up a bond with the public; they still need to demolish the ethos of their opponents. They still need to invoke a crisis in order to legitimize themselves; they still need good sound-bites. *Der Untertan* remains relevant because it reveals brilliantly how language is used to pursue economic agendas, suggesting that backroom lobbying and media management are essential aspects of both business and politics.

3: Organizing Speech in Gabriele Tergit's *Käsebier erobert den Kurfürstendamm,* 1931

> *Non omne quod nitet aurum est.*
> [All that glitters is not gold.]
> —Proverb

Introduction: Liberal Critique

GABRIELE TERGIT (1894–1982), born Elise Hirschmann, was a respected journalist and court correspondent for the *Berliner Tageblatt* (Berlin Daily News) from 1924 to 1933. *Käsebier erobert den Kurfürstendamm* (1931; Käsebier Conquers the Kurfürstendamm), her first novel, is set against the background of the Wall Street crash of October 24, 1929, and its devastating consequences for Germany.[1] The novel is also informed by a Berlin corruption scandal that began on September 26, 1929. The three Sklarek brothers, clothing retailers, had a government contract to supply clothes for civil servants; they forged receipts somewhere in the region of ten million marks. The scandal provided considerable fuel for National Socialist propaganda.[2] In early 1932 Tergit reported on the trial of Moritz Rosenthal, a business partner of the Sklareks, pointing out that he was at the same time an administrator and beneficiary of public funds.[3] The emerging details of the Sklareks' backroom deals certainly influenced the composition of *Käsebier.* The novel depicts German liberalism in crisis. The collapse of the monarchy in 1918 had led to a "Sinnkrise" (crisis of meaning) for the educated middle classes, as they lost the special entitlement they had enjoyed in the Wilhelmine state; the idea of Bildung was stripped of its prestige and was replaced by the worship of money.[4] That year the liberal author Carl Sternheim commented on the intellectual bankruptcy of the German nation, remarking

> daß alle Welt in Deutschland von der obersten Spitze bis zum letzten Arbeiter entschlossen stand, jeden menschlichen und mitmenschlichen Akt von seiner ziffernmäßigen Bedeutung abhängig zu machen, das heißt einfach jedes Geschehen nach seinem pekuniären Erfolg wertete.[5]

[that every social class in Germany, from the highest elite to the lowest worker, was determined to judge every human action in terms of its profitability, put simply, to judge every event in terms of its financial return.]

Sternheim argues that humanist values such as *Geist* (a term that combines aspects of "intellect" and "spirit" and will henceforth be left untranslated) and Bildung have been replaced with economic rhetoric:

Allmählich schwand natürlich auch die Fähigkeit, mit Geist überhaupt umzugehen. Die Sprache bildete nur für wirtschaftliche Phänomene noch ausreichende Begriffe und damit war etwas anderes als Ökonomisches in Deutschland überhaupt nicht mehr lebendig.[6]

[Gradually, of course, the ability to use our Geist disappeared. Language still provided adequate concepts for dealing with economic phenomena alone, and when that stage had been reached, it was only in economic affairs that any vitality could still be found in Germany.]

For Tergit, writing in 1931, this situation had become even more exacerbated. The contemporary rejection of Geist is typified in *Käsebier* by the careerist Willi Frächter.[7] Frächter declares scornfully: "Mit Geist lockt man keinen Hund vom Ofen. Geist? Wer will Geist?" (*Kb* 147; You won't catch a dog with Geist. Geist? Who wants Geist?). Frächter's view that Geist is obsolete is linked to his cynical view of human beings as dogs. For Frächter, liberal narratives about human dignity no longer apply.

In *Käsebier* this decline in liberal values is exemplified by the decline in journalistic standards. In the first chapter Schröder, an aging journalist, predicts that the government will fall and the far right will come to power (*Kb* 11). He complains that journalists are no longer capable of delivering an informed, principled critique of the state and how it operates: "Wir haben ein parlamentarisches System ohne einen Etatkritiker" (*Kb* 12; We have a parliamentary system without a critic of the state). His younger colleague, Gohlisch, responds: "Wozu? Skandalmachen trägt mehr ein. Beziehungen und ein Pöstchen" (*Kb* 12; Why bother? Reporting scandals is more profitable. Connections and a nice little position). Instead of doing something about the situation, Gohlisch accepts it with an ironic shrug. This exchange neatly draws attention to the contradictory, ambivalent role of news media. On the one hand, newspapers are supposed to safeguard the democratic process by informing their readers and giving balanced, differentiated accounts of events. On the other hand, they are businesses that have to make a profit, which means that they will tend to value sensational headlines more than serious, critical reporting. Intense competition can have a negative effect on quality journalism because it forces media to cater to the most tepid "mainstream" interests, becoming depoliticized so as not to offend readers.[8] Most publications at this time were owned by three companies: Ullstein, Mosse, and Scherl. The *Berliner Tageblatt*, for which Tergit wrote, was owned by Mosse and served as the model for the fictional *Berliner Rundschau* (Berlin Review) in *Käsebier*. Mosse's competitor Scherl was taken over in 1916 by the industrialist, far-right politician, and media mogul Alfred Hugenberg (1865–1951),[9] thus making print media increasingly subject to corporate interests. From 1928 onward Hugenberg's tabloid *Berliner Nachtausgabe* (Berlin Evening News) openly supported the Nazis.[10] Tergit's novel goes to the heart of these problems, depicting journalists who are so desperate to keep their jobs that they toe the editorial line, abandoning pluralistic political coverage.[11] As Gohlisch puts it: "Wozu Talent? Nicht-Talent mit etwas Sadismus gewürzt bringt viel mehr Geld ein. Ein genotzüchtigtes Mädchen ist beliebter als ein Satz von Goethe" (*Kb* 15; What's the point of talent? Nontalent spiced with a little sadism is more profitable. A brutalized girl is more popular than a quotation from Goethe). Gohlisch, however, also worries that he has betrayed his class and that he has become a hack (*Kb* 284). Throughout the novel the journalists lament the seedy realities of their trade, the hackwork and the superficial gossip. But if journalists are corrupt, so, too, are the other characters: "Große Worte klangen: 'Nieder mit dem Kapitalismus!'—'Für deutsche Freiheit!' Aber dahinter stand für jeden einzelnen die nagende Sorge, ob er seinen Platz, seinen engen oder weiten Platz, würde im Leben halten können" (*Kb* 337; Grand words were used: "Down with capitalism!"—"For German freedom!" But behind these words, for each person there was the gnawing worry whether he would be able to maintain his position, small or large, in life). In this way, Tergit's text encourages its readers to be critical, alerting them to the material interests underlying public rhetoric.

Käsebier indicts the corruption of society in general, particularly the banking sector, the construction industry, and local government. In chapter 2 the journalist Augur declares that

> nirgends mehr kommt es auf die Leistung an, weil die keiner zu schätzen weiß, sondern nur auf die Organisation des Geredes darüber. Statt einer Cliquenwirtschaft, der des Offizier- und Studentenkorps, haben wir jetzt hundert nebeneinander, nationale Clique, soziale Clique, katholische Clique, Cliquen fürs Verdienen, Cliquen für Pensionen. Kurzum, wer nicht die Hintenherumwege kennt, ist verloren. (*Kb* 26)

> [nowadays what counts is not the achievement itself (which nobody appreciates), but the organization of gossip about it. Instead of a clique economy run by officers and student fraternities, we now have a hundred cliques existing side by side: a national clique, a social clique, a Catholic clique, cliques for earning money, cliques for pensions. In short, anyone who doesn't have any connections behind them is lost.]

This is a situation in which the most important form of work is networking. When Augur tries to blame capitalism for this situation, however, Gohlisch replies that the terror of communism is much worse (*Kb* 27). Tergit's characters are worried by the political successes of the far right, but they are also appalled by the show trials taking place in the Soviet Union (*Kb* 17). Politically, they no longer know which way to turn.

This opening sets the tone for what is to come as the novel shows its liberal characters in disarray, their humanist values mocked as outdated. The main characters, the journalists Georg Miermann and Fräulein Dr. Lotte Kohler, are *Bildungsbürger* (members of the educated class) who find that education no longer commands respect. The situation is particularly ironic for Lotte Kohler who, like Tergit herself, is representative of the first generation of German women to complete doctoral dissertations. This generation of women struggled to acquire Bildung for the very first time precisely when it was being devalued.[12]

Given that *Käsebier*, like *Der Untertan*, charts the defeat of liberalism by corporate capitalism, it is fitting that the initial inspiration for Tergit's novel was a newspaper article by Heinrich Mann, "Lachbühne in Berlin N" (Comedy Theater in North Berlin), reviewing a comedy show starring Erich Carow (1893–1956) and his wife, Lucie Carow (1892–1953).[13] Mann described Carow as a genius and his work as "übersinnliche Komik" (metaphysical comedy).[14] Carow received permission to reproduce the article in a publicity brochure, where it appeared together with texts by other well-known writers. This actual event—a media splash made by a small-time cabaret artist—served as the starting point for Tergit's novel. The folk singer Georg Käsebier becomes an overnight sensation when his show is reviewed by the eminent writer Otto Lambeck. Success soon turns to failure, however, and the hype around Käsebier reflects the inflated prices that preceded the Wall Street crash. In her memoirs Tergit emphasizes that Käsebier is unimportant as a character; rather, he serves as a peg on which to hang all the other characters.[15] The true subject of the novel is the feeding frenzy which occurs around him. As Fiona Sutton observes, Tergit envisaged Käsebier as an instrument to expose corruption.[16] He is the pretext for an analysis of the socioeconomic networks and media circles of the time.

Käsebier explores language both as an instrument of manipulation and as a means to expose this manipulation. In this sense, it is appropriate that the main protagonists are journalists, because they are acutely aware of the potential of language both to liberate and to oppress. Before we consider rhetoric in *Käsebier*, let us begin with some comments on narrative technique, showing the extent to which the novel is implicated in the mass media it criticizes.

The Feuilleton Novel

Andreas Huyssen thinks that the feuilleton form is perfectly suited to capturing the fragmentation of experience that characterizes modernity.[17] It is precisely this genre that Tergit deploys in *Käsebier*. Indeed, Tergit's literary production continually crosses and recrosses the borders between fact-based journalism and literary fiction.[18] *Käsebier* also adopts the journalistic forms of the character sketch and reportage. In *Der Untertan* the narrative is interwoven with the public statements of the kaiser; in *Käsebier* the narrative comprises a mosaic of Tergit's own feuilletons. According to Christiane Schultze-Jena, Tergit uses seventeen of her feuilletons in *Käsebier*; according to Petra Gute, the number is twenty-five.[19] Juliane Sucker notes the presence of many other intertextual borrowings in the novel, including newspaper headlines, biblical quotations, popular songs, advertising slogans, and numerous literary references (most notably to Heine, Fontane, Goethe, and Thomas Mann).[20]

Käsebier is divided into forty tightly compressed chapters, each of which could stand on its own as a journalistic sketch or reportage. The abrupt transitions from one chapter to the next convey a sense of what Elizabeth Boa calls "the throwntogetherness of city life."[21] Many of the chapters are composed almost entirely of dialogue among two or more members of a particular social group. In formal terms the novel is like a register of various business transactions. For much of the work the disembodied third-person narrator is a detached observer who simply transcribes the conversations and the actions as they occur, letting them speak for themselves. Often a chapter ends with a scrap of dialogue: an opinion or an observation that hangs in suspension without any commentary. This, too, conveys the impression of conversations overheard. At other times the dialogue is followed by a brief comment from the third-person narrator that communicates a sense of inexorable movement from one financial catastrophe to the next. These observations are characterized by their brevity; e.g., at the end of chapter 24: "Die Premiere des Tonfilms 'Käsebier' war ein furchtbarer Durchfall" (*Kb* 258; The premiere of the sound film *Käsebier* was a terrible disaster); or, at the end of chapter 36: "Der Konkurs ging seinen Gang" (*Kb* 359; The bankruptcy took its course).

At times the detached narrative voice makes this novel seem like a sober transcription of the "Cliquenwirtschaft" (*Kb* 26; clique economy). The narrative voice does not always remain neutral, however: at key moments it articulates a distinct moral perspective of its own.[22] To a certain extent, the narrator's personality is even implied by her resolve to maintain a critical, discreet distance from the social wheelings and dealings she observes: for example, at Margot Weißmann's salon, where deals are sealed between sexual partners and business associates. The important things here are to see and be seen and to maintain one's valuable social connections. Käsebier's concerts are just another pretext for high society to gather. Even Miermann's funeral in chapter 33 turns into the usual social enterprise: "Es war eine mondäne gesellschaftliche Unternehmung. . . . Es war nichts anderes als bei einem Rout bei Margot Weißmann" (*Kb* 329; It was a fashionable social undertaking. . . . It was no different from a soirée at Margot Weißmann's).

In contrast to these movers and shakers, the journalists in *Käsebier* come across for the most part as bystanders. The dialogues among Kohler, Miermann, and Gohlisch register the political and economic developments with concern or gloss the action with bitter jokes such as their preferred greeting, an ironic variation of the Hitler salute: "Heil und Sieg und fette Beute" (*Kb* 28; Hail and victory and fat profits). For the most part, the journalists function rather like the chorus in Greek tragedy: they comment sadly on the action, but they cannot change its course. Adhering to bourgeois liberal values, they are condemned to observe the deterioration of those values. There is, however, a striking discrepancy between the political content of the journalists' private conversations and their published articles.[23] Arguably, the journalists' lack of political engagement means that they are a part of the problem they diagnose. Even so, their conversations sketch out a moral framework for the narrative. The reader is invited to share their perspective on events and to interpret information in accordance with it. This feature becomes particularly important toward the end of the novel, when Miermann and Kohler attain tragic insights into their situations. This move toward classical tragedy, with its central moment of recognition, implies a moral condemnation of the entire age and a rejection of the fashionable concept of *Sachlichkeit* (objectivity).

Beyond *Neue Sachlichkeit*

The term *Neue Sachlichkeit* (New Objectivity) implies a new dispassionate gaze at reality after the turbulence of the years 1914 to 1923.[24] Juliane Sucker argues that Tergit's novel does not conform to the conventions of Neue Sachlichkeit because the two main characters, Miermann and Kohler, represent nonobjective viewpoints.[25] Far from being dispassionate, these two figures are marked by their emotional investments. Distanced, critical observation is undermined by the recurrence of subjective factors linked to Miermann and Kohler.[26] For Sucker, *Käsebier* resists both "Versachlichung" (objectification) and the "Vermännlichung" (masculinization) that is often associated with it: she sees the text as ironically rehearsing some of the macho slogans associated with Neue Sachlichkeit, precisely in order to show that this masculine ideology of "neutrality" is suspect.[27] Although *Käsebier* rehearses several tropes associated with Neue Sachlichkeit, the novel concludes with a decisive condemnation of this detached perspective. Indeed, *Käsebier*'s dense, allusive, and ironic style shows profound affinities with the works of Theodor Fontane and Thomas Mann. Miermann's advice to Gohlisch is eloquent in its simplicity: "Lesen Sie Fontane" (*Kb* 33; Read Fontane). The connections with *Buddenbrooks* are obvious; for example, when Frau Waldschmidt tells her daughter, "Tenue, Ella, Tenue, die Dehors wahren, du bist eine Waldschmidt" (*Kb* 268; Posture, Ella, posture; keep up appearances, you are a Waldschmidt). The final chapters of *Käsebier*, in which the Kohlers have to auction off their furniture, can be read as an amplification of the house sale in *Buddenbrooks*. There is an even deeper affinity between *Käsebier* and *Buddenbrooks* in terms of the contradiction between liberal ideals and actual business practices. While the merchants in *Buddenbrooks* try to conceal the brutal realities of business life with a veil of sentimentality, Miermann and Lotte Kohler cling to their cherished illusions until life forces them to recognize the actual conditions under which they live. Tergit's novel, however, implies that perhaps these characters are right to hang onto their beliefs and that it is good to have values and principles, even if this makes a person less "objective."

Another commentator who warns against seeing *Käsebier* as a confirmation of "objectivity" is Inge Stephan. She quotes Otto Flake's critique of Neue Sachlichkeit:

> Die Gefahren, die einer Zeit drohen, lassen sich aus ihren Schlagworten herauslesen; so auch aus dem der Sachlichkeit. Dieser Begriff besticht, er verführt. Aber man braucht nur ein wenig zu überlegen: von dem Sachlich-machen ist bloß ein winziger Schritt zum Zur-Sache-machen. Macht man aus der Liebe eine Sache, so ist alles aus.[28]

> [The dangers that threaten an era can be interpreted from the buzzwords of the time, and this also applies to "objectivity." This word is seductive and corrupting. Just think about it a little. If you start by treating things objectively, it is only a small step to turning them into objects. If you turn love into an object, then all is lost.]

The danger diagnosed here is that "objectivity" becomes a code word for the objectification and commodification of everything, even the most personal values. The invitation to "be objective" and to take an unsentimental view of "the facts" can translate into a ruthless, self-serving mentality in which other people are regarded as objects or stepping-stones. This mentality is embodied in *Käsebier* by Willi Frächter and Käte Herzfeld, who apply the "sachlich" (objective) approach to love itself. Their behavior seems to confirm the narrator's melancholy opinion that "Berlin hat kein Klima für die Liebe" (*Kb* 90; Berlin does not have a climate for love). Thus, Frächter falls in "love" with the heiress Ella Waldschmidt simply because she can further his career ambitions (*Kb* 293). Käte Herzfeld's relationships, too, are devoid of emotional attachment: "Merkwürdig . . .,

daß ich immer nur Beziehungen zu Männern habe, die ich nicht liebe"
(*Kb* 61; It's funny that I only have relationships with men I don't love).
But Käte Herzfeld is much more complex and ambivalent than her male
counterpart. She may have mercenary tendencies, but, as a "new woman,"
her independence is also genuinely important to her. At one point Käte
describes the dating game explicitly as a "ganz munterer Betrieb" (*Kb* 59;
very lively business), showing the extent to which she regards her personal
relationships as a form of doing business. On the one hand, she is a mercenary who sleeps with the banker Winkler because she needs credit (*Kb*
61); on the other, she earns her own living precisely because she thinks it
is immoral for women to remain financially dependent on men (*Kb* 183).
She regards the institution of marriage as "Wahnsinn" (*Kb* 302; madness),
and argues that extramarital sex is preferable because there are no strings
attached (*Kb* 184). At one point she declares, "Seele! Kann unsereiner
nicht vertragen" (*Kb* 57; Soul! People our age can't stand that sort of
thing). In this way, the most "objective" characters in *Käsebier*, Frächter
and Herzfeld, are also the most unappealing.

At the same time, however, there is a sense of awe at their sheer
resourcefulness. Chapter 19 contains an appreciation of Käte Herzfeld's
qualities as a saleswoman:

> Käte . . . war ein ungeheuer kaufmännisches Talent. Sie brachte alles
> dafür mit, die Überzeugtheit von ihren Waren—alles übrige war
> Schund, was sie hatte, war immer erstklassig—, die große Rednergabe,
> die Schönheit, den Sexappeal, die rasche Klugheit und das
> Rechnenkönnen. Sie wurde überall vorgelassen, sie war liebenswürdig
> und hatte sofort einen leicht erotischen Ton, der nie aufdringlich war.
> (*Kb* 212–13)

> [Käte . . . had enormous talent as a saleswoman. She brought all the
> right qualities to the role: conviction about the excellence of her
> products—everything else was crap, hers were always first-class—
> great eloquence, beauty, sex appeal, quick wit, and arithmetic skill.
> She was welcomed everywhere, she was charming, and she had at
> once a soft erotic tone that was never obtrusive.]

There is something "ungeheuer" (which can be translated as "monstrous"
as well as "enormous") about her talent. She brings great conviction to her
role, combining ethos, pathos, and logos, all wrapped up in a gentle, erotic
package. Like an Aristotelian orator who knows that *ethos* (character) is the
strongest proof, Käte Herzfeld uses her personality to sell her products. In
fact, her personality is itself her greatest product.

In contrast to this "objective" approach adopted by the careerist characters, Miermann and Kohler appear sympathetic precisely because they are
capable of genuine feeling. Although the narrative satirizes Miermann's
old-fashioned humanism, it remains largely sympathetic to a humanist

position. In a post-Nietzschean world of moral relativism, in which traditional moral values are dismissed as "outmoded" or not "sachlich" enough, the narrative ultimately sides with those who fail to keep step with the new times. In spite of the valedictory tone, however, these humanist characters are depicted with considerable ambivalence. Kohler's pathetic devotion to the manipulative Oskar Meyer-Paris seems hopelessly naive, inviting readers to reflect on which is more damaging: Käte's cynicism or Lotte's naivety. Miermann's collection of humanist values includes old-school sexism, and his relationship with Käte reveals his sexual double standards. Although he regularly cheats on his wife, he recoils against Käte's insistence on her own sexual independence. Miermann is doomed by his macho pride. In a moment of desperation and confusion, he rapes Käte: "Es war eine Vergewaltigung gewesen. Sie würde ihm das nie verzeihen" (*Kb* 303; It was rape. She would never forgive him).

Both Miermann and Kohler are shown to be limited in their outlooks. And yet the narrative focalization remains attached to them, presenting them as worthy of attention. In this capacity, they invite our sympathy as readers. The narrative builds up to moments of pain in which Miermann and Kohler are unable to be "objective," and emotion supersedes reason. These emotional climaxes present a sharp contrast to the daily routine in the rest of the novel. At these moments the business of making money seems to grind to a halt, and a dimension of human feeling intrudes. When Kohler discovers that her lover, Meyer-Paris, is leaving her and going to America without even saying goodbye, she turns pale and feels like "eine Gestorbene" (*Kb* 287; a dead woman). She feels desperate and wishes that she had a gun (*Kb* 289). A few days later, she has regained a sense of composure and admits to her friend that she is "ein hoffnungsloser Fall" (*Kb* 290; a hopeless case). She wants to change and tries to make a new start by getting a short haircut. Soon afterward, she and her mother are plunged into financial ruin.

As for Miermann, he seems genuinely devastated by what he has done, as is evident in his speech at the funeral of Augur's daughter (*Kb* 304–7). And his subsequent demise is so pathetic that it makes him seem pitiable. The narrative takes care to remind readers that Miermann has always been a good friend and mentor to Kohler and Gohlisch: they even wrote their articles as if they were private letters to him (*Kb* 321).[29] Shortly afterward, Miermann is fired by Frächter and suffers a mental and physical collapse in the street. As he breaks down, Miermann is acutely aware of the human misery all around him: "Er hatte das Gefühl, daß die Häuser auf ihn fielen. Und diese ganzen Häuser waren von unten bis oben mit nichts gefüllt als Menschensorgen" (*Kb* 324; He felt as if the houses were falling down on him. And these entire houses were filled from top to bottom with nothing but human sorrows). At this point the narrative reads like an apocalyptic painting by Ludwig Meidner or a poem by Georg Heym. The dominant idiom here is not Neue Sachlichkeit at all but the wild pathos of German Expressionism. And Miermann's last words are a Jewish prayer that he has not spoken for thirty-five years (*Kb* 326).[30] The religious dimension that enters the narrative at the moment of Miermann's demise represents a break with the stylistic gestures toward Neue Sachlichkeit that preceded it. It is true that the sufferings of Miermann and Kohler are still described in a restrained manner, but this does not make their agony less poignant. As the novel draws to a close, its attention to the ruined lives of its main characters can be read as an indictment of "objectivity." The closing sections of *Käsebier* are by no means objective or detached; on the contrary, they are loaded with pathos. In this way, *Käsebier* ultimately has a cathartic power that goes far beyond the cool clichés associated with Neue Sachlichkeit.

Two Versions of Liberalism

The rejection of Neue Sachlichkeit in *Kasebier* is also shown by the longest quotation in the novel, in chapter 17. The quotation is not aligned with any one of the characters, which means that it can be seen as an expression of the narrator's own position.[31] It is taken from a work by the political economist and sociologist Gustav von Schmoller (1838–1917). Schmoller is identified by name, and the date of the text, 1886, is also given. Schmoller was the leading opponent of Max Weber in the *Werturteilsstreit* (value-judgment dispute) that took place at the 1909 Vienna conference of the Verein für Sozialpolitik (German Economic Association). The dispute was about whether the social sciences should enjoy *Werturteilsfreiheit* (freedom from value judgment).[32] The key question was: Should sociologists allow their research to be informed by ethical and political considerations or not? The background to the debate was Weber's conviction that Schmoller's faith in Prussian bureaucracy was misplaced. Weber thought that Prussian dirigisme was holding back German expansion; like his mentor, the liberal politician Friedrich Naumann, Weber wanted Germany to emulate Anglo-American free-market capitalism.[33] By asking his colleagues to abstain from value judgments, Weber hoped to put an end to the mixture of social science and paternalistic conservative politics represented by Schmoller and his school.[34] Interestingly, Tergit's decision to include the Schmoller quotation suggests that she opposes Weber's economic liberalism, aligning herself with the paternalist conservatism represented by Schmoller. Here is the quotation in full:

> Die heutige Gesellschaft nötigt die unteren Schichten des großstädtischen Fabrikproletariats durch die Wohnverhältnisse mit absoluter Notwendigkeit zum Zurücksinken auf ein Niveau der Barbarei und Brutalität, der Roheit und des Rowdytums, die unsere

Vorfahren schon Jahrhunderte hinter sich hatten. Ich möchte behaupten, die größte Gefahr für unsere Kultur droht von hier aus. Die besitzenden Klassen müssen aus ihrem Schlummer aufgerüttelt werden, sie müssen endlich einsehen, daß, selbst wenn sie große Opfer bringen, dies nur eine mäßige, bescheidene Versicherungssumme ist, mit der sie sich schützen gegen die Epidemien und gegen die sozialen Revolutionen, die kommen müssen, wenn wir nicht aufhören, die unteren Klassen in unseren Großstädten durch ihre Wohnungsverhältnisse zu Barbaren, zu tierischem Dasein herunterzudrücken. (*Kb* 201–2)

[Today's society, through its poor housing conditions, forces the lower classes of the urban proletariat inescapably to revert to a level of barbarity, brutality, roughness, and thuggery that our ancestors left behind centuries ago. I contend that this represents the greatest danger for our culture. The propertied classes must be woken from their slumber, they must finally realize that—even if they make great sacrifices—this is only a modest, moderate insurance payment, one that will protect them against the epidemics and social revolutions that must occur if we do not ameliorate the living conditions of the lower classes of our great cities, conditions that reduce them to barbarity and an animal level of existence.]

Tergit sides with Schmoller in her refusal of Weber's scientific neutrality. Like Schmoller, she regards the social security system as an essential safeguard against the possibility of revolutionary violence. If social security is abolished, the result will be a descent into barbarism. The prominence of the Schmoller quotation in chapter 17 suggests that although Tergit was politically a liberal, she supported the idea of a strong state, one that would take an active role in implementing social security for the working classes. Her liberalism did not extend to the economic sphere.

The Decline of Liberal Values

The decline of traditional values is a recurring theme in the novel: for example, when we read about a homeware designer named Fräulein Götzel, who is "tüchtig" (capable) but who has "kein künstlerisches Gewissen" (*Kb* 212; no conscience as an artist). This description seems to imply that business capability excludes artistic conscience. Kitsch sells, and the decline in aesthetic standards suggests a similar decline in moral standards. This pattern is repeated when the contract for the building design is awarded to the unscrupulous Karlweiß rather than to Oberndorffer. Oberndorffer reflects, "Die Leute haben kein Gefühl mehr für die Qualität" (*Kb* 245; People no longer have a feeling for quality). The pattern is reinforced when Franz Rohhals, a partner in the carpentry firm Feinschmidt & Rohhals, shoots himself. This was an excellent firm that once worked for the great Prussian architect Karl Friedrich Schinkel himself. Unfortunately, nobody is willing to pay for quality craftsmanship anymore, and the firm has been undercut by its cheaper competitors:

> Die haben alles gemacht, was gut ist in Berlin. . . . Alles, was gut ist, geht zugrunde. . . . Man muß doch kalkulieren! Sonst geht man doch selber vor die Hunde. (*Kb* 275–76)

> [They made everything that is good in Berlin. . . . Everything that is good goes under. . . . You have to be calculating! Otherwise, you just go to the dogs yourself.]

There is a sense of a race to the bottom here. Those who work according to the highest standards will go under, and those who lower their standards to the bare minimum will succeed. As Fiona Sutton has shown, first, these references touch on contemporary debates about the threat to German *Wertarbeit* (quality work) from mass production,[35] and second, they imply that there is a connection between the decline in quality and the rise of Nazism.[36] This connection occurs when the construction manager Max Schulz is compelled to award the contract for fitting the plumbing and gas pipes to the lowest bidder, who is a Nazi: "Max Schulz mußte den Auftrag an Staberow Söhne geben, trotzdem ihm Staberow höchst unsympathisch war, so 'n moderner schneidiger Nazi, der Geschäfte mit 'n Hakenkreuz im Knopfloch machte" (*Kb* 252; Max Schulz had to give the contract to Staberow and Sons, in spite of his deep dislike of Staberow, a fashionable modern Nazi who did business with a swastika in his buttonhole). In this way, the narrative associates National Socialism with the triumph of style over substance.

The connection between fascism and superficial style is also suggested when the reporters discuss their acquaintance, Dr. Krone, who is too honest for his own good. For example, he once confessed that he did not know what the problem was with a patient. The journalists regard this as an embarrassing admission, which could damage his reputation. As Augur puts it, "Der Erfolg ist eine Sache der Suggestion und nicht der Leistung" (*Kb* 28; Success is a matter of suggestion, not achievement). Gohlisch responds, "Dieser einzige Satz erklärt den ganzen Faschismus, ihr seid feige Sklaven, ihr braucht Autorität" (*Kb* 28; This one sentence explains the whole of fascism: you are cowardly slaves, you need authority). In other words, advertising depends on a pessimistic view of human beings, assuming that they are ignorant herd animals who can be easily led. Tergit's description of *Käsebier* as an updated version of Hans Christian Andersen's fairy tale "The Emperor's New Clothes" is appropriate here as an analysis of fascist propaganda.[37] When everyone follows the Führer, it no longer matters that he is a fake. As long as no one dares to dissent, then the illusion of authority remains complete. Telling lies can be highly successful, especially if people are too afraid to expose them.

Later in the text, the ruined banker Frechheim makes a similar complaint, declaring that Berlin is a place "wo die Lumpen nach oben schwimmen und die Anständigen untergehen" (*Kb* 360; where the scum rises to the top, and decent folk go under). Nice guys finish last, and "nur glatte Höflinge kommen weiter" (*Kb* 23; only smooth courtiers get ahead). In this way, the novel depicts an intensified form of competition in which the old rules of doing business no longer apply, and anything goes. Business is now a contest in which no holds are barred, and bourgeois moral values appear as a form of luxury that people can no longer afford. This cutthroat situation anticipates the mood of Brecht's *Threepenny* projects, in which the drive to make money takes precedence over all other considerations, and morality is reduced to an ostentatious sales pitch, a ruse, or a feint.

Much as in Thomas Mann's *Buddenbrooks*, the traditional bourgeois characters appear trapped by their moral values. They subscribe to an ethical system that seems outdated and even ridiculous in a context where individuals are determined to make a profit by any means at their disposal. When Kohler tells her widowed mother that their life savings are endangered because Muschler's bank has declared bankruptcy, the mother suggests that they could make a living by running a guesthouse. The narrative comments dryly: "Sie dachte immer noch, daß man es mit Fleiß und Sparsamkeit schaffen müßte" (*Kb* 339; She still thought that hard work and frugality were the best ways to get along). Ironically, bourgeois virtues such as hard work and frugality no longer count for much in a world where hard-earned savings can disappear overnight into the hands of unscrupulous bankers like Muschler. The collapse of Muschler's bank ruins hundreds of people, but it does not ruin Muschler himself because he still has a private Swiss bank account that he can rely on (*Kb* 352). One of the victims, Dr. Krone, complains: "Erst hat einen der Staat betrogen, jetzt die Bankiers. Alle fünf Jahre werden einem die Ersparnisse gestohlen. Glatt gestohlen! . . . Soll man doch gleich bolschewisieren, weiß man, woran man ist" (*Kb* 354; First you are fleeced by the state, now by the bankers. Every five years your savings are stolen. Plain theft! Perhaps we should just let the Bolsheviks nationalize everything; then we would know where we were). There is a sense of middle-class desperation here: private property, it seems, is not only under attack in the Soviet Union, it is also endangered by speculative capitalism itself.

When the final bankruptcy occurs, it ruins Muschler's partner, Frechheim, who complains that the younger generation of businessmen no longer display any allegiance to their own firms. They make a clear distinction between the firm's capital and their own private funds:

> Früher ... war ein Unternehmen der große Stolz, für das man sparte
> und in das jeder erübrigte Pfennig hineingesteckt wurde, da hatte der
> Kapitalist den Mehrwert, weil er auch das Risiko hatte. Aber diese
> Leute, für die ihr Unternehmen eine Art Börsenpapier ist, das eine
> Rente abwirft, diese Herren sind allerdings zur Bolschewisierung reif.
> (*Kb* 361)

> [Previously a firm was a source of great pride; you saved for it and you
> put every last cent into it. The capitalist enjoyed the surplus value
> because he took the risks. But these people who treat their firm like a
> share certificate to be sold off at a profit, these gentlemen are ripe for
> a Bolshevik revolution.]

The contrast between this attitude to business and the ethos of Thomas
Mann's Buddenbrooks could hardly be more pronounced. Commercial
ventures no longer last for generations; they no longer require a lifetime's
dedication: instead, they are increasingly regarded as short-term investments, to be liquidated without hesitation.

All of this amounts to a catastrophe for liberalism. The rise of the
bourgeoisie relative to the aristocracy in the nineteenth century had been
predicated on an ideology of honesty and hard work. Tergit's characters,
however, bear witness to an economic situation where *Leistung* (achievement) and Wertarbeit do not count, and success is largely based on nepo-
tism and networking. In this way, high-risk capitalism seems to lead to a
regressive situation, one in which the liberal principle of economic reward
based on merit is increasingly hollowed out.[38]

Business Scandals

One of the most scandalous figures in *Käsebier* is the construction mag-
nate Otto Mitte, an expert networker who has built an entire construction empire through his government contacts. The text describes Mitte
repeatedly (three times in quick succession) as follows: "Er war untertan
der Obrigkeit" (*Kb* 202–3; His allegiance was to the authorities). The
repetition of this phrase emphasizes the real secret of his success. Mitte's
lobbying of government officials consists of bribery, as the following
statement indicates: "[Mitte] baute Gartenstädte, nicht sehr erstklassig,
nie mit guten Architekten, sondern immer mit solchen, die Fühlung,
Geldfühlung mit Stadträten hatten" (*Kb* 202; Mitte built garden sub-
urbs, not very first-class, never with good architects, but always with
architects who had contacts, financial contacts, with city officials). This
is confirmed by the fact that Mitte's favored architect, Karlweiß, has
worked for the Steglitz housing department, where he awarded contracts to his own firm, and, although he was removed from this office,

he is still a member of the housing assistance committee (*Kb* 180). This is the point in Tergit's novel where the parallels with the Sklarek scandal are most apparent. As in the Sklarek case, the novel shows the state being effectively milked by private contractors who use lobbying and bribery to corner the market. As the chorus of journalists reflect on Karlweiß's success, they come to the realization that "ein bißchen korrupte Genialität [ist] besser als eine korrekte Unfähigkeit" (*Kb* 181; a little corrupt ingenuity is better than legitimate inability). In other words, what really matters is success, even if the means are dishonest. The main difference between Karlweiß and the Sklareks is the scale of their corruption. Karlweiß's fraud is relatively low-key, whereas the Sklareks' was huge (the case for the prosecution ran to several volumes). At one point in *Käsebier*, it even transpires that the Sklareks donated money to the Deutschnationale Volkspartei (DNVP, German National People's Party), which was used to print a political poster denouncing them (*Kb* 294–95). Tergit's text thus depicts the ironic spectacle of Jewish businessmen directly funding anti-Semitic attacks upon themselves.

While the real-life Sklarek scandal related to the clothing industry, Tergit focuses on the building industry. She was well placed to do this, since her husband, Heinrich Julius Reifenberg, was an architect, and she was a friend of Werner Hegemann, a Berlin city planner who, in 1930, published *Das steinerne Berlin* (Berlin, City of Stone), a five-hundred-page study of Berlin housing.[39] Reviewing the book, Walter Benjamin highlighted its political implications, observing that it presented the architectural history of Berlin as a series of corrupt deals between state officials and private landowners who were permitted to build enormous *Mietskasernen* (tenements; literally, "rental barracks") to maximize their rents.[40] Benjamin's review compares Hegemann to Robespierre, saying that he shares the Jacobin leader's "unbestechliche Witterung für Korruption" (incorruptible nose for corruption).[41] According to Benjamin, Hegemann's achievement is to have revealed history itself as a scandal: "die ewig aktuelle Geschichte, mit anderen Worten, die Skandal-Geschichte" (ever-present history, in other words, scandal history).[42] The construction deal in *Käsebier* accords well with a Benjaminian reading of history as a series of scandals. Although the Käsebier apartments are supposed to be of high quality, the standards are soon compromised, and the residents' quality of life is not considered. As the investor Muschler puts it: "beim Bauen ist der Bau gar nicht so wichtig" (*Kb* 211; when you build, the building is not so very important). In this sense, *Käsebier* is a *Skandalgeschichte* (scandalous story) that depicts the pursuit of profit regardless of the human cost. But scandals are complex things, because they are always filtered through, and sometimes even created by, the media.

The Organization of Speech

The media do not simply report events; they create facts, and they provide a perspective from which to view reality. In 1921 Kurt Tucholsky observed that "die Reproduktion der Wirklichkeit [ist] unendlich wichtiger als das Geschehnis selbst" (the reproduction of reality is incomparably more important than the event itself).[43] In 1922 the American author Walter Lippmann (1889–1974) published *Public Opinion*, in which he argued that information flows could be selected and "tailored" in order for political elites to "set the agenda."[44] John Hartley provides a list of criteria used by news media to select which items to feature: these include the "size" of the event, its "cultural proximity," and whether it can be reduced to a clear message—for example, a dispute between "us" and "them."[45] *Käsebier* offers similar insights. As the journalist Augur observes in chapter 2, what matters in economic terms is no longer hard work or achievement but "die Organisation des Geredes" (*Kb* 26; the organization of speech). *Gerede* (talk, gossip, chatter) is a pejorative word; it could also be translated as "chit-chat." It is close in meaning to *Geschwätz* (drivel, hogwash, guff), and it could also be translated in an informal register as "crap" or "bullshit." Thus, according to this statement, the decisive economic factor is not the commodity itself, not the "facts" of the matter, but, instead, the way in which those facts are selected and presented in order to set the agenda for the discussion that follows. For example, in *Käsebier* the influence of the builder Otto Mitte is so great that Professor Schierling's "independent" report fails to mention the serious flaws in the architectural plans for the new development (*Kb* 210–11). Mitte's dominance in the construction industry enables him to "organize" the discourse within the profession.

The chief "organizer of speech" in *Käsebier* is Willi Frächter, who embodies the new type of careerist. Frächter knows the importance of observing "the niceties": "Das sind so Nuancen, die Frächter alle kannte und auf die es ankommt" (*Kb* 126; Those are the nuances, Frächter knew all of them, it's the niceties that matter). For Frächter, it is only the externalities of business that count. He is a skilled self-publicist, opportunist, and trend-spotter who uses Käsebier as a stepping-stone to launch his own media career. Frächter's sales pitch to the newspaper publisher Cochius in chapter 15 is slick. He starts by reciting his experience in commercial advertising and the brand names that he has personally fostered in support of his claim that "Ich bin kein kaufmännischer Laie" (*Kb* 187; I am not a layperson when it comes to business). He promises to bring in new advertising revenue and to boost circulation to a hundred thousand—of course, the two go hand in hand. In addition to a fixed salary, he wants a percentage share of any increase in profits (*Kb* 187). Frächter plans to rationalize the business by laying off workers, and he boasts of his ability to create new desires: "das Wesen des modernen Betriebsfachmanns ist es, schlummernde Bedürfnisse zu wecken" (*Kb* 188; the essence of a modern business expert is to awaken dormant needs). On his appointment as editor, Frächter turns the fictional *Berliner Rundschau* into a sensationalist rightwing tabloid similar to those published by Alfred Hugenberg's Scherl. Frächter is a composite character: Dieter Wrobel describes him as a fictional disciple of Hugenberg;[46] Erhard Schütz thinks that he is modeled on the literary editor of the *Berliner Tageblatt*, Fred Hildenbrandt, who had Nazi connections.[47] Frächter, however, also has certain affinities with the Nazi propaganda minister Joseph Goebbels. Like Goebbels, Frächter began his career as an Expressionist poet, and the description of Frächter's early career in *Käsebier* (*Kb* 280–81) certainly bears comparison to Goebbels's.[48] The affinity between Frächter and Goebbels is also suggested by Tergit's statement to Jens Brüning that her intention was to reveal the dangers of advertising:

> Ich wußte doch von Anfang an, daß . . . die Reklame eine Leben zerstörende Angelegenheit [ist]. Hat sich ja auch erwiesen, als dann Herr Goebbels das Ministerium für Reklame aufgemacht hat.[49]

> [I knew from the beginning that . . . advertising is a business that destroys lives. This was confirmed when Mr. Goebbels opened his propaganda ministry.]

In *Käsebier*, the journalists discuss Frächter and observe that although he is not a Nazi, he has the potential to become one: "Warum ist Frächter nicht Naziintellektueller geworden? . . . Hätt' er auch werden können . . . er ist es zufällig nicht geworden, wird er wahrscheinlich noch" (*Kb* 283; Why hasn't Frächter turned into a Nazi intellectual? He could have. It is a matter of chance that he did not; probably he will later on). The journalists' discussion then turns to politics. Lotte Kohler objects to the socialists' fanatical insistence on the class struggle between bourgeoisie and proletarians, which she argues will lead to the most frightful witch hunts (*Kb* 284). Miermann raises the subject of fascism and describes it as "Die Form als Inhalt" (*Kb* 285; Form as content). This predates Walter Benjamin's similar diagnosis in his famous "Kunstwerk" essay of 1936, where he states that fascism pursues "die Ästhetisierung der Politik" (the aestheticization of politics).[50] Despite this similarity, Tergit and Benjamin offer different accounts of fascism, as Fiona Sutton has shown. While Benjamin's essay presents fascism as harnessing the aura, offering expression to the masses while conserving oppressive structures within society, Tergit, in *Käsebier*, associates the success of fascism with the destruction of aura and authenticity.[51] And while Benjamin's essay welcomes the loss of the aura, Tergit's novel laments its passing.

Modes of Oratory: Confession; Eulogy; Liturgy

As the novel proceeds toward its catastrophic finale, a religious dimension enters the text. As a counterpoint to the "sachlich," "morally neutral" economic rhetoric of the business figures, the text increasingly adopts emotional, moral, and religious rhetoric. When Muschler's bank collapses, Lotte Kohler passes a church and thinks, "Würde die Kirche offenstehen . . ., würde ich hineingehen und mich ausruhen" (*Kb* 340; If the church were open, I would go in and have a rest). The religious pathos provides an alternative narrative framework that explodes the conventions of Neue Sachlichkeit and harks back to the eschatology of German Expressionism. In the final chapters of *Käsebier* there is a religious sense of moral judgment on the vanities of the Weimar bourgeoisie. At the same time, the vestiges of pre-First World War imperial Germany are also found wanting. Tergit's portrayal of late Weimar is thus highly ambivalent. *Käsebier* may be critical of the present, but it also expresses the recognition that imperial Germany deserves to remain in the past. Its values, as embodied in its heavy, ostentatious furniture and rigid gender roles, are too restrictive. In chapter 35 Kohler stares at the (now worthless) family furnishings from before 1914, and she has a moment of tragic recognition: "War sie nicht ebenso blind für das Echte gewesen wie alle anderen?" (*Kb* 347; Hadn't she been as blind as all the others about the truth?) The key word here is the adjectival noun "das Echte" (truth, authenticity, genuineness). The free indirect discourse does not specify precisely what is meant by "das Echte," and this challenges readers to interpret it—what is the "truth" that Lotte has failed to recognize? The appeal to "truth" and "authenticity" here signals an appeal to moral absolutes, and to the religious frameworks in which they are traditionally defined and understood. The "truth" that Lotte has missed, it seems, is the difference between right and wrong, between good and evil. Like her contemporaries, she has been blinded by her own vanity; she has been seduced by trivial things.[52] This interpretation is confirmed by the narrator's reference to "Jahrmarkt der Eitelkeit" (*Kb* 331; vanity fair), which calls to mind William Makepeace Thackeray's novel (1847–48), which takes its title from a scene in John Bunyan's *Pilgrim's Progress* (1678). Taken together, this reference suggests that what really matters to the narrator of *Käsebier* is not worldly success at all, but moral integrity.

The critique of "vanity" plays out movingly in the final chapters of *Käsebier*. As the two liberal characters, Kohler and Miermann, lose their dignity, there is a sense of poetic justice as their hubris is punished. Lotte and her mother, who pride themselves on their family's social status, have to sell off their family heirlooms, which are revealed as worthless junk. Miermann, who prides himself on his humanist sensibility, commits rape.

Miermann's crime seems motivated by his nineteenth-century values: he cannot cope with being ridiculed by Käte (*Kb* 302–3), and punishes her for her desire to remain unattached. This incident clearly shows that some aspects of modernity, such as equal rights for women, are to be welcomed unequivocally.

Miermann has enough of a liberal conscience to be crushed by the crime he has committed. As Boa points out, Miermann's guilt is compounded when the daughter of a low-paid colleague dies from "an illness that a little money to pay the doctor's bill could have cured. But none of the editorial team noticed until it was too late."[53] At the girl's funeral in chapter 30, Miermann gives a speech that amounts to both a personal confession and an indictment of his entire generation. There is an unmistakable sense of divine retribution here: "Wir hier unten, die wir Sünder sind allzumal,[54] die wir ohne Not gelogen haben und betrogen, die wir uns der Macht gebeugt, dem Guten verschlossen und unseren Vorteil gesucht haben, die wir unseren Nebenmenschen nicht geliebt haben" (*Kb* 306; We down below, we who have all sinned and lied and betrayed without cause, we who have submitted to the powerful, rejected goodness, sought our own advantage, we who have not loved our fellow men). No wonder the listeners feel uncomfortable: "Miermanns Rede war merkwürdig gewesen, fanden die meisten Anwesenden" (*Kb* 307; Most of those present found Miermann's speech rather strange). It is amusing for readers as these jaded urban sophisticates are shocked to the core to hear a fellow liberal like Miermann having recourse to ancient concepts of sin and penance ("religiöse Formeln zweier Jahrtausende" [*Kb* 307; religious formulations of two millennia]). Miermann's closest friends, Lotte Kohler and Gohlisch, sense that this speech is not only a personal confession by Miermann but also an admission of defeat, an abdication (*Kb* 308).

The contrast between Miermann and Frächter, between authenticity and inauthenticity, is ultimately revealed in the two contrasting funeral orations in chapters 30 and 33. If Miermann is a penitent rapist, then Frächter is a hypocrite who, in the German phrase, "über Leichen geht" (walks over corpses). Frächter's speech at Miermann's funeral is a classic eulogy, but as readers we know that Frächter precipitated Miermann's demise by firing him. Frächter flatters his audience by expressing his admiration for the dignity of journalism, but his praise of Geist rings false because, as we already know, he scorns it (*Kb* 147). With affected piety, he pays tribute to Miermann's quality journalism: "Wir Verleger, wir Geschäftsleute sozusagen, wir sind nur die Handlanger, die den Journalisten, dem Geiste helfen wollen. Denn letzten Endes ist der Inhalt das Wichtigste, der Kern, nicht die Schale" (*Kb* 330; We publishers, we businesspeople as it were, we are only the servants who want to promote journalists and Geist. For in the final analysis content is what is most important; it is the heart of the matter). Coming from Frächter, this is, of course, a blatant falsehood. His hypocrisy reaches its zenith when he describes Miermann as "den mir liebsten, den mir nächsten Mitarbeiter" (*Kb* 329; my dearest, my closest colleague). Perhaps what is most outrageous about this tissue of lies is that Frächter gets away with it; no one dares to challenge him.[55] As Miermann's friends Gohlisch and Kohler leave the cemetery, Gohlisch comments, "Es haben nur solche gesprochen, die er nicht ausstehen konnte" (*Kb* 331; The only people who spoke were the ones he could not stand). The juxtaposition of the funeral orations in chapters 30 and 33 reveals the shocking contrast between a moral reckoning and amoral self-congratulation. It invites readers to see that there is a world of difference between authentic speech and inauthentic speech.

Miermann's collapse occurs immediately after he has witnessed a Nazi making a scene in an ice-cream café. The man explodes with rage because he has had to wait to be served. He starts shouting and banging the table with his fist. Shortly afterward, Miermann lies dying in the arms of his wife. The master wordsmith is now reduced to the silent language of physical gestures: "Er drückte ihr die Hand und bewegte die Lippen" (*Kb* 326; He pressed her hand and moved his lips). Miermann's last words are those of an ancient prayer, the Shema Yisrael, the centerpiece of Jewish daily prayers: "Es kamen die 35 Jahre ungesprochenen Worte von seinen Lippen, das uralte Sterbegebet der alten Juden: 'Schmah isroel, adonoi elohenu adonoi echod.' 'Höre, Israel, der Ewige, unser Gott ist der eine Gott.'" (*Kb* 326; Words came from his lips that he had not pronounced for 35 years, the ancient dying prayer of the Jewish people: "Hear, O Israel, the Lord our God, the Lord is one"). It is a moment of intense pathos, as the assimilated, acculturated Jew, the secular humanist, the epicure versed in the worldly, sensual poetry of Horace and Goethe, suddenly returns to the austere religion of his ancestors. At this point Miermann represents an entire generation of assimilated German Jews who suddenly rediscovered their Jewishness as hard-won emancipation and assimilation were canceled out almost overnight. In this way, the text depicts the collapse of liberal cosmopolitanism and a reversion to ethnic affiliations.

Miermann's words of prayer signal the return of the repressed. Religion and morality, which have been declared passé by various sophisticated and superficial readers of Darwin, Nietzsche, and Marx and rejected by many Weimar intellectuals as being incompatible with the contemporary ethos of Neue Sachlichkeit, suddenly return with a vengeance. Far too late, the leading characters of *Käsebier* realize that what they really need to do is to find "das Echte" and learn to tell the difference between right and wrong.[56] Thus *Käsebier* ends with a denunciation of worldly success and the manipulative rhetoric used to achieve it. The statement "Bei der Zeitung kommt's nicht mehr auf den Inhalt an" (*Kb* 275; The content of a newspaper no longer counts) expresses the fashionable idea that form is more important than content. Tergit's text concludes, on the contrary, it is not form but moral content that matters.

4: Seeing through the Rhetoric in Bertolt Brecht's *Dreigroschenroman*, 1934

> *It is more desirable to seem*
> *just than to be just.*
>
> —Aristotle

Introduction: The Black Book of Clichés

IN *DIE LITERARISCHE WELT* (The Literary World) of May 21, 1926, German authors were asked to respond to the following question: "Welche stilistische Phrase hassen Sie am meisten?" (Which stylistic cliché do you hate most?). Bertolt Brecht (1898–1956) responded, "Die Phrasen, die hassenswert sind, sind Legion. Es wäre falsch, eine beliebige herauszufischen. Man müßte eine Enzyklopädie, ein Schwarzbuch der Phrase herausgeben" (The clichés worth hating are legion. It would be mistaken to select one random phrase. What is needed is an encyclopedia, a black book of clichés).[1] Eight years later, he published a novel that can be read as precisely that: the *Dreigroschenroman*. David Bathrick has noted that Brecht's works often consider the problem of manipulation in mass society.[2] This is especially true of the *Dreigroschenroman*. As a refugee from Hitler from 1933 onward, Brecht developed an acute diagnosis of the ideological manipulations of the Nazi party in his plays, poetry, and prose writings. *Dreigroschenroman*, written in the winter of 1933–34 with the assistance of Margarete Steffin, is the first major work Brecht produced in exile. It explores the connections between language and power, analyzing linguistic strategies used by economic and political actors alike in order to influence the public.

In August 1934 Brecht instructed his Amsterdam-based publisher, Allert de Lange, to print passages of the *Dreigroschenroman* in italics to convey the impression that certain phrases were being quoted and exhibited (*BFA* 28:433). Walter Benjamin, in his 1935 review of the novel, emphasized Brecht's use of italics, observing that Brecht had created "eine Sammlung von Ansprachen und Sentenzen, Bekenntnissen und Plädoyers . . ., die einzig zu nennen ist" (a collection of addresses and maxims, affirmations and pleas, which is unique).[3] This chapter argues that the *Dreigroschenroman* is a novel that exhibits certain types of discourse to show how language is used to exert political and economic influence. George Orwell made a similar point in the essay "Politics and the English Language" (1946), where he observes: "Political language . . . is designed to make lies sound truthful and murder respectable, and to give an appearance of solidity to pure wind."[4] *Dreigroschenroman* is a critique of political ideology, a corporate thriller with fascism as a subtext. Wolfgang Jeske has shown that Brecht incorporated transcripts from Hitler's radio speeches into the novel.[5] Unfortunately, much research on the work has tended to focus on politically neutral questions of genre.[6] This chapter, in contrast, focuses on the economic and political uses of language in the *Dreigroschenroman*. It draws in part on Cornelie Ladd's interpretation of the novel in terms of classical rhetoric. From this perspective, language is a source of power that largely supersedes physical force.[7]

Rhetoric and Ethos

In an unpublished PhD thesis of 1991 titled "Fictions of Power, Powers of Fiction" Cornelie Ladd has demonstrated how Brecht's *Dreigroschenroman* draws on the classical tradition of rhetoric and oratory as exemplified by Cicero. Her reading of the novel argues that "the conventions of classical rhetoric are shown to replace physical force as a source of power in 'threepenny' London."[8] Brecht's interest in Ciceronian oratory is shown by the fact that his library contained works by Cicero,[9] and Cicero also features in Brecht's unfinished novel *Die Geschäfte des Herrn Julius Caesar* (1938–40; *The Business Affairs of Mr. Julius Caesar*). According to Ladd, Brecht's characters use the techniques of classical rhetoric to exploit the expectations of their audience. Brecht's plays often investigate how audiences respond, as Laura Bradley has recently shown.[10] In the novel Brecht develops the idea of Macheath as an orator, always depicting him as speaking to an audience. Almost every time he appears, he is working on a particular audience in order to impose his own agenda. The audience is often represented by the hapless veteran George Fewkoombey, who is intended as a counterexample for the readers: his gullibility leads him to the gallows.

Macheath and Peachum use forensic rhetoric to get the legal system to work in their favor: they evade justice "by means of the very discourse that is responsible for allocating it."[11] Peachum employs forensic discourse when he stands accused of selling damaged ships to the government for use as troop carriers. Questioned by the police about the sinking of the *Optimist*, Peachum stresses the fact that he always worked closely in conjunction with the authorities. Then he sets out two possible explanations for the disaster: either the ship sank as a result of criminal negligence on the part of the authorities and the suppliers, or, given the excellence of the authorities and British firms, it was an accident.[12] Obviously, version two is preferable to the authorities. If they conclude that Peachum is a crook, then they become accessories to the crime: they cannot prosecute Peachum without causing trouble for themselves. In this way, Peachum's discourse implicates his audience in the crime. There are few audiences or juries who would be willing to find themselves guilty. The novel also presents Peachum as an orator in his dealings with Macheath. Peachum runs through in his head all the arguments he could use against Macheath. The point here is that Peachum shapes his speech with a view to manipulating his listeners. When he speaks, he has already calculated the effect that his speech is likely to have.

Aristotle regards *ethos* (character) as the most effective means of persuasion.[13] Brecht's alter ego, Herr Keuner, agrees, when he tells a philosopher: "Sehend deine Haltung, interessiert mich dein Ziel nicht" (*BFA* 18:439–40; "I see your bearing and so I am not interested in your goal").[14] The "Haltung" (bearing) of the speaker is the decisive factor here. Given the centrality of *ethos* in classical rhetoric, it is no wonder that much forensic and legal discourse is concerned with establishing character. *Ethos* is, however, not simply a quality of the speaker. It expresses the relation between speaker and audience.[15] As a businessman, Macheath constantly presents himself to his audience as a man of good character and positive intentions. He knows that credibility is an essential part of every sales pitch.

The Macheath of the *Dreigroschenroman* is no longer the small-time hoodlum of the *Dreigroschenoper* (1928; *Threepenny Opera*); he is busily reinventing himself as a respectable businessman. What matters most is the public perception of his character. Much as the classical orator had to appear as a *vir bonus dicendi peritus* (good man skilled in speaking), Macheath knows that he requires a good reputation:

> Wie alle Begüterten mußte er einen ausgezeichneten moralischen Ruf haben. Er brauchte ihn, damit man ihm gestattete, die Eigentümer der B.-Läden zu betrügen. (*D* 141)

> [Like all well-to-do people, he had to have an irreproachable moral reputation. And he needed it, in order to be able to swindle the B. shop owners without interference.[16]]

Only those who are considered to be "respectable" can attract investors, or charge top dollar for their services. In this way, the text draws a parallel between classical *ethos* and applying for a loan. A businessperson who asks the bank for a loan must demonstrate that his or her character is impeccable. At the beginning of book 2, Miller of the National Deposit Bank tells the story of Nathanael Rothschild, who introduced the concept of honesty (*Ehrlichkeit*) into the world of finance. This concept is described as a new "trick" (*D* 133–34; *TN* 121–22).[17] Whether or not one is considered to be "of good character" is a decisive factor when it comes to doing business. The figures in the novel thus seek to influence the framework in which economic decisions are made by manipulating their audiences' perception of *ethos*.

Brecht's knowledge of oratory and *ethos* is particularly evident in book 2, chapter 8 of the *Dreigroschenroman*, when Macheath makes a pitch to the investment bankers Jacques and Henry Opper at their stately home, "Warborn Castle" (*D* 157; *TN* 143). Oratory is invoked at the beginning of the scene when we read that Jacques Opper is working on a biography of the orator Lycurgus. The editors of the *BFA* think that Brecht is referring to Lycurgus of Athens (ca. 390–24 BC), a logographer and one of the ten great Attic orators. Such was his skill in oratory that he was appointed three times as the manager of public revenue of Athens—moving in career terms from speechwriter to central banker.[18] The way in which Lycurgus of Athens combines the roles of orator, politician, and banker exemplifies the argument of this monograph: namely, that rhetoric, politics, and finance are all related enterprises.

Jacques Opper's favorite word is "Persönlichkeit" (*D* 158; "personality," *TN* 145), and this shows the importance he accords to *ethos*. Of course, a banker does not define *ethos* in terms of moral goodness but in terms of credit worthiness, and this is the point that Brecht is trying to make. Opper listens intently as Macheath explains how he plans to extract the maximum profits from his employees. After the meeting, Macheath mocks the hypocrisy of these upper-class bankers, who claim they want to test his "Charakter" ("character") but really only care about his "Warenlager" (*D* 159; "warehouses," *TN* 146). This misses the point that the bankers judge a person's "character" in terms of his or her financial resources. In fact, Opper checks Macheath's actual business figures very carefully indeed, but because he belongs to the social elite he expresses Macheath's high credit score in terms of classical *ethos*: "Er verlangt völlig zu Recht die voll ausgebildete *Persönlichkeit* beim rechten Verkäufer; Kollokakadia! als er ihn beschrieb, sah ich Alkibiades vor mir" (*D* 160; "He demands, quite rightly, the fully developed, harmonious *personality* of the salesman. Collocacadia, as he said it, I saw Alcibiades before me," *TN* 147). The Greek word used here is *kalokagathia* (καλοκαγαθία), meaning "a perfect gentleman"; it derives from the phrase for "gentlemanly personal conduct" (*kalos kagathos*, καλὸς κἀγαθός). This is the distinctive value of classical Greek civilization, according to the historian Jacob Burckhardt, who defines *Kalokagathie* as the "Einheit von Adel, Reichtum und Trefflichkeit" (unity of aristocracy, wealth, and excellence).[19] Burckhardt's historical narrative serves as a convenient justification for Opper's professed disdain for money (*D* 158; *TN* 145). Burckhardt, however, argues that while the Greeks disdained wealth, they made an exception for the richest merchants: "die großen Kaufleute [waren] so ideal gesinnt als irgend eine Aristokratie" (the great merchants were as high-minded as any noble house).[20] In essence, this amounts to the belief that money is to be scorned in very small quantities, but it is to be respected when it is possessed in huge amounts. Opper is in line with his mentor Burckhardt here. When Opper compares Macheath to the ideal of gentlemanly virtue, this is a coded way of saying that they can do business: ideal virtues are invoked as code words for huge profits. Here the narrative points toward an ideology that equates financial wealth with goodness of character. In this context, the discourse of "good character" boils down to the credit rating: a high valuation of character can be converted into financial wealth, and vice versa.

Like any good businessman, Macheath does not rule out the possibility of public office:

> "Meiner Meinung nach, es ist die Meinung eines ernsthaft arbeitenden Geschäftsmannes, haben wir nicht die richtigen Leute an der Spitze des Staates. Sie gehören alle irgendwelchen Parteien an und Parteien sind selbstsüchtig. Ihr Standpunkt ist einseitig. Wir brauchen Männer, die über die Parteien stehen, so wie wir Geschäftsleute. Wir verkaufen unsere Ware an Arm und Reich." (*D* 340)

> ["In my opinion, which is the opinion of a hard-working business man, we haven't got the right men at the head of the country. They all belong to some party or other, and parties are, of necessity, self-seeking and egotistic. Their outlook is one-sided. We need men who stand above all parties, something like us business men. We sell our wares to rich and poor alike." (*TN* 318)]

As a hard-working businessman, he claims that he is free of the dirty "politics" of the established parties. His status as a businessman enables him to present himself as a political outsider who is free from the taint of corruption that is associated with central government. The idea that the world of business is removed from the world of politics is absurd, as is the idea that businesspeople are less corrupt than politicians. But the rhetoric of the plain, honest businessman works very well: Donald Trump used the same strategy in his presidential election campaign of 2016 to capitalize on the American public's distrust of the established political elite in Washington, DC. Sometimes it is not political policy (*logos*) that counts, but the public persona (*ethos*) an orator is able to project. Brecht's Macheath is well aware, however, that *ethos* is a performative construction. It is a gesture rather than a *habitus* (group characteristic) or inherent essence: "Es hat heutzutage nur noch wenig Sinn, sich eine Persönlichkeit zuzulegen" (*D* 283; "It's really very little use nowadays trying to have personality," *TN* 263). In other words, to be successful as a public speaker you do not need to have a good character or a stable personality, but you need to appear as if you do. What really counts in terms of *ethos* is not consistency of character but the ability to rise to the occasion and perform as if you did have a consistent character.

Arguably the most direct allusion to Cicero in the *Dreigroschenroman* is the moment when Macheath discusses the ignorance of the public and claims that the salesman must be a teacher: "*Verkäufer sein . . . ist: Lehrer sein. Verkaufen heißt: die Unwissenheit, die erschütternde Unwissenheit des Publikums bekämpfen*" (*D* 136; "*To be a salesman . . . is to be a teacher. 'To sell' means: to fight the ignorance, the terrible ignorance of the public*," *TN* 123). Ladd emphasizes the verb "bekämpfen" (fight) here and points out: "Macheath compares his economic strategy to war. This same agonistic quality is present in Macheath's definition of the salesman, where he speaks of 'battling' the ignorance of the consumer. Like the salesperson, Macheath indeed fights with the ignorance of those who listen to him: their ignorance is his weapon."[21] Macheath's discussion of the public's ignorance alludes to Cicero's definition of oratory in *De oratore*:[22]

> Knowing, then, that oratory is a subject that relies on falsehood, that seldom reaches the level of real knowledge, that is out to take advantage of people's opinions and often their delusions, I shall speak about it.[23]

Here Cicero admits that the orator must exploit his audience's ignorance. The allusion to Cicero highlights the irony of Macheath's statement. Macheath does not want to reduce the ignorance of his customers but to increase it, in order to make a profit. The same applies to Peachum's idea of selling Bildung to the common worker: "Sie müssen ihm auch *Bildung* verkaufen" (*D* 373; "You must sell him *culture*," *TN* 349). When Peachum and Macheath join forces at the end, Peachum explains that it is because they both wish to serve the working classes and says, "Das ließ in mir sogleich eine verwandte Saite klingen" (*D* 372; "This immediately struck a corresponding chord in myself," *TN* 348). This is double-talk: Peachum and Macheath do not intend to serve but to exploit their customers.

Stock Phrases as Capital

At the beginning of the *Dreigroschenoper* Peachum, the King of the Beggars, reflects on the biblical quotations he paints on placards and uses as the tools of his trade; e.g., "Geben ist seliger als Nehmen" (It is more blessed to give than to receive, *BFA* 2:233). He wonders how much value he can extract from each quotation before it is used up. Filch enters and comments: "Ja, das sind Sprüche! Das ist ein Kapital!" (*BFA* 2:234; Yes, those are sayings! That is a capital!). Certain phrases, it seems, have monetary value because they can persuade the public to part with their money. For Peachum, the Bible is essentially a source of advertising slogans, its proverbs are a form of capital, and the act of quotation is the investment of linguistic capital in the service of public relations.[24] In this way, Peachum converts phrases into cash, and Filch is right when he identifies Peachum's stock phrases as a form of capital. The term "stock phrases" accurately conveys the sense that certain phrases have commercial value.

This insight can, of course, be traced back to classical rhetoric, which often relies on commonplaces to develop an argument. Commonplaces are part of the audience's cultural vocabulary, a mental place where one goes to find a store of arguments. Cicero argues that orators must familiarize themselves with commonplaces, either by means of long experience or by listening carefully to people:

> For you may bring me someone as learned, as sharp-witted and intel-
> ligent, and as ready in delivery as you like: if, for all that, he is a
> stranger to the customs of his community, its precedents and models,
> its traditions, and the character and inclinations of his fellow citizens,
> then those commonplaces, from which arguments are produced, will
> not be of much benefit to him.[25]

By using these commonplaces, the speaker will be able to appeal to the widest possible audience, using the lowest common denominator in order to address the largest demographic. Commonplaces can enable a speaker to reach both sides of the audience in any given debate; this was the practice of developing arguments *in utramque partem* (for both sides), compelling speakers to take stock of situations from more than one perspective.[26]

Brecht shows his awareness of the power of commonplaces very clearly in the *Dreigroschenroman*. Many of the characters adopt certain forms of verbal *habitus* like costumes. They put on and shed their linguistic attitudes as easily as a person changes clothes. William Coax's suits are "von der Stange" (off the rack; ready-made); his business associates are "ready-made," as is the shipyard where he buys his rotten ships (*D* 35–36; *TN* 30–31). And Coax's phrases are "ready-made" commercial pitches designed to suit the widest possible audience. In other words, Coax and his fellow businessmen are adept at using rhetorical commonplaces. This is not necessarily a bad thing: in "Musik von der Stange" (Ready-Made Music), a Herr Keuner story first published posthumously in 2004, Keuner speaks approvingly of ready-made clothes: "Berufskleider können Kleider von der Stange sein" (working clothes can be ready made). If we apply this dictum to Coax's phrases, we may respond with admiration: this stock of phrases may be cheap, clichéd, and even corny, but they are also effective and adaptable to almost any given situation.[27] When it comes to persuading an audience, what is required is not originality but familiarity.

Steve Giles has compared the two different versions of the *Dreigroschenoper* and shown that in the later version of 1931 there is more discontinuity between words and actions as the figures of the drama self-consciously distance themselves from their own verbal behavior patterns.[28] This tendency toward discontinuity is even stronger in the *Dreigroschenroman*, where the figures use language in a highly calculated way to gain the maximum effect. The way that Macheath, Peachum, and Coax use language in Brecht's novel seems to anticipate the term "post-truth politics," which was coined by David Roberts in 2010 to describe "a political culture in which politics (public opinion and media narratives) have become almost entirely disconnected from policy (the substance of legislation)."[29] Recent debates about "post-truth politics" are, however, superficial if they do not take classical rhetoric into account. Classical oratory tells us that substance of policy (*logos*) does not always win a debate. To succeed, speakers also need *ethos* and *pathos*, and they also need to formulate their arguments in terms that the audience can relate to. This consideration enables us to see that the *Dreigroschenroman* is not simply an encyclopedia of clichés; in fact, it is a sophisticated handbook of rhetorical commonplaces.

From the Orator to the Demagogue

Brecht was interested in Hitler's rhetoric, and he parodies it in his play *Der aufhaltsame Aufstieg des Arturo Ui* (1941; *The Resistible Rise of Arturo Ui*) when the Hitler figure is trained by an actor. In the *Dreigroschenroman*, too, National Socialist rhetoric is an important subtext.[30] It is certainly possible to see parallels between the rise of Macheath and Hitler's ascent to power. Hitler was a talented orator who had a whole stock of rhetorical commonplaces at his disposal.[31] He chose his words carefully, mastering the "language of the post-war little guy."[32] Clearly, on one level the *Dreigroschenroman* is concerned with the mechanisms of persuasion used by the Nazis. Nevertheless, Macheath is different from Hitler: he is a businessman, not a politician. He uses anti-Semitic rhetoric when it suits him to do so, but only to advance his own business agenda.

If Macheath resembles any historical figures, then he is much closer to the German industrialists who also engaged in nationalist politics—for example, Baron Carl Ferdinand von Stumm-Halberg, Hugo Stinnes, and Alfred Hugenberg.[33] Hugenberg, the former director of Krupp Steel, built a media empire and became the leader of the Deutschnationale Volkspartei (DNVP, German National People's Party) in 1928. His alliance with the Nazis in 1929 gave them a respectability they had not possessed before.[34] As for Hugo Stinnes, there was a legend that he ate only an egg for breakfast.[35] The *Dreigroschenroman* refers to this legend when Macheath eats an egg for breakfast with great care (*D* 348–49; *TN* 325–26). A few pages later, the theme is developed when Grooch says of Macheath, "Ich habe gehört, er lebe so einfach. . . . Irgendwer hat gesagt, daß er Vegetarier sei" (*D* 351; "I have heard that he lives quite simply. . . . Someone has even told me that he is a vegetarian," *TN* 327). This is clearly an allusion to Hitler, a vegetarian and a self-styled common man. But this form of self-stylization can actually be traced back to business leaders such as Stinnes and Cornelius Vanderbilt, who projected the image of a modest lifestyle (*BFA* 16:465). This is the lineage Brecht explores in the *Dreigroschenroman*. When Macheath cites Rudyard Kipling's phrase "Der kranke Mann stirbt und der starke Mann ficht" (*D* 164; "The sick man dies and the strong man fights," *TN* 150),[36] it recalls the social Darwinism of Baron von Stumm-Halberg's publicist, Alexander Tille, who proclaimed that "die Untüchtigsten unfehlbar zugrunde gehen" (the most incapable never fail to go under).[37] Brecht is studying not only Hitler's rhetoric but also that of the right-wing populists and business leaders who preceded him. It is no accident that business leaders often tend to be right-wing populists, or that the two groups often club together, since it is convenient to blame social inequality and poverty on ethnic minorities rather than on big business.

Hitler was not the first nor the last to foster ignorance and then capitalize on it. Brecht reflects on the political uses of ignorance in "Ein Problem für die Marxisten" (1938; A Problem for Marxists), which raises a question for Marxists: how can they persuade members of the petit bourgeoisie (a class that tended to be profascist) that Hitler does not represent their interests? Much of Hitler's rhetoric was directed at the German *Mittelstand*, the petty-bourgeois businesspeople whose livelihoods were threatened by large-scale commercialization. Macheath, too, claims to champion the rights of German retailers.[38] "Ein Problem für die Marxisten" suggests a Ciceronian solution to the problem of how to address the petty bourgeoisie:

> Ein Problem für die Marxisten ist es, zu den Kleinbürgern zu sprechen. . . . Gegen den Faschismus muß man sich ihrer Vorurteile bedienen, ihren Glauben an den Führer könnte man am besten bekämpfen, wenn man an ihren Aberglauben appellierte. Da wir das nicht können, haben wir es schwer. (*BFA* 22.1:416–17)

> [A problem for the Marxists is speaking to the lower middle classes. . . . To oppose fascism, we need to use their prejudices. The best way fight their belief in the Führer is to appeal to their superstition. Because we cannot do this, things look difficult for us.]

Like Cicero, Brecht recognizes that an orator has to adopt the vocabulary and the prejudices of the audience. He thus advises Marxists to appeal to German nationalist prejudices. He is not the first Marxist to have had this dangerous idea. During the Ruhr crisis of 1923, the Communist leader Karl Radek proclaimed Albert Leo Schlageter as a martyr. Schlageter was a right-wing activist who was executed by the French authorities on May 26, 1923; Radek celebrated him in order to recruit nationalists to the Communist cause.[39]

Brecht's fragment "Ein Problem für die Marxisten" gets to the heart of the matter, showing how the Nazis manipulated the prejudices of their voters. By blaming Jews for the consequences of capitalism, they were able to misdirect people's attention:

> Alle Lösungen, die aus dieser Ecke kommen, sind Lösungen auf dem Papier. Da wird eine Brieftasche bei einem Mann mit krummer Nase gefunden, und von nun an wird auf krumme Nasen Jagd gemacht. . . . Daher kommt der klassische Vorschlag, das Wort *Börse* durch ein anderes, "sauberes" Wort zu ersetzen, da dem *Wort* Börse ein schlechter Geruch anhaftet. (*BFA* 22.1:417)

> [All the answers from this corner are paper answers. They find a brief-case on a man with a hooked nose, and now they are hunting hooked noses. . . . This is where they get the classic idea to replace the word *stock exchange* with another, "cleaner" word, because the *word* stock exchange has a bad odor.]

Brecht's analysis here accords fully with Kenneth Burke's analysis of Hitler's rhetoric in *Mein Kampf* (1925–26; *My Struggle*). According to Burke, Hitler provided "a noneconomic interpretation of economic ills," deflecting the attention of his audience away from economic factors "by attacking 'Jew finance' instead of *finance*."[40] Instead of blaming property speculation for the crisis, the Nazis blamed the Jews. They also found new words to disguise exploitation, such as *Volksgemeinschaft* (folk community). In the novel Macheath uses a similar strategy of misdirection in order to fool his own employees. In this way, Brecht's text alerts readers to the economic and political agendas that lurk behind the rhetoric of inclusion and exclusion. As Brecht noted laconically in the margin of Alfred Forke's translation of *Mê Ti* (1922; Mozi): "das gasthaus ist nicht / gastlich der gastlichkeit / wegen, sondern des verdienstes / wegen" (the guesthouse is not hospitable out of hospitality, but to make a profit).[41]

Brecht's Language Criticism

As noted in this book's introduction, Brecht's work often draws on modernist Sprachkritik. Around 1930 Brecht remarks: "Erkenntnistheorie muß vor allem Sprachkritik sein" (*BFA* 21:413; cognitive science must focus above all on language criticism). From 1930 to 1932 Brecht engaged with the logical empiricism of the Wiener Kreis (Vienna Circle); the Brecht archive contains his annotated copies of *Erkenntnis* (Cognition), the group's journal. Brecht's linguistic criticism has received remarkably little attention. W. F. Haug notes intellectual affinities between Brecht and Ludwig Wittgenstein but does not comment on their shared interest in the Vienna Circle.[42] A fuller picture is provided by Herbert Claas and Steve

Giles, who survey Brecht's study of Vienna Circle thinkers such as Rudolf Carnap, Hans Reichenbach, and Otto Neurath.[43] Giles comments that Brecht was "not uncritical" of these authors and finds that Brecht's position on truth and language is closer to the pragmatism of C. S. Peirce.[44] As we might expect, Brecht considers language in terms of its use value as an instrument of manipulation or distraction, i.e., as a gesture. In a note of 1931 Brecht observes: "Die auftretenden . . . Sätze müssen da gefaßt werde, wo sie als ein Verhalten wirken, also nicht nur einseitig als Spiegelungen, Ausdrücke, Reflexe" (*BFA* 21:525; As sentences appear, they must be grasped at the point where they function as behavior, not one-sidedly as reflections, expressions, reflexes). This remark suggests that sentences function as actions in their own right, each with its own behavioral attitude. Brecht alludes to Carl von Clausewitz's dictum that "Der Krieg ist eine bloße Fortsetzung der Politik mit anderen Mitteln" (War is the continuation of politics by other means)[45] in the *Dreigroschenroman* when Hale describes politics as the continuation of business by other means: "Politik ist die Fortführung der Geschäfte mit anderen Mitteln" (BFA 16, 173; "Politics is the pursuit of business by unbusiness-like methods," *TN* 159). War, politics, and business all involve the pursuit of material interests. In the *Dreigroschenroman* the principal means of doing business is via language: protagonists use speech to outmaneuver opponents. Brecht is drawing on Nietzsche's Sprachkritik here. Schooled in classical rhetoric, Nietzsche sees language as an arsenal of persuasive techniques. Brecht's early reading of Nietzsche leads him to similar conclusions. In a diary entry of September 6, 1920, he describes words as potential weapons: "Das Schlimmste, wenn die Dinge sich verkrusten in Wörtern, hart werden, weh tun beim Schmeißen, tot herumliegen. Sie müssen aufgestachelt werden, enthäutet, bös gemacht, man muß sie füttern und . . . abrichten" (*BFA* 26:158; Worst of all is when things become encrusted in words and become hard, so that they hurt if you throw them, or lie around lifeless. They need to be provoked, skinned, angered; you have to feed them and . . . train them).

Brecht's writings of 1933–34 onward continue these reflections on language, with specific reference to Nazi propaganda. Upon completion of the *Dreigroschenroman* in the summer of 1934, Brecht began work on *Buch der Wendungen* (1965; *Me-Ti: Book of Interventions into the Flow of Things*), a series of parables drawing on the work of the ancient Chinese philosopher Mozi—known in Forke's German translation of 1922, which Brecht possessed, as Mê Ti.[46] Many of the texts in *Buch der Wendungen* reflect on Hitler's use of language; e.g., "Aussprüche des Anstreichers" (1934; The Housepainter's Slogans), which dissects Hitler's slogan "Gemeinnutz geht vor Eigennutz" (*BFA* 18:49–50; Help the community before yourself). Another text, "Katalog der Begriffe" (Catalogue of Concepts, possibly written in the late thirties) reflects on ideological terms used by the Nazis: *Natur* (nature), *Boden* (soil), and *volkstümlich* (popular)—although the last term was also used by the Popular Front organized by the Soviet Union (*BFA* 18:116–17).[47] This idea of a "catalogue of concepts" recalls the notion of an "encyclopedia of clichés" that Brecht mooted in 1926. In *Buch der Wendungen* we are told that it is important to study the ruling classes in order to see how they rule so effectively (*BFA* 18:127). In this text, as in the *Dreigroschenroman*, Brecht is weighing up the ideological techniques of his opponents—for example, when we learn that the banker Jacques Opper is writing a biography of Lycurgus of Athens. The fact that a banker is studying a classical orator is no accident, since bankers need to be skilled in the art of persuasion. One of Brecht's alter egos in *Buch der Wendungen* is the poet Ken-jeh, of whom Brecht says: "Wenn er einen Wald sieht, jammert er sofort über die Zeitungen, die aus dem Holz gemacht werden und das Volk verdummen" (*BFA* 18:117; "Whenever he sees a forest, he moans straightaway about the newspapers printed from its wood that fool the people"[48]). This implies a critique of the mass media as propaganda. As in classical oratory, language is a practical tool, perhaps even a weapon: "Der Dichter Kin erkannte die Sprache als ein Werkzeug des Handelns" (*BFA* 18:79; "The poet Kin saw language as a tool for taking action"[49]). Certain sentences can even be viewed as allies in the struggle against fascism: "Wir stellen allerhand Sätze zusammen, wie man Verbündete wählt für den Kampf" (*BFA* 18:89; "We construct lots of sentences about how to choose allies for the struggle"[50]). And if some sentences are allies, "Sätze von Systemen hängen aneinander wie Mitglieder von Verbrecherbanden" (*BFA* 18:95; "Sentences within systems are connected to each other like members of criminal gangs"[51]). Given that the first composition phase of *Buch der Wendungen* was 1934, the same year as the *Dreigroschenroman*, it is plausible to argue that two texts share a concern with the rhetorical use of language.

The linguistic considerations of *Buch der Wendungen* suggest that Macheath employs his sentences like tools or implements, or like "Mitglieder von Verbrecherbanden" (members of criminal gangs). When he asserts that he is happy to do business with anyone—"Wir verkaufen unsere Ware an Arm und Reich . . . ohne Ansehen der Person" (*D* 340; "We sell our wares to rich and poor alike. Without regard for standing," *TN* 318)—he proclaims the principle of the free market, in which (theoretically) each individual is treated fairly and equally. Macheath's rhetoric anticipates the Hayekian neoliberalism of our own time that claims that free markets are "fairer" than politics because they function according to universal principles. Such rhetoric condemns politics as biased and corrupt because it serves particular interest groups. Markets—so the argument goes—distribute goods "freely" according to impartial general rules, unlike politics, which is supposedly tainted by ideology. This ignores the fact that markets (and politics) offer an enormous advantage to those with capital at their disposal, as Wolfgang Streeck points out.[52] In the *Dreigroschenroman* the critique of economic manipulation and the critique of political manipulation are therefore intertwined.

Economic Rhetoric and Ideology

Much neoliberal economic theory today derives from the work of Friedrich August von Hayek (1899–1992). Hayek argues that governments should guarantee the rule of law but avoid direct intervention in the economy, e.g., through price controls, because such controls would not "allow the market to function adequately."[53] He warns against the pursuit of distributive justice, claiming that it will lead to a command economy.[54] Hayek's neoliberal successors since the 1970s have taken this to mean that free markets distribute wealth more fairly than elected governments and that markets should be freed from state intervention. Recent decades have seen the growth of multinational corporations and a return to the monopoly capitalism of the 1920s. Hayek himself dismisses private-enterprise monopolies as a problem "of little importance" and warns against any government action against them.[55] Although Hayek considers monopolies to be a "minor" problem, they were a major problem in Brecht's lifetime. They repeatedly threatened the stability of Weimar democracy. In 1920 the brinkmanship of the industrialist Hugo Stinnes almost provoked the Allies to occupy the Ruhr; as a result, Stinnes became a nationalist hero (he died in 1924).[56] In 1927 Hermann Bücher, the general manager of the Reichsverband der Deutschen Industrie (German Steel and Industry Association) declared that the weakness of the German state was a welcome opportunity "zu einer unternehmerischen Revisionspolitik" (for an entrepreneurial revisionist policy)—a code phrase for the restoration of an autocratic regime.[57] In 1931 large donations from German industrialists boosted the NSDAP (Nationalsozialistische Deutsche Arbeiterpartei [National Socialist German Workers' Party; i.e., Nazi Party]) substantially.[58] In November 1932 several German business leaders wrote to President Paul von Hindenburg, asking him to appoint Hitler as chancellor.[59] During World War II the chemical cartel IG Farben equipped the gas chambers at Auschwitz.[60] Brecht's journal entry of April 13, 1948, reads: "Die Vergasungslager des IG-Farben-Trusts sind Monumente der bürgerlichen Kultur dieser Jahrzehnte" (*BFA* 27:268; The gas chambers of the IG Farben Trust are monuments of the bourgeois culture of these decades).

Pace Hayek, the reality of how markets work is that they tend to form monopolies, as the big fish eat the little fish. Brecht's story "Wenn die Haifische Menschen wären" (*BFA* 18:446–48; If Sharks Were People) illustrates this point. Indeed, the *Dreigroschenroman* even reflects on this tendency, with specific reference to the book of Matthew. The Matthew Effect, as it has become known, was coined in 1968 by the sociologist Robert K. Merton and takes its name from the Parable of the Talents in Matt. 25:29: "For unto every one that hath shall be given, and he shall have abundance: but from him that hath not shall be taken even that which he hath."[61] Merton used the term to describe how eminent scientists tended to accrue more credit than lesser-known colleagues. More generally, it describes the phenomenon that the more resources and connections you have, the more you get. In economics it is known as cumulative advantage.[62] The conclusion of the *Dreigroschenroman* delivers an analysis of the Matthew Effect. Fewkoombey dreams that he is a judge. The defendant is Jesus Christ. The case for the prosecution is based on Matt. 25. The prosecution argues that the biblical parable has been used to justify inequality, and that it is false because it implies that everyone is given a talent—everyone has a fair chance. The judge declares: "Daß aber *alle* Menschen ein Pfund mitbekämen, das erklärte das Gericht als nicht erwiesen" (*D* 385; "But the statement that *all* men received a pound was not accepted by the court as proved," *TN* 359). This dream sequence implies that the market is not free and fair, because the odds are always weighted in favor of those who start off with greater resources. And if some people have nothing except their bodies, then they are forced to make their own bodies available for exploitation. Fewkoombey realizes that "Der Mensch [ist] des Menschen Pfund!" (*D* 391; "Man is the pound of man!" *TN* 364). Human beings exploit each other, and themselves, as capital.

This is the reality that liberal rhetoric of the free market either conceals or describes as regrettable but inevitable. In order to justify the free market as the natural order of things, various authorities tend to be invoked, including the Bible, Adam Smith, and Charles Darwin. Adam Smith's notion of an "invisible hand" is often taken out of context and used to present the market as a self-correcting mechanism, one that functions according to the laws of supply and demand.[63] Decisions by the market are then regarded as natural or inevitable, to the extent that they seem to fall from the sky without human intervention.[64] If thousands are made destitute, such rhetoric implies that no one can be held personally responsible, because it is only the self-correcting operation of the market. Brecht's novel makes a similar point when Macheath is accused of murdering Mary Swayer. Macheath's lawyer argues that Mary's death was the result of general economic laws (*D* 264–66; *TN* 245–47). His waffle obscures the facts of the case: that Macheath, as Mary's employer, bled her dry. Translated into the language of Brecht's Herr Keuner, the lawyer's rhetoric implies that sharks eat little fish, but little fish should allow themselves to be eaten, because it is a law of nature for sharks to eat little fish. Or, as Macheath puts it, in crude social Darwinist terms: "Der kranke Mann sterbe und der

starke Mann fechte. So sei es immer gewesen und werde es immer sein"
(*D* 194; "The sick man dies and the strong man fights. It had always been
and always would be so," *TN* 180).

Communication and Business

In the *Dreigroschenroman* we read: "Wohlstand [war] nur die andere Seite
der Armut. Was war der Wohlstand der einen anderes als die Armut der
andern?" (*D* 309; "prosperity was only the reverse side of poverty. What
was the prosperity of one man but the poverty of another?" *TN* 289).
Language performs the essential function of disguising exploitation in
economic exchanges. Behind this camouflage, the real battles happen in
secret. Macheath must maintain around himself the "Halbdämmer, in dem
man fett werden konnte" (*D* 219; "that convenient twilight in which a
man can grow fat and prosperous," *TN* 203). As a legal form of robbery,
according to Brecht, business deals are best concluded in half-darkness. As
the Latin phrase *caveat emptor* (let the buyer beware) implies, buyers generally have less information about what they are purchasing than the sellers
do. Brecht's characters meet in a restaurant called the "Tintenfisch"
(squid, cuttlefish). This is an animal that blinds its opponents with ink during combat: an appropriate symbol for Brecht's capitalist characters, who
use words to conceal their true intentions. Dialogue here is a defense
mechanism to conceal aggression. For example, Peachum claims he is
doing "everything" for his daughter but then prostitutes her to the broker
William Coax.

The novel deploys several means of linguistic estrangement. Italics
draw attention to key speeches, the characters' actions often contradict
their verbal gestures, and the third-person narrator highlights the artificiality of the characters' spoken language by inserting comments such as:
"Hätte er [Fewkoombey] sich Gedanken gemacht, wären ungefähr dies
seine Gedanken gewesen . . ." (*D* 73; "Had he been thinking, his thoughts
would have been somewhat as follows . . .," *TN* 67); "Wäre er [Peachum]
gebildet gewesen, hätte er ausrufen können . . ." (*D* 97; "Had he been
educated, he might have cried out . . .," *TN* 90). Then there is the portrayal of language as a force of nature. Macheath's speech affects Mary
Swayer much like a blizzard or a storm at sea: "Für sie war Macs Redekunst
ungefähr dasselbe, wie die Schneikunst der Wolken im Winter, das, was die
Zerschmetterkunst der Sturmwogen für das Schiff ist" (*D* 200; "Mac's
powers of oratory meant about the same to her as the power of the clouds
to snow in winter; but in reality it threatened her as the destructive power
of the storm threatens a ship at sea," *TN* 185–86). This is another allusion
to classical oratory, namely the description of Odysseus in Book 3:220–23
of Homer's *Iliad*: "When he liberated that great voice from his chest and

poured out words like the snows of winter, there was no man alive who could compete with him."[65]

Eloquence translates into wealth; for example, in the description of the lawyer's office, which contains "die dicken Teppiche, die seine Beredsamkeit ihm eingebracht hatte" (*D* 312; "the thick carpet which past eloquence had earned for him," *TN* 291). Rhetoric is most effective, however, when the audience is vulnerable. Mary Swayer falls prey to Macheath's eloquence because she does not understand how business works. A powerful opponent cannot be swayed by eloquence alone, and this is when bribery, blackmail, extortion, or violence become necessary. For example, when Peachum wants Macheath to divorce Polly, he rehearses speeches but eventually realizes that in this case only violence will work (BFA 16, 230; *TN* 213). But words can still serve as traps for the unwary.

Populism and Marketing

Macheath uses public relations to pursue his interests. He recognizes that many small traders wish to preserve their "Selbständigkeit" (independence). He gives newspaper interviews in which he claims that his B-stores are all independent, and he calls independence a fundamental drive of human nature, suggesting that modern man has a particular need to prove that he is capable (*D* 51; *TN* 46). But the stores still belong to Macheath as part of his franchise. The B-store owners think that they are independent, but effectively they are employees with no fixed wages, who receive only commissions as payment. Their so-called independence makes them more dependent than ever on Macheath. If the store makes a profit, he gets most of it. But if the shopkeeper goes bankrupt, he or she loses everything, and the store reverts to Macheath, who simply leases it to a new "owner." Macheath's claim that "Das System sollte ganz und gar dem *kleinen Mann* zugute kommen" (*D* 52; "The system was purely for the benefit of the *small man*," *TN* 47) is only a trap for the shopkeeper.

Macheath wants to squeeze the maximum profit out of the B-store owners, but he does not want to be the target of their resentment. Accordingly, he uses ideological manipulation in order to steer his employees' perceptions of their own situation. He makes them believe that independence is in their own interest and offers them a scapegoat when things go wrong: the Jewish-owned department stores. In one scene, Macheath and Polly visit a B-store in Liverpool, where the shopkeeper and his wife look utterly miserable and undernourished. When the man tells Macheath he cannot settle his rates this month, Macheath starts blaming Jewish bankers (*D* 100; *TN* 92). Macheath misdirects the man's resentment so that he does not blame his own employer for his dire situation. This is clearly a comment on anti-Semitic propaganda of the Nazis, which presented the party as the champion of the Mittelstand (midsize companies). The National Socialist manifesto of May 1920 demanded special protection for the Mittelstand and immediate nationalization of larger (Jewish) department stores.[66] Like Hitler, Macheath exploits existing resentments to gain political mastery over the petty-bourgeois salespeople he exploits.

At one point, Macheath makes a speech to the B-store owners in which he announces his new collaboration with Aaron, the Jewish department store owner. Macheath presents Aaron as a powerful Jewish capitalist who is out to exploit the "little people," German shopkeepers with blue eyes: "Warum sollte der mächtige Aaronkonzern mit uns kleinen Geschäftsleuten künftig zusammenarbeiten wollen? . . . nicht wegen der *blauen Augen* der Billigkeitsläden!" (*D* 163; "Why should the mighty Aaron combine want to work together with us small shopkeepers? . . . Not because of the *blue eyes* of the Bargain shops!" *TN* 149). Macheath warns his audience against Aaron and claims that he, Macheath, will fight to defend their interests because he believes in an "idea." In this way, Macheath presents himself as the champion of a Germanic Volksgemeinschaft against an enemy identified as a Jew. This act of misdirection obscures the fact that Macheath plans to extract maximum profit from "his" shopkeepers, as he has just told his bankers: "Die eigentliche Einnahmequelle sei und bleibe der Angestellte" (*D* 159; "The real source of profit was, and would always be, the employees," *TN* 145). Macheath accuses his competitor, Aaron, of being motivated by purely material interests:

> "Wohin wir blicken in der Natur, geschieht *nichts ohne materielle Interessen!* Wo immer einer zu dem andern sagt: ich meine es gut mit dir, wir wollen zusammen . . . usw., da heißt es aufgepaßt! Denn die Menschen sind eben menschlich und keine Engel und sorgen vor allem erst einmal für sich selber." (*D* 163)

> ["Wherever we look in nature, *nothing* is done *except for material profit!* Whenever one person says to another: I want to help you, let's start together and . . . etc., that means, Look out! For men are only human beings and not angels, and they think first of all of themselves." (*TN* 149)]

Here Macheath presents himself as warning his audience about Aaron's tactics. But at the same time, he is describing his own tactics. Macheath proclaims his decision to devote himself entirely to the service of the B-store owners: "Und darum habe auch ich mich entschlossen, in Zukunft meine ganze Kraft Ihnen und den B.-Läden zu widmen, nicht aus materiellem Interesse heraus, sondern weil ich an die Idee glaube" (*D* 163; "And therefore I, too, have decided to dedicate in the future all my powers to you and to the B. shops. Not for reasons of material gain, but because I believe in the ideal," *TN* 149). Macheath's claim that he is not pursuing material interests contradicts his previous statement that every action is motivated by material interests. What counts is that Macheath assures his audience that he is united with them against a Jewish competitor. The audience ignores his previous warning, assuming that he will champion their collective interests. Soon after telling the storeholders that he is sacrificing himself for their benefit, Macheath increases the rates they have to pay him because it is time for them to show "was in ihnen stecke" (*D* 194; "what they were made of," *TN* 180).

Businessmen in the *Dreigroschenroman* use mystification in order to promote their interests, and the media helpfully oblige by circulating their claims—e.g., the lie that they are not motivated by money but by something more profound, such as the love of sport, or by a "dämonisch" ("daemonic") drive (*D* 129; *TN* 116). Rulers often falsify history, carefully shrouding themselves in legends (*D* 127; *TN* 115). Such mythmaking directs attention away from material transactions toward a putative higher plane. The banker Jacques Opper even claims that "Die eigentliche Triebkraft der Menschheit ist das Bedürfnis, sich auszudrücken, das heißt seine *Persönlichkeit* zu verewigen" (*D* 158; "The real motive power of humanity is the necessity of self-expression, that is, the perpetuation of *personality*," *TN* 145). The two key words, "dämonisch" and "Persönlichkeit," are highlighted by extra spacing between the letters to draw attention to the fact that they are forms of self-mythologizing.[67]

Another way to deny one's own self-interest is to claim that one is merely acting as a trustee for someone else. Peachum likes to say that he is doing everything for his daughter. Miller and Hawthorne of the National Deposit Bank stress that the bank does not belong to them but to a seven-year-old girl: "Die Bank gehört nicht uns, sondern der kleinen Talk, übrigens ein ausnehmend reizendes kleines Mädchen!" (*D* 138; "The bank doesn't belong to us but to the little Talk, an exceptionally charming child!" *TN* 126).[68] The corrupt civil servant Hale claims that his primary motivation is to serve his country (*D* 172; *TN* 158). A director of a company can always point out that he has a responsibility to his shareholders. Capitalists like to appear in the role of guardians or trustees who enrich others, not themselves.

Macheath's favorite lie is that he always works for the benefit of the consumer. In one interview, he claims that he will defeat his competitors thanks to his tireless efforts in the service of his customers (*D* 213; *TN* 197). Here is a particularly flagrant example of Macheath's doublespeak, one in which he appears in the guise of a martyr to his work:

> "In dem unaufhörlichen Bestreben, dem Publikum zu dienen, legen wir uns Beschränkungen auf, die nur *die Stärksten* von uns aushalten. Wir sind zu billig. Unsere Gewinne sind so winzig, daß wir selber darben. Wir sind vielleicht zu fanatisch darauf aus, dem kleinen Käufer gute Waren zu erschwinglichen Preisen zu bieten." (*D* 267)

["In our unceasing endeavor to serve the public, we make demands on ourselves which only the *strongest* can endure for long. We sell too cheaply. Our profits are so small that we have to face privation. Perhaps we are too fanatical in our efforts to supply the poor purchaser with the best articles at reasonable prices." (*TN* 248)]

Macheath claims that he shares the misery of his colleagues (in fact, he is the principal cause of their misery). Occasionally, he lets the mask slip: when he describes himself as one of the "strongest" traders, he presents himself not as a servant but as a master. This talk of self-martyrdom is a justification for the price increases he is going to announce.

Conclusion: Blunt Thinking

What conclusions can be drawn from this? In the *Dreigroschenroman*, economic and political interests are intertwined. Macheath and Peachum are accomplished orators who ensnare their listeners with stock phrases that imply a collective identity.[69] These gestures toward shared identity are hooks for the audience. They invoke the idea that the speaker and the listeners have mutually shared interests, in order to obscure the fact that opposing interests are at stake. It is no coincidence that the penultimate chapter is called "Nebel" ("Fog"), since the ruling elite in this novel is adept at clouding the understanding of the public with decorative phrases. References to absolute principles (as in the bishop's eulogy near the end of the novel) act as a smokescreen, distracting from the dirty deals that have been done.

There are double standards here. The leaders of society want to spread confusion; at the same time, they take information-gathering very seriously in respect of their material interests. They read newspapers, they send out scouts, they reconnoiter the terrain (e.g., when Macheath goes to the barbershop, *D* 214; *TN* 198–99). The *Dreigroschenroman* shows that precise information-gathering is essential for business; but it is equally important to prevent one's competitors from learning about one's own actions. We have a situation in which all of the figures try to get the maximum information about the others, while simultaneously obscuring their own activities as much as possible. If they discover that others are trying to find out about their affairs, they are outraged. For example, Police Commissioner Brown gets annoyed about Communists who talk about corruption in the ministries and even claim that the police force is not impartial. He argues that the Communists see everything in terms of black and white:

"*Solche Schwarzweißmalerei macht alles, was diese Schmutzaufwirbler vorbringen, einfach unglaubwürdig.*"
"Wenn jetzt einer mitschriebe, was du daherredest," sagte Macheath bedächtig, "wäre es auch Schwarzweißmalerei." (*D* 339)

[*"Painting things in such black and white terms makes all these mud-slingers' claims seem quite unbelievable."*
"If anyone was to write down what you've been saying," said MacHeath thoughtfully, "it would also be painting things in black and white terms." (*TN* 317)[70]]

Macheath's answer here can be understood as a form of *Verfremdung* (distancing) or metacommentary. The text reflects on its own activity, its own exposure of corrupt verbal, political, and economic practices. The Communists are supposed to be so blinded by their ideology that they view everything in terms of material interests—the question of property is described by Marx and Engels as the principal question of the Communist movement.[71] In this respect, "Schwarzweißmalerei" could be seen as a variant of Brechtian "plumpes Denken" (blunt thinking).[72] This concept is mentioned in the novel by Hale:

> *"Als der deutsche Kaiser an den Präsidenten Krüger telegrafierte, welche Aktien stiegen da und welche fielen? Natürlich fragen das nur die Kommunisten. Aber unter uns, doch nicht nur sie: die Diplomaten auch. Es ist freilich plump gedacht, aber der Wirklichkeit ist dieses Denken sehr nahe. Die Hauptsache ist, plump denken lernen. Plumpes Denken, das ist das Denken der Großen."* (GBA 16, 172–73)

> [*"When the German Kaiser telegraphed to President Kruger, do you know which stocks rose and fell? No! Of course, only the communists ask that. But between ourselves, it is not only the communists; the diplomats want to know too. That's rather a blunt example, but the idea is very near the reality. The chief thing is to learn to think bluntly. Blunt thinking is great thinking."* (*TN* 158–59)]

It is not only the Communists who focus on the question of property; it is also the elite. Walter Benjamin interprets this passage as Brecht's commentary on his own method, arguing that blunt thinking is useful because it applies theory to practice: "Ein Gedanke muss plump sein, um im Handeln zu seinem Recht zu kommen" (A thought must be blunt, in order to come into its own as an action).[73] Benjamin points out that Marx was the first to illuminate the relations between human beings under capitalism, relations that had previously been obscured. Marx was a great teacher of satire because he was able "die Verhältnisse zwischen Menschen aus ihrer Erniedrigung und Vernebelung in der kapitalistischen Wirtschaft wieder ans Licht der Kritik zu ziehen" (to take the relations between human beings out of the degradation and fog of capitalist economics and bring them back into the light of criticism).[74] To summarize: blunt Marxist thinking can be a great antidote to hot air. Or, as Cicero puts it: "Cui bono?" (Who stands to gain?)[75]

5: Giving an Account of the Self in Ingeborg Bachmann's *Malina*, 1971

> *daß sich neuerdings die*
> *Geschichte im Ich aufhält*
> [these days, history resides
> inside the self]
> —Ingeborg Bachmann

Introduction: A Sociopolitical Approach to *Malina*

*M*ALINA, BY INGEBORG BACHMANN (1926–73), centers upon the enigma of a split personality: the female narrator (Ich), who is gradually supplanted by her male alter ego, Malina. Most interpretations of the novel have focused on the gendered aspect of this dislocation in the self, and indeed, the novel thematizes the imbalances of power as enshrined in normative binary models of gender relations. Georgina Paul, for example, reads Malina's appropriation of the narrative subject as a work of mourning for the lost "feminine" aspect within *himself* and takes the novel's absence of closure (i.e., the enigma of its final words, "Es war Mord" ["It was murder"][1]) as an affirmation of a "feminine" plurality.[2] Anyone studying *Malina* today must take account of the exponential growth in Bachmann scholarship if one-sided interpretations are to be avoided. As early as 1992, Sara Lennox and Leslie Morris asked feminist readers to abandon "wishful thinking" about Bachmann's politics, and to stop trying "to make her conform to our ideas."[3] More recently, Dirk Göttsche suggests that "it is time to move beyond the notion that there could be one single privileged approach or key to the meaning of Bachmann's work."[4] Like Kafka's, Bachmann's work is fundamentally open.[5] But the fact that Bachmann's work resists interpretive closure does not mean that anything goes. Politicizing Bachmann may be a risky business, but to focus solely on aesthetics, without reference to the political and historical contexts in which they are embedded, is also questionable. In 1995 when Susanne Baackmann proposed a political approach to Bachmann's work, Albrecht Holschuh called for a "purely literary" reading.[6] The tension in Bachmann scholarship between political and "apolitical" readings resembles an exchange between Ich and Ivan in the novel.

Ich tells Ivan: "Gerade habe ich erfunden, wie ich die Welt doch noch verändern kann!" (*M* 105; "I've just invented a way to change the world after all!" *Ma* 64). Ivan replies scornfully: "Was? du auch? die Gesellschaft, die Verhältnisse? das muß ja heutzutage der reinste Wettbewerb sein" (*M* 105; "What? you too? society, relationships? these days that has got to be the biggest game around," *Ma* 64).

This chapter considers *Malina* in debate with canonical thinkers: Weber, Marx, Elaine Scarry, Brecht. It concludes with an analysis of the rhetorical dimension in *Malina*, which stresses the importance of open-ended debate. Obviously, taking a political approach to *Malina* risks endangering its aesthetic polysemy. Bachmann's discretion as an artist was so great that she avoided tackling political questions directly. As she put it in an interview in 1971: "Und wenn ich zum Beispiel in diesem Buch 'Malina' kein Wort über den Vietnamkrieg sage, kein Wort über soundso viele katastrophale Zustände unserer Gesellschaft, dann weiß ich aber auf eine andere Weise etwas zu sagen—oder ich hoffe, daß ich es zu sagen weiß"[7] (*GuI* 90–91; And if for example I don't say a word about the Vietnam War in *Malina*, not a word about our catastrophic social conditions, well then I do know how to say something in another way—or at least I hope I do). Bachmann's is an art of indirectness.[8] Much Bachmann scholarship studiously avoids direct political reference. Her 1949 dissertation on Heidegger is often cited,[9] as is her reception of Wittgenstein,[10] Nietzsche,[11] and Benjamin.[12] French theory in the shape of Roland Barthes is sometimes allowed a look-in. Sigrid Weigel reads *Malina* in Barthesian terms as the victory of the third-person narrator over the first person.[13] Áine McMurtry reads *Malina* in terms of Barthes's *Fragments d'un discours amoureux* (1977; *A Lover's Discourse: Fragments*) and of Nietzsche and Theodor Adorno. She interprets the Ich-Malina dichotomy as an opposition between the Dionysian female and the Apollonian male protagonist, thus identifying a feminist cultural critique at the heart of Bachmann's poetics and opening up a debate about the politics of aesthetic representation.[14] Yet although McMurtry mentions "the socio-cultural roots" of the individual crisis, she steers clear of unpacking the wider socio-political implications of Bachmann's work.[15] Michael Minden's reading of *Malina* is framed by Eric Santner's view of modernity as the passage from the "vertical" authority of the single sovereign to the "horizontal" sovereignty of the crowd.[16] Minden reaffirms Bachmann's place within the tradition of German modernism as informed by Nietzsche's metaphysical crisis and "sympathy for the abyss,"[17] and it is true that the narrator of *Malina* owns a copy of Nietzsche's *Ecce Homo* (*M* 175; *Ma* 110). Unlike Nietzsche, however, Bachmann depicts the sovereign deity as a monster; and she foregrounds human suffering. If Bachmann's novel implies a form of negative theology, then it is closer to Adorno's negative dialectics than to Nietzsche's "vertical," elitist concerns. Tellingly, Bachmann alludes not to the Nietzsche who denounces pity but to the Nietzsche who intervened when a horse was being flogged, as the narrator of *Malina* attempts to help a suffering horse (*M* 24; *Ma* 11).

This chapter attempts a reading of *Malina* that maintains its focus on suffering bodies but also places them within socioeconomic frameworks. In Bachmann's first Frankfurt lecture on poetics in 1959, she stresses the multiple value systems to which the modern subject is exposed:

> Unsere Existenz liegt heute im Schnittpunkt so vieler unverbundener Realitäten, die von den widersprüchlichsten Werten besetzt sind. . . . Sie können sich allen gleichzeitig anvertrauen, wenn Sie sich nur darauf verstehen, in der Praxis alles säuberlich getrennt zu halten. Hier Innerlichkeit und Sinnbezüge, Gewissen und Traum—da Nützlichkeitsfunktion, Sinnlosigkeit, Phrase und sprachlose Gewalt. (*KS* 268–69).

> [Our existence today is at the intersection of so many unbound realities, which are occupied by the most contradictory values. . . . You can entrust yourself to all of them simultaneously, but only if you know how to keep them all hygienically separated from each other in practice. Here interiority and allusiveness, conscience, and dream—there utilitarian function, senselessness, cliché, and mute violence.]

This anticipates the sense of the divided self that is so central to *Malina*; indeed, the lecture tries to reject a facile separation of these spheres: "Moral ist Moral, Geschäft ist Geschäft und Krieg ist Krieg und Kunst ist Kunst" (*KS* 269; Morality is morality, business is business, war is war, and art is art). Any art that accepted such a separation, Bachmann declares, would amount to a declaration of bankruptcy: art and morality, she says, must not remain cut off from business and politics (*KS* 269). Since her evocation of colliding values stems from Max Weber, it makes sense to begin with Weber.

Reading *Malina* through Weber: Disenchantment and Conflict

Bachmann was familiar with Weber's opposition between enchantment (*Zauber*) and disenchantment (*Entzauberung*). Weber opposes "magic" and "rationality" as two endpoints along a continuum of possible explanatory models. In her 1949 doctoral dissertation on Heidegger, Bachmann names Weber, the representative of "scientific philosophy," as the chief witness against Heidegger's mystic philosophy of being.[18] Bachmann's 1953 poem "Große Landschaft bei Wien" (Great Landscape near Vienna) stages the confrontation between mystic thought and modern, instrumental rationality:

träum dein Geschlecht, das dich besiegt, träum
und wehr dennoch mystischer Abkehr im Protest.
Mit einer andern Hand gelingen Zahlen
und Analysen, die dich entzaubern.
Was dich trennt, bist du.[19]

[dream your lineage, which masters you, dream
and yet still, in protest, resist the mystic's retreat.
In a different manner numbers and analyses
win, and they disenchant you.
What separates you, is you.[20]]

In his otherwise fine translation Peter Filkins opts for "lineage" rather than "gender" in translating "Geschlecht." If we adopt the alternative, the change of meaning is startling: the 1953 poem announces a gendered dislocation at the heart of the modern subject and links it to the Weberian disenchantment of the world. The dichotomy between the female Ich, characterized by her dreams, and her male alter ego, Malina, characterized by distanced analysis, is prefigured here almost twenty years before the publication of the novel.

The dislocation of the self outlined here can be traced back to Max Weber's diagnosis of modern life as characterized by "value collisions." In his lecture "Wissenschaft als Beruf" (1917; "The Vocation of Science"), Weber interprets the crisis of secular modernity as eternal warfare between opposing value systems or between different "gods." Weber is not an uncritical champion of scientific rationality; on the contrary, he states that science is "irreligious" and can tell us nothing at all about the meaning of the world. Science enables us to control life technically, but it cannot tell us whether or not we should do so. Modern specialization, the argument goes, has led to the development of competing institutional and ideological spheres of science, law, economics, religion, art, etc. In consequence, "die verschiedenen Wertordnungen der Welt [stehen] in unlöslichem Kampf untereinander" ("the different value systems of the world stand in [insoluble] conflict with one another").[21] Every individual is faced with the battle between the gods of the different systems and values.[22] And the outcome? Life itself becomes subjected to extraordinary strain:

Die vielen alten Götter . . . entsteigen ihren Gräbern, streben nach Gewalt über unser Leben und beginnen untereinander wieder ihren ewigen Kampf. Das aber, was, gerade dem modernen Menschen so schwer wird, und der jungen Generation am schwersten ist: einem solchen *Alltag* gewachsen zu sein. Alles Jagen nach dem "Erlebnis" stammt aus dieser Schwäche. Denn Schwäche ist es: dem Schicksal der Zeit nicht in sein ernstes Antlitz blicken zu können.[23]

[The many gods of old . . . rise up from their graves, strive for power
over our lives and begin once more their eternal struggle among
themselves. But what is difficult for modern man, and most difficult
of all for the younger generation, is to meet the demands of such an
everyday life. All hunting for "experience" stems from this weakness,
for not to be able to look the destiny of the time full in the face is a
weakness.[24]]

Weber's questioning of "experience" strikes a chord with contemporary
feminist debates, in which experience "is always contested, always therefore political."[25] And the crisis of everyday life faced by the modern subject
that Weber describes anticipates Ich's inability at the beginning of *Malina*
to think about or write the word "heute'" ("today"). According to Weber,
we live in the midst of value relations that are without a common denominator.[26] This forces us to recognize "the tragic, strife-torn character of
life" and "to choose our own fate."[27] But the choice Weber offers at the
end of his lecture is clear-cut: either embrace the painful uncertainties of
modern science or "return to the open, compassionate arms of the old
churches."[28]

Reading *Malina* through Weber would suggest that Ich attempts to
flee the violence and disenchantment of modernity and seeks redemption
through love.[29] She loads her relationship with Ivan with all the religious
fervor of a saint or a martyr. Her love for Ivan is "diese stärkste Macht
der Welt, weil die Welt eben krank ist" (*M* 35; "this most powerful force
in the world, simply because the world is sick," *Ma* 18). Their love is a
force that could heal the sick world; or, conversely, were their love to
spread like an epidemic, it would help the world (*M* 32–33; *Ma* 17). She
waits for Ivan's telephone calls like a Muslim on a prayer mat, her fore-
head pressed to the ground (*M* 41; *Ma* 23). Alas, Ivan prefers women
who think less and are merely amusing: "Lach mehr, lies weniger, schlaf
mehr, denk weniger" (*M* 104; "Laugh more, read less, sleep more, think
less," *Ma* 64). Thus for Ich love is a religious, transformational force, but
for Ivan it is a pleasurable pastime to be enjoyed during leisure from
work.[30] In contrast to Ich's religion of all-enveloping love, Malina's separation of the spheres represents the scientific position. Reading in this
way, Ich and Malina represent the dialectic between enchantment and
disenchantment.

The Weberian position is to face up to the fact of eternal warfare and
to accept one's tragic destiny. As Malina tells Ich:

Malina: Es gibt nicht Krieg und Frieden.
Ich: Wie heißt es dann?
Malina: Krieg. . . . In dir ist kein Frieden, auch in dir nicht.
Ich: Sag das nicht, nicht heute. Du bist furchtbar.
Malina: Es ist Krieg. Und du bist der Krieg. Du selber. (*M* 193)

[Malina: It isn't war and peace.
Me: What is it then?
Malina: War. . . . There is no peace in you, not even in you.
Me: Don't say that, not today. You're terrible.
Malina: It's war. And you are the war. You yourself. (*Ma* 120–21)]

Here Malina, like Weber, sees struggle as an intrinsic component of modern existence. And, like Weber, Malina responds with the scientific detachment of the professional academic. As a military historian, his business is the study of warfare. Like the Weberian scientist, Malina remains patiently detached in the face of the collision of values. He refuses to adhere to any one value system and questions all ideologies. His independence of mind is disturbing and makes him hard to pin down. As Stephanie Bird argues, Malina struggles "against normalization"; "his conformity is external and largely illusory."[31] Accordingly, she suggests, Malina is capable of causing a rupture in Viennese society: "Er webt nicht an dem großen Text mit, an der Textur des Verbreitbaren, das ganze Wiener Gewebe hat ein paar kleine Löcher, die nur durch Malina entstanden sind" (*M* 315; "He is not weaving his contribution into the grand text, expanding the texture of the network, the few small holes in the Viennese net only exist thanks to Malina," *Ma* 198). Malina cannot therefore simply be dismissed as an ideologue or apparatchik, because his engagement has a subversive quality.

Is Malina, perhaps, a scholar in Weber's idealized sense, a figure of intellectual integrity who brings an inquiring mind to all forms of social practice, even religious dogma and superstition? He certainly sounds like it:

Malina wendet sich allem mit einem gleichmäßigen Ernst zu, auch Aberglauben und Pseudowissenschaften findet er nicht lächerlicher als die Wissenschaften, von denen sich in jedem Jahrzehnt herausstellt, auf wieviel Aberglauben und Pseudowissenschaftlichkeit sie beruht haben. . . . Daß Malina sich allem leidenschaftlos zuwendet, den Menschen und den Sachen, das charakterisiert ihn am besten (*M* 261)

[Malina treats everything with a uniform seriousness, he doesn't find superstitions and pseudo-sciences any more ridiculous than the sciences which themselves really rely on superstitions and pseudo-sciences, as every passing decade reveals more and more clearly. . . . Dispassionate is the best way to describe how Malina devotes himself to everything, people as well as ideas and things (*Ma* 163–64)]

On this account, Malina seems like the model researcher, even the model psychoanalyst. His subversive qualities do not necessarily make him an opponent of capitalism, however, since capitalism itself is fundamentally subversive according to Joseph Schumpeter, who describes it as a process of "creative destruction."[32] Malina's intellectual vocation could suggest that he acts as an outrider or servant of the establishment. Perhaps the capitalist system welcomes Malina's subversion because it thrives off it. Capital needs researchers and developers to rationalize production and open up new markets. Malina's skeptical approach certainly has affinities with Weber, who recommends the scrutiny of existing social practices, because "gerade das 'Selbstverständliche' (weil anschaulich Eingelebte) [pflegt] am wenigsten 'gedacht' zu werden" (We often neglect to to think out clearly what seems to be obvious, because it is intuitively familiar).[33] This recalls Malina's motto: "Ruhe in die Unruhe bringen. Unruhe in die Ruhe" (*M* 327; "Calm the commotion. Disturb the calm," *Ma* 205). Perhaps Malina represents the subversive spirit of contestation. Or, his attitude could be seen as a form of quality control, one that makes it possible to rationalize existing practices and to seek out new ones, finding gaps in the (conceptual) market. Malina sees that most current ideas and concepts are bought and sold: "Malina würde sagen: 'Die alle, mit ihren gemieteten Ansichten, bei diesen hohen Mieten, die werden teuer bezahlen'" (*M* 133; "Malina would say: All these people renting opinions, and at such high rates, they'll wind up paying dearly," *Ma* 82).

Malina has a strong affinity with the Weberian thinker who can detach himself or herself from conventional viewpoints. He exemplifies disenchantment because he "objectifies every situation" (*GuI* 74). Weber's famous dictum that disenchantment is the fate of the modern age occurs near the end of "Wissenschaft als Beruf":

> Es ist das Schicksal unserer Zeit, mit der ihr eigenen . . . Entzauberung der Welt, daß gerade die letzten und sublimsten Werte zurückgetreten sind aus der Öffentlichkeit. . . . Es ist weder zufällig, daß unsere höchste Kunst eine intime und keine monumentale ist, noch daß heute nur innerhalb der kleinsten Gemeinschaftskreise, von Mensch zu Mensch, im pianissimo, jenes Etwas pulsiert, das dem entspricht, was wir früher als prophetisches Pneuma in stürmischen Feuer durch die großen Gemeinden ging und sie zusammenschweißte.[34]

> [It is the fate of our age, with its . . . disenchantment of the world, that the ultimate, most sublime values have withdrawn from public life. . . . It is no accident that our greatest art is intimate rather than monumental, nor is it fortuitous that today only in the smallest groups, between individuals, something pulsates *in pianissimo* which corresponds to the prophetic *pneuma* which formerly swept through great communities like fire and welded them together.[35]]

If the fate of modernity is disenchantment, then what happens to the spirit (*pneuma*)? According to Weber, it is banished to the most private, intimate sphere, where it still pulses and vibrates in pianissimo. Here is another connection: at the climactic point of both Weber's essay and Bachmann's novel—the depiction of the desperate plight of the human spirit in modernity—both have recourse to Italian musical notation. For Weber, the spirit can only manifest itself in pianissimo, very softly. In *Malina*, the modality of pianissimo only occurs once, when Ich speaks the name of her lover, Ivan. Malina tells her: "Ich fürchte wirklich, du bist verrückt" (*M* 311; "I really am afraid you're crazy," *Ma* 195), and she replies: "Nicht so sehr. Und nicht sprechen wie (piano, pianissimo) Ivan" (*M* 311; "Not too crazy. And don't talk like (piano, pianissimo) Ivan," *Ma* 195). The extreme softening of Ich's voice sounds wounded; both of the men in her life are turning against her. The musical direction *piano* occurs once more in the novel, when Ich states: "(piano) Auch wenn es das Unverzeihliche ist, will ich mich immer verzetteln, verirren, verlieren" (*M* 330; "[piano] Even if it is unforgivable, I'm still always wanting to spread myself too thin, to lose my self, to lose my way," *Ma* 208). In Malina's functional, disenchanted world, Ich's attachment to Ivan seems "crazy," "unforgiveable." The correspondence of Ich and Malina with Weber's distinction between enchantment and disenchantment implies opposing forms of narrative economy. Malina's disenchantment is cumulative and acquisitive. It permits him to objectify situations and therefore to accumulate knowledge and cognition. Ich's fundamental attitude, in contrast, is self-sacrificing and self-negating. She has invested her entire being in Ivan, and her principal regret is that Ivan does not require her sacrifice (*M* 266; *Ma* 166). Her ethos of self-expenditure can be read as an attempt to restore magic and enchantment to the modern world. In economic terms, her desire for self-sacrifice is like Georges Bataille's analysis of potlatch as the attempt to access a sovereign state of being through the negation of material property.[36]

If Malina is the disenchanted scholar, an enabler of knowledge who avoids cognitive closure, then he could appear as an emancipatory figure. But any utopian potential is countered by his daily activity as a civil servant in the military museum. Even if he performs his day job "Aus Gründen der Tarnung" (*M* 7; "As a disguise," *Ma* 1), the fact is that he works in service of the state. His official duties include going to an auction of weapons at the Dorotheum, the largest auction house on the continent (*M* 88; *Ma* 53). That makes him an arms dealer, even if these antique weapons are not intended for actual use. And the museum remains in close contact with the Austrian Ministry of Defense. Once again, this suggests parallels with Weber. There were limits to Weber's ethics of disenchantment. Despite proclaiming the value of disenchantment, Weber openly sanctioned the value of "charisma" in politics. In "Die drei reinen Typen der legitimen Herrschaft" ("The Three Types of Legitimate Rule"),[37] the third type of legitimate rule proposed by Weber is charismatic rule: "kraft affektueller Hingabe an die Person des Herrn" ("on the basis of affectual surrender to the person of the lord").[38] In the thirties and forties the American sociologist Talcott Parsons attempted to present Weber, who died in 1920, as a "good," liberal German, tainted neither by Nazi collaboration nor Marxist sympathies. This sanitized transatlantic view was decisively challenged in 1959 by Wolfgang Mommsen, who reconstructed Weber's unsentimental politics of power, exposing his fondness for militarism and charismatic leadership. As Mommsen notes, although Weber condemned the Kapp Putsch, there is an elitist, aristocratic element to his theory of charismatic leadership. Weber failed to anticipate the development of the charismatic totalitarian ruler.[39] Mommsen recalls Weber's Freiburg inaugural address of 1895, in which he called for "a German world power policy."[40] If *Malina* is cast in a Weberian mold, then perhaps he, too, has a preference for the charismatic ruler and imperialist realpolitik. One might ask, as a reader: if Malina is really so independent of mind, then why is he working for a subsection of the Austrian Ministry of Defense?[41]

Malina's interest in warfare shows yet another affinity with Weber. In Weber's *Wirtschaft und Gesellschaft* (1921–22; *Economy and Society*), the eighth fundamental concept of sociology is conflict ("Kampf"), understood in terms of selection ("Auslese") of the fittest, i.e., the general struggle for existence in terms of individuals' opportunities ("Lebenschancen"). Weber sees all forms of conflict, from physical violence to economic competition, as forming a continuum.[42] He regards social life as characterized by never-ending antagonism: "'Ewig' ist die Auslese deshalb, weil sich kein Mittel ersinnen läßt, sie völlig auszuschalten" ("Selection is inevitable because apparently no way can be worked out of eliminating it completely").[43] Although the family unit might seem to exclude "selection" and violent conflict, Weber comments: "Vergewaltigung jeder Art [ist] innerhalb auch der intimsten Vergemeinschaftungen gegenüber dem seelischen Nachgiebigeren durchaus normal" ("coercion of all sorts is a very common thing even in the most intimate of such communal relationships if one party is weaker in character than the other").[44] The nightmares in *Malina* perhaps confirm Weber's somber diagnosis. If so, this would support the argument that the dreams do not refer to actual, specific incidents. Rather, they show forth violent, pathological structures embedded within all human society. In any case, the competition for opportunities is, according to Weber, never-ending. Since Malina, too, considers war to be the most salient aspect of life, he emerges as a clear-sighted theorist of constant warfare, innovation, and economic competition (conjoined aspects of the contemporary global order). This is a view of reality as an undeclared state of permanent warfare. As Bachmann asserts in one of her interviews: "Ja, haben Sie denn da einen Zweifel? Daß in dieser angeblich zivilen Welt, zwischen Menschen, die sich scheinbar gut benehmen, im Verborgenen ein permanenter Kriegszustand herrscht?" (*GuI* 111; Yes, do you doubt it? That in this allegedly civilized world, between people who are apparently well-behaved, in secret, a permanent state of warfare prevails?).[45] In *Malina*, however, dystopian and utopian elements go hand in hand. In order to elucidate these, let us now turn to Marx and Scarry.

Reading *Malina* through Marx and Scarry: Hurting and Making

In *Malina* there is a pervasive sense of "universal prostitution," which Sara Lennox interprets in "materialist feminist" terms, arguing that material and discursive practices are interlinked.[46] The phrase, which occurs four times in *Malina* (*M* 78, 274, 289; *Ma* 47, 172, 181), is a quotation from the *Paris Manuscripts* of 1844,[47] in which Marx describes the general prostitution of the laborer.[48] "Universal prostitution" first appears in *Malina* in French— which is a red herring, almost as if Bachmann had wanted to disguise its provenance by slipping it into a lecture on de Sade's *100 Days of Sodom*. Ich reacts by laughing uncontrollably and walking out noisily (*M* 79; *Ma* 47). The second time the phrase appears, it seems more threatening, and she regrets having laughed. In Vienna after 1945 there were rumors of a "Menschenhandel" ("slave trade"), and it seemed to her as if anyone with a job was a prostitute without knowing it (*M* 274; *Ma* 172). In those years, "Alle haben einen Gebrauch voneinander gemacht" (*M* 289; "Everyone slept with everyone else, everyone used each other," *Ma* 181). From here, it is a short step for Ich to postulate the existence of a universal black market:

> Eines Tages soll angeblich kein schwarzer Markt mehr existiert haben. Aber ich bin davon nicht überzeugt. Ein universeller schwarzer Market ist daraus entstanden. . . . Der Markt überhaupt ist schwarz, so schwarz kann er damals gar nicht gewesen sein, weil ihm eine universelle Dichte gefehlt hat. (*M* 276)

> [One day the black market ostensibly ceased to exist. But I'm not convinced. A universal black market resulted. . . . the whole market is black through and through, it can't have been that black before because it still lacked a universal density. (*Ma* 173)]

The concept of the "universal black market" can be seen as a judgment on the new world order after 1945. The principle of unregulated economic competition now permeates every aspect of human life.[49] In Bachmann's text this "dark field" assumes nightmarish proportions, to the extent that Ich is overcome by nausea when she goes into a department store; the products go black before her eyes:

> Tausende von Stoffen, Tausende von Konservendosen, von Würsten, von Schuhen und Knöpfen, diese ganze Anhäufung von Waren, machen die Ware schwarz vor meinen Augen. In einer großen Zahl ist alles sehr bedroht, eine Menge muß etwas Abstraktes bleiben, muß eine Formel aus einer Lehre sein, etwas Operables, muß die Reinheit der Mathematik haben, nur die Mathematik läßt die Schönheit von Milliarden zu, eine Milliarde Äpfel aber ist ungenießbar, eine Tonne Kaffee spricht schon von zahllosen Verbrechen. . . . (*M* 276)

[Thousands of fabrics, thousands of tin cans, of sausages, shoes and buttons, the whole mass of items blackened each single item before my eyes. Everything is much too threatened by large numbers, a mass has to remain something abstract, has to be the postulate of a theory, has to remain operable, it has to have the purity of mathematics, only mathematics allows billions to be beautiful, a billion apples, on the other hand, is unpalatable, a ton of coffee in itself testifies to countless crimes. . . . (*Ma* 173)]

The passage clearly invokes a Marxian perspective. The human origins of the products have been concealed.

Bachmann's concern to reveal the suffering body behind the commodity is in line with Marx, as interpreted by Elaine Scarry. Scarry argues that joy and pain are closely connected in labor; she sees hurting (in which the external world impacts the self) and making (in which the self acts upon the world) as two interrelated aspects of human existence. Her approach is compatible with a feminist critique: at stake in both approaches is the violence done to human subjectivity. Marx understands men's and women's "fundamental human identity to reside in their existence as 'creators,' 'imaginers,' and 'makers.'"[50] Any social system that departs from this basis is fundamentally opposed to the creative essence of humans. In the fifth notebook of Marx's *Grundrisse* (1939–41; *Foundations of the Critique of Political Economy*), the cultivated land is described as a prolongation of the worker's body; it forms an aspect of human sentience.[51] For Marx, being alive comprises social activity. To alienate people from their labor is to deny their sentience. Scarry describes *Das Kapital* (1867; *Capital*) as "an elaborate retracing of the path along which the reciprocity of artifice has lost its way back to its human source."[52] Lennox identifies a similar Marxist analysis in one of Bachmann's drafts for the *Todesarten* (Ways of Dying) project, the "Wüstenbuch" (Desert Book).[53] When Franza visits Luxor, she sees the artisans working in their shops. For the first time since childhood, she witnesses the production of commodities: the making of shoes, the baking of bread. She considers the consequences of living in the developed world, in which this connection is usually invisible:

Es ist kein Gefallen am einfachen Leben, sondern bloß der Gedanke, daß wir nie mehr etwas zu sehen bekommen von der Entstehung der Dinge, die wir brauchen, daß unsre Kinder weder wissen, wo ihr Essen herkommt, wo ihre Kleidung, daß sie mit Spielzeug abgefertigt werden, das ihre Phantasie falsch beschäftigt, daß im Ansatz schon alles verfehlt ist, daß ihr Wissen kein Basis hat.[54]

[It's not fondness for the simple life but rather the thought that we no longer see anything of how the things which we need are created, that our children know neither where their food comes from, nor where their clothes come from; they are fobbed off with toys that

stimulate their imagination in a way that is false, so that it is all wrong
from the start, their knowledge has no basis.]

The word "basis" underlines the Marxist connection, recalling the relation
between "base" and "superstructure" as defined by Marx in his preface to
Zur Kritik der politischen Ökonomie (1859; *A Contribution to the Critique
of Political Economy*). People living in the developed world have lost a
sense of the connection between base and superstructure. The use of the
personal pronoun to makes the message more urgent: "we" are blinded,
"our" children are misled.

    Malina hinges on a dislocation in the self between Ich and Malina,
and this self-division resonates with Marx's account of alienation. As Scarry
puts it, "For Marx it [capitalism] entails a serious dislocation in the species
itself, for it announces that the original relation between sentience and
self-extension (between hurting and imagining, between body and voice,
or body and artifice) has been split apart and the two locations of self have
begun to work against one another."[55] This diagnosis could certainly be
applied to *Malina*: Malina reaps the benefit as Ich is gradually exhausted
and finally destroyed by her emotional labors. He takes possession of Ich's
narrative and her emotional life. In this way, he appropriates her entire
human sentience: "Ich: Ich habe nur ein Leben. / Malina: Überlaß es mir"
(*M* 233; "Me: I only have one life. / Malina: Leave it to me," *Ma* 146).
How does this occur? Ich contends that in a heterosexual relationship, the
woman must generally take on the emotional workload for both partners:
"Das Denken daran nimmt tatsächlich den größten Teil der Zeit jeder Frau
in Anspruch" (*M* 284; "Such thoughts really do consume the greatest part
of every woman's time," *Ma* 178). What appears to be an emotional problem is actually a division of labor, or, more precisely, a transfer of sentience
from one person to another. As Ich tells the father in one of her dreams:
"Du hast uns doch immer alle verschachert" (*M* 191; "You always did auction off each one of us," *Ma* 119). Here the theme of universal prostitution returns. As Scarry puts it, the distribution of property involves the
distribution of sentience itself: "To summarize this . . . as the problem of
'the haves and have-nots' is inadequate . . . unless we understand that what
is had and had not is the human body."[56] Applied to *Malina*, this suggests
that the split in Ich's consciousness results from the sacrifice of her sentience, as her spirit is gradually expropriated: "Gibt es eine geistige
Enteignung?" (*M* 131–32; "Is there such a thing as the expropriation of
intellectual property?" *Ma* 81). When Malina assumes the position of edi-
tor/narrator, he takes possession of her human essence and its expression
in writing.

    Ich becomes increasingly desperate to remove herself from the cycle of
exploitation. She develops an aversion to the simplest financial transactions. Toward the end of the novel she cannot utter the phrases used to

buy groceries: "Es waren die Worte dafür, die ich nicht hören konnte. Zwanzig Deka Kalbfleisch. Wie bringt man das über die Zunge?" (*M* 340; "It was the words for these things that I could not bear to hear. Half a pound of veal. How can you get that past your tongue?" *Ma* 214). One conversation with Malina plays on the double meaning of *handeln*, which means "to act" but also "to trade":

Ich: (diminuendo) Ich habe doch nie gern gehandelt.
Malina: Aber gehandelt hast du. Und hast mit dir handeln und dich behandeln lassen, auch über dich verhandeln lassen. (*M* 329)

[Me: (diminuendo) I've never liked acting anyway.
Malina: But you have acted. And you have allowed others to act on you, against you, use you in their own actions and transactions. (*Ma* 207)]

While Ich is open to manipulation, Malina appears impossible to grasp. In the dialogues between Ich and Malina, Italian musical directions are used exclusively for Ich, never for Malina. This gives Ich an embodied quality that Malina lacks. At the end of the novel, Ich's sentience is gradually consumed until she vanishes into a crack in the wall. Malina, by contrast, is exempted from productive suffering. As her executor, he inherits her writings, and as her editor, he completes her transformation into a commodity.

Scarry's idea that pain and imagination are counterparts is implied by the double meaning of the word *travail* as both "work" and "pain" (in German *Mühe*, "effort" and "trouble").[57] She posits a continuum between passive suffering and the controlled suffering of labor.[58] Accordingly, she sees pain and imagining (or hurting and making) as the extremes between which the human psyche can be mapped out.[59] In Bachmann's text, Malina advises Ich to spare her tears of pity: "Wein also nicht über andere. . . . Sie brauchen nicht Tränen made in Austria" (*M* 326; "So don't cry over others. . . . They don't need tears 'Made in Austria,'" *Ma* 205). He has no interest in imagining the pain of others. From Scarry's perspective, this is Malina's greatest shortcoming. His ethic of restraint blinds him to the extremes of pain and imagination. This is, arguably, why he is fascinated by Ich and wishes to preserve her insights. The incongruence between them is highlighted when Ich visits the astrologer Senta Novak, who describes the opposition between them as "die Produktivität und die Selbstzerstörung" (*M* 261; "productivity and self-destruction," *Ma* 163). Novak's diagnosis, however, misses the point that creation and destruction are two sides of the same process. As Göttsche has shown, Malina and Ich represent the confrontation between two different forms of narrative, each of which is insufficient in itself. This is the productive tension at the core of the novel, which constantly refers readers back to the incommensurability yet necessity of the two narrative positions.[60] Ich's traumatic abjection is not necessarily weakness, however. Pain is an instance of being human and, for Scarry, a condition of creation. Whether we as readers prefer Malina's restraint or Ich's agonized intensity, the two of them are undeniably interdependent.

Reading *Malina* through Brecht: The User and the Used

In an interview of March 23, 1971, when asked about the doppelgänger motif in *Malina*, Bachmann stated: "Das Doppelgängermotiv habe ich ja nicht erfunden. Es ist uralt. Nur meine Variation ist anders: Das Ich, weiblich, hat ein männliches Gegenüber" (*GuI* 74; I have not invented the doppelgänger motif. It is ancient. Only my variation is different: Ich, feminine, has a masculine counterpart). Bachmann does an injustice here to Brecht, for she knew Brecht's play *Der gute Mensch von Sezuan* (1943; *The Good Person of Szechwan*) well enough. It features a protagonist divided into two personalities, female Shen Te and male Shui Ta. Bachmann had borrowed aspects of this text for her own radio play, *Der gute Gott von Manhattan* (1957; The Good God of Manhattan).[61] Both *Malina* and *Der gute Mensch* feature a woman who lives with her male doppelgänger. In both, the male half deals with the practical world because the female seems incapable of doing so. In both, the male half stands accused of murdering the female half. Although Karen R. Achberger noted these parallels in 1991, this connection has not been followed up.[62] Achberger points out that "Shen Te's reaction to the circumstances, namely to silence her female voice and emerge as the male Shui Ta, is exactly the course which Malina chooses."[63]

The parallels between Bachmann and Brecht do not stop there, of course. Let us consider a few before discussing the *Malina–Der gute Mensch* connection in more detail. It is widely acknowledged that the title of Bachmann's planned novel cycle, *Todesarten*, derives from Brecht's *Buch der Wendungen (Mê Ti)*:

VIELE ARTEN ZU TÖTEN
Es gibt viele Arten zu töten. Man kann einem ein Messer in den Bauch stechen, einem das Brot entziehen, einen von einer Krankheit nicht heilen, einen in eine schlechte Wohnung stecken, einen durch Arbeit zu Tode schinden, einen zum Selbstmord treiben, einen in den Krieg führen und so weiter. Einiges davon ist in unserem Staate verboten. (*BFA* 18:90)

[MANY WAYS TO KILL
There are many ways to kill people. You can stab someone in the guts with a knife, you can take away their bread, you can deny them hos-

pital treatment, you can house them in a slum, you can work them to
death, you can drive them to suicide, you can lead them to war, etc.
Some of this is forbidden in our country.]

Bachmann is arguably less interested in the collective than Brecht, and
more interested in the individual. Nevertheless, Bachmann's critique of
bourgeois hypocrisy often resembles Brecht's. In her short story "Alles"
(Everything), for example, the male narrator plans to educate his children
"wie die Zeit es erfordert, halb für die wölfische Praxis und halb auf die
Idee der Sittlichkeit hin"[64] (as is required these days: half for dog-eat-dog
practice and half for the idea of morality).[65] And Bachmann, like Brecht,
wants to show society in a radically new way: "[Die] Gesellschaft . . . muß
sich radikal anders zeigen" (*GuI* 72; Society must show itself . . . in a
radically different way). Both writers engage in Sprachkritik (language
criticism) and suspect the "black magic" of words (*M* 152; *Ma* 95).
Indeed, Bachmann undertakes Sprachkritik explicitly in her "Entwürfe zur
politischen Sprachkritik" (*KS* 368–77; Notes toward a Critique of Political
Language).[66]

Both authors put moments of disruption at the center of their literary
aesthetic, with a view to activating the audience's intelligence and imagination. As Wolfgang Iser argues, cognitive gaps induce the reader to participate in renegotiating the multiple possibilities latent in the texts.[67] Brecht's
poem "Verwisch die Spuren!" ("Cover Your Tracks!") is programmatic in
this respect. A text must have cognitive gaps if it is to excite the audience's
intellectual hunger.[68] The cover blurb on the first edition of *Malina* sets
up the reader as detective:[69]

> Mord oder Selbstmord? Es gibt keine Zeugen. Eine Frau zwischen
> zwei Männern. . . . Ein Leichnam, der nicht gefunden wird. Das ver-
> schwundene Testament. . . . Das Papierkorb, von niemand durch-
> sucht. Verwischte Spuren. Schritte. Jemand also, der noch auf und ab
> geht, in dieser Wohnung—stundenlang: MALINA (*TP* 3.2:742)

> [Murder or suicide? There are no witnesses. A woman between two
> men. . . . The body cannot be found. The testament: disappeared. . . .
> No one searched the waste-paper basket. The traces: covered. Steps.
> Someone still paces up and down in the apartment—for hours:
> MALINA]

The phrase "Verwischte Spuren" (covered tracks) here announces the
novel's debt to Brechtian aesthetics.[70]

There are a number of remarkable parallels between *Malina* and *Der
gute Mensch von Sezuan*. (1) Each text explodes its genre. *Malina* is a novel
that begins with a list of dramatis personae, observes the classical unities of
space (Vienna) and time (today), and contains a number of dialogues presented like a playscript. *Der gute Mensch*, like most instances of epic

theater, foregrounds the narrative exposition of the action, rather than the action itself. (2) Each text is punctuated by dream sequences that function as a commentary on the remainder of the text. (3) Each text contains musical interludes—key lines are not spoken but sung. (4) These features, and the many sudden jumps in genre, mood, and tone in both texts work as alienation effects that invite critical reflection on the action. (5) *Der gute Mensch* is a text about a prostitute, Shen Te; *Malina* is a text about a female author in a patriarchal world who reflects on "universal prostitution." (6) Both texts explore a triangular relationship among a woman (Ich, Shen Te), her male alter ego (Malina, Shui Ta), and another man (Ivan, Yang Sun) whom she loves but who mistreats her. (7) The burned hand is a central image in both texts: in *Der gute Mensch* the barber Shu Fu attacks Wang the water-seller with a pair of hot curling tongs and cripples his hand; in *Malina* there is the Gustave Flaubert quotation "Avec ma main brûlée, j'écris sur la nature du feu" (*M* 96; "With my burned hand, I write on the nature of fire," *Ma* 58).[71] (8) In both texts a mysterious trio of figures motivates the action: *Der gute Mensch* features a trio of gods, who are incompetent, cowardly bureaucrats; *Malina* features a trio of murderers, later designated as a quartet of murderers. (9) The heroine in both texts has an ambivalent relationship with her female servant.[72] (10) Both texts allude to the biblical story of Sodom and Gomorrah: Brecht's play uses it as a framework, Bachmann's novel alludes to it via a reference to de Sade's *120 Days of Sodom* (*M* 78; *Ma* 47). (11) In each text the male alter ego takes care of the finances because the female persona is too generous. (12) In each the female persona's initial career success (Shen Te gets a tobacco shop, Ich is a famous writer) causes her to be overwhelmed by petitioners and supplicants, who have to be warded off by the male persona. (13) In each text the female persona fails utterly in her attempt at living "a good life." (14) In each text the male persona suppresses the female persona and stands accused of her murder. (15) Both texts conclude by presenting the audience/readers with a problem they are expected to solve.

The fact that each text is punctuated by nightmare sequences that serve as a commentary is particularly significant. In *Der gute Mensch* Wang the water-seller reports a nightmare he has just had:

> [Ich] träumte und sah meine liebe Schwester Shen Te in großer Bedrängnis im Schilf des Flusses, an der Stelle, wo die Selbstmörder gefunden werden. . . . Auf meinen Anruf rief sie mir zu, sie müsse den Ballen der Vorschriften ans andere Ufer bringen, daß er nicht naß würde. (*BFA* 6:252–53)

> [I was dreaming and I saw my dear sister Shen Teh in great distress amongst the reeds by the river, at the spot where the suicides are found. . . . When I called to her she called back that she must carry

the whole bundle of precepts across to the other bank, keeping it dry
so that the ink should not run.[73]]

Here, as in *Malina*, the heroine is physically crushed by the burden of
patriarchal orders. And there is an even closer intertextual link when we
recall that in *Malina* the motif of "der Friedhof der ermordeten Töchter"
(the cemetery of the murdered daughters) derives from the "Friedhof der
Namenlosen" in Vienna, where the unidentified bodies of people who
have drowned in the Danube are buried (*TK* 2:481). Both texts are also
ambivalent about the demise of the female protagonist: is she driven to
commit suicide, or is this a murder? In Brecht's play the gods have created
a world that is "unbewohnbar" (uninhabitable; *BFA* 6:269). Read in this
light, the dream sequences in *Malina* suggest that Ich, like Shen Te, is
trapped in a hostile (patriarchal, capitalist) world ruled over by sadistic
bullies.

In both texts the female persona is assigned the role of the sympathetic
dupe, whereas the male persona manages the finances.[74] Just as Shen Te is
overwhelmed by freeloaders, Bachmann's Ich is overwhelmed by people in
need of assistance (*M* 113; *Ma* 69–70). Malina allows Ich to perform small
acts of charity, often shaking his head in silent disapproval. But if the charity threatens to become too expensive, Malina intervenes:

> In solchen Momenten sagt Malina entschieden: nein! . . . Malina
> rückt mit dem Geld heraus und sagt ja, aber bei den ganz großen
> Katastrophen und Unternehmen sagt Malina nein. (*M* 113–14)

> [At such moments Malina says decidedly: no! . . . Malina pulls out the
> money and says yes, but he says no to the really big catastrophes and
> undertakings. (*Ma* 70)]

Ich is unable to say "no" because she speaks from the position of the
human soul.[75] Her function as a narrator is to give voice to subjective
human impulses. Malina, in contrast, finds it easy to say "no" because his
primary concern is to bring order where there is chaos ("Ruhe in die
Unruhe bringen"). Together they represent the ultimate irreconcilability
between subjective emotion and objective practice. For Malina, everything
boils down to the question of finance: "Malina hat keine Theorie, für ihn
richtet sich alles nach der Frage 'Haben oder Nicht-haben'" (*M* 114;
"Malina doesn't have any theory. For him everything divides into 'having
or not having,'" *Ma* 70). He sneers at Ich's generous impulses: "Das kann
eben nur dir passieren, ein Dümmerer findet sich nicht" (*M* 114; "That
could only happen to you, you couldn't find anyone dumber," *Ma* 70).
Ivan behaves in a similar way when Ich encounters a Bulgarian who is suffering from Buerger's disease and pays for his treatment. We as readers are
encouraged to share in Ivan's verdict: "Da hast du dich wieder hereinlegen
lassen" (*M* 118; "You've let yourself get taken in again," *Ma* 73).[76]

Conversely, from Ich's perspective, Ivan's and Malina's indifference to other people's suffering is potentially fatal: "Denn es wäre unmenschlich, so gar nichts zu tun" (*M* 327; "It would be inhuman to do nothing," *Ma* 205).

Ivan and Malina express indifference to others with almost Brechtian cynicism. Malina states that there is no point in crying for other people (*M* 326; *Ma* 205). Indifference is a key concept for Bachmann, who points out that it can be murderous.[77] Indifference in *Malina* is foregrounded by a quotation from Kant, which occurs twice:[78] "Es ist umsonst, Gleichgültigkeit in Ansehung solcher Nachforschungen erkünsteln zu wollen, deren Gegenstand der menschlichen Natur nicht gleichgültig sein kann" (*M* 340, 351; It is pointless to feign indifference in the light of such research, the object of which cannot be indifferent to human nature).[79] Joachim Eberhardt argues that the quotation serves a plot function: that Ich reads the quotation first, then it anticipates Malina's takeover of Ich.[80] Maria Behre, however, interprets the quotation as a call for an attitude that is informed by emotional and affective values.[81] Kant himself seems ambivalent about the value of indifference. On the one hand, he stresses that there are certain questions we cannot be indifferent about. On the other hand, he asserts that if a branch of knowledge lacks foundations, then indifference, doubt, and criticism are to be welcomed.[82] If Malina resembles the Kantian disinterested and detached theoretician, Ich perhaps resembles the Kantian individual caught in the moral agony of the categorical imperative: something must be done. What matters to Ich are the ethics of the present. She is aware that she belongs to "einer nicht satt zu bekommenden, immer im Notstand lebenden Bevölkerung" (*M* 278; "an insatiable population living in a constant state of emergency," *Ma* 174). This is why she spends the last of her money in Paris on buying bottles of wine for the tramps in the Rue Monge (*M* 278; *Ma* 174). It is a beautiful gesture, like Shen Te giving cigarettes to an unemployed worker or buying a cup of water from Wang the water-seller in the middle of a downpour. What is striking is the small scale of these actions. But this does not make them insignificant.

The climax of Brecht's play is the courtroom scene, in which Shui Ta stands accused of the murder of Shen Te.[83] He reveals that he is Shen Te and explains that she/he was torn into two people by the command to do good and to live. The split personality is caused by the incompatibility of morality and survival. Something similar occurs in Brecht's *Die sieben Todsünden der Kleinbürger* (1933; *The Seven Deadly Sins of the Petit-Bourgeoisie*), in which the protagonist is split into Anna I, the manager and saleswoman, and Anna II, the commodity who is forced into prostitution. The piece hinges on the question: "can one survive in a society that hypnotizes us with false goals and 'needs'? . . . Do we listen to our soul or do we sell it?"[84] This suggests that Malina's silencing of Ich is an act of selling out, much as Shui Ta sells Shen Te, or Anna I sells Anna II. Another example: Arnold Schoenberg's opera *Moses und Aron* (1932–33; Moses and Aaron), another possible model for *Malina*, also hinges on the opposition between the soul and the voice. In Exod. 4:10–16 Moses tells the Lord that he is not good with words and begs not to be chosen as a messenger, and so God assigns his brother, Aaron, to be his mouthpiece. In the opera, Aaron betrays and falsifies Moses's message. The gifted orator resorts to manipulation and utterly compromises his brother's moral purpose.[85] In all of these intertexts or possible models for *Malina* there is a split between the speaking, selling subject and the silent victim of betrayal. In this way, Bachmann and Brecht show us that we exploit ourselves: often we are both sellers and sold.

In the final sections of *Malina* the text sets up a close parallel between financial exploitation and linguistic manipulation, suggesting that words and coins are both instruments of abuse. This is why the words required to buy and sell things start to stick in Ich's throat. When she tries to buy groceries, it feels as if a coin is stuck in her mouth: "Eine Münze, ein Schilling etwa, rollt für mich auch nicht das Problem des Geldverkehrs . . . auf, sondern ich habe plötzlich einen Schilling im Mund, leicht, kalt, rund, einen störenden Schilling zum Ausspucken" (*M* 341; "A coin, something like a schilling, does not unleash the problem of cash commerce . . ., it's just that suddenly I feel a schilling in my mouth, light, cold, round, a bothersome schilling to spit out," *Ma* 215). Words and coinage both weigh heavily on her tongue; they symbolize two compromised systems of exchange from which she would like to remove herself. The closing references to Ich's testament reinforce this parallel. Sensing the end approaching, Ich wants to put her financial affairs in order and writes to her lawyer, Herr Dr. Richter: "Es handelt sich ja nicht um Geld, da ich keines mehr habe, ich bin ja in Wien völlig isoliert, abgetrennt von dem Rest der Welt, in dem man Geld verdient und ißt" (*M* 346; "It has nothing to do with money, since I don't have any left, I am fully isolated in Vienna, cut off from the rest of the world where people earn money and eat," *Ma* 218). Here, Ich attempts to portray herself as entirely removed from the world of economic circulation. Tthe logic of writing a testament, however, forces her to reflect on financial value, even as she tries to assert that her *Nachlass* (estate) is completely worthless: "Es sind allerdings Papiere ohne Wert, Wertpapiere habe ich nie besessen" (*M* 347; "They are all without any value, I have never owned any papers of value, no stocks and bonds," *Ma* 218). This is a pun: "Wertpapiere" can mean both "valuable papers" and "stocks and share certificates." But the joke here is on Ich: although she refuses to contemplate her testament in economic terms, she cannot escape the logic of finance. After all, the whole point of writing a will is to dispose of one's earthly goods. Ironically, Ich's last words and actions cannot escape the logic of the market, because they refer to the property she will leave behind.[86]

Viewed in the light of Weber, Marx/Scarry, and Brecht, the central dichotomy between Malina and Ich appears in different ways. From a Weberian perspective, Malina could stand for disenchantment, Ich for enchantment. From Scarry's perspective, Malina could represent a controlled, gradual form of hurting, Ich the extremes of hurting and imagining. Alternatively, in Brechtian terms, Malina could be interpreted as the canny entrepreneur, Ich as the overgenerous philanthropist whose kindness needs to be curbed. From this perspective, Malina is the line manager who "manages" Ich but who dismisses her when she can no longer function. Perhaps Ich—like Brecht's Shen Te—does not die but merely goes on extended leave? When Ich disappears into the wall, she is moved off the books like an unauthorized expenditure, taken out of circulation like a dud coin. The books are balanced, but the human being slips away between the cracks.

Conclusion: An Account of the Self

Malina continually alerts its readers to problems of language. "Ich" is only a word, after all.[87] As Malina says to the narrator: "Du magst es noch immer in den Mund nehmen, dieses Ich? Erwägst du es noch? Wieg es doch!" (*M* 331; "You still want to take this into your mouth, this 'Me'? Are you still weighing it over? Go ahead and weigh it on a scale!" *Ma* 208). Ich would like to give an account of herself, but she cannot do so. Giving an account of yourself is an economic and juridical procedure. According to Judith Butler, when we reflect upon ourselves we are already participating in our own subjection along ideological lines: "The 'I' is always to some extent dispossessed by the social conditions of its emergence."[88] The experience of the narrator in *Malina* seems to confirm these insights as Ich is subjected to a barrage of discourse from the male figures, each one trying to define her in his own terms. Whether it is Ivan telling her what to write, or the father silencing her, or Malina prodding her with his questions, all too often it is the male figures who dictate the terms of the dialogue. Ich's reflection on her own story makes it easier for the men to classify her and seize control of her narrative.

There is an exception, however, and it occurs in the interview with Herr Mühlbauer of the *Wiener Nachtausgabe* (Vienna Evening News).[89] To the extent that the journalist attempts to cajole the narrator into participating in his discursive game, he resembles the other male figures in *Malina*. In this case, however, Ich succeeds in turning the tables on him. Mühlbauer tries to manipulate Ich into embodying a domesticated cliché of femininity, for example, by asking her to talk about her cats; but she responds that she does not have a favorite animal or insect (*M* 93; *Ma* 57). Then she delivers some home truths about Austria that make his jaw drop

(*M* 97; *Ma* 59). When she mentions uncomfortable aspects of Austrian history, such as the *Justizpalastbrand* (July Revolt) of July 15, 1927, his response is to delete the recording (*M* 91; *Ma* 55). Again, when Mühlbauer asks her where she feels at home, instead of responding with domestic clichés, she explains the multiethnic character of her home region (*M* 101; *Ma* 62). Having studied law for four semesters (*M* 90; *Ma* 55), the narrator is well prepared for Mühlbauer's cross-examination. As she refuses to be rushed, she delivers a profound critique of the limitations of journalism itself, which is designed for quick consumption. As she says to the journalist: "Ich weiß nicht, ob Sie mir noch folgen wollen, Ihre Zeit ist ja so begrenzt und Ihre Spalte in der Zeitung auch" (*M* 99; "I don't know if you still want to follow me, since your time is so limited and your column in the paper as well," *Ma* 60). Her speech explodes the confines of the light-entertainment genre in which Mühlbauer operates. He beats a hasty retreat, calling it a wasted afternoon—he does not intend to publish the interview. As readers, however, we can observe that Ich has beaten the journalist at his own linguistic game. Ich's great eloquence in the interview means that her protestations of weakness should not be taken at face value.

Malina is a work of great rhetorical and stylistic verve, which shunts from one position to the next with astonishing rapidity. This argumentative switching of position is the essence of the rhetorical process, according to Michael Billig.[90] He points out that the Sophist Protagoras is held to be "the first person who asserted that in every question there were two sides to the argument exactly opposite to one another."[91] Ich and Malina embody opposing truths. Only when they enter into a debate do the sparks fly. The oppositional debate between them is central to the text, because it implies that there can be no absolute refutation of either perspective. Stephanie Bird regards Malina as, at least partially, a positive figure, and believes that he represents the need to accept conflict "to undermine the destructive consequences of intransigent opposition."[92] Bird points out that "Bachmann's portrayal of unresolvable ambiguities is fundamental to the *creative momentum* [italics added] in which the search for change and utopia lies."[93] This suggests that the absence of closure in *Malina* is what makes it so significant: it is too radically open to fit into a newspaper column. The relentless questioning and switching from one subject position to the other, the insistence on dialogue between opposites, is what gives it such momentum. In an interview of March 22, 1971, Bachmann, perhaps in echo of Kafka, described the novel as a process: "Wenn man so will, ist es ein geistiger Prozeß, der stattfindet" (*GuI* 71; You could say that there is a mental process taking place). The word "Prozeß" also means "trial," and, as in Kafka's novel, there is a sense of moral, ethical, and legal arbitration in *Malina*. If *Malina* is a process, it is a process driven by the questions exchanged by the two main figures. As Billig puts it: "The switching of a stance . . . can represent a process of self-discovery for the individual."[94] Bachmann states that it is important for writers to keep switching positions: "Denken Sie nicht aus *einem* Grund, das ist gefährlich—denken sie aus vielen Gründen" (*KS* 269; Don't think from *one* basis, that is dangerous. Think from several bases). This accords with the model of rhetorical debate proposed by Billig, who argues that each locus of argument has its opposing place. For example, in the debate between Romantics and Classicists, the opposition can lead to a productive dialogue.[95] Motion is an important aspect of Bachmann's poetics. In her 1969 preface to a planned collection of Brecht's poetry she praises Brecht for "the pace at which his spirit marched" ("Geistmarschschritt," *KS* 459). Like Brecht, Bachmann strives for dialogic openness in her work. For Bachmann, the task of the writer is to give to the language "a new way of moving" ("Gangart," *KS* 263). The fascination of *Malina* owes much to the fact that there are two narrative economies in play. It is the clash between Malina's restraint and Ich's emotional abandon that makes the novel so compelling and that keeps the debate alive. This is an account that will never be closed.

6: Negotiating Bureaucracy in Hermann Kant's *Das Impressum*, 1972

In oratory it is the worst possible fault to deviate from the ordinary mode of speaking and the generally accepted way of looking at things.
—Cicero

Introduction: The Critical Apologist

THIS CHAPTER CONSIDERS the use of business rhetoric in Hermann Kant's *Das Impressum* (1972; *The Imprint*). It might be objected that the word *business* is out of place here. Can the term be applied to the centrally planned economy of the German Democratic Republic (GDR)? Yes, it can. Even in the planned economy there was room to maneuver. Admittedly, most industrial enterprises were *Volkseigene Betriebe* (Publicly Owned Operations), or VEBs, under the control of the state. The VEBs were, however, given considerable autonomy in the 1960s as part of Walter Ulbricht's economic reforms aimed at making the economy more competitive.[1] Furthermore, many independent private businesses existed, as historians such as Agnès Arp and Peter Karl Becker have shown.[2] Even in the GDR, there were certain economic freedoms. The historical record shows that lines of questioning that contrast "free" and "unfree" markets risk reducing complex phenomena to ideological oppositions. No market has ever been entirely "free"; every economy is, to a certain extent, planned and regulated by the state. Indeed, UK and US governments have very often championed protectionist policies.[3]

Obviously, the GDR socialist economy was much more tightly controlled than a capitalist economy. Crucially, price mechanisms were determined by the state, not by supply and demand.[4] Decades before, Max Weber warned that workers in a socialist system, far from being emancipated, would be "faced with an all-embracing state bureaucracy, incomparably more powerful than private entrepreneurs."[5] Weber also predicted that ideology would impede the operation of such an economy, leading to "a decrease in the formal, calculating rationality" characteristic of capitalist economies.[6] Any discussion of economics and business in the GDR needs to acknowledge its complex, multilayered administrative structures. Although the Sozialistische Einheitspartei Deutschlands (Socialist Unity Party of Germany), or SED, determined state policy, officially the party and the state were separate, and this meant that citizens could deal with state officials without dealing directly with the SED itself.[7] This was a state that Mary Fulbrook describes as a "participatory dictatorship," in which citizens were, to a certain extent, allowed to participate actively in power structures.[8] She criticizes binary models of the GDR, arguing that "the dichotomy between 'state' and 'society' does not hold up; the battle lines are more complex and difficult to delineate."[9] Similarly, in a study of GDR writers Sara Jones identifies a "need to take a more nuanced approach to the examination of intellectual interaction with power within these structures and to avoid ready-made epithets."[10]

This applies even in the case of Hermann Kant (1926–2016), a loyal SED functionary, vice-president of the GDR Writers' Union from 1969 to 1978, and president of the Writers' Union from 1978 to 1990. In that last capacity he helped to control and administer cultural production in the GDR for over two decades.[11] He belonged to the founding generation of the GDR, who were intensely loyal to the SED because they regarded it as antifascist. Heiner Müller once observed that Kant, like many of his generation who had served in World War II, had a profound sense of guilt, and he tried to atone through dedication to the state.[12] But, even for Kant, loyalty and criticism sometimes went hand in hand. This is evident in *Das Impressum*, a novel that strikes a delicate balance between affirmation of party doctrine and occasional critical reflection upon it. The novel is loosely based on Kant's experience of editing a student newspaper, *Tua res* (Your Business), between 1957 and 1959.[13] The novel's publication history is worth briefly summarizing, because it shows that there was a considerable degree of complexity in Kant's relationship with the SED. *Das Impressum* was written from 1967 to 1969, and early sections of the novel were serialized in the journal *Forum* from April to July 1969. At this point serialization was halted, and the novel was not published in book form until 1972. The first official report on *Das Impressum*, produced by Lucie Pflug, head of the Publishing Section in the Central Committee Department for Culture, dated July 24, 1969, points out that the novel calls party policy into question: it trivializes the idea of class struggle, it does not denounce the convergence of East and West, and it mocks the procedure for acceptance into the party. The second report on the novel, this time an anonymous assessment dated November 27, 1969, accuses Kant of deviating from the socialist idea of man and, more seriously, taking a basic "antidogmatic" line throughout the book, which includes satirical criticism of senior party members and the suggestion that there is a contradiction between workers and intellectuals.[14] Kant's problems were compounded when he gave an interview, published on November 6, 1969, to the West German SPD magazine *Vorwärts* (Forward), in which he contradicts the official party line that recognition of the GDR by West Germany is a precondition of talks between the two states.[15] This comment could have led to official measures against him, but shortly afterward he published a retraction in the official SED newspaper, *Neues Deutschland* (New Germany).[16] Jones interprets this piece not as opportunism but as a demonstration of commitment to the party.[17] She points out that Kant's recorded interactions with the secret police agency, the Ministerium für Staatsicherheit (Ministry for State Security), or Stasi, actually gave him an unofficial channel, which he used to express criticism of SED policy.[18] She concludes that Kant's actions demonstrate the desire "to create increased room for dialogue" and "a gradual widening of the boundaries of the possible" within the structures of the GDR.[19] In contrast, Wolfgang Emmerich argues that Kant's fiction promises more than it delivers: every time it appears to be about to touch on a taboo subject, it retreats. All too often, what seems like an act of rebellion collapses into an accommodation.[20] Is Kant's fiction genuinely critical, or are his occasional critical gestures merely a fig leaf? Every authoritarian organization has its approved critics, who are there to make it seem as if criticism is possible. The hesitancy of Kant's criticisms invite us to see him as critical apologist for the GDR.[21]

Kant knew that criticism was possible, but only to a certain extent, and only if phrased "within the dominant value system of official discourse."[22] In classical rhetoric, this means that the speaker must use commonplaces (accepted wisdom) in order to get the message across. According to Cicero (see the epigraph at the beginning of this chapter), the cardinal sin for the orator is to depart from the forms of everyday usage that are approved by the community. This does not, however, rule out the possibility of political reform. Indeed, Eugene Garver has shown that Machiavelli advises politicians to make an appeal to traditional values in order to install new political values.[23] This chapter argues that Kant uses precisely this method in *Das Impressum* to advocate new ways of doing politics. His work strikes a delicate balance between advocating moderate reform and delivering a mildly critical apology for the East German regime.

Workers and Managers

The basic argument in this chapter (as throughout this book) is, first, that language can be used rhetorically to influence political and economic decisions, and, second, that fiction as a medium is particularly well suited to showing how language operates in the service of such purposes. Kant's *Das Impressum* is pervaded by an awareness of the power of rhetoric. The protagonist, David Groth, is a newspaper editor who works with language on a daily basis. Chapter 1 is narrated by David in the first person. Although much of the novel uses third-person narration, the narrative perspective is closely aligned throughout with David's. Occasionally, the focus shifts to his wife, Franziska, a photographer whose career has taught her that it is not enough to have truth on your side. In order to persuade, truth requires eloquence and sometimes an occasional white lie: "Sie erfuhr etwas . . . von der Macht des richtigen Wortes, von der Gunst, der sich die treffende Lüge erfreut, von den Künsten, derer die Wahrheit braucht" (She learned something about the power of the telling phrase, about the favor accorded to an appropriate lie, about the arts that the truth requires).[24] The couple both work at the *Neue Berliner Rundschau* (New Berlin Review).[25] This is not an explicitly economic context, but, as the narrator makes clear, "So ein Verlag ist auch ein Betrieb" (*DI* 212; A publishing house is also a business). Indeed, Kant's depiction of the newspaper's editorial process allows him to make general points about the mechanisms of decision making in the GDR. From the very start of *Das Impressum* it becomes apparent that the novel's central theme is how bosses and workers relate to each other. On the first page, we learn that David has just been invited to become a government minister. His initial reaction is to refuse because, although ministers are supposed to be humble servants of the state, they are also very powerful people capable of bearing and acting on grudges. David describes himself as having an "Elefantengedächtnis" (*DI* 12; memory of an elephant) and a considerable degree of "persönliche Empfindlichkeit" (*DI* 13; personal sensitivity). These character traits mean that if he were appointed as minister, he could use the opportunity to settle some personal scores. He still dreams of taking revenge on one of his readers, Alfred Kleinbaas, who wrote a damning critique of David's first big article (*DI* 13–14). What scores might David settle if he were a minister (*DI* 15)?

Right from the start, *Das Impressum* draws attention to the fact that the relationship between workers and managers has plenty of potential pitfalls. Workers are required to behave in certain ways. For example, when the boss is coming, the workers have to look busy. David thinks back to when he joined the newspaper as a messenger boy and recalls the advice of his first manager there. Ratt, the head of the message room, tested David by asking how fast a messenger should be. The correct answer is: if the editor in chief decides to come down to message room and check on how things are going, then the message boy must be quick enough to whisper a warning to his manager that the editor is coming, so that the manager can take his feet off the chair, open his eyes, and tell the staff to get busy (*DI* 22). Not surprisingly, GDR censors were annoyed by this sort of antiauthoritarian humor.

The critique of authority in Kant's text is never outspoken or confrontational, however; it is always couched in sympathetic anecdotes that emphasize the humanity of both managers and workers. Chapter 1 draws to a close with an anecdote about Xaver Frank, the newspaper's sports editor. At an editorial meeting Frank loses his temper: he declares that he hates boxing; the sport should be banned because it causes brain damage (*DI* 32–34). The point of this story is that managers resemble the rest of humanity; it is an "Aberwitz" (superstition) to believe that "unsere Oberen sind anders als wir" (*DI* 35; our superiors are different from us). Unfortunately, this superstition is extremely widespread. It continues to separate workers and managers even in the GDR, where, according to socialist theory, class differences had been overcome. In this way, chapter 1 of *Das Impressum* implies that there is a gulf between socialist theory and "real existing socialism." By focusing readers' attention on the complex relationships between workers and their managers, it implies that GDR citizens need to learn how to deal with this hierarchy on an everyday basis.

Talking around Corners

The unequal power relationships between workers and managers suggests the need to choose language carefully. Speech is a powerful instrument in any context, but it was especially powerful in the context of the GDR. Official discourse in the GDR tended to have a binary structure and to invoke certain foundational narratives about the state itself.[26] Language use in the GDR was often evaluated in terms of whether or not it conformed to or contravened these discursive codes. The GDR censorship system ensured that three topics in particular remained taboo: first, criticism of the USSR; second, criticism of the SED and its leadership; third, criticism of the socialist system.[27] Jones cites Wolfgang Bialas's argument that GDR citizens had to deal "with the existence of two levels of reality, an official one, present in the media, social organizations and parties, and the everyday one of their lifeworld."[28] This suggests that GDR citizens adapted their discourse depending on whether the context was private or official.

Whether in the East or West, communication is the key to getting things done. Classical orators had to project the appropriate *ethos* (character) and use the appropriate commonplaces (shared reference points) to reinforce a sense of community and belonging. In a Western business context, this means affirming one's loyalty to the company; in the GDR context it meant affirming one's loyalty to the party. In the Eastern bloc until 1990, citizens were expected to be dedicated to socialist values; nowadays in the West, employees are expected to be "passionate" about company values. Classical orators learned to craft their speech to fit the specific occasion and to affirm a close bond with their listeners. Applied to the context of the GDR, this meant that speech had to be modulated not only according to whether the occasion was official or private but also according to the logic of the relationship between participants in a discussion and according to the nature of the interests involved.[29] Communication problems within the SED were further exacerbated by the fact that everyone was supposed to be following the same party line, so that differences of opinion could not be expressed without risking penalties.

Speaking and writing in a context in which conflicts of interest are taboo presents particular problems. How can disputes be negotiated and resolved if they must simultaneously be denied or played down? Problems that arose within the party had to be settled discreetly and with circumspection. As Brecht's Mother Courage puts it: "Mit dem Kopf kann man nicht durch die Wand" (*BFA* 6:49; "No good banging your head against a brick wall").[30] Instead of tackling internal problems head on, it seems that party members had to develop linguistic strategies to approach difficult subjects sideways. Such situations require particular types of rhetorical strategy. Four obvious strategies are: (1) circumlocution, which enables a speaker to talk around a difficult subject; (2) ellipsis, where the speaker alludes to a subject by not mentioning it; (3) euphemisms; and (4) anecdotes or parables, where the speaker tells a story in order to illustrate a moral point. It is hardly surprising that Kant and his protagonist frequently use all four of these techniques.

David Groth learned his art of circumlocution from his father, Wilhelm, who died in Dachau. David cherishes Wilhelm's memory and his ability to "talk around corners":

> David lernte mit dem Um-die-Ecke-Denken bald auch selber, mit seinem Vater um die Ecke zu reden, und er fand heraus, daß diese Redeart nicht nur Spaß machte, sondern auch Schutz bot, Deckung gegen andere und vor sich selber. (*DI* 87)

> [David soon learned to think around corners, and he also learned how to talk around corners just like his father. And he discovered that this way of speaking was not only fun, it also gave protection, it provided cover against other people, and it also covered your own tracks as well.]

This is a moment of metanarrative reflection in which the narrator evaluates the reasons for his digressive style. It also recalls Brecht's famous poem "Verwisch die Spuren" ("Cover Your Tracks"). And the narrator claims that David and his father prefer "Sorgfalt und Sparsamkeit im Ausdruck" (*DI* 87; care and economy of expression). At this point, however, readers are entitled to disagree. Neither David nor the narrator are sparing in their use of words. On the contrary, they are chatty and loquacious. David's wife, Franziska, tells him that he is "redselig" (*DI* 113; talkative), and surely she should know. Circumlocution allows David to seem open and frank; it lets him say a lot without giving too much away. Direct points are unlikely to persuade party officials: "Die Leitung . . . läßt sich nicht so erreichen von seinen Silbendolchen, Wortbeilen und Satzspießen" (*DI* 324; Party leaders . . . will not be moved by his knifelike syllables, his axe-like words, and his spearlike clauses). Circumlocution is often more effective than confrontation. The need to avoid the direct route when planning the trajectory of one's argument reflects the ambivalence about rhetoric in *Das Impressum*, suggesting that rhetoric is both a danger and, sometimes, a necessary tool.

This ambivalence about rhetoric is developed in chapter 3 when David associates his suspicion of high-flown rhetoric with the abuses of rhetoric in the Third Reich. He also, however, links his mistrust of grand rhetoric with his resolution to "talk around corners" and to "filter" everything he says consciously before he says it:

> [David] gab nach Möglichkeit keinen Buchstaben von sich, der nicht durch die Filter hellwacher Kritik gelaufen wäre, und baute somit zugleich tiefstes Mißtrauen in sich auf gegenüber allem Großton, mit dem man ihn zu etwas veranlassen oder von etwas zurückhalten wollte. (*DI* 88)

> [Wherever possible, David did not give away a single letter that had not been passed through the filter of conscious criticism; consequently, and at the same time, he cultivated a profound mistrust of every boastful way of speaking that was intended to make him do something or prevent him from doing something.]

Ambivalence about rhetoric is all too evident here. The two halves of the sentence are causally connected, suggesting that David's awareness of his own rhetorical performance makes him all the more alert to other people's maneuvers. Awareness of rhetoric turns him into a keen observer of his own words and those of others.

Anecdotes and Mediation

One of Kant's favorite taboo subjects is the black market in the GDR.[31] He considers it in *Das Impressum* and in the brilliant short story "Der dritte Nagel" (1981; The Third Nail), which lifts the lid on the GDR's informal economy of mutual favors and backhanders, showing how people used personal networks in order to procure desirable goods.[32] In *Das Impressum* Kant uses the picaresque mode to tell the story of Richard Kist, a retired railway worker who becomes an "Unternehmer" (*DI* 124; businessman). It begins harmlessly enough, when Kists's daughter asks him to bring her some "Kaffesahne" (*DI* 122; coffee cream). Kist starts supplying cream and other groceries to the whole neighborhood on the black market. When the authorities find out, they classify the case as "REBEA, was heißt: Rentner-Beschaffungs-Aktion" (*DI* 127; REBEA, meaning "pensioner procurement action"). Kist is prosecuted for counterrevolutionary activity, but he tells the court that he was simply applying the organizational principles he learned as a railway worker; he certainly did not intend anything counterrevolutionary (*DI* 129–30). Kant thus plays down black-market activity by presenting it in anecdotal form as the action of a lone pensioner. One of the first reviewers of *Das Impressum*, Hermann Kähler, remarked that Kant's anecdotal feuilleton style is both intimate and public: it neatly fuses the personal and the political. It can bring a political spirit into private conversations and a more friendly tone into public debate.[33] Western scholars have tended to criticize Kant for his use of anecdotes,[34] but Kähler reminds us that an anecdotal style enables an author to make controversial points in a friendly way.

This "light-touch," anecdotal style is not just of literary interest; it also has practical uses in political and business contexts. A socialist functionary needs rhetorical skills to liaise successfully with colleagues. Middle managers in US industry, too, have to communicate continually with superiors and subordinates, as well as administrators, technicians, and experts based in other departments.[35] Similarly, functionaries in the GDR had to mediate between different sets of interests by using a different "expressive style in different situations."[36] Toward the end of the novel David learns that his old friend Gerhard Rikow has just died suddenly. Rikow is described as an exemplary party functionary precisely because he mediated among farmers, industrial engineers, and the government (*DI* 436). This suggests that party functionaries require practical experience of dealing with people at every level of the social hierarchy. Franziska tells David that she is bothered by his "Patriarchenton" (*DI* 113; patriarchal tone), and here she speaks for many GDR intellectuals who saw this tone as symptomatic of rigid bureaucracy. David can only excuse himself by saying that if he did not adopt this tone, people would not take him seriously: "Mitarbeiter erwarteten nun einmal von ihren Chefs eine Art Belehrung; auch wenn sie es nicht mochten, erwarteten sie es doch" (*DI* 114; Colleagues just expected some kind of mentoring from their bosses; even if they didn't like it, they still expected it). He concedes, however, that managers should also be willing to learn from their subordinates (*DI* 279). He would like the relationship between workers and managers to be a mutual learning process.

Bureaucrat's Blues

Das Impressum shows the workings of party bureaucracy through the succession of editors who run the *Neue Berliner Rundschau*. GDR literature often depicts two opposing types: the "partisan" and the "functionary."[37] Partisans belong to the older generation who have experienced war, persecution, or exile and are of more independent mind. Functionaries belong to a younger generation who lack this experience; they are less independent and more disciplined. David tries to mediate between these two types.[38] He is mentored by Johanna Müntzer, a "partisan" character with great independence of mind, loosely based on the writer Anna Seghers. Although she performs the duties of the editor in chief, she is never appointed to this rank because she is a woman. Instead, Heinrich Meyer is appointed editor in chief, despite having no experience as a journalist (*DI* 217–18). The narrator calls this "eine Art historischen Irrtums" (*DI* 217; a kind of historical error). The implication here is that party officials would do well to listen more carefully to outspoken women. As the novel develops, Müntzer and Meyer both act as mentors to David. Müntzer forces him to think and act independently (*DI* 252), and Meyer reminds him that at the end of the day, loyalty to the party is what counts (*DI* 342). Meyer is not a typical functionary, however, having previously worked as a coachman for a brewery, a heavyweight wrestler, and a driver and bodyguard for Karl Liebknecht (*DI* 218). He is a veteran of the class struggle.

The rule-bound party functionary is presented in a much more negative light: the next editor in chief, Herbert Bleck, is appointed because he is the antithesis of a practical person. The committee decides that

> die Mitarbeiter dort . . . waren vor allem zu sehr Praktiker, und der Praktizismus stand zu jener Zeit weit oben im Katalog der die Entwicklung hemmenden Gefahren. Ein theoretischer Kopf mußte her, ein Mensch mit Bewußtsein und Geschichtsbewußtsein, ein nicht nur geschulter, sondern auch studierter Mann. (*DI* 234)

> [The colleagues there . . . were, above all, too practical in their approach, and at that time practicality was very high on the list of dangers obstructing socialist development. What was needed was a theoretician, a man with consciousness and historical consciousness, not only a man who had been schooled, but a man who had studied.]

This passage criticizes party leaders' tendency to prefer dogma to practicality, although it softens its criticism by saying that this rigidity was of its time, i.e., it typified an earlier stage in GDR history. Even so, it is still striking for twenty-first-century readers to learn that practicality was considered a threat. It soon becomes apparent that Bleck is a narrow-minded apparatchik who hates "practical types." One of his favorite phrases is "vorgefundene Menschen" (*DI* 233; people as we find them); he blames them for holding back the development of the GDR. The photographer, Gabelbach, has to explain the journalistic process step by step to Bleck because he has no idea how the newspaper is actually put together (*DI* 236–48). He is succeeded as editor by a nameless individual, referred to simply as "Nachfolger III" (*DI* 253; successor III) or "Chef III" (*DI* 279; boss III). This becomes a running gag. But Kant softens the implied criticism of "boss III" because he shows a willingness to learn. At the end of a long editorial meeting, he takes the time to listen to Johanna Müntzer and even says, "'Lernen können wir alle noch'" (*DI* 279; "We can all learn things"). Johanna agrees very warmly indeed: "'Es freut mich, solche Worte von dir zu hören. . . . Es stimmt ja so sehr!'" (*DI* 279; "I am glad to hear you say that. . . . You are so very right!"). The narrator presents this as a significant moment because, for once, the functionary shows awareness that running a business operation does not rely on ideology but on a willingness to learn from the workers on the ground.

Kant tries to address the problem of bureaucracy even more directly in chapter 11, when he considers the question of whether or not there are contradictions between party bureaucrats and workers or between intellectuals and workers in the GDR. We know that Kant was forced to soften the tone of this chapter in particular, as evidenced by an unsigned and undated statement produced by an official in the Main Office for Publishing and Book Trade and sent to Kurt Hager, the Politburo member responsible for culture, on July 24, 1969.[39] In chapter 11 David concedes there is an "Unterschied" (*DI* 358; difference) between intellectuals and workers. He adds, however, that it would be wrong to turn this distinction into a "Gegensatz" (*DI* 358; opposition). Once the question is raised, it will not go away and dominates the rest of the chapter. David reflects on Che Guevara, who gave up the ministerial post that Fidel Castro offered him to go and fight as a guerilla in Latin America. David decides, however, that the priority is for Cuba to become an economic success, and this requires functionaries, not revolutionaries (*DI* 365). The narrative turns inward as David conducts the debate with himself:

> Meinst du, ich bin begeistert von mir, wenn ich mir melden kann: Nun ja, es läuft, keine besonderen Vorkommnisse, auf Posten nichts Neues? Das soll Glück sein, mein Glück: Die Maschine arbeitet, das Fließband fließt, keine Stockungen und keine Katastrophen? (*DI* 366)

> [Do you think I feel inspired when I can tell myself: well, things are coming along, no incidents, nothing to report? That is supposed to be happiness, my happiness: the machine is working, the conveyor belt is moving, no interruptions and no catastrophes?]

David here admits that the work of a functionary is repetitive and machine-like. Then he attempts a more exciting metaphor, noting that every successful spaceflight requires a ground crew: "Kein Höhenflug ohne Ordnung am Boden, aber Glück ist wohl anders" (*DI* 366; No high flight takes place without organization on the ground, but happiness is something else). Knowing that this is subversive, the narrator interrupts himself and anticipates the orthodox objection: "Sehr fragwürdig, Meister Groth, sehr fragwürdig, deine Ansicht! . . . Wohin siedelst du dann deinen Glücksbegriff?" (*DI* 366; Your opinion is very questionable, Master Groth, very questionable! . . . Where, then, do you locate your concept of happiness?). A party member should be happy to serve the state. But the narrator persists. He is seeking a more measured response: "Nun ja, jubeln—das wäre affig, aber nörgeln, weil zu den Pflichten, in die man sich selbst gebracht hat, auch die Wiederholung gehört, das ist wohl lächerlicher noch" (*DI* 366; Well, it would be ridiculous to rejoice, but it would be even more ridiculous to grumble just because one of the commitments you have made involves repetition). This shows the narrator's concern to strike a balance between a critique of bureaucracy and a defense of it. "Ein bißchen Wehmut ist erlaubt" (*DI* 366; A little melancholy is permissible)—but not too much, because everyone has to work together: "tu deinen Teil (*DI* 380; do your bit). In classical rhetoric this sort of debate is called *refutatio* (refutation): the part of the speech devoted to answering the counterarguments of your opponent. The narrator adopts the perspective of the opposition in order to answer their objections more effectively. But nagging doubts remain. In the following chapter, chapter 12, the rigidity of party bureaucracy is explained with reference to the uprising of June 17, 1953. The official Fritz Andermann was nearly killed by a mob during the uprising, and this experience has made him determined to prevent it ever happening again. He resolves to be hard and "den Vorwurf der Enge nicht fürchten" (*DI* 408; not to fear the reproach of narrowmindedness). In this way, the narrator conveys the viewpoint of the GDR elites that their bureaucratic rigidity was justified because the country was under siege from the capitalist West.[40]

Negotiating with the Party on Its Own Terms

Machiavelli advises the modern prince to make an appeal to old traditions and values in order to legitimize his new methods. What is required is "the usurpation of tradition."[41] Kant adopts a similar strategy in *Das Impressum*, always presenting new ideas from within an orthodox framework.[42] Every time he mentions V. I. Lenin, he uses the Soviet leader to legitimize his critique of the bureaucracy; for example, "Bereits Lenin habe gesagt, nur wer überhaupt nichts tue, begehe keinen Fehler" (*DI* 7; Lenin said that only a person who does nothing at all makes no mistakes). This militates against the rigidity of SED practice. Lenin is invoked again to underline the importance of listening to the people: "Leserbriefe [boten] einer gelegentlichen Äußerung Lenins zufolge günstige Gelegenheit zur Erforschung von Volksmeinung" (*DI* 216–17; According to a casual remark by Lenin, readers' letters offered a great opportunity to study the opinion of the people). This comment draws on the authority of Lenin to argue that party officials must be open to criticism. In this way, the novel uses socialist shibboleths to legitimize its humble requests for a relaxation of party rigor. It makes the classic point that every politician must be closely in touch with the mood of the polis.[43] It also suggests that willingness to learn is a "Tugend" (*DI* 248, virtue) that party officials need.[44] At one point David even carries out an opinion survey, interviewing members of the public to discover their hopes and ideas for the future.

Lenin is not the only Soviet authority invoked by Kant; he also references the Soviet educationist Anton Semyonovich Makarenko (1888–1939), who pioneered alternative forms of participatory education in the 1920s.[45] The party functionaries who have read Makarenko are more tactful; they soften their instructions by using modal verbs or the subjunctive instead of the imperative: "Vielleicht könnte man es folgendermaßen anpacken . . . oder: Ich überlege gerade, ob nicht . . . oder: Was meinen Sie, wäre es nicht denkbar, daß . . .?" (*DI* 114; Maybe you could tackle this way . . . or: I wonder if you couldn't . . . or: What do you think, is it possible that . . .?). This contrasts with the direct orders used by the military. *Das Impressum* presents Makarenko's democratic pedagogy as a good example. Similarly, to justify his ambitions for the newspaper in a language that the party leaders will understand, David uses the comparison of an Olympic trainer (*DI* 213). International sport was, of course, one arena in which the party did encourage intense competition.[46]

Das Impressum also gives an example of how persuasion can work in an official context. In chapter 8 David learns that the British Gunsmith Association has invited a representative of the GDR to attend an event in London. David himself once worked as a gunsmith's apprentice and wants to attend. But first he has to get permission. At the editorial meeting David and Johanna manage to persuade their colleagues by inviting them to consider the benefits of the trip. David lets Johanna do most of the talking. She hints that the trip will promote the technological achievements of the GDR to an international audience. Once the idea is mentioned, various colleagues realize that the trip will generate journalistic material that can be used in all the different sections of the newspaper at once. Everyone will benefit. The scene shows Makarenko's pedagogy in action: instead of dictating a course of action, colleagues are invited to work out the benefits for themselves. The editor in chief objects that they require a correspondent with a technical background. Only then does Johanna let slip that David is a trained gunsmith (*DI* 259). Then she starts apologizing for her poor memory—actually, she is allowing time for the penny to drop. Instead of declaring her idea from the start, Johanna feeds clues to the boss, encouraging him to come up with the idea himself, so that he can take the credit (*DI* 260). Here *Das Impressum* suggests that it is possible to negotiate successfully with party officials and get results, but only by framing the message in an appropriate manner.

Conclusion: The Insider's View

Kant's status as a loyal and well-connected party functionary gave him some privileged insights into the workings of the SED. *Das Impressum* can be read as a handbook for managing party elites. Of course, it could also be read as an apology for the SED regime. Although the authorities hesitated for three years before allowing it to be published, and despite the novel's ever-so-gentle criticisms, in fact it establishes the *ethos* (character) and loyalty of its author beyond question. The criticisms are smuggled in, carefully covered by a mass of socialist commonplaces. *Das Impressum* is an entertaining insider's view of how to negotiate with the state-socialist bureaucracy. It is not just a period piece, however. Many of its insights into the mechanisms of power and persuasion could be applied to any complex organization today.[47]

7: Corporate Discourse in Friedrich Christian Delius's *Unsere Siemens-Welt,* 1972

> *Ingenuity for life*
> —Siemens advertising
> slogan used in 2017

Introduction: Business and Bureaucracy

THIS CHAPTER EXAMINES Friedrich Christian Delius's representation of corporate rhetoric and bureaucracy in his pioneering work of post-1968 documentary fiction. Whereas Hermann Kant writes from within the GDR establishment, Delius (b. 1943) was, until 1971, a doctoral student and an activist associated with the *Außerparlamentarische Opposition* (Extra-Parliamentary Opposition) in the Federal Republic of Germany (FRG). While Kant writes in a realist mode, Delius's early work belongs to the genre of *Dokumentarliteratur* (documentary literature) developed in the 1960s and 1970s by East and West German authors, including Rolf Hochhuth, Maxie Wander, Peter Weiss, Heinar Kipphardt, Günter Wallraff, Irina Liebmann, and Erika Runge. Practitioners of the genre called for the politicization of literature and for writers to engage with the facts of the modern industrial world.[1] Although Kant and Delius are writing from opposite sides of the Cold War divide and using different literary forms, to a certain extent they have a shared preoccupation: the inevitably bureaucratic nature of modern life.[2] For some West German writers in the 1970s, the growth of the capitalist corporation was a major concern. This preoccupation was reflected in Wallraff's polemics against industry and big business;[3] in Mathias Scheben's science-fiction novel *Konzern 2003* (1977; Corporation 2003) most of Western Europe is ruled in 2003 by the giant Zannen Corporation.[4] Seen from this perspective, there seemed to be a number of parallels between the bureaucracy of the Soviet states and what President Dwight D. Eisenhower called "the military-industrial complex" of the US in his farewell address of January 17, 1961.

Unsere Siemens-Welt (Our Siemens World) seems to invite such parallels. For example, considering Siemens in the late nineteenth century, the narrator notes approvingly that "das Betriebsklima entsprach dem einer staatlichen Behörde, es herrschten alle Vorzüge eines 'kalten militärischen Tons'" (the atmosphere of the firm was equivalent to that of a government agency; it had all the advantages of a "cold military tone").[5] Even the notorious Stasi has a counterpart in Delius's corporate world, in which there is a confidential personnel file on every employee. At one point the narrator regrets that the new employment law allows employees to apply to view their files, but he adds that the corporation will find ways to ensure that certain data remain confidential.[6]

It was Max Weber who pointed out that private companies and political parties have one thing in common: both rely upon a highly developed bureaucracy. In the state sphere, this structure is known as a bureaucratic agency (*Behörde*); in the private sector, it is known as a firm (*Betrieb*).[7] Weber draws a parallel between the modern entrepreneur who conducts himself as the "first official" of the company and the modern ruler (e.g., Frederick II of Prussia) who speaks of himself as "the first servant of the state." In contrast to neoliberalism, which views the state and enterprises as fundamentally opposed, Weber asserts their fundamental similarity: "Die Vorstellung, daß staatliche Bürotätigkeit und privatwirtschaftliche Kontortätigkeit etwas innerlich wesensverschiedenes seien, ist europäisch-kontinental und den Amerikanern im Gegensatz zu uns gänzlich fremd" ("The idea that the bureau activities of the state are intrinsically different in character from the management of private offices is a continental European notion and, by way of contrast, is totally foreign to the American way").[8] Weber argues that states and businesses have to rely on bureaucracy because it is technically superior to other forms of organization and faster in terms of response time.[9] Particularly relevant for this chapter is Weber's distinction between bureaucracy's impersonal function, on the one hand, and its typical ideological halo or transfiguration (*Verklärung*), on the other hand.[10] In other words, each bureaucracy requires an ideological justification to inspire its functionaries with loyalty to their office (*Amtstreue*). Delius's early works are important precisely because they investigate this process: Delius unpicks, or scratches away at, the discursive veneer or "halo" with which the modern corporation seeks to gild itself.

The full title of Delius's text is *Unsere Siemens-Welt: Eine Festschrift zum 125jährigen Bestehen des Hauses S.* (Our Siemens World: A Festschrift on the Occasion of the 125th Anniversary of the House of S.). While the text proclaims itself to be a "Festschrift," a commemorative publication, it is, in fact, a sophisticated satire on corporate publicity. As we shall see, perhaps the most controversial aspect of the work is its handling of Siemens's role in World War II and the Holocaust. When the book was published on October 19, 1972, the Siemens corporation swiftly filed for an injunction against Delius and his publisher, Rotbuch. The legal dispute was finally settled in 1976, with Delius claiming a victory on points over Siemens: the court confirmed that publication of the book could continue, subject to nine deletions. The verdict is reprinted in the recent *Werkausgabe* edition, together with a timeline of the trial and details of the court costs, which were divided in half between Siemens and the accused (*USW* 335–42).

Although *Unsere Siemens-Welt* is not technically a novel, it offers a thrilling narrative. Indeed, I would argue that it can be designated as a "protonovel" for two reasons. First, it tells a dramatic story in which the heroic characters are the House of Siemens and its various directors, and the villains are the "Störenfriede" (*USW* 307; troublemakers) and "betriebsfremde Gewerkschaftsvertreter" (*USW* 308; trade unionists who are external to the company); second, because it laid the structure and groundwork for Delius's first novel, *Ein Held der inneren Sicherheit* (1981; A Hero of Internal Security). The protagonist of that novel is Roland Diehl, a ghostwriter whose boss, Alfred Büttinger, president of the "Verband der Menschenführer" (Association of Leaders), is kidnapped by left-wing terrorists. The events are loosely modeled on the kidnapping and murder of Hanns-Martin Schleyer by the Red Army Faction during the "German Autumn" of 1977. Diehl's official function is to write "Marktwirtschaftssprüche" (market economy slogans).[11] Although the terrorist actions of 1977 are the subtext, *Ein Held der inneren Sicherheit* is interpreted by Keith Bullivant as primarily "an examination of the language of power and of those who wield it."[12] This statement could be applied just as easily to *Unsere Siemens-Welt*. Indeed, the anonymous narrator of *Unsere Siemens-Welt* anticipates the figure of Diehl: he, too, is a copywriter whose job is to praise the company that employs him. The representation of the managers in the two texts is also remarkably similar: Büttinger, the fictional manager of *Ein Held der inneren Sicherheit*, is essentially a pragmatist whose watchword is "Leistung" (achievement, performance).[13]

This chapter focuses on the early satire, *Unsere Siemens-Welt*, because this work engages closely with an actual existing corporation and its corporate discourse or *Selbstinszenierung* (self-presentation).[14] The chapter argues that *Unsere Siemens-Welt* is important because of its alertness to language, rather than its economic analysis. Delius comments, "Der Autor . . . ist kein Wirtschaftsfachmann, mehr als allem andern muß er seiner Sensibilität gegenüber den Wörtern trauen" (*USW* 345; The author . . . is not an economic expert; above all, he has to trust his sensibility for words). That is, he brings a literary sensibility to corporate publicity, enabling him to unravel some of the contradictions in the firm's attempt to control its own public image. Before addressing the content of the firm's narrative, this chapter will situate *Unsere Siemens-Welt* in terms of genre and Delius's wider project of linguistic criticism.

Sprachkritik, Genre, and Narrative Voice

As noted in the introduction to this volume, Delius owes a debt to the tradition of Sprachkritik (linguistic criticism): he often displays an awareness of the instrumental qualities of language. Indeed, the "Zusammenhang von Sprache und Macht" (connection between language and power) has been seen as the main thread that runs through Delius's works.[15] This connection goes back as far as Aristotle, who distinguishes between three genres of oratory: *deliberative* (debating future intent), *forensic* (establishing a past cause), and *epideictic* (apportioning praise and/or blame). Delius's works often explore the celebratory and festive mode of epideictic oratory: this characterization applies to *Wir Unternehmer* (1966; We Entrepreneurs), and to his satirical textbook *Konservativ in 30 Tagen* (1991; Conservative in 30 Days), which analyzes the (often sententious) discourse of Germany's leading conservative daily newspaper, the *Frankfurter Allgemeine Zeitung* (FAZ; Frankfurt General Newspaper). It also applies to his celebrated novellas of the 1990s, *Die Birnen von Ribbeck* (1991; The Pears of Ribbeck), which hinges on a celebration of German reunification, and *Der Sonntag, an dem ich Weltmeister wurde* (1994; The Sunday I Became World Champion), which juxtaposes the emotive power of Lutheran sermons with Germany's victory in the World Cup Final of 1954. The epideictic genre is associated with praise, but it still involves argumentation, as it is required to circumvent unspoken criticism. The genre requires the speaker to maneuver carefully to avoid any suggestion of censure or blame.

Wir Unternehmer was Delius's first big step in the direction of Sprachkritik and corporate satire. It comprises extracts from the proceedings of the Economics Conference of the CDU/CSU (Christian Democratic Union of Germany/Christian Social Union in Bavaria) in Düsseldorf in 1965. It is basically a series of eulogies dedicated to the German "economic miracle," combined with a series of dire warnings against Social Democrats and trade unionists who threaten to undermine the achievements of German entrepreneurs. The speeches are broken up into verse form to draw attention to the ideological maneuvers of the speakers.[16] These entrepreneurs are well aware that they are engaged in political propaganda; one of them even calls for "eine Neubildung der Sozialsprache" (*USW* 81; a new formation of social language).

A key tactic in *Wir Unternehmer*, as Delius notes in his preface, is the use of truisms (*Binsenwahrheiten*) and commonplaces (*Gemeinplätze*), which are so obvious that they imply that critical reflection is unnecessary.[17] Rhetorical commonplaces are essential to classical rhetoric. They are the "places" (*loci* or *topoi*) of arguments, the stock phrases comprising audiences' cultural vocabulary. Cicero advises orators to learn commonplaces (*loci communes*) so that they have a stock of arguments ready to use:

"We must have at hand specific commonplaces that . . . occur to us on the spot."[18] Such phrases are effective because they elicit recognition and assent from the audience. As Aristotle puts it, maxims are persuasive because audiences "love to hear [the speaker] succeed in expressing as a universal truth the opinions which they hold themselves about particular cases"; he adds that maxims give a "moral character" to a speech.[19] In other words, commonplaces and maxims are sententious: they flatter the audience by confirming its beliefs.[20] Delius's preface to *Wir Unternehmer* shows his awareness that commonplaces invite the audience to be uncritical and to accept at face value whatever claims are being made.[21] His mistrust of commonplaces signals his debt to Karl Kraus, who wrote,

> Abgründe dort sehen zu lehren, wo Gemeinplätze sind—das wäre die pädagogische Aufgabe an einer in Sünden erwachsenen Nation; wäre Erlösung der Lebensgüter aus den Banden des Journalismus und aus den Fängen der Politik.[22]

> [To educate people to see the abysses lurking beneath commonplaces—that would be the pedagogic task for a nation which has been raised in sin; that would be the salvation of our best values from the bonds of journalism and the clutches of politics.]

Delius's work continues Kraus's tradition of educating readers to read between the lines. The fact that Delius sees himself as an educator is apparent from his comments on the purpose of *Unsere Siemens-Welt*:

> Der Nutzen dieser Dokumentarsatire könnte darin liegen, . . . dem Leser das Bewußtsein zu schärfen, diese Sprache der raffinierten Selbstrechtfertigung als Herrschaftstechnik zu durchschauen. Ich hoffe, dem Leser dadurch ein gewisses Vergnügen zu verschaffen, daß er diesen ständigen Formulierlügen . . . immer weniger auf den Leim geht. (*USW* 329)

> [The use of this documentary satire could be . . . to sharpen the consciousness of the reader to see through this language of refined self-justification and to recognize it as a means of dominance. By doing this I hope to entertain readers and help them to be taken in less and less by these continual false formulations.]

Like Kraus, Delius hopes to inoculate his readers against propaganda. The affinities between Delius and Kraus can also be observed on the level of method. Gerwin Marahrens describes Kraus's procedure as the tactile, sonic scrutiny of individual words: "[Seine] rhetorischen Methoden und Praktiken dienen ihm lediglich dazu, die Worte zu drehen und zu wenden, sie abzuklopfen und abzuhören, um ihre wahren Herztöne zu vernehmen" ([His] rhetorical methods and practices enable him to twist and turn words, to tap them and listen to them carefully in order to discern their

true heartbeat).[23] Delius's description of his own linguistic procedure in
Unsere Siemens-Welt is remarkably similar, invoking Elias Canetti's dictum
that a poet's task is to take words down from their pedestals: "Ein Dichter
. . . wäre also einer, der von Worten besonders viel hält, . . . sie befragt und
betastet, streichelt, zerkratzt, hobelt, bemalt" (*USW* 345; A poet is a person who thinks a lot about words, . . . who questions them and touches
them, strokes and scratches them, planes them down and paints them).
The writer's engagement with language is thus a tactile process; there is a
sense of grappling with the words in order to find out how they operate
and what they are really doing.

One particularly slippery category of words is the pronoun, because
they function to include and exclude people. Pronouns are used discur-
sively to define group identities, and discourse analysts consider shifts in
pronouns to be symptomatic of conflict between different discourses.[24]
Delius is well aware of the integrative function of the pronoun *wir* (we).
In the preface to *Unsere Siemens-Welt* the reader encounters the firm's
founder, Werner von Siemens, not in his capacity as an entrepreneur or an
inventor but in his role as a master of language:

> Der Verfasser . . . erlaubte sich, den Stil dieser Schrift—insbesondere
> die Form des schon von Werner von Siemens geforderten integrier-
> enden Wir—der Redeweise nachzubilden, die bei festlichen Anlässen
> üblich und als rhetorisches Mittel partnerschaftlicher Verbundenheit
> unentbehrlich ist. (*USW* 144)

> [In particular, the author has presumed to adopt the word "we": it
> has an integrative power; it has been the required mode of address
> ever since Werner von Siemens. The author has modeled the style of
> this work on this manner of speaking, because it is commonly used at
> festive occasions and is indispensable as a rhetorical means of affirm-
> ing the bonds of partnership.]

In this way, the preface sends a clear warning signal for readers to beware
of pronouns such as *wir* and *unser* (our) because they are rhetorical instruments used to affirm the existence of shared interests. These inclusive pronouns are a good way to cover up any conflicts of interests under a rhetoric
of partnership. The problematic status of "we" and "our" runs right
through the text. It is present in the title, too. At first glance, *Unsere
Siemens-Welt* (Our Siemens World) sounds reassuringly positive, an assertion of cooperation and shared enterprise. It affirms a sense of team spirit
and harmony, suggesting perhaps that Siemens and its employees are constantly working diligently to make the world a better place. A second look
at the title, however, could lead to a sense of irony and unease. What is that
pronoun *Unsere* really doing? Whom does it include, and whom does it
exclude? One possible interpretation of the phrase could be that it expresses
the viewpoint held by Siemens managers that the world belongs to them.

Read in this way, against the grain, the title of the book evokes a narcissistic fantasy, a pathological claim that the entire world belongs to Siemens.

Another rhetorical, or ideological, strategy that Delius explores is the familiar claim "daß Wirtschaft und Politik oder gar Ideologie nichts miteinander zu tun haben" (*USW* 245; that economics and politics or indeed ideology have nothing to do with each other). Such statements are themselves highly ideological, and they are undermined when we observe Siemens working closely with banks and with its own rivals to minimize the risks of a free market (*USW* 167) and lobbying for state intervention in the market (*USW* 194–95). Coexisting with the call for a free market is the call for preferential treatment within that market: Siemens only wants the market to be free when it suits the firm. By juxtaposing contradictory statements in this manner, Delius alerts readers to the fact that the rhetoric of freedom and inclusion is often used in pursuit of an exclusively profit-driven agenda.

As a Festschrift, the rhetorical operation of *Unsere Siemens-Welt* is related to classical Greek eulogy, in which the celebration of the dead serves as a pretext "to project and reinforce a specific ideology of patriotism, collectivity and citizenship."[25] For example, Pericles's oration for the war dead in 431 BC was intended "to forge a sense of identity and values."[26] In the hands of the skilled orator, the eulogy becomes an instrument or political tool to serve the present. In terms of genre, then, *Unsere Siemens-Welt* is epideictic: a text that apportions praise and/or blame. In fact, this duplicitous text does both: it blames under the cover of praise. As Michael Billig puts it, behind every panegyric lurks the potential for blame; indeed, the whole point of the panegyric is to drive away "the anti-logoi of criticisms."[27]

In the afterword Delius says he selected the literary form of the Festschrift because it offered an effective way to handle the dense economic material that would be "sprachlich angemessen, vielleicht sogar vergnüglich" (*USW* 343; linguistically appropriate and even entertaining). As a genre, the company Festschrift is typically an uncritical celebration. This laudatory function evokes the figure of a hack writer, hired by Siemens to produce a vanity publication in line with the firm's self-image:

> der Autor muß sich nur in einen von Siemens beauftragten Festschriftsteller verwandeln, der die Geschichte und Aktivitäten des Konzerns fast besinnungslos rühmt und in seinem Eifer auch vieles ausplaudert, was in Festschriften normalerweise verschwiegen wird. (*USW* 343–44)

> [All the author had to do was transform himself into someone commissioned by Siemens to write a commemorative publication; someone who praises the history and the activities of the corporation almost senselessly and, in his zeal, divulges that which is normally kept secret in a Festschrift.]

Figuring the narrator as an overzealous hack who cannot refrain from blabbing about the company secrets is a convenient narrative device. It creates a movement whereby excessive praise tips over into accusation and blame. The narrative says more than it wants to, more than it is supposed to. Satirically, it enlarges its subject until its moral absurdities become apparent. But this raises the question: why would a writer who is paid to praise his employer be stupid enough to present his employer in such a bad light? Bernard Dieterle suggests that Delius exploits the genre itself: the requirement to draw up a list of the subject's merits invites the speaker to use superlatives and to reveal excessive details.[28] In generic terms the eulogy is dangerously close to its counterpart, invective, and Delius's text takes full advantage of this proximity. Readers of *Unsere Siemens-Welt* can spot the disjunctions between the high-flown rhetoric and the base activities that are being related. Readers can also enjoy the experience of watching the slippages and ruptures in the glossy narrative. The pleasure of the text is linked to these moments when the mask slips and the tone of self-congratulation slips over into an involuntary admission. Put simply, the narrative economy of *Unsere Siemens-Welt* relies on the unreliable narrator, who undermines his own apparent loyalty to Siemens by saying too much. The text invites readers to observe and enjoy as the narrator continually oscillates between loyalty and disloyalty. This is evident if we compare Delius's subversive text with the bland, officially approved Festschrift by the historian Wilfried Feldenkirchen, which was published in 1997 to mark the 150th anniversary of the Siemens corporation.[29] Feldenkirchen's previous monograph (1995) acknowledged the company's use of slave labor during the early forties,[30] but his official Festschrift makes no mention of it. Furthermore, Feldenkirchen was working as a Siemens project manager at the time of his death in a car accident in 2010.[31] Feldenkirchen's career trajectory from historian to Siemens employee raises the question of scholarly independence, and his official Festschrift certainly reads like a hagiography. In contrast, Delius's text delights in exposing the cracks in the corporate facade; e.g., when he juxtaposes the firm's "Menschlichkeit" (humanity) with its founder's advice to his sons on how to deal with the employees: "Brecht was nicht biegen will" (*USW* 150; If they don't bend, break them).

Corporate Identity and Brand Technique

The Siemens corporate brand was established in the 1930s by the brand manager Hans Domizlaff (1892–1971), the first director of the Hauptwerbeabteilung (Main Advertising Department), or HWA, which was set up in 1935. The Festschrift introduces Domizlaff as a figure who should "nicht unerwähnt bleiben" (*USW* 185; not remain unmentioned). Until 1935, advertising had been dispersed among various divisions; as Feldenkirchen puts it, however, between 1918 and 1939 "public relations and advertising steadily gained in significance for corporate policy, whereas technology assumed more of an auxiliary function."[32] The corporation's new public image was carefully curated by Domizlaff, whose textbook, *Die Gewinnung des öffentlichen Vertrauens: Ein Lehrbuch der Markentechnik* (1939; How to Build Public Trust: A Textbook of Brand Technique), is a standard work and still in print today.[33] Influenced by Gestalt psychology and early mass psychology, Domizlaff regarded each brand as a living organism, an "Ideenorganismus" (idea-organism) with its own will (in today's terms, this might be called a meme). According to this theory of *Markentechnik* (brand technique), a public gathers around a particular achievement, and it is the task of the brand manager to nurture this clientele and to win its trust.

Domizlaff begins his study with a contrast between two character types: the "Jahrmarktsverkäufer" (carnival trader) and the "Kaufherr" (head of a merchant house). He compares the "Reklame" (blatant, gimmicky advertising) of the twenties to the cheap tricks of the salesman at a traveling fair. In contrast to this he proposes the style of "der ortsangesessene Handelsherr" (the established head of a merchant house), who cultivates the reputation and prestige of his house with dignity.[34] Domizlaff's description of how the head of a merchant house should present himself almost reads as if it were an excerpt from Thomas Mann's *Buddenbrooks*:

> Der Kaufherr sucht seine Kunden durch Gewinnung ihres Vertrauens zu binden. Seine würdige Lebenshaltung, gemessen und befangen in einem ganz bestimmten Rahmen, seine unaufdringliche Art, die Vornehmheit seines Geschäftsgebarens, die Zuverlässigkeit seiner Empfehlungen und die suggestive Kraft einer selbstsicheren Persönlichkeit sind die wesentlichsten Mittel.[35]

> [The head of a merchant house seeks to bind his customers by winning their trust. His dignified lifestyle, appropriate and yet embedded in a very specific framework, his unobtrusive, discreet manner, the refinement of his way of doing business, the reliability of his recommendations, and the suggestive power of his self-assured personality are the most essential means.]

In this view of corporate branding, it is not cheap advertising tricks that count but the prestige of the firm and the quality of its personal connections. The requirements of *Buddenbrooks*—the need to maintain the correct facade, the need for the firm's director to represent it at the highest levels of society—are still in force. They just need to be modernized in line with the latest branding techniques.[36]

In the light of Domizlaff's theory we can observe the ideological connections between the patrician merchant house and the official designation
for the Siemens corporation, "das Haus Siemens" (the House of Siemens).
Carl Friedrich von Siemens conceived the organization as a family of companies closely cooperating, symbolized by the term *Haus* (house), which
he chose in preference to the foreign-sounding technical term *Konzern*
(corporation, group of companies).[37] Feldenkirchen thinks that "the historical significance of the term 'House of Siemens' as a supporting device
cannot be overestimated" because it evokes the symbolic unity of the different firms, which have a shared focus in terms of electrical engineering.[38]
We should, however, also note the linguistic associations of the term: "das
Haus Siemens" emphasizes the *Bodenständigkeit* (down-to-earth, Germanic
quality) of the Siemens corporation by harking back to the proud merchant houses of the early modern period in Germany. Much as Renaissance
merchants established economic empires to rival the aristocracy, the phrase
"das Haus Siemens" has aristocratic and dynastic connotations. It is not so
far away from "the House of Austria" that is an enduring presence for the
narrator of Ingeborg Bachmann's *Malina*. In this way, the official designation for the company subliminally ratifies its aristocratic and imperial
ambitions.

Domizlaff's theory of brand technique, with its blend of the medieval
and the modern and its Nietzschean admiration for the elite merchants of
the Renaissance, exemplifies the German Expressionist context from which
it emerged. Indeed, Domizlaff's biography typifies the close connections
among modern art, commercial advertising, and political propaganda. A
disciple of the German symbolist painter Max Klinger (1857–1920), he
spent the 1920s working as an advertising consultant for the Reemtsma
cigarette company. He hoped that his book *Propagandamittel der
Staatsidee* (1932; Propaganda for the Idea of the State) would gain him a
position as an adviser to the government of Heinrich Brüning. As Delius
puts it, this book gave Joseph Goebbels some "wichtige Ideen" (*USW*
185; important ideas), and there was a meeting between Goebbels and
Domizlaff in 1936.[39] Domizlaff joined Siemens in 1934 and left in 1940—
according to Delius's narrative, because by this time the House of Siemens
was working "fast ausschließlich" (almost exclusively) for the National
Socialist state, and there was no longer any need for advertising (*USW*
185). In 1945 Domizlaff was interned by the British authorities for six
months; he rejoined Siemens as an advertising consultant in 1947. At this
critical moment when the firm's future was in question, Domizlaff cam-
paigned to protect Siemens from being dismantled.[40] He contributed significantly to the firm's postwar "makeover" (*USW* 189). And yet in 1957
he privately published a polemic asserting the principle of white supremacy,
which suggests strongly that his personal "denazification process" was far
from complete.[41]

Publicity and Complicity

The greatest public relations challenge that Siemens has ever faced is how to narrate its complicity in the Holocaust. Feldenkirchen tried to address this issue in an attempt to "help Siemens come to terms with its role in this period."[42] More recently, S. Jonathan Wiesen has produced a fascinating case study of how Siemens tried to deal with this period in its history.[43] Wiesen distinguishes two phases of the Siemens forced-labor program: (1) At the beginning of the war in 1939, Berlin Jews and Polish civilians were drafted to work in Siemens's Berlin factories. By the beginning of 1943 all of the Berlin Jewish Siemens workers (approximately 2,000) were transported to Auschwitz, where most of them were gassed on arrival. (2) In the later stages of the war Siemens used Jewish and non-Jewish Eastern European concentration-camp inmates as slave laborers. Siemens obtained 2,700 laborers from Auschwitz; the company's largest forced-labor enterprise was at the women's concentration camp Ravensbrück, comprising 2,300 prisoners.[44] The Conference on Jewish Material Claims against Germany, which represented the survivors, concluded: "The Siemens concern reaped the full benefit from this slave work without any pecuniary compensation for the victims or the least care for the victims."[45] The conference came to a financial settlement with Siemens AG in 1962, although Siemens insisted that the payments did not represent the admission of any legal or moral obligation.[46]

The involvement of Siemens in the forced-labor program means that in 1945, Siemens executives urgently needed to put a positive gloss on their actions. This quest for a new narrative exemplifies what Paul Betts has termed "a crisis of cultural representation for post-fascist society."[47] Soon after VE-Day, May 8, 1945, Siemens was accused of war crimes and faced the real prospect of dismemberment by the Allied powers. Confronted with its complicity, Siemens had to construct a narrative of noncomplicity.[48] Siemens held a board meeting on July 16, 1945, to discuss its response to the allegations. A counternarrative to present Siemens in a positive light was launched by Fritz Jessen and taken up by Hanns-Henning von Pentz. They emphasized the peaceful and humanitarian aims of the company, its progressive treatment of its workers, and its internal "opposition" to the National Socialists. By July 31, 1945, Pentz's team had produced the first draft of the document, and in the days that followed Pentz and Wolf-Dietrich von Witzleben worked hard to finesse it. They exchanged and proofread drafts, polishing and nuancing the language. Wiesen comments that this "meticulous crafting" shows that Germans in the summer of 1945 "embraced any rhetorical device that could mitigate the severity of the claims against them and their country."[49] The situation forced Siemens to construct an alternative and positive history of the Siemens Geist (spirit).

This Siemens counternarrative tried to stress the personal integrity of the firm's director, Carl Friedrich von Siemens, who had died in 1941. It highlighted the isolated instances in which Carl Friedrich sought to distance himself from Nazi policy, at the same time playing down his cooperation with the regime. For example, Feldenkirchen describes Carl Friedrich as "an opponent of National Socialism," despite the fact that he was appointed to the Generalrat der Wirtschaft (General Council of the Economy) in 1933.[50] Feldenkirchen's evidence for Carl Friedrich's "opposition" to the Nazis is that he delivered a speech in support of Chancellor Brüning at the General Electric Company in New York on October 27, 1931, in which he criticized the Nazis;[51] in the November 1932 elections he gave financial support to the national-liberal Deutsche Volkspartei (German People's Party), or DVP;[52] after 1933 he had "numerous conflicts with those in power";[53] and when he died in 1941, no official representative of the government was present at his funeral.[54] Delius's account of the New York speech of 1931 is different. In Delius's version, Carl Friedrich criticizes Brüning for going easy on the trade unions and comments favorably on Hitler's use of "starke Disziplin" (*USW* 178; strong discipline) in the fight against Communism. Delius's text presents Carl Friedrich as an "einstiger Demokrat" (*USW* 179; former democrat) who had no choice but to find an accommodation with the Nazis. Of course, Carl Friedrich disapproved of Hitler's "beschränkte[r] Nationalismus" (*USW* 183; narrow nationalism), because the firm exported a third of its products; and he certainly disagreed with Hitler's "kurzsichtige[r] Antisemitismus—man half also, solange das ging, leitenden Juden bei ihrer Ausreise!" (*USW* 183; short-sighted anti-Semitism—as long as we could, we helped leading Jews to emigrate). According to Delius's narrator, the aspect of National Socialism that upset Carl Friedrich the most was that it stopped him from being "Herr im eigenen Haus" (*USW* 183; master of his own house); he felt that the all-powerful state suffocated "gesunden Unternehmensgeist" (*USW* 183; healthy entrepreneurial spirit). This implies that Carl Friedrich's principal grievance against the Nazis was the challenge to his authority and the autonomy of his company. Noticeable by its absence is any acknowledgment of the suffering and death of the victims of Nazism.[55] Delius's text thus draws attention to the self-serving quality of the Siemens narrative of the part it played in World War II, which makes its attempts at *Vergangenheitsbewältigung* (coming to terms with the past) so superficial.[56]

Rationalization Policies

The conduct of Siemens in the early forties can be understood better in the context of the progressive social policies the firm had developed in the interwar period.[57] As early as 1917, Carl Friedrich von Siemens had announced that *Arbeitsleistung* (work performance) was closely connected to the living conditions of Siemens employees.[58] His social policies were influenced by the work of Richard Ehrenberg (1857–1921), an economics professor who promoted the idea of an "Arbeitsgemeinschaft" (work community) based on a commonality of interests between entrepreneurs and workers—a convenient concept for smoothing over any potential conflict of interest.[59] In 1921 Carl Friedrich von Siemens was a founding director of the Reichskuratorium für Wirtschaftlichkeit (Reich Advisory Board for Cost Effectiveness), or RKW,[60] and in 1924 the Siemens corporation was one of the founding members of the Reichsausschuß für Arbeitszeitermittlung (Reich Committee for Working-Time Investigation).[61] These initiatives were part of the wave of rationalization that occurred in twenties Germany as entrepreneurs sought to organize their firms on rational principles to maximize efficiency. It gradually became apparent to experts that any attempt to rationalize production had to take the social dimension into account.[62] As a Reichstag representative from 1920 to 1924, and as head of the firm from 1919 to 1940, Carl Friedrich von Siemens was at the forefront of efforts to promote the health and hygiene of the working classes. Carola Sachse describes the social policy of Siemens as a "double strategy" intended to optimize production flows within the firm and to serve as a model for state policy directed toward the industrial rationalization of society as a whole.[63] While Siemens was progressive in its social policies, however, it attempted to shape the family lives of its workers along conservative lines, to the extent of discriminating against female employees.[64]

In the context of company social policy during the National Socialist regime of the 1930s we see a similar ambivalence between progressive and retrograde tendencies. The framework for this period was set out by Robert Ley's Deutsche Arbeitsfront (German Labor Front), or DAF, which was first established on May 10, 1933, to supersede the banned labor unions by implementing policies of social rationalization. An important subsidiary of the DAF was Albert Speer's Schönheit der Arbeit (Beauty of Labor) Bureau, which promoted the renovation of factories and workplaces with the aim of restoring the "Würde" (dignity) of labor.[65] This rhetoric of "dignity" went hand in hand with the dissolution of organized labor, and, to a certain extent, the beautification projects were "a palliative for poor wages."[66] But they had substance, too. Paul Betts describes the Beauty of Labor program as an unprecedented "state-level effort to marry labor and aesthetics" and points out that it adopted many of the principles of Weimar modernists such as Peter Behrens, Walter Gropius, and the Werkbund (Association of Craftsmen).[67] The program included new day-care facilities intended to "ease the adjustment of women to the factory."[68] In his denazification trial, Wolf-Dietrich von Witzleben, the Siemens personnel chief during the Third Reich, said he was proud of the fact that in 1933 Siemens had already achieved many of the goals the DAF wanted to pursue.[69]

Although the Siemens corporation was to a certain extent the model pupil of the DAF, there were limits to this cooperation. In fact, Siemens repeatedly attempted to block the intrusions of the DAF into its rationalization policy.[70] This raises the question of whether disputes between Siemens and the DAF could be described as "resistance" (*Widerstand*). Carola Sachse rejects this claim, arguing that debates between the two organizations focused solely on rivalry between spheres of influence, in terms of deciding whether the firm's social policy was to be driven by productivity concerns or racial concerns.[71] Each organization had different priorities: in regard to selecting candidates for company-owned apartments, the chief concern of the DAF was to optimize racial hygiene, whereas Siemens wanted to optimize the production flow, and this divergence led to frequent debates between them.[72] The two organizations shared certain selection criteria, however, including health, working-life expectancy, "joy in work" (*Arbeitsfreude*), work performance, ambition for promotion, and hygienic and moral homelife.[73]

The ultimate convergence in the rationalization processes of Siemens and the DAF occurred in the forced-labor program, although Siemens often did its best to promote the health and the survival of its forced laborers. According to Sachse, the Siemens forced laborers were protected to a certain extent, because illness and death represented "disruptions" (*Störungen*) in the production process.[74] Delius's text makes a similar point: from the management point of view, deaths were regrettable because they disturbed the production flow.[75] Since many laborers were sent to concentration camps, the result was "eine für die kontinuierliche Produktion nicht sehr förderliche Fluktuation" (*USW* 186; a fluctuation that was not very conducive to production). And yet the rationalization process required the selection of prisoners. According to Delius's narrator, this had the result that "jeden Monat wurden die jeweils 100 Schwächsten zwecks anderweitiger Verwendung ins KZ Sachsenhausen überführt" (*USW* 187; every month the weakest hundred laborers were transferred to Sachsenhausen to be used for other purposes). Of course, the narrator does not dwell on such unpleasant details. Instead, he shrugs off any sense of responsibility with a convenient phrase: it was merely the "Zeitumstände" (*USW* 186; circumstances of the time) that turned these Jews and foreigners into forced laborers.

The Rhetoric of War and Logistics

Delius's Festschrift traces the corporation's involvement in military technology from the Crimean War of 1853–56, in which it supplied both Britain and Russia (*USW* 149), to the 1970s. Delius links the firm's early success to Werner von Siemens's contacts in the Prussian military, and he suggests that the expansion of the firm in the early twentieth century was guided by Prussian military philosophy. The motto of Arnold von Siemens, eldest son of Werner, was "Getrennt marschieren, vereint schlagen!" (*USW* 165; March separately, strike in unison!). The motto, describing how Arnold divided his responsibilities with his brother Wilhelm, is, in fact, a quotation from the Prussian General Helmuth von Moltke, describing the pincer strategy he used at the Battle of Königgrätz in 1866. Arnold became the chairman of Siemens & Halske, Wilhelm the chairman of the Siemens-Schuckertwerke. And while Arnold concentrated on networking at the highest levels of Wilhelmine society, Wilhelm focused on management (*USW* 165–66).

One of the most interesting features of Delius's text, however, is its analysis of the ongoing militaristic ethos among West German businessmen in the period after 1945. There is a memorable moment in *Wir Unternehmer* when the Lutheran bishop Hanns Lilje remarks that the entrepreneur belongs to the "Stoßtrupp" (*USW* 33; shock troops) of development today. This logic is continued in *Unsere Siemens-Welt* in the description of Egon Overbeck: a member of the Siemens *Aufsichtsrat* (supervisory board) and the director of Mannesmann AG, he is a former army officer who regards his activity as a manager as a continuation of his previous career as a military strategist:

> Als Major im Generalstab a.D. ist der heute 54jährige überzeugt, daß die als Truppenführer erlernte Kriegskunst mit Nutzen im Management von heute eingesetzt werden kann: "In beiden Bereichen gilt die Ökonomie des Mitteleinsatzes—da Blut, hier Geld; auch wenn man den Vergleich scheut, ist es schon so." (*USW* 265)

> [As a former major in the general staff, the 54-year-old is convinced that the art of warfare he learned as a troop commander can be usefully deployed in management today: "Both fields depend on the economic deployment of resources—in that case blood, in this case money; even if people shy away from this comparison, it is still true."]

This statement implies that the wartime logic of the production flow has continued to inform Siemens policy after 1945.[76] The irony is obvious when the chairman of the board, Dr. Bernhard Plettner, and his approach to management reform, are compared to the leadership style of Hitler's favorite general, Erwin Rommel: "Plettner geht à la Rommel an die Front!" (*USW* 272; Plettner goes straight to the front, like Rommel!).

Unsere Siemens-Welt examines the rhetoric of an organization that is one of the chief beneficiaries of the nuclear arms race. We are told that the West German government has invested ten billion DM into atomic research, and a significant portion of this money has gone to Siemens (*USW* 196). Delius mentions a partnership with the Westinghouse Corporation in the USA[77] and adds that the nuclear industry is one of "der lukrativsten und zukunftsträchtigten Weltmärkten" (*USW* 197; one of the most lucrative world markets, with a most promising future). The fact that the nuclear industry has close links to the military is obvious: "versteht sich für den Kenner der Materie von selbst" (*USW* 197; An expert on this subject will know that this is self-evident). Here the text invokes an unspecified "expert" authority to justify the shift from nuclear power to nuclear weapons technology and continues, "Das vielfältige Ineinander von Kerntechnik, Raumfahrt- und Rüstungstechnik läßt es uns auch geraten erscheinen, die Ratifizierung des Atomwaffensperrvertrages nicht zu fördern" (*USW* 197; Given the multiple interconnections between nuclear engineering, space technology, and defense technology, it seems advisable to us not to encourage the ratification of the Nuclear Nonproliferation Treaty). The scientific, measured register of the language allows the narrator to sound impartial: it seems "geraten" (advisable) to continue the nuclear arms race because it propels the space race (for example, in terms of the similar technology used for nuclear missiles and space rockets, or in terms of the satellite technology employed both for military and exploratory purposes). To dispense with nuclear technology, it is argued, would harm scientific progress in general. Accordingly, the text justifies military production in terms of both scientific progress and profit margins: "Denn zum einen ist die militärische Technik immer noch der Hauptschrittmacher der technischen Entwicklung, zum andern sichert der Rüstungssektor immer noch die ertragreichsten Geschäfte" (*USW* 205; First, military technology still sets the pace in terms of technical innovation; second, the defense sector still guarantees the most-profitable contracts). Ironically, the narrator believes that a thousand new fighter jets will bring "emancipation" (*USW* 206), which is conceived here in terms of military superiority. The other strategy the narrator uses to exclude ethical concerns is his claim that "kein Unternehmen von der Größe unseres Hauses kann es sich heute leisten, die rüstungstechnische Entwicklung zu ignorieren" (*USW* 205; today, no enterprise of our magnitude can afford to ignore developments in defense technology). Here the logic of magnitude takes over: the bigger the company, the more imperative it is to participate in arms manufacturing in order to maintain its dominant market share. This implies that the bigger the business, the less it can afford to care about ethics.

Delius examines other contrived arguments for nuclear weapons in *Konservativ in 30 Tagen*, which is composed mainly of quotations from the *Frankfurter Allgemeine Zeitung*. According to the *FAZ*, old fashioned concepts of "war" and "peace" are misleading:

Die Perspektiven von Krieg and Frieden selber haben längst die althergebrachten Gesinnungsfarben verloren. Ehedem galt, daß Rüstung auf Krieg, Abrüstung auf Frieden zuliefe. Nun haben wir erfahren, daß die Atomwaffen wenn nicht den Frieden, so doch eine Epoche des Nicht-Krieges gewährleistet haben.[78]

[Perspectives on war and peace have lost their traditional colors of thought long ago. Formerly armament was considered to be a move toward war, disarmament a move toward peace. Now we have learned from experience that although nuclear weapons do not guarantee peace, they have certainly guaranteed an era of nonwarfare.]

According to this logic, the best way to guarantee peace is to be armed to the teeth; pacifism is dangerously naive; and denuclearization would be a tragedy because it would leave Europe exposed to the risk of Russian invasion.[79] The central argument here is: "Soldaten leisten für den Frieden mehr als die Wehrdienstverweigerer" (Soldiers achieve more for peace than conscientious objectors).[80] By means of such clever inversions, military invasions are justified as humanitarian interventions, and pacifists are dismissed as dangerous lunatics. Of course, this military logic requires a constant build-up of arms and regular weapons upgrades, which increases the profits of corporations such as Siemens.

This rhetoric of militarization is already in place in *Unsere Siemens-Welt* when the narrator observes that technology has developed to such an extent that it is now almost impossible to make a clear distinction between civil and military production: "Auch wenn sich die Grenze zwischen der zivilen und militärischen Produktion und Forschung immer weniger exakt ziehen läßt . . ." (*USW* 205; Even if it is becoming increasingly difficult to draw a line between civil and military production and research . . .). It has become easy to retool civilian technology for military purposes:

in unserer hochtechnisierten Gesellschaft [sind] die Grenzen zwischen militärischen und nichtmilitärischen Produkten so fließend geworden, daß wir bei Bedarf beispielsweise in unseren Kernforschungszentren in relativ kurzer Zeit eine Atombombe herstellen oder einen Wettersatelliten auf militärische Ziele umpolen können. (*USW* 207–8)

[in our highly technologized society the boundary between military and nonmilitary production has become so fluid that, if need be, we could produce an atom bomb relatively quickly in one of our nuclear research centers, or we could refunction a weather satellite for military purposes.]

In this military-industrial complex, human concerns are subordinated to the military logic of the production flow.[81]

Conclusion: The Rhetoric of Cooperation and Partnership

Recent study of transnational corporations (TNCs) refutes the liberal economic theory of the self-regulating "free" market. In the global economy of the early twenty-first century the so-called free market tends to be dominated by a small number of large corporations that maintain close links to governments through lobbying and personal contacts.[82] *Unsere Siemens-Welt* shows that the firm has always preferred this way of doing business. The firm's priority is "verstärkte Bemühungen um staatliche und öffentliche Aufträge" (*USW* 213; intensified efforts to gain state and public contracts). We learn that before Werner von Siemens founded Siemens, he was an army officer and government official with a place and a vote on the Prussian telegraph commission, which enabled him to award himself his own contracts (*USW* 148). When he stood down from this role, he was replaced by a close friend (*USW* 148). The firm expanded with the financial assistance of his cousin Georg Siemens (1839–1901), cofounder and director of Deutsche Bank (*USW* 153). Werner von Siemens also had a hand in the new German patent law of 1877, which ensured that his firm could exploit any new patents registered (*USW* 156).[83] As the anonymous narrator comments: "[Das zeigt] die Potenz einer Firma, die ihre kommerziellen und technischen Interessen außergewöhnlich taktvoll auf die des Staates und seiner führenden Männer abzustimmen wußte" (*USW* 162; [This shows] the potency of a firm that knew, with extreme tact, how to harmonize its commercial and technical interests with those of the state and its leading men.) It is worth noting the double meaning of the verb "abstimmen" here: it can mean "to harmonize" and "to vote"; in this way the verb suggests a musical metaphor ("reading from the same hymn sheet") as well as political lobbying. The associated noun "Stimme" can mean both "voice" and "vote." This chain of associations suggests that the success of Siemens is based on the political skill of its directors, who, like politicians, achieve power and influence by means of the orchestration of voices and votes. This is the point of the section in *Unsere Siemens-Welt* on the directors of Siemens and their many positions of influence, detailing the "viele Beziehungen auf vielen Ebenen" (*USW* 275; many connections on many levels) the firm enjoys. Thanks to this networking, Siemens is "verhaftet" (*USW* 275; embedded) into the political and economic landscape of Germany. As Quintus Tullius Cicero, brother of the famous orator, once advised in a political campaign manual written in 64 BC, *Commentariolum petitionis* (*How to Win an Election*): "You should work with diligence to secure supporters from a wide variety of backgrounds. Most important among these are men with distinguished reputations. . . . Make friends with any man who holds great influence."[84] Or, as Colin Crouch observes: "Political power and economic wealth are mutually convertible currencies."[85] Whether ancient or modern, the essential strategy remains the same: businessmen and politicians must continuously extend influence and support in order to succeed. This strategy applies to the media, as well: the narrator remarks that magazines that print negative publicity can be threatened with a boycott (*USW* 249).

The narrator boasts that the Siemens corporation owes much of its success to its ability to win government contracts:

> Unsere Stärke gründet u.a. darauf, daß wir sowohl die Wünsche der öffentliche Hand (Post, Bahn, Militär, Verwaltung, Energieversorgung) wie die der Industrie (Investitionsgüter) als auch die der Privatverbraucher (Konsumgüter) erfüllen. (*USW* 194)

> [Our strength is based inter alia on the fact that we fulfill the wishes of public spending (postal service, railways, military, governance, energy supplies), those of industry (capital goods), as well as those of the private consumer (consumer goods).]

From the narrator's perspective, every "Marktposition" (market position) is also a "Machtposition" (position of power) that gives the firm a greater say ("Mitsprache") in political and economic decisions (*USW* 195). These are not new insights, but they are particularly relevant in the context of twenty-first-century "governance," the business-management equivalent of political organization, as state functions are increasingly exercised by private companies and other international organizations.[86] The narrator of the Festschrift confidently embraces the rhetoric of international cooperation and global economic liberalization, as if to imply that Siemens is working "für unser aller Wohlstand" (*USW* 228; for the prosperity of all). But such phrases ring hollow when juxtaposed with Siemens's collaborations with white South Africa and support of the Portuguese dictatorship and its military adventures in Angola (*USW* 228). If we read between the lines of this smooth discourse, the underlying motive appears:

> Immer interessanter werden auch die Möglichkeiten einer noch stärkeren internationalen Kooperation . . . um den finanziellen und politischen Gegebenheiten des Weltmarkts und den Notwendigkeiten seiner optimalen Aufteilung Rechnung zu tragen. (*USW* 233)

> [Ever more interesting are the possibilities for stronger international cooperation . . . in order to take into account the financial and political conditions of the world market and the necessity for it to be shared out optimally.]

The key phrase here is "optimale Aufteilung" (optimal sharing). What is to be "optimized" here is not solutions to problems facing humanity such as poverty, war, disease, and pollution, but a share of the market. At such moments, the marketing discourse is revealed as a cynical ploy. What counts is not the substance of the project but the substance of the pitch.[87]

Business rhetoric always works best if you already have the audience in your pocket. *Unsere Siemens-Welt* delights in tracing a web of close partnerships between corporations and government. The risk of monopoly formation here is obvious.[88] In 2007 Siemens and ten other companies were investigated by the European Commission for price fixing in EU electricity markets between 1988 and 2004. Although Siemens was alleged to play a leadership role in these activities, it received full immunity from fines because it was the first company to come forward with information about the cartel.[89] That same year, however, it was fined €396,562,500 in another cartel case.[90] In December 2008 Siemens agreed to pay $1.34 billion in fines to American and European authorities "to settle charges that it routinely used bribes and slush funds to secure huge public works contracts around the world."[91] Greek state prosecutors are still pursuing sixty-four Siemens executives who are accused of bribing Greek officials to secure exclusive contracts in the 1990s and during the 2004 Olympic Games in Athens.[92] There is plenty of material that could be used to write a contemporary update of Delius's Festschrift. Since it was published in 1972, our world has become more corporate than ever.

8: Producing Ethos in Kathrin Röggla's *wir schlafen nicht*, 2004

> *weil das natürlich für unternehmen*
> *sehr entscheidend sei—die frage "wie*
> *kommuniziere ich"* . . . *wie man*
> *vertrauen herstellen könne*
> [because of course that was really
> decisive for companies—the question
> "how do I communicate" . . . how one
> could manufacture trust]
> —Kathrin Röggla

Introduction: No More Rest Periods

IN AN INTERVIEW published in the *Frankfurter Allgemeine Zeitung* on November 14, 2015, Janina Kugel, personnel director of Siemens, explained that employment law needs to be changed in response to digitalization, adding that she often debates this issue with government representatives. Kugel argued that "die vorgeschriebenen Ruhezeiten" (mandatory rest periods) are "Unsinn" (nonsense) because of flextime.[1] According to Kugel, it is not efficient to calculate whether or not the employee was offline long enough to comply with the rest periods— quite an ironic statement, given that Siemens specializes in data processing. Therefore, she says, rest periods should be abolished: "Das passt nicht mehr in die Zeit" (It is no longer appropriate today).[2] This genre of managerial discourse is echoed and examined by Kathrin Röggla (b. 1971) in *wir schlafen nicht* (2004; *We Never Sleep*), which derives from a series of interviews she conducted with German-speaking finance experts based in New York. Her first interviewee was an investment banker for Morgan Stanley, whom she visited in his office in midtown Manhattan.[3] Although *wir schlafen nicht* is ostensibly set at a trade fair in Germany (the location is most reminiscent of Düsseldorf), Röggla's use of US-based source material is justified by the global interconnectedness of the German economy. Like Delius's *Unsere Siemens-Welt* in the previous chapter, *wir schlafen nicht* is documentary fiction and represents an investigation into a particular genre of corporate rhetoric. The economic environment changed considerably, however, in the three decades between Delius's text and Röggla's, particularly in terms of deregulation.

From the 1980s onward there have been successive waves of deregulation and privatization in Western economies. The collapse of the Soviet bloc in 1989–90 and the reunification of Germany intensified this process. Since the 1980s, "deregulation" is often promoted as a way to make industries more competitive, although, as David Graeber has noted, it usually meant the opposite, marking a shift from "managed competition between mid-sized firms" to a situation where "a handful of financial conglomerates . . . dominate the market."[4] For Graeber the word *deregulation* itself is a convenient fiction, affixed to each new regulatory measure in order to frame it as a way to reduce bureaucracy.[5] At the same time, the "new credo" is that "everyone should look at the world through the eyes of an investor."[6] In *Unsere Siemens-Welt* the Siemens management is fundamentally opposed to collective bargaining, preferring to negotiate separately with each individual employee. In *wir schlafen nicht* there is a sense that this situation has been fully achieved: the characters have no sense of solidarity, no trade union affiliation. Indeed, these management consultants are paid to rationalize businesses (i.e., to fire people). They typify what Ulrich Beck has called "a generalization of employment insecurity."[7] This is the brave new business world that Röggla investigates in *wir schlafen nicht*, a world in which every job is constantly under threat. In *wir schlafen nicht* the characters know that their jobs can be restructured out of existence at any time. They know this because it is their job to restructure other people's jobs out of existence.

Initial research on *wir schlafen nicht* focused on linguistic features, such as the text's frequent use of the subjunctive mood, especially in reported speech (*Konjunktiv I*), which is well suited to conveying the sense of insecurity and backbiting that characterizes this workplace.[8] The next phase of the novel's reception is characterized by sociological readings.[9] David Clarke and Elaine Martin have stressed the way the characters seem trapped in a kind of undead, zombielike existence.[10] Anna Katharina Schaffner is ambivalent about the novel's use of the subjunctive; for her it is both a symptom of alienation and dislocation and a potentially liberating, distancing Brechtian *Verfremdungseffekt*.[11] In short, the subjunctive achieves a disconnection from lived experience, whether for better or for worse. This chapter takes the sociology of crisis and Sprachkritik as its starting points, but its main purpose is to draw out some affinities between the novel's "bwler-deutsch" (*wsn* 219; "business admin jargon," *WNS* 195) and classical rhetoric (*bwl* is an acronym for *Betriebswirtschaftslehre*, business administration). It starts with a brief discussion of the historical context and the linguistic context and then moves on to consider the relevance of classical rhetoric to modern business communication, specifically in terms of self-presentation, the projection of *ethos* (character), and the anticipation of audience response.

Crisis and the Restructuring of the Job Market

Röggla's corporate world is characterized by a sense of constant crisis. Like Delius, she is well aware that an economic crisis can be useful as an instrument of leverage. Delius calls this "das Phänomen der Krise als kalkulierbares Instrument" (*USW* 262–63; the phenomenon of the crisis as a calculable instrument). The idea that capitalism is linked to crisis is not new. Joseph Schumpeter argued that capitalism involves creative destruction, as the means of production are constantly revolutionized.[12] In an essay first published in 2009, soon after the financial crisis of 2007–8, Röggla cites Naomi Klein's point that companies can make capital from political crises.[13] Röggla also reports on a talk entitled "Das Unerwartete managen" (Managing the Unexpected), in which the speaker, Kathleen Sutcliffe, argues that the elite crisis-management teams—the "high-reliability teams" deployed in catastrophic situations (natural or man-made disasters)—should serve as a model for normal businesses.[14] Röggla concludes, "Die Katastrophenbewältigung ist nicht mehr alleine an den Ausnahmezustand gebunden, sondern ist in den unternehmerischen Alltag geraten" (Crisis management is no longer associated solely with a state of emergency; instead, it has become part of everyday business practice).[15]

wir schlafen nicht, published in 2004 before the global financial crisis, already reflects a sense of crisis that was in the air after the Enron scandal of 2001. Chapter 9 of the book is titled "pleiten" ("bankruptcies"). It features five of the six characters: the partner, the senior associate, the tech assistant, the online editor, and the key account manager. They almost form a chorus, suggesting that rumors of insolvencies are everywhere. The online editor complains, "das krisengerede, das permanente, habe sie auch langsam satt" (*wsn* 65; "she was also getting sick of the constant crisis talk," *WNS* 57). As Jonathan Crary points out, in a crisis there is no time to sleep, and this informs the new office culture in which employees are expected to work around the clock and keep their rest periods to a minimum.[16] The constant threat of firing is a powerful motivational tool. *wir schlafen nicht* features a character known as the "McKinsey king," who works for the McKinsey consultancy firm and is described as a snake eyeing up a bunch of rabbits (*wsn* 42; *WNS* 38).[17] McKinsey is known for its policy of "up or out," which requires staff to achieve promotion within a fixed time limit to keep their jobs. As a result of this personal review cycle, first introduced in 1954, only one in five new employees stay at the company for five years or more.[18] McKinsey has similar schemes for senior management, too, titled: "grow or go," "lead or leave." Such punitive performance reviews are now widely used in many sectors, with most forms of employment becoming increasingly precarious. At one point, the IT technician sees a group of technicians looking for work and assumes that they come from developing countries or from Russia. The key account manager replies that they might not be foreigners—there are plenty of unemployed locals, as well (*wsn* 41; *WNS* 37).

In *wir schlafen nicht* it is the figure of the "praktikantin" (intern) who embodies the sense of exhaustion and hopelessness about the job market. In section 12, "erst mal reinkommen" ("getting a foot in the door"), she complains that her biggest problems are her lack of connections and the fact that she does not have the right kind of parents. Her competitors benefit from having "ihre steuerberatereltern und wirtschaftsprüfereltern" (*wsn* 88; "their tax-consultant parents and their cpa parents," *WNS* 77). People tell her that she needs mentors, but she disagrees: mentors do not help very much (*wsn* 89; *WNS* 77). She is expected to do an internship, but it is hard to get one that is financed (*wsn* 89; *WNS* 78). Her job is idiotic, and it is completely unpaid; she cannot even pay into a health insurance scheme (*wsn* 89; *WNS* 78). But her situation could be much worse: increasingly, people have to pay to do an internship: "zahlen, daß man arbeiten darf" (*wsn* 90; "pay for the privilege of working," *WNS* 78). Charging for internships is justified by citing expenses, overheads, or training costs: "sie verkauften jetzt eine arbeit immer als ausbildung" (*wsn* 90; "now they always sold a job as training," *WNS* 78). Paying to be allowed to work: at first glance it seems outrageously unfair, even criminal. The intern can, however, see the logic behind this way of thinking. Why shouldn't a leading company seek to capitalize on its own prestige? "das liege doch auf der hand, daß auch ein attraktiver arbeitsplatz einen marktwert habe und an den meistbietenden verkauft werden könne" (*wsn* 90; "of course it was obvious that even an attractive job had a market value and could be sold to the highest bidder," *WNS* 79). The intern is so disillusioned that she starts to doubt whether a job market exists anymore: "als wäre nichts geschehen, als gäbe es noch einen arbeitsmarkt" (*wsn* 158; "as if nothing had happened, as if there were still a job market," *WNS* 139). Toward the end of the novel the intern's story descends into the realms of gothic horror. She describes a world where executives walk over the corpses of failed job applicants: "wie sie bewerbungsleichen geflissentlich übersähen, ja, direkt über sie stolperten, weil sie ihnen langsam den weg versperrten" (*wsn* 158; "the way they deliberately overlooked the job application corpses, yes, actually tripped over them because they were slowly beginning to block the way," *WNS* 139). Here the narrative suggests the uncanny viciousness of the rat race, inviting comparisons with Christian Petzold's film *Yella* (2007), in which the protagonist bullies a cash-strapped *Mittelständler* into committing suicide. The partner declares that he has "nur das gefühl, durch eine permanente katastrophe zu gehen, einen permanenten kriegszustand wahrzunehmen" (*wsn* 215; "only the feeling of going through a constant catastrophe, to be aware of the constant state of war," *WNS* 191), which recalls the statement in Ingeborg Bachmann's *Malina* that "es gibt nicht Krieg und Frieden. . . . Es ist

Krieg" (*M* 193; "it isn't war and peace. . . . It's war" *Ma* 120–21). When the key account manager says that she did not emerge alive from her experiences (*wsn* 151), it recalls the undead existence of Petzold's Yella, who only achieves a white-collar career after she has died in a car crash.

Sprachkritik for the Twenty-First Century

Classical rhetoric often becomes decisive at a time of crisis, when quick decisions are required.[19] Although Röggla does not refer explicitly to classical rhetoric, she is influenced by contemporary discourse analysis and the new management idiom that emerged in the 1990s, "full of bright, empty terms like vision, quality, stakeholder, leadership, excellence, innovation, strategic goals, or best practices."[20] Röggla deserves credit for the critical attention she brings to bear on this sort of corporate jargon, which harks back to the modernist tradition of Sprachkritik.[21] She explains that when she conducted the interviews for *wir schlafen nicht*, she decided to adopt an entirely uncritical attitude: "Ich hatte den Eindruck, als würde diese Art der hysterischen Affirmation sie in ihre eigenen Widersprüche hineintreiben" (I had the impression that this type of hysterical affirmation would get them entangled in their own contradictions).[22] This remark neatly encapsulates the narrative technique of *wir schlafen nicht*, in which the interview material has been carefully stylized and poeticized by the author in order to exaggerate its own inherent contradictions.

This does not mean, however, that the narrative voice is able to escape the exploitative logic of the system she describes. It might seem that the narrator/interviewer does have a form of independence: when she finally appears in person at the end of the novel, the word *ich* (I) is used for the very first time. Until this point, all the characters have avoided using the first-person pronoun, using instead the impersonal pronoun *man* (one), which suggests a loss of individuality and a submersion in the crowd. The shift from *man* to *ich* at the end appears to promise some kind of liberation, and this possibility is supported by the title of the final chapter: "wiederbelebung: ich" (*wsn* 219; "revival," *WNS* 195). Röggla has rejected this interpretation, however, pointing out that the narrator/interviewer is just as manipulative as the characters she interviews: "Der Erzählergeist war der diabolische Geist der Unternehmensberater selbst. . . . Die Erzählinstanz nimmt so gesehen nur scheinbar eine Außenperspektive ein" (The spirit of the narration was the diabolical spirit of the management consultants themselves. . . . Thus the narrative instance only appears to adopt an outside perspective).[23] The fact that the narrator/interviewer herself is implicated in the process of manipulation and exploitation means that the narrative is inherently unreliable, and no one is to be trusted, not even the narrator herself. And, although the characters go on strike against the narrator in the penultimate chapter, refusing to comment any further, we should note that this is only a symbolic strike, as there is no mention of any employment contract between the narrator and the characters. The question of whether the narrator is exploiting her characters remains unresolved.

No one is impartial here, and particularly not the management consultants, despite the fact that they try to insist on their impartiality: "Und doch pocht gerade diese Branche auf ihre Neutralität" (And yet it is precisely this industry that insists on its own neutrality).[24] Neutrality is, almost always, a convenient fiction that disguises a personal agenda. Professionals like to profess their dedication to their duty, concealing the motive of personal profit. The more "professional" you appear, the more you can charge for your services. Röggla's executives thus pride themselves on their professionalism and constantly invoke their business expertise. The McKinsey consultant always insists on the basic principles of business management, stating, "das ist grundkenntnis" (*wsn* 44; "that's basic knowledge," *WNS* 40). He puts down his rivals by telling them that they need to "einen grundkurs in bwl absolvieren" (*wsn* 45; "pass a basic course in business administration," *WNS* 40). Professionalism is closely related to what the classical theory of rhetoric calls *ethos* (character), the most powerful means of persuasion.[25] Technical jargon reinforces *ethos* and is an effective way to confuse the uninitiated: "Jede Fachsprache [übt] ihren Reiz aus" (Every technical language has its own particular charm).[26]

Wir schlafen nicht takes the reader on an entertaining tour of *Bwl-Deutsch* (business admin jargon), an arcane professional discourse that thrives on Anglicisms and neologisms. Although she belongs to this executive class, the online editor expresses her outrage at the slick patter of her peers. She is surprised that these words do not stick in people's throats: "allein der jargon. es wundere sie ohnehin, daß man den ungestraft auf dauer anwenden könne. es wundere sie, daß da nichts passiere, daß da niemand explodiere oder ersticke an den sachen" (*wsn* 115; "just the *jargon* alone. she was amazed that you could use it constantly with impunity. she was amazed that nothing happened, that no one exploded or choked on the things," *WNS* 98–99).[27] Readers of *wir schlafen nicht* could well find themselves sharing the online editor's outrage—this is German, but not as we know it. It is a German of the business elites, and it shows clearly how elites can fence themselves off by employing an exclusive register of language. The language of financial elites is just as bureaucratic as that of any government administration.

The job titles of these consultants are ostentatious: "ja, das ist schon eine ganz schöne show mit den bezeichnungen" (*wsn* 33; "you know, it's really quite a *show* with the titles," *WNS* 30). They also have handy phrases at their disposal to cover up any contentious issues, phrases that are intended to give the impression of professionalism:

man spreche von "unterschiedlichen unternehmenskulturen," weil
niemand genau sagen könne, was das sei, und deswegen alles in
diesem erklärungsmodell untergebracht werden könne. "unter-
schiedliche unternehmenskulturen" seien genauso wie "harte bwl"
schimären. aber so was behalte man, wie gesagt, besser für sich.
(*wsn* 56)

[people talked about "different corporate cultures" because no one
could say exactly what that meant, and that's why everything could
be subsumed under this explanatory model. "different corporate cultures" are chimeras, just like "solid business administration practices."
but it was better to keep such things to oneself. (*WNS 49*)]

The partner's view that the notion of "different corporate cultures" is a
hoax is echoed by Wolfgang Streeck, who argues that the "varieties of
capitalism" theory is misleading because the dominant trends have always
come from the USA.[28] But there is also a more subversive suggestion here:
namely, that "solid business administration practice" itself is a mirage.
There is a sense of the Emperor's New Clothes here. Moray MacLennan,
the CEO of the international advertising agency M&C Saatchi, makes the
same point in a much more offensive way: when he became a company
director at age twenty-six, "I was helped by management guru Tom Peters
who said, 'There is only one thing that you ever need to know in business—no one has a f***ing clue what they are doing.'"[29] Provocations
aside, it is evident that in Röggla's text the characters use business rhetoric
as a smokescreen, to prevent other people from getting too close. They are
performing according to the accepted rules of a game. One rule is that the
semblance of teamwork must be maintained at all costs:

man gerate ja auf so projekten immer in eine ganz eigene gesprächslogik
und gesprächsmuster hinein, also beispielsweise würde man nur noch
insiderwitze reißen. ja es seien dann insiderwitze und insidergespräche,
das bekomme durchaus was sektenhaftes, wenn man so wolle.
(*wsn* 73)

[on these kinds of projects you fell into a completely different conversational logic and conversational register, for example you'd only tell
insider jokes. yes, there were *insider* jokes and *insider* conversations,
it really did become something like a sect, if you will. (*WNS* 64)]

Language here is not a tool used to communicate with people; it is a
defense mechanism designed to keep people out, to distance people and
prevent them asking too many challenging questions. Behind every conversation there is an agenda: "den strategischen anteil, der jedes gespräch
durchziehe" (*wsn* 83; "the strategic component that ran through every
conversation," *WNS* 72). The default genre of discourse is the sales pitch:
"hier werde ja nur noch in kategorien von werbung und öffentlichkeitsar-

beit gedacht, jeder ansprechspartner wird hier doch automatisch zum kunden oder zu einer art kunde, einem 'klienten,' wie sie sagten. ob das noch nicht aufgefallen sei?" (*wsn* 114; "around here, the only framework they thought in anymore was advertising and publicity. every contact automatically became a customer or at least a sort of customer, a 'client' as they said. haven't you noticed?" *WNS* 98). Given that this is the dominant mode of interaction, it is hardly surprising that many characters try to avoid having discussions with each other. The key account manager complains that her colleagues cannot be bothered to listen to her, and they find various excuses to avoid having to listen: "im grunde sei sie von lauter unansprechbarkeiten umgeben" (*wsn* 118; "in reality, she was just surrounded by nothing but aloofness," *WNS* 102).

There is a sense of fatalism in *wir schlafen nicht*, as Röggla's characters seem doomed to rehearse the commercial language that imprisons them. Only occasionally do they attain glimmers of insight into their situation; e.g., when the online editor asks, "die frage sei doch die: in wessen durchhalteparolen stecke man drin? ja, in wessen durchhalteparolen halte man sich versteckt?" (*wsn* 189; "that was the question: whose never-say-die slogans were they stuck in? yes, whose never-say-die slogans were they hiding behind?" *WNS* 167). The employees seem trapped within their own discursive practices: "man hat sich nur immer in dem ewigen beraterwitz aufgehalten . . . da hat man sich eine ganze weile aufgehalten" (*wsn* 41; "we did also talk about the ever-popular consultant joke . . . we spent a pretty long time on that," *WNS* 36). The repetition clearly conveys the interminable, tautological nature of this discourse. In this way, the employees are stuck in the "durchhalteparolen" ("never-say-die slogans") of their managers.[30] These mantras with which they encourage themselves are not their own phrases; rather, they have internalized the instructions of their managers. In Freudian terms this would be the superego, but Röggla is working within a Foucauldian framework. Foucault has shown the way in which Enlightenment discourses of self-actualization can lead individuals to internalize mechanisms of control. Röggla cites Foucault's 1978 essay on "governmentality," which examines how people are governed by means of "self-governing" techniques.[31] According to Foucault, truth-finding discourses are an essential component of the exercise of power.[32]

Röggla's reading of Foucault leads her to see management discourse as part of an omnipresent ideology. She defines this management discourse as

> ein Herrschaftsinstrument, dem wir nicht entkommen können. Überall stoßen wir, in Managementdiskursen wie in den Lebenshilfetipps der Frauenzeitschriften, auf Konzepte, Programme und Rationalitäten mit all ihren Widersprüchen, deren prominentester das Suggerieren von Freiheit, Entscheidungsfreiheit und Partizipation ist.[33]

[an instrument of control that we cannot escape. In management discourses and in the lifestyle tips of women's magazines, everywhere, we encounter concepts, programs, and rationalities with all their contradictions, the most prominent one being the suggestion of freedom, freedom of decision and participation.]

Here, Röggla picks up on the contradiction involved when advertisements tell us to be free and "just do" what we want. This connects with Foucault's point that ideology invokes the spirit of liberation precisely in order to tie people down more firmly. He argues that the project of self-realization becomes a means of control as individuals choose freely to subordinate their will to authorities and institutions.[34] Foucault's analysis of voluntary subordination is echoed in Röggla's text when the characters discuss the question of whether or not they have been kidnapped:

—und außerdem: man ist ja nicht direkt hierher entführt worden, nein, das kann man nicht sagen, man ist ja aus freien stücken hierhergelangt.
—nein, von einer entführung kann man nicht reden. . . .
—wenn, dann müßte es sich um eine länger angelegte entführung handeln, als eine, die schon länger am laufen ist. (*wsn* 128)

[—and besides that: no one has been kidnapped and brought here against their will. no, you couldn't say that, they had all come here here of their own free will.
—no, you couldn't call it a kidnapping . . .
—if it were, then it would have to be about a kidnapping with a longer term of investment, one that had been going on for a longer period of time. (*WNS* 112)]

In this way, the characters' quest for freedom has transformed into its reverse. Ideology invites us to collude, and we do the rest of the work. As Karin Krauthausen puts it, "Auch Freiheit und konsensuelle Handlungsformen sind in die Untersuchung von Machtverhältnissen einzubeziehen" (Freedom and consensual forms of action also need to be included in the investigation of power relations).[35] Röggla explores the ways in which the language of freedom can be used to keep people in captivity.[36]

Producing and Dismantling *Ethos*

Although Röggla does not refer explicitly to classical rhetoric in her work, its principles are implied in a lecture given in 2007 where she explains that credibility is created by means of gestures that can be learned: "Dabei weiß jeder, dass Glaubwürdigkeit in den Medien ein Effekt ist, von Rahmungen und Kontexten abhängig und über kommunikativen Gesten hergestellt" (Everyone knows that credibility in the media is an effect that depends on framing and contexts, and is produced by means of communicative gestures).[37] The affinities between Röggla's work and classical rhetoric are thus evident in her view of top managers as "top convincers" who are paid to "create credibility": "Die Topüberzeuger wissen jedenfalls eine Menge zu erzählen über die Erzeugung von Glaubwürdigkeit oder ihre Demontage, es ist ja auch ihr Geschäft" (In any case, the top convincers can tell you a lot about how to create credibility or how to dismantle it—it is their job, after all).[38] "Glaubwürdigkeit" (credibility) relates to the classical conception of *ethos* (character), which, according to Aristotle, is the strongest and most effective proof of oratory.[39] In *wir schlafen nicht* the key account manager knows that her most important professional competence is communication, and, specifically, the ability to create trust: "wie man vertrauen herstellen könne" (*wsn* 52; "how one could manufacture trust" *WNS* 46). Röggla's "top persuaders" are thus the modern counterparts to classical orators, and their instruments remain the same: rhetoric, and, specifically, the production of *ethos*. *Ethos* is of paramount importance because it expresses relations of shared interest and sympathy between the speaker and the audience. *Ethos* takes precedence over *logos* (argument) because it establishes the framework of interests within which arguments will be interpreted. Röggla expresses this awareness when she writes,

> Sie [die Topüberzeuger] wissen, dass nichts allein für sich faktischen Charakter hat, sondern stets in Interessens- und Interpretationsverhältnissen steht, was sie natürlich ungerne öffentlich sagen. Denn die Öffentlichkeit, und sei es nur die Betriebsöffentlichkeit, bleibt der Ort, wo man lieber den "Fakten, Fakten, Fakten"—Ruf eines Herrn Markwort inszeniert, zumindest, wenn man eine Situation beherrschen möchte.[40]

> [They [the top persuaders] know that nothing has a factual character by itself alone, but that it is always related to interests and interpretations. They do not like to admit this in public, of course. Because the public sphere, even if it is only the company employees, is the place where they prefer to stage Mr. Markwort's demand for "facts, facts, facts," at least when they want to control a situation.]

In other words, these modern orators know that facts are actually secondary to the persona the orators project, the rapport they have with the audience, and the interests that are at stake. While they use this knowledge to inform their rhetoric, however, managers must be careful not to reveal these tricks. They like to present themselves as practical individuals with a strong grasp of the facts, and they say things like "gegen verkaufszahlen lasse sich eben nicht anargumentieren" (*wsn* 48; "one couldn't argue against sales figures," *WNS* 42). Actually, though, the emphasis on "facts" and "figures" directs attention away from conflicts of interest; it directs attention away from more delicate issues, and, at the same time, it bolsters the speakers' personal *ethos*. It is not so much the facts and figures themselves but, rather, the impression of objectivity and professionalism that is at stake. What business managers require above all is *ethos*: they must personify the professional values they preach. As the business expert Fritz J. Roethlisberger puts it, a successful middle manager must, above all things, be an example for others.[41] In this respect, modern management wisdom is in accordance with Aristotle.

The characters in *wir schlafen nicht* build up their own *ethos* by continually asserting their eagerness to work. For example, the intern suggests that she would pull out all the stops to get a job: "nein, sie wisse nicht, zu was sie bereit wäre, um einen job zu kriegen, das wisse sie nicht, sie vermute mal zu einigem" (*wsn* 92; "no, she didn't know what she'd be preapred to do to get a job. that she didn't know for sure but she guessed she would be willing to go quite far," *WNS* 80). The partner says that he could not imagine ever being unemployed (*wsn* 172; *WNS* 152). The key account manager seems proud of the fact that she cannot take it easy: "'deine leistungsmentalität, die dich eines tages begraben wird,' habe man gesagt, und diese leistungsmentalität habe man schon bei ihrer mutter festgestellt" (*wsn* 199; "'your performance mentality, that's going to bury you some day,' they had said, and they had also seen this performance mentality in her mother," *WNS* 177). She is proud of her determination to perform, even if it could cause her early death through a work-related illness. The partner goes a step further and boasts that he has no sense of his own mortality: perhaps he just left it lying around somewhere. Because he lacks a sense of his own mortality, he is able to get his workload done (*wsn* 200; *WNS* 178).

Achieving this level of performance requires almost superhuman efforts. The online editor admits that there is something almost fascistic about this doctrine of self-sacrifice: "sie selbst sei ja schon so ein bißchen eine faschopersönlichkeit (*lacht*)" (*wsn* 144; "she was a bit of a fascistic personality herself [laughs]," *WNS* 127).[42] She tries to turn this into a joke, but it has the ring of truth. The profession is like a war of attrition in which only the most resourceful will survive. What matters is the rhetoric of self-discipline: "also leistung, effizienz und durchsetzungskraft seien bei ihr positiv besetzte werte, und es sei auch schon wahr, sie bewundere menschen durchaus, die sich überwinden könnten" (*wsn* 144; "productivity, efficiency, the ability to get things done are positive values. and it was also true that she admired people who could push beyond their own limits," *WNS* 127). In other words, the job requires people to act as if they are *Leistungsethiker* (those with a strict performance ethic) or perhaps even Nietzschean supermen. This uncompromising professional *ethos* affirmed by Röggla's characters seems, on one level, to be an exaggeration of the Protestant work ethic of worldly asceticism that Max Weber described over a century ago. Of course, Röggla's consultants have to play hard as well as work hard, which arguably makes things even more exhausting. A comparison with *Buddenbrooks*, however, suggests that, if anything, Röggla's characters are even more ascetic: the Buddenbrook family motto insists on the need to sleep soundly at night, but Röggla's faceless executives are denied this luxury. Thomas Buddenbrook fears he is becoming an actor, but Röggla's key account manager fears that she is becoming a machine: "[eine maschine] wolle sie nicht sein. nur einigermaßen klappen sollen die abläufe, da müsse man schon ein wenig dahintersein und sich auch anpassen an die erfordernisse, die gerade so entstünden" (*wsn* 148; "she really didn't want to be a machine. it's just that the daily operations had to work out, more or less. so you had to get behind it somewhat and you had to adapt to the demands that ensued," *WNS* 130). On the one hand, this suggests a mechanical existence; but on the other hand, the verb *sich anpassen* (adapt) highlights the fact that these managers have to be far more flexible and adaptable than any machine. Actually, the machine metaphor is of very limited relevance here, because business managers need to communicate with other human beings. The machine metaphor is only one facet of the management persona; it is more important for managers to demonstrate "soft" skills such as communication and networking.

Business managers, like classical orators, have to build their personal authority. The Latin term for this is *auctoritas*, which defined as "an elusive but vital mix of personal impressiveness and charisma with influence and connections."[43] Röggla's characters like to rehearse their connections because it enhances their authority, asserting a sense of belonging to the financial elite:

> verwandtschaftsgeschichten würden immer dazugepackt, kleine anekdoten, zielanekdoten, würde sie sagen, deren einziger sinn und zweck sei zu beweisen, wie sehr man schon in dieser verwandtschaft parke, ja, geradezu in ihr versenkt sei. (*wsn* 157)

> [yes, relationships were spoken about to which she had no access, and stories about these connections and relationships were always packed into the narrative. little anecdotes, anecdotes with a moral, she would say, whose only point and purpose was to prove to her how well placed the others already were in these relationships. (*WNS* 138)]

The neologism *zielanekdoten* (literally, "targeted anecdotes") here is particularly telling. "Targeted anecdotes" serve a practical purpose: they assert the speaker's connections and ability to command the support of those who matter. Politicians often use anecdotes for precisely this reason: to show that they are in touch with common people.[44]

Classical rhetoricians advocated the continual practice of speechmaking, in order to refine the orator's skills. In a similar fashion, Röggla's characters like to take every opportunity to practice their persuasion skills. They test each other by inventing hypothetical scenarios and asking for the other person's opinion. This sets up a form of role-play: a simulation of a job interview. The persons asking the questions assert their authority, and at the same time, they test and potentially undermine the competence of the persons being interviewed. The intern dreams of escape, asserting that she has had enough of being invited to play such games: "sie verlasse jetzt diesen ewigen assessment-rausch, diesen test-modus, in dem alle gefangen seien. sie habe keine lust auf diese schein-situationen, diese bewerbungsspielchen" (*wsn* 156–57; "she was leaving this eternal *assessment* rush, this testing mode that everyone was caught up in. she had no desire to be caught up in this illusory situation, these little job application games," *WNS* 137). An example of these role-play situations is: "ich bin jetzt siemens, und du willst eine tochter von mir kaufen" (*wsn* 158; "now i'm siemens, and you want to buy one of my subsidiaries," *WNS* 138). These role-playing exercises are remarkably similar to the exercises Quintilian recommends as training for orators. In the *suasoria* exercise, students were asked to imagine themselves as a figure from history or mythology and to present an argument outlining their choice of action—for example, the question of whether Cato should marry.[45]

The importance of role-play in Röggla's text reflects the understanding that *ethos* is not an innate quality but a performative relation that emerges within a specific context or occasion. The key account manager explicitly distances herself from her public persona. She says "daß sie für lebendig gehalten werde, wo es nicht stimme" (*wsn* 198; "she was taken for being alive when it wasn't even the case," *WNS* 175). She even had the feeling that people were using her as a "lebendigkeitscreme" (*wsn* 198; "aliveness salve," *WNS* 176), applying her to any occasion in order to enliven the event, as if she were a cosmetic cream. This suggests that she often projects an *ethos* that she considers fake; her liveliness conceals her inner feeling of lifelessness.

Although the internet has led to an increase in visual communication, it also facilitates the transmission of the human voice, whether by Skype, podcast, online video, or vlog. Röggla's characters see themselves as public speakers, as orators, and this is shown when the partner describes his voice as "sein wichtigstes werkzeug" (*wsn* 107; "his most important tool," *WNS* 92). The chief instrument of the orator is the voice, and this shows the partner's awareness that public speaking, oratory, is the most essential aspect of his profession. Voices have great emotional and musical potential; they can be modulated to maximize the effect on the listeners. This is why the partner finds his sudden voice loss so devastating: "ja, er habe über nacht seine stimme verloren . . . und in seinem job müsse man eben eine stimme haben, ohne stimme laufe da gar nichts" (*wsn* 107; "yes, he had lost his voice . . . and in his *job* you really had to have a voice, without a voice nothing worked at all," *WNS* 92). This recalls the oral problems of the Buddenbrook family: without a voice you cannot get people to do what you want, because you have no voice to persuade them with. Given the centrality of the voice to communication, it is hardly surprising that there is a whole branch of medicine dedicated to the treatment of voice disorders (dysphonia).[46] It is significant that the tonality of the voice makes an emotional appeal to the listener. For this reason, it is appropriate that the partner's voice loss is cured by a nonrational means: hypnosis therapy (*wsn* 174; *WNS* 154). Since he uses his voice essentially as a form of hypnosis, it is fitting that his voice can only be restored by a professional hypnotist.[47] Because these consultants use their voices all the time, voice loss seems to be one of the principal forms of repetitive strain injury that goes with the job—the key account manager, too, has lost her voice temporarily (*wsn* 182; *WNS* 161). For the practiced orator, *ethos* is not an innate, intrinsic aspect of the personality but an interpersonal relationship that relies principally on the voice, on a projection of the voice.

Pitching to the Audience, Pleasing the Managers

In classical rhetoric, orators were required to know the audience extremely well so that they could pitch their speeches accordingly. Cicero remarks that the orator must "have his finger on the pulse of every class, every age group, every social rank."[48] A similar point is made by business expert Fritz J. Roethlisberger, who argues that the modern business manager must learn to communicate with various interest groups. Every one of these relationships involves a different set of interests and entails a different mode of communication.[49] According to Roethlisberger, communication skills are the key requirement of the managers and administrators of the future, and, specifically, they need to "have appreciation for a point of view different from their own."[50] Like Roethlisberger's foremen, Röggla's management consultants have to face a number of different audiences. Röggla discusses the consultants' multiple allegiances and the different audiences to whom they have to appeal:

> Berater haben schließlich als Auftraggeber einen Vorstand eines Unternehmens und müssen mit dessen einzelnen Abteilungen arbeiten. Sie sind außerdem ihrem eigenen Unternehmen verpflichtet und zudem manchmal den Interessen von externen Geldgebern, was natürlich in der konkreten beruflichen Alltagserfahrung zu ständigen Konflikten führt.[51]

[After all, consultants get a commission from the managing director of a company, and they have to work with the individual departments of that company. They also have to pursue the interests of their own firm, and sometimes, in addition to this, they also have to serve the interests of external funding agencies. Of course, this leads to continual conflicts in practice, in terms of everyday professional experience.]

Consultants are required to serve several different interests, and therefore they need to change perspective continually: "Unternehmensberater . . . müssen auch ihrer Position wechseln können bzw. unterschiedlichen, einander widersprechenden Interessen dienen" (Management consultants must be able to change their position, or rather, to serve different and conflicting interests).[52] Röggla's consultants need to shift their perspective constantly, depending on whether they are addressing colleagues from their own firm, or clients—managers and employees of the company they are being paid to advise or restructure—or technical specialists, or their own managers. The "flexibility" required of modern managers involves a similar competence to that of classical orators and lawyers, namely, the ability to put yourself into somebody else's position and formulate your language accordingly. Training in classical rhetoric involved the composition of *controversiae*, fictional law cases in which the student had to "act" either for the defense or the prosecution.[53] This exercise was designed to teach students "to see ourselves as others see us," to use Robert Burns's formulation.[54] The key account manager in Röggla's text expresses this idea as follows:

> ihre kollegen könnten schon ganz gut über sich lachen, und die könnten sich durchaus mal von außen sehen, und das müßten sie auch. die müßten sich ja auch alles anziehen können, das sei ja ihr job, positionen einzunehmen und wieder zu relativieren. (*wsn* 142)

> [her colleagues. they were all very able to have a good laugh at themselves. they could absolutely take a detached look at themselves, and they had to too. they also had to be able to wear different guises, that was their job. to take positions and then to relativize them again. (*WNS* 125)]

Like lawyers, these consultants have to weigh up different positions in a debate and articulate different arguments in line with those different positions. The Roman orator Cicero was trained as a lawyer, and the legal profession embodies a sense of continuity from classical rhetoric to modern business. Much like lawyers, consultants need to anticipate possible objections in advance. They must have the ability to put themselves in someone else's shoes, and this requirement implies an ethical dimension.[55]

In this respect, there are striking similarities between business management and classical rhetoric. The key account manager in *wir schlafen nicht* has designed structured questionnaires to study attitudes of clients and colleagues:

> weil das natürlich für ein unternehmen sehr entscheidend sei—die frage "wie kommuniziere ich nach außen, wie kommuniziere ich nach innen," und da hätten sie einige tools entwickelt, mit denen man das feststellen könne. wie man durch strukturierte fragetechniken quantifizierbare info, aber auch qualitative gewinnen könne. (*wsn* 52)

> [because of course that was really decisive for companies—the question "how do i communicate externally, how do i communicate internally," and they had developed several tools with which one could determine this. how one could gain quantifiable *info* through structured methods of questioning, but also how one could gain qualitative *info*. (*WNS* 46)]

Here, the marketing techniques used by the key account manager—questionnaires and focus groups—are essentially methods of investigating audience habits and responses that are in accordance with the wisdom of classical oratory.[56]

Obviously, the most significant audience that these characters need to impress is their own managers. Much of what they say is calibrated to appeal to any managers who may be listening. Röggla's consultants invest considerable energy in trying to guess what their bosses are thinking.[57] In Chapter 19, "anpassen" ("adapting"), we are told that learning how to identify with managers is part of one's professionalization process: "ja, einübung ins mitleid mit managern, das ist doch das, was hier passiert" (*wsn* 140; "yes, practicing sympathy with managers, that's what's going on here," *WNS* 123). And there is a very important distinction here: employees should not identify with the company itself, but only with the company executives. As the key account manager puts it,

> normalerweise habe auch niemand etwas dagegen, daß man sich übermäßig engagiere, solange der eigene ansatz mit den interessen des vorstandes konvergiere, wohlgemerkt nicht der firma, sondern des vorstandes, wenn nicht, dann heiße es schnell "überidentifikation" (*wsn* 49)

> [normally no one had anything against it if someone was excessively engaged, as long as their own approach converged with that of their superiors. not the company, mind you, but the supervisors. if not, then right away they called it "over-identification" (*WNS* 43)]

What matters here is that decisions by senior management will not be questioned. When the key account manager challenges the decision to hire McKinsey, she thinks she is defending the interests of the company. Her managers disagree, however; she is accused of "overidentification" and fired (*wsn* 48; *WNS* 42).

The consultants carefully control their performance and speech. Direct disagreement with senior management is out of the question; so, too, are expressions of awkwardness, weakness, or inability. Before they speak, they ask themselves how their audience is likely to respond. The online editor describes her previous job as a TV editor:

> "du mußt dich zusammenreißen, das geht doch nicht, daß du hier jetzt losheulst, daß du da durchdrehst. denn das interessiert deine interviewpartner nicht. . . . das interessiert auch die kamera nicht, daß du fertig bist. und dein team hat auch kein interesse daran, daß du schon 20 stunden am arbeiten warst." (*wsn* 147)

> ["you have to pull yourself together, it really won't work for you to start bawling here, for you to have a breakdown here. because the person you're interviewing couldn't care less. . . . the camera also couldn't care less that you're a wreck. and your *team* couldn't care less either that you've been working straight through for twenty hours." (*WNS* 129–30)]

Here and elsewhere in the novel we see how the characters consider the audience response before they speak. They ask themselves: will these people be interested in what I have to say? This is particularly pertinent when addressing a manager: "einen vorstand von daimler-chrysler interessiert so was nicht" (*wsn* 135; "the board at daimler-chrysler wouldn't be interested in anything like that," *WNS* 118); "das interessiert einen vorstand nicht! damit geht man nicht hin. das behält man für sich!" (*wsn* 193; "that doesn't interest management at all! don't take that stuff to them. you keep that sort of thing to yourself!" *WNS* 170–71). The characters try to anticipate the priorities of their audience and tell them what they want to hear. They know what they are expected to say:

> wisse man doch: man müsse diesbezüglich den mund halten, sich zumindest etwas zurückhalten mit der eigenen meinung. wisse man doch: was dürfe man sagen und was nicht. . . . und wenn jemand nur noch ja-nein-entscheidungen am tisch haben möchte, dann wirst du ihm auch nur ja-nein-entscheidungen auf den tisch legen! (*wsn* 32–33)

> [everyone knew: you had to keep your mouth shut when it came to this, at least hold back somewhat with your opinions. everyone knew: what you could say and what you couldn't. . . . and when someone wants to be presented with nothing but yes-no decisions, then you'll do nothing but present them with yes-no decisions! (*WNS* 29)]

Röggla's consultants have to be economical with the truth. The senior associate knows that the narrative of a company has to be airbrushed so that it appears in the best possible light: "ach, die firmengeschichte, ja, da paßt auch nicht alles rein . . . auch da muß eine auswahl getroffen werden" (*wsn* 193; "oh, right, the history of the firm, it was true that not everything fit in there . . . there too choices had to be made," *WNS* 171).

Röggla's consultants feel compelled to talk constantly to demonstrate that they are taking the initiative, or to maintain their networks so that they do not miss any important information. The online editor admits that she uses her phone almost continually: "ach, sie stünde dann unter redezwang" (*wsn* 124; "she just felt compelled to talk," *WNS* 108). Communication thus becomes the central aspect of the job. For the most part, however, this is not a form of communication that involves teamwork but a performance for the benefit of the managers. Before they speak they always try to anticipate their manager's response: "man hört sich immer noch reden, denn jemand sieht zu, daß man auch das richtige macht, das wird dann der herr belting sein" (*wsn* 23; "you still hear yourself talking because someone's making sure that you're doing the right thing, and that is mr. belting," *WNS* 21). In other words: when the manager is coming, look busy.

In conclusion, an analysis of *wir schlafen nicht* reveals how the discourse of freedom is often used to maintain a state of unfreedom. Many fashionable concepts have entered the boardroom, including "Kreativlösungen, flache Hierarchien" (creative solutions, flat hierarchies).[58] Despite these assertions of creative freedom, however, Röggla's text suggests that essential hierarchies are still very much in place. Indeed, the characters are ranked in a strict order (*wsn* 84–85; *WNS* 73–74), suggesting that the management hierarchy is entrenched and nonnegotiable. None of the characters expect loyalty or gratitude from their colleagues: there is no honor among thieves. And yet the fiction of teamwork has to be maintained, for the sake of those all-important appearances. Nobody trusts anybody else, and this means that people have to work even harder to build trust. The absence of trust and certainty does not render rhetoric superfluous. On the contrary: in a crisis, when evidence is lacking and action is required, rhetoric actually becomes even more important.[59] The centrality of communication in *wir schlafen nicht* indicates that doing business in the twenty-first century still relies on the production of credibility and the need to convince many different audiences (superiors, subordinates, stakeholders, colleagues, clients, and customers). Businesspeople still use classical techniques such as projecting *ethos* and studying audiences to make their arguments more persuasive. In other words, the "new" economy of the twenty-first century is remarkably similar to the "old" economies of previous centuries.

9: Communicative Contests in Philipp Schönthaler's *Das Schiff das singend zieht auf seiner Bahn*, 2013

> *reden ist besser als schweigen*
> [speaking is better than not speaking]
> —Philipp Schönthaler

Introduction: Training the Corporate Communicator

DAS SCHIFF das singend zieht auf seiner Bahn (The Ship That Goes Singing on Its Way), by Philipp Schönthaler (b. 1976), focuses on consultants who "develop" personnel, and employees who "develop" themselves, in line with company selection procedures. Like Delius's *Unsere Siemens-Welt*, Schönthaler's novel is a documentary satire.[1] It is set in a fictional cosmetics company, "Pfeiffer Beauty Kosmetik," in Stuttgart. This is appropriate because the novel depicts a world in which employees are expected to be "attractive" to employers.[2] The plot hinges on a series of job interviews, mentoring sessions, staff meetings, and corporate presentations. The third-person narrator recedes behind the characters and their discourse. This is significant, given that Schönthaler wrote his doctoral thesis on the figure of the narrator in the works of Thomas Bernhard, W. G. Sebald, and Imre Kertész.[3] Perhaps Schönthaler's decision in *Das Schiff* to avoid using a narrator who says "I" is an attempt to distance himself from these authors. Nevertheless, Bernhard's influence is evident when moments of physical lapse bring the characters' professional facade crashing down, e.g., when Rike Njlhouz starts farting uncontrollably during a job interview (*DS* 6), or when List, a fraud investigator making a sales pitch, accidentally swings his briefcase into the human resources director's private parts (*DS* 83).

Das Schiff is saturated with the discourse of "continuing professional development" (CPD). Schönthaler's interest in Bildung (education) and *berufliche Weiterbildung* (professional development) signals an intellectual affinity with Thomas Mann, which is confirmed by Schönthaler's short story "Nach oben ist das Leben offen" (2012; Life Opens Up toward the

Top), set in a "Sportheim" (sports facility) in the Swiss Alps that offers motivational sports training for high fliers.[4] One member of the staff is Dr. Behrens, an allusion to Mann's *Der Zauberberg* (1924; *The Magic Mountain*), which is set in a Swiss sanatorium run by a Dr. Behrens. This connection takes the present monograph full circle, suggesting that there are long-term continuities in depictions of the business world by German authors.

Both Mann and Schönthaler have a certain baroque verve. The early modern image of the *Totentanz* (Dance of Death) appears both in *Buddenbrooks* and in *Der Zauberberg*,[5] and a review of Schönthaler's *Das Schiff das singend zieht auf seiner Bahn* compared it to Sebastian Brant's Renaissance satire *Das Narrenschiff* (1494; *The Ship of Fools*).[6] The comparison is justified not only in terms of the titles, because *Das Schiff* is populated by a legion of *Fachidioten* (specialists with tunnel vision). But there is another aspect of Schönthaler's text that connects even more profoundly with the early modern period: namely, its performative aspects, which link to the axiom of baroque drama that "parler, c'est agir" (to talk is to act).[7] Conventional management wisdom, with its emphasis on communication, unwittingly rehearses the positions of the baroque era, in which communication was highly formalized around the courtly art of *werben* (to court, to solicit). The modern sense of *werben* is "to advertise," "to recruit," and the changing usage of the verb suggests that there is a continuity between the classically trained eloquence of the baroque courtier and the presentation skills of the modern businessperson. Schönthaler's focus on the *Bewerbungsgespräch* (job interview) is very much in this courtly tradition: the modern job applicant is in a similar position to the petitioner at an early modern court.

This chapter argues that *Das Schiff* depicts a world of corporate athletes and accomplished orators: elite communicators, trained by a battalion of career coaches and motivational experts with a view to maximizing their performance.[8] Much like the athletes and orators of the ancient world, modern business executives are required to train continually in order to develop their resilience as well as their communication skills. In *Das Schiff* the power struggle no longer takes place in the classical forum, senate, or stadium but in the meeting room or the assessment center.

The assessment center is a world in which individual performance is reviewed and evaluated using an array of tests. The tests depend upon a wide variety of parameters and performance indicators. In this situation the decisive factor is, arguably, communication. Much as Roman orators would train for hours before giving their speeches, Schönthaler's businesspeople train fastidiously to prepare themselves for interviews and presentations. *Das Schiff* cites a fictional psychologist and "motivation researcher," Albert Bandura, who claims, "Erst wenn wir unsere Ziele konkret formulieren können, sind wir für einen kommunikativen Auftritt hinreichend gewappnet" (*DS* 58; We are only sufficiently armed for a communicative encounter if we can formulate our goals precisely). The adjective *gewappnet* (steeled, prepared), is etymologically related to *bewaffnet* (armed); it casts the businessperson as a soldier preparing for combat. Another expert, Prof. Dr. Simonia Thavhoff, appears on a glossy brochure for Succo Consulting Zurich. Under her photo is a quotation from Sun Tzu's military treatise, *The Art of War*: "Nur wer den Gegner und sich selbst gut kennt, kann in 1000 Schlachten siegreich sein" (*DS* 234; Only he who knows his enemy and knows himself can be victorious in a thousand battles). The use of this slogan shows the extent to which Schönthaler has been studying contemporary management handbooks.[9] The phrase appears in several handbooks written by the organizational psychologist Alexander Thomas, who translates Sun Tzu's insight into modern business parlance as "Nur wer den fremdkulturell geprägten Partner und sich selbst in seine kulturellen Bedingtheiten erkennt, kann in allen Kommunikations- und Kooperationssituationen erfolgreich sein" (Only he who knows the partner who is shaped by a foreign culture and who knows himself can be successful in all situations of communication and cooperation).[10] The repeated references to Sun Tzu suggest that "situations of communication and cooperation" are essentially the modern equivalents of battlefields. Sun Tzu also said, however: "The best general is the one who never fights." In other words, public speech and diplomacy are often the most effective weapons of all. It is no accident that Quintilian often evokes military metaphors as a subtext in his *Institutes of Oratory*: a great orator displays the "luster" and the "authority" of a military leader.[11]

An examination of *Das Schiff* shows the continuing relevance of classical oratory for modern business communication. In his essay *Porträt des Managers als junger Autor* (2016; Portrait of the Manager as a Young Author) Schönthaler observes that global corporations are investing in storytellers, because stories draw people in: they are an effective means to promote identification.[12] Like Friedrich Nietzsche and the Greek authors he admired, corporations evaluate communication primarily in terms of its *Wirkung* (effect, impact).[13] The classical model is also relevant in terms of the Greek concept of *agon* (competition, whether in athletics, chariot racing, music, poetry, or oratory), which arguably functions as a structural principle for Schönthaler's text. The Latin term for *agon* is *ludus* (play, game, sport); the German equivalent is *Spiel* (game, play). According to Jacob Burckhardt, ancient Greek culture centered entirely on the competitive principle of *agon*: "Agon . . . ist es, welcher die Trefflichkeit . . . manifestiert . . . die volle Entwicklung des Individuums war davon abhängig, daß man sich unaufhörlich untereinander maß und verglich" (*Agon* . . . is the manifestation of excellence . . . the full development of the individual depended on the fact that they measured and compared themselves against each other without pause).[14] A similar competitive culture of constant measurement informs the human resources methods depicted in *Das Schiff*.

The characters in *Das Schiff* are corporate athletes who compete relentlessly with each other in terms of career success. Their agonistic engagement is defined in terms of classical athletics and oratory, as contests of physical athleticism and verbal performance. Cicero conceives of oratory as a verbal combat, and he compares training an orator to training an athlete in the palaestra (wrestling school or gymnasium):

> we must shape our orator with respect to both words and thoughts, so that he will act like those who fight with weapons or in the palaestra: they believe that they should not only take account of how to strike and dodge, but also of how to move with grace, (and the orator must likewise make sure that he uses words and thoughts not only for proof and refutation, but also to charm).[15]

Communication is understood here as a beautiful form of combat. Cicero wants orators to deliver their lines with the grace and timing of athletes. This is also the message at the start of Schönthaler's novel, which stresses that first impressions count. *Das Schiff* begins with a "precredit sequence": six pages of narrative are inserted before the book's title page and front matter. This paratext emphasizes the importance of making the correct opening maneuver, as the personnel manager declares: "Was man am Anfang versäumt, ist auch später verloren . . . 30 Sekunden reichen . . . für einen guten Personaler aus, um das Leistungsniveau des Gegenübers intuitiv zu erfassen" (*DS* 3; What you neglect at the start cannot be compensated for . . . thirty seconds are sufficient for a good personnel manager to grasp intuitively the performance level of the person opposite). Battles are sometimes won in the first thirty seconds, as the opponents take each other's measure. The arena in which these modern contests take place, and the principal locus of *Das Schiff*, is the modern assessment center.

The Assessment Center: Selection and Rejection

The assessment center is the place of the *Auswahlverfahren* (selection procedure), where candidates are rigorously graded and rated in accordance with the latest scientific procedures. The assessment center tests both mind and body: it requires candidates to demonstrate mental agility and stamina while retaining their physical and emotional poise. In *Das Schiff* the human resources director Dr. Frederick Quass proclaims that "Die Leistung, nicht die Herkunft soll als egalitäres Selektionskriterium dienen" (*DS* 32; It is not your background, but your performance that serves as an egalitarian selection criterion). This ignores the fact that high performance often results from a privileged background and an elite education. Although the assessment center claims to be based on egalitarian principles, its aim is highly elitist. Dr. Quass welcomes a cohort of interview candidates by giving them a brief history of the assessment center. He starts by mentioning the Hamburg-born psychologist William Stern (1871–1938), who invented the IQ test in 1910. Quass then proceeds,

> Das Assessment-Center wie wir es heute kennen und für Sie veranstalten, verdankt sich schließlich psychologischen Testverfahren, die Dr. Johann Baptist Rieffert erstmals in den 1920er Jahren zur neutralen Auswahl von Offizierswärtern in der Weimarer Republik entwickelte (*DS* 32).

> [The assessment center as we know it today, and to which we now welcome you, owes its existence to the test procedures that were initially developed by Dr. Johann Baptist Rieffert in the 1920s for the neutral selection of officer candidates in the Weimar Republic.]

The reference to Johann Baptist Rieffert (1883–1956) and the claim that his techniques were "neutral" is tendentious. Quass's airbrushed narrative elides the uncomfortable details of Rieffert's career, which are worth outlining here. Rieffert completed his PhD in Bonn on Arthur Schopenhauer in 1910 and his Habilitation, "Zur Genealogie des Beziehungsbewußtseins" (On the Genealogy of Relational Consciousness), in Berlin in 1919. From 1919 to 1925 he was an expert in military psychology at the University of Berlin and from 1926 to 1931 director of the psychological division of the Reichswehr;[16] during the latter period he developed a selection procedure based on a holistic, integrated approach to the candidate.[17] This process was extended by his successor, Max Simoneit (1896–1962). From 1927 onward, no Reichswehr officer could be appointed without having received satisfactory results in the *heerespsychologisches Auswahlverfahren* (armed forces psychological selection procedure),[18] and by 1941 more than 450 psychologists were working in various branches of the German military.[19] Rieffert joined the Nazi Party and the SA (Sturmabteilung) in 1933, and in 1934 he was rewarded with a personal chair in psychology and *Charakterkunde* (Characterology) at the University of Berlin; his new research focus was racial psychology and what he called the "Anpassungstechnik" (adaptation technique) of the Jews.[20] In 1936 he was expelled from the NSDAP, allegedly for concealing his previous membership in the Social Democratic Party, and dismissed from his chair. His appeal of the dismissal was rejected in 1938, and in 1940 he found work in the Borsig factory in Breslau.[21] In 1945 the Americans classed Rieffert as a Nazi supporter of low significance and even allowed him to share his personality tests with the US Navy.[22]

Rieffert's career, with its various stations—philosopher, military psychologist, racial psychologist, and industrial-recruitment consultant—suggests uncomfortable parallels between human resources and Nazi racial selection. His career trajectory reminds us that the essential purpose of a selection procedure, whether military or civilian, is to grade human beings in terms of their usefulness or nonusefulness. In the Third Reich, being rated as undesirable often had fatal consequences. It should be noted that Schönthaler's text only refers to Rieffert in passing, and *Das Schiff* does not engage directly with the National Socialist past at any point. Even so, the reference to J. B. Rieffert and the military origins of the assessment center is telling, and it is also highly significant that the headquarters of Pfeiffer Beauty are constructed on the grounds of an old US Army barracks: "Das es sich ursprünglich um eine Kaserne handelte, ist kaum noch zu erkennen" (*DS* 43; It is barely possible to recognize that this estate was originally a barracks). These references ensure that a sense of Germany's violent military past lingers in the background.

Schönthaler's theme, however, is not the administered genocide of the mid-twentieth century, which categorized people in terms of their racial characteristics, but the administered elitism of modern assessment centers, which rate people in terms of their economic "performance." The key criterion is no longer racial purity but economic viability. The consequence of failure is no longer a death sentence but unemployment. This distinction is subverted on the very first page of Schönthaler's novel, however, as Rike Njlhouz tries to calm herself before her interview: "Rike japst, sie weiß, dies ist keine Hinrichtung, nur ein Vorstellungsgespräch" (*DS* 1; Rike yelps; she knows this is not an execution, only a job interview). Far from being reassuring, this phrase just hangs there, without a period to mark the end of the sentence. It implies that if Rike is unsuccessful in the interview, then she will indeed die a symbolic social death: being sentenced to poverty is a symbolic form of death sentence. In this way, the theme of human resources indicates its own flip side, namely, that some human beings are categorized as worthless and undesirable in economic terms. As Zygmunt Bauman puts it, "The production of 'human waste,' or more correctly wasted humans . . . is an inevitable outcome of modernization."[23] Or, to quote Karl Marx's ironic commentary on John Stuart Mill's claim that workers should be sparing in the number of children they produce, "Es giebt zu *viel* Menschen. . . . Die Production des Menschen erscheint als öffentliches Elend" (There are too *many* people. . . . The production of people appears as public destitution).[24] Although crude social Darwinism has been discredited, corporate staffing policy suggests that more complex forms of social discrimination have continued into the twenty-first century. The categorization of people into "human resources" and "human waste" is exemplified in the fates of the novel's two main characters: Erik Jungholz is the "good example," the corporate athlete who scales the career ladder, while Rike Njlhouz is the "bad example" whose inability to communicate effectively renders her unemployable.[25] These different outcomes show how companies measure performance in terms of communication skills and athleticism. In the next two sections we will consider each of these criteria in turn.

Communication and Oratory: Business Experts Rediscover Aristotle

The first words of Schönthaler's novel, capitalized in the original text, are "IN SACHEN KOMMUNIKATION" (*DS* 1; ON THE SUBJECT OF COMMUNICATION). Globalization and the internet have reinforced the centrality of communication to business. Communication now occurs across multiple media and platforms. It often still relies on public speaking, however, whether face-to-face, on video, or via Skype. The internet's ability to disseminate speech instantly around the globe makes classical oratory more relevant than ever. Chris Anderson, "curator" of the company TED, which provides "idea-based talks," argues that the spoken word is undergoing a renaissance: "Just as the printing press massively amplified the power of authors, so the web is massively amplifying the impact of speakers."[26] Anderson's guide to public speaking shows how communications experts are returning to the classical theorists of oratory and rhetoric, Aristotle and Cicero.[27]

A recent German handbook on international business communication uses Aristotle's *Rhetoric* as a foundation; it is edited by Alexander Thomas, one of the experts referenced in Schönthaler's text. The handbook contains a digest of Aristotle's theory by Stefan Kammhuber, a personnel consultant whose starting point is Aristotle's definition of rhetoric as "the faculty of observing in any given case the available means of persuasion."[28] The speaker must have an intimate knowledge of the audience and its values in order to determine which persona to adopt (*ethos*), which emotions to elicit (*pathos*), and which content and structure to employ (*logos*).[29] Just as Sun Tzu counsels the general to know the enemy, so, too, does Aristotle advise the orator to get to know the audience well.[30] Kammhuber echoes Aristotle's argument that knowledge of the conventions of the specific *Zielkultur* (target culture) is indispensable.[31]

As this suggests, intercultural communication is now an established theme within global business studies. At one point in *Das Schiff* Erik Jungholz reads a brochure titled *Intercultural Competence* offering a crash course in Russian culture before he does business with Russian business partners: after all, he might be invited on a bear-hunting expedition (*DS* 236–40). The brochure is an obvious example of Orientalism as defined by Edward Said, in which Western "experts" construct crude stereotypes of Easterners. Klaus Antoni argues that "intercultural communication" primers often reduce complex, changing cultures to positivist, essentialist stereotypes.[32] The Orientalist stereotypes current in contemporary intercultural communication studies suggest uncomfortable parallels with the Western imperialism of the nineteenth century. Here, identity politics are used to construct and project cultural stereotypes; for example, an image of Germanic quality and business expertise.

Ethos refers to the speaker's relationship with the audience. In *Das Schiff* Erik Jungholz knows that he has to establish a close rapport: "Zunächst gilt es die Verbindlichkeiten zu steigern" (*DS* 4; First you have to ensure that bonding takes place). He observes all the niceties, seeking eye contact, making compliments: "Schön hier!" (*DS* 4; It's great here!). Getting the "chemistry" right is all-important: "Die Kommunikation scheitert nicht an der Substanz, sondern an der Akzeptanz . . . ist hingegen die Akzeptanz gegeben, kann man beginnen, über die Substanz zu reden (*DS* 4; Communication does not fail due to substance but due to acceptance . . . if acceptance is established, then you can begin to talk about the substance).

When it comes to planning a speech, preparation is essential. Aristotle's term for this is *heurisis*, Cicero's is *inventio*. Although it is often translated as "invention," Catherine Steel argues that it would be more helpful to translate *inventio* as "research" to convey the point that careful research is required to find the best methods of persuasion to use in any given context.[33] Schönthaler's novel demonstrates this understanding of *inventio* in the description of Esser, a medical student who neglects his patient because he is busy preparing a speech for his *Burschenschaft* (student fraternity). Esser is sifting through a pile of sourcebooks to find the raw materials for his speech:

> Er befindet sich im Grunde noch im ersten Stadium seiner Arbeit, der *inventio*, damit beschäftigt, Material und Anregungen aus einem Stapel von Büchern zu sammeln, darunter Dantes *Vita Nova*, . . . Moritz Freiherr Knigge: *Spielregeln: Wie wir miteinander umgehen sollten*, . . . Brigitte Nagiller: *Klasse mit Knigge: Stilsicher in allen Lebenslagen* und *Harenbergs Lexikon der Sprichwörter und Zitate*. (*DS* 54)

> [He is still basically in the first stage of his work, *inventio*; he is busy collecting materials and ideas from a pile of books, including Dante's *Vita Nuova*, Moritz Freiherr Knigge's *Rules of the Game: How to Get Along with People*, . . . Brigitte Nagiller's *High Class with Knigge: How to Be Stylish in Every Situation*, and *Harenberg's Dictionary of Sayings and Quotations*.]

Classical authors are absent here, and Dante's *Vita Nuova* is only included because Esser's brief is to prepare a toast for the ladies who will be present. Instead of the conversation manuals of Adolph Knigge (1752–96), we have contemporary best sellers by Moritz Freiherr Knigge (b. 1968) and

Brigitte Nagiller that popularize the works of Adolph Knigge for a twenty-first-century audience.[34] These book titles offer a sketch of the transmission of classical oratory and rhetoric, via eighteenth-century manuals of courtly conduct, to contemporary lifestyle coaches.

Voice and Body Language

Classical oratory emphasizes the importance of nonverbal signals: voice, body language, physical appearance. Modern corporations, too, are becoming increasingly sensitive "to the interaction between the organization and the customer through the 'service encounter' offered by the employee."[35] There is now a growing field of research dedicated to the study of "aesthetic labor," i.e., the time, money, and energy people invest in their professional appearance.[36] At the beginning of *Das Schiff* the recruitment psychologist Zander explains that verbal content only accounts for a small part of interpersonal communication:

> Wissenschaftliche Untersuchungen belegen, dass der Inhalt weitgehend zu vernachlässigen ist: Das sind fünf, allenfalls zehn Prozent. . . . Entscheidend sind vielmehr die paraverbalen Faktoren, das Wie, die Expertin zählt die Faktoren auf: erstens Stimme, zweitens Tonfall, drittens Klangmelodie—diese Parameter fallen mit 30 bis 35 Prozent ins Gewicht. . . . Entscheidend für einen wirklich guten Auftritt—wir sprechen von 50 bis 60 Prozent—ist jedoch die Körpersprache, das bedeutet: Körperhaltung, Gestik, Blickkontakt, das muss absolut sitzen. (*DS* 5)

> [Scientific studies prove that the content should be largely neglected: content only counts for five, at most ten percent. The decisive factors are paraverbal factors: "how" it is delivered. The expert lists the factors: firstly voice, then tone of voice, then the musicality of the voice—these parameters count for around 30–35 percent. The most decisive factor for a really good presentation, however, is body language—let's say around 50–60 percent. That means: posture, gestures, you must make definite eye contact.]

Classical authors were well aware of the importance of these factors, and Aristotle discusses vocal delivery in detail at the beginning of *Rhetoric*, book 3. Although the subject is "unworthy," Aristotle thinks that orators "cannot do without it" and that they have much to learn from professional actors, who have now superseded the poets in terms of their vocal skill.[37] Aristotle's word for "vocal delivery" is *hupokrisis*, which originally meant "acting" or "gesturing."[38] Vocal delivery is thus related etymologically to hypocrisy and dissembling, which explains Aristotle's reluctance to address the subject.

Schönthaler's novel shows no such hesitation: "Grundsätzlich ist eine kräftige, sonore Stimme . . . von Vorteil, eine gepflegte Sprache, gepflegter Ausdruck, Äußeres" (*DS* 1; As a basic principle, a powerful, sonorous voice is an advantage, polished language, polished expressions, externalities). *Das Schiff* thus begins with a programmatic statement that business communication requires careful modulation of the voice. Schönthaler's managers resemble the classical orators who trained rigorously to improve their vocal delivery, exercising daily and often learning speeches by heart.[39] A good accent is essential, and Cicero recommends cultivating a Roman one (i.e., from the city itself); rural and foreign accents are to be avoided.[40] The modern word for this practice is elocution: elocution lessons have long been perceived as a pathway to success. In Germany one of the leading voice coaches was the music teacher Julius Hey (1831–1909), who trained the singing parts for Richard Wagner's first festivals in Bayreuth.[41] Hey's manual for actors, singers, and speechmakers, *Der Kleine Hey* (1912; The Small Hey), is still in print, and it is referenced in *Das Schiff* when Rike Njlhouz has speech therapy.

Rike's therapist is Sunny Reichart. In spite of the upbeat name, there is something intimidating about her. The first session is devoted to the pronunciation of the letter "A." Unfortunately for Rike, she is told to recite an ominous verse from *Der Kleine Hey*: "Barbara saß nah am Abhang" (*DS* 125; Barbara sat near to the slope). In this verse, "Barbara" sits close to a precipice, and this situation resembles Rike's own precarious position as she teeters on the verge of a nervous breakdown. Worse still, Sunny does not engage in a dialogue with Rike but lectures her in a patronizing fashion, without letting her get a word in edgewise. We might expect a speech therapist to encourage the client to speak, but in this case the only voice that gets exercised is the therapist's. Rike would probably be better off with another therapist, one who allowed her to say something. The element of intimidation is most noticeable when Sunny says that Rike is free to reject her advice:

> Wobei sie [Sunny] ihre Kundinnen zu nichts zwingen wolle, sie mache nur Angebote—es liege an ihr, Rike, das Angebot anzunehmen oder nicht, schließlich wird hier keiner zu irgendetwas gezwungen. (*DS* 121)

> [She [Sunny] does not want to force her customers to do anything, she only makes offers—it is up to her, Rike, whether to accept the offer or not. After all, no one is being forced to do anything here.]

It is telling that Sunny denies *twice* that any force is being used. The more she denies the use of force, the less we believe her. There is an element of coercion here: the client is free to conform or to fail. Given Sunny's condescending approach, it is hardly surprising that Rike lapses into stunned silence. Much like Hanno and his failed poetry recital in Thomas Mann's *Buddenbrooks*, it is Rike's lack of ability as an orator that proves that she is unsuitable for a business career.

Corporate Athletes and Their Coaches

As George Lakoff and Mark Johnson have argued, metaphors have the power to shape our experience of reality.[42] Schönthaler's characters live by the guiding metaphor of the corporate athlete, informed by the modern reception of classical civilization. In the nineteenth century the historical example of Sparta was adopted as a model that informed the development of nationalism, militarism, and public-health policy, and this culminated in the first modern Olympic Games in 1896. The emphasis on participation that characterizes the modern Olympics is, however, very different from their classical precedent: for the ancient Greeks, "only winning mattered; arriving second offered little consolation."[43] Given the prestige of sports and athletics in modern culture, it is hardly surprising that business experts have turned to athletics as a model for business. In an influential article published in 2001, Jim Loehr and Tony Schwartz argue that business executives are "corporate athletes" who "train in the same systematic, multilevel way that world-class athletes do."[44] They believe "the real enemy of high performance is not stress, which . . . is actually the stimulus for growth. Rather, the problem is the absence of disciplined, intermittent recovery."[45] Loehr and Schwartz teach their business clients to incorporate "recovery rituals" into their daily routine.[46] They conclude that companies "cannot afford to ignore" the "physical, emotional, and spiritual well-being" of their employees.[47] Some leading global IT companies have taken up these recommendations, introducing workplace health programs that encourage employees to regard themselves as corporate athletes and to undergo monitoring procedures that can be used to inform decisions about promotions and layoffs.[48] "Corporate athlete" discourse implies the ethical "injunction to move toward *athleticism* as the norm."[49] Business culture has shifted from Weber's Protestant asceticism to the athleticism of the twenty-first century. In *Buddenbrooks*, the family members are determined to maintain their "Haltung" (*B* 452; "self-control," *Bu* 403). Schönthaler's characters, too, are concerned with maintaining the "richtige Haltung" (correct posture), but now they emulate the dynamic poise of the athlete.[50]

The ambitious manager Erik Jungholz is distinguished from the outset by his competitive spirit and his bodily awareness. He compares the interview room to a soccer field: "Er ist hier nicht auf dem Rasen, beim Fußball" (*DS* 2; He is not on the football pitch here). Recent psychological research has suggested that the best soccer players have considerable cognitive flexibility in terms of shifting focus, choosing what to ignore, and, if necessary, suppressing unwanted behavior.[51] This reinforces the parallel between athletes and business managers: in both fields, mental self-discipline is essential. For this reason, Erik Jungholz adjusts his attitude very carefully before he gives a presentation before his colleagues: "Er . . . wirft den Kopf in den Nacken, strafft seinen Rücken. Natürlich weiß er, in dieser Situation muss er erst mal einen Gang runterschalten, sein Adrenalin zügeln" (*DS* 2, 116; He tilts his head upward and tenses his back; naturally, he knows that in this situation he has to start by shifting into a lower gear and containing his adrenalin). The fact that this sentence is repeated shows the extent to which these actions are part of his daily routine.[52] He starts his day with qigong exercises, listening on his headphones to an aerobics instructor who declares, "Das kämpferische Zusammenspiel von Bewegung, Vorstellung und Atmung stärkt die innere Kraft für die täglichen Konflikte; mit Qi Gong können Sie Ihren regenerativen Energien gezielt nachspüren" (*DS* 17; The martial interplay between movement, imagination, and breathing boosts your inner life energy, preparing you for daily conflicts; with qigong you can focus on reconnecting with your regenerative capacities). This corresponds to the "recovery rituals" advocated by Loehr and Schwartz.[53] Pamela Smaart's preferred ritual is to tap against her cheekbone so that her glass eye pops out, then put it back in—this stress relief has become "unentbehrlich" (indispensable) for her (*DS* 41). Erik Jungholz has a number of such rituals that he incorporates into his daily routine: they include smoothing his tie with his left hand (*DS* 1, 22) and repeating a positive mantra to himself: "Er ist wirklich gut, er weiß, dass er gut ist—bei dem Gedanken steigert sich seine Stimmung zusätzlich" (*DS* 1, 22, 68; He's really good, he knows that he's good—at this thought his mood brightens even more).[54] Another ritual that can offset feelings of stress is listening to music.[55] Erik Jungholz plays rock and roll on his car stereo to get pumped up before a presentation (*DS* 18–20). On his way to a game of golf, he listens to rap music (*DS* 62–63). He is always ready for action: "Wie immer ist Jungholz schlagbereit, als sein Kollege erst beginnt, sich spielfertig zu machen" (*DS* 68; As always, Jungholz is ready to take his shot, while his colleague is still getting ready for the game).

Given the high stakes, it is hardly surprising that some employees try to cheat, e.g., by inflating their CVs. *Das Schiff* features a fraud investigator named List who discovers that one of the applicants to Pfeiffer Beauty, Marcus Vestlund, has lied about living in Paris for two years (*DS* 40); List has a range of interrogation techniques that he uses (*DS* 91–93). Erik Jungholz is too intelligent to fake his CV, but he does break the rules to win a game of golf; the CPD consultant, Pamela J. Smaart, has a smartphone video that shows him cheating (*DS* 47–48). This does not lead to a reprimand, however; instead, she gives him coaching sessions to moderate his behavior. She tells him to work on his "Teamfähigkeit" (*DS* 49; team spirit). He has to modulate his approach: "Alphatiere, die mit gehobenem Hinterlauf ihr Revier markieren, das ist passé. Es weht ein anderer Wind: Was Sie bis hierher gebracht hat, wird Sie nicht weiterbringen" (*DS* 49; Alpha animals who mark their territory by raising their hind leg are passé. A new wind is blowing: the qualities that have gotten you this far will not take you any farther). In order to keep up with the latest trends, Jungholz will have to pay even more attention to his soft skills.[56] The emphasis on "soft skills" and "teamwork" recalls once again the analogy with athletics: just as soccer players have to pass the ball, businesspeople have to work effectively together. But the demand for soft skills does not mean that rigid hierarchies in the workplace have been abolished. It just means that they are less obvious than before. In *Das Schiff* the unwritten rules of the golf course suggest that hierarchies are not soft, after all. As the players assume their positions, "der CEO [hat] sämtliche Ärsche im Blick" (*DS* 68; the CEO can see everyone's ass). Here the emphasis on "teamwork" replaces older, class-based notions of "solidarity" and serves to mask existing hierarchies.

The call for teamwork is, at least on one level, a motivational tool that enforces compliance. For the sake of "the team," everyone has to "do their best" so as "not to let the team down." It is an effective form of peer-group pressure that calls for dedication to the project of "self-development." As an article in *Die Zeit* puts it, attending counseling is no longer viewed as a sign of weakness but as an indication of employability:

> Wer heute einen Coach, Therapeuten oder Mentaltrainer in Anspruch nimmt oder ein Kommunikationsseminar besucht, gilt nicht mehr als krank oder gestört—sondern als klug oder bestrebt, etwas für das eigene Glück zu tun.[57]

> [These days, someone who employs the services of a coach, therapist, or motivational trainer, or who visits a communication seminar, is no longer regarded as sick or dysfunctional but as intelligent and striving to improve oneself.]

The metaphor of the corporate athlete justifies the need for human resources consultants "who provide the expertise, the techniques and the rituals that promise to facilitate the ongoing development and success of the self."[58] In *Das Schiff* the most prominent career consultants are Pamela J. Smaart and Dr. Beate Posner. Smaart and Posner are the motivational experts who "develop" employees in order to enhance their value to the employer. The name "Smaart" is fitting, because annual performance reviews are often structured in terms of "SMART" targets; the acronym stands for "Specific, Measureable, Achievable/Aligned, Relevant, Time Bound." Note that the priority here is not to develop people, but professionals (the *P* in *CPD* stands for "professional," not "personal"). This assumes that development of the individual coincides with the interests of the company. Consultants help employees to imagine that their employer's "interest in performance and productivity matches [their] own concerns for health and well-being."[59] The underlying narrative is that if employees succeed in aligning their own interests with the interests of the firm, then they will be rewarded in terms of career progression. Unfortunately, in the precarious job market of the twenty-first century there are no guarantees. As Oliver Nachtwey points out, the liberal principle of economic reward based on performance has been "hollowed out" in recent decades, as profits are divided less and less equally.[60] At the same time, the discourse of "equal opportunity" and "personal responsibility" means that poverty is no longer viewed in terms of class inequalities but, instead, solely as a matter for the individual. "Equal opportunities" imply that if you do fail, it is your fault. Nachtwey concludes, "The more a society insists upon equal opportunities, the more unequal it becomes and the more legitimate inequalities become."[61] If corporate athletes fail to win a race, they have no one to blame but themselves. Furthermore, since athletes tend to have short careers, then employees who identify as athletes are less likely to complain about being fired. The metaphor of the athlete also signals that the new ideology of "self-realization" produces a culture that is surprisingly homogenous.[62] Much as nineteenth-century Bildung failed to live up to its promise of individual development, often serving as a form of indoctrination,[63] contemporary berufliche Weiterbildung (CPD) promises "self-realization" while delivering more docile employees. The metaphor of the corporate athlete is a powerful way to manufacture social consent.[64]

Playing the Game

The athleticism of the characters in *Das Schiff* emphasizes the idea that business does not involve cooperation, but competition. Teamwork is acknowledged in sport, but at the end of the day, winning the game is more important. At the beginning of the novel Erik Jungholz knows the rules of the game: he knows the criteria by which he will be judged, including the "Knock-out-Kriterium" (*DS* 2; knockout-criterion). He also knows the script he is supposed to stick to: "Er kennt seinen Text" (*DS* 2; He knows his lines). This phrase is so important that it is repeated at the end of the novel, as Beate Posner approaches the podium: "Sie kennt ihren Text" (*DS* 274; She knows her lines). This statement, which effectively opens and closes the novel, announces that the recruitment business is a game with a specific set of rules—or, rather, a form of public spectacle.

Given that game-playing and competition are paramount in *Das Schiff*, it is significant that Schönthaler has published an essay on Jean Baudrillard's concept of play: "Die Theorie ins Spiel bringen" (2013; Bringing Theory into Play). In his essay Schönthaler observes that Baudrillard wishes to subvert communication.[65] Language games, for Baudrillard, are intrinsically *agonal* (competitive).[66] Baudrillard thus embraces the agonal quality of speech, i.e., its persuasive function as a practical intervention. Much as orators adapt their speeches according to the subject matter, the radical theorist's intervention should be guided by the object in question: "dem Gleichen mit dem Gleichen begegnen" (meeting like with like). Baudrillard emphasizes game-playing to escape the Marxist logic of work and production—incidentally, this misrepresents Marx, who makes no clear distinction between (nonalienated) labor and creative play.[67] Instead of work, Baudrillard wants play; and instead of "production," he wants "seduction."[68] According to Baudrillard, illusion is positive because it is a precondition for the game-playing that, for him, constitutes culture. The players of the game do not need to believe in the rules; they merely accept the rules and accept that the game is worth playing.[69]

Baudrillard's game theory is problematic, because game models have become part of the status quo. In the twenty-first century, economic activity is no longer defined in terms of industrial production but in terms of competition and innovation. Creative economies and "creative solutions" are so prevalent nowadays that they have become embedded in institutional practices across the globe.[70] Play, innovation, and spontaneity are no longer dismissed as anarchic or subversive: on the contrary, they are welcomed as examples of "best practice."[71] The game model of society also legitimates social inequality: for there to be winners, there must also be losers. Moreover, as Michael Billig points out, game-based social theories "bypass the very essence of rhetoric," which resides "not in the sense of organized competition, but in the sense of argumentation."[72] The gaming metaphor, with its focus on rules, has little to say about how rules are created and changed by means of argument.[73] Furthermore, with all due respect to Baudrillard, life is not a game.

Despite these reservations, Schönthaler's engagement with Baudrillard has had a positive influence on *Das Schiff*, which adopts the jargon of human resources consultants in order to oppose "like with like."[74] Schönthaler wants to engage with the corporate system on its own terms ("Die Phänomene immanent, gemäß ihrer eigenen Logik herauszufordern"; Challenge phenomena immanently, according to their own logic).[75] Indeed, Schönthaler's attention to social conventions in *Das Schiff* is insightful, showing clearly that social game-playing is almost inescapable. When Beate Posner visits Professor Bender, her retired former supervisor, he seems a shadow of his former self. When he retired, he was so shocked that nobody was interested in him that he acquired a dog, which gives him the unquestioning devotion he is used to (*DS* 226). The dog is there to provide a substitute for human society—in this case, the students and research assistants who once looked up to Bender.

Even more ironic is the fate of Rike Njlhouz. When she drops out of the employment market, she cannot escape the game-playing. The mental institution she checks into is just another organization with its own set of rules. Rike's new roommate, Leoni, explains to her that

> es gebe gute Kranke und schlechte Kranke und es gebe solche, die die Regeln kennen und sich dazu verhalten können: Das seien die wirklich Guten, die können das Ganze für sich arbeiten lassen, nicht umgekehrt. Aber das müsse man erst mal hinkriegen, das sei nicht ohne, da müsse man stark sein, wissen, wie der Hase läuft. (*DS* 255)

> [there are good patients and bad patients and ones who know the rules and who behave accordingly: they are the really good people, they let the whole system work for them, instead of the other way around. But it takes a bit of practice, it's not that easy, you have to be strong, you have to know the score.]

As Leoni explains, it pays to know the score, because if you do, then you can play the system. And if you do not "play ball," there are consequences. Even losing the game does not mean that you can stop playing. Often, a lost game is just the prelude to the next game. To quote the soccer coach Sepp Herberger: "Nach dem Spiel ist vor dem Spiel" (After the game is before the game). Human beings are social animals, and the next social game is always just around the corner.

Consultants and the Self as Enterprise

The army of consultants in *Das Schiff* recall Michel Foucault's lectures on governmentality. Foucault observes that in the ancient world, consultants would provide medical and moral advice for a fee. These consultants offered spiritual, moral, and philosophical "direction," self-analysis, and prescriptions for improvement.[76] They dispensed advice on every aspect of a person's lifestyle, including food, clothing, relationships, and politics; they would even offer group consultations.[77] These ancient practices clearly anticipate the contemporary self-improvement industry, in which lifestyle experts are always on hand to offer guidance. It is a situation that Immanuel Kant would have deplored.[78] Indeed, the epigraph to *Das Schiff* is a quotation from Robert Musil, observing that we are often surrounded by interfering experts.[79] Of course, it could be argued that the expert training regimes of the twenty-first century are necessitated by the constantly changing forms of economic competition. In Schönthaler's novel Rike cannot control her thoughts and emotions, and perhaps counseling is appropriate in such a case.

Perhaps it is not the counselors themselves who are so problematic, but the unquestioning acceptance of "competition" as a value. Joseph Vogl argues that the principle of "competition" has become so pervasive that contemporary economic regimes deliberately encourage individuals to view themselves as fully-fledged businesses or "microenterprises," complete with corresponding motivational structures.[80] In this way, the economic principles of modern societies invite people to see themselves as microbusinesses. The quest for self-improvement is motivated by the quest for greater economic returns. This is the ideological subtext to the corporate culture Schönthaler depicts in *Das Schiff*.

Employment consultancy is a growth industry. Career advisers play an essential role within the regimes of economic austerity pursued by Western governments since the financial crisis of 2007. Operating particularly in postindustrial regions of Europe with high levels of unemployment, career counselors help to manage the transition from Fordist industrial economy to the new postindustrial service economy of "soft skills" and part-time, flexible "minijobs." Career services render the workforce more flexible and adaptable to the new requirements of the twenty-first-century workplace. Wanda Vrasti argues that career consultancy "repurposes the working population for the needs of financialized just-in-time production flows," creating "a permanent, state-subsidized, reserve army of cheap labour."[81] According to Vrasti, the postindustrial restructuring of the economy has been "contained and concealed" by a "seductive skills revolution."[82] With deliberate irony, she describes employment consulting as "a benevolent, pastoral task" that enables people "to better sell themselves":[83]

> Consulting is not a profession that requires a specific education or concrete skills. The expertise consists in the consultant's ability to embody a vision of entrepreneurial success to which the client aspires.[84]

Consultants are paid to embody a vision of success. This performative aspect of consultancy refers us back to classical tutors of rhetoric and oratory. Embodying a vision of success relates to the Aristotelian concept of *ethos* (character). Consultants must project the desired *ethos*, coaching employees on how to present themselves and polishing the résumés and the interview techniques of their clients. In this respect, twenty-first-century career advisers are not so very unlike the logographers and rhetoricians of the ancient world. Like their predecessors, they do not teach specific competences; instead, they are moral guides who encourage their clients "to embark on a process of transformation" and to accomplish "an all-round transformation in people's self-perception and general orientation to life."[85] This project of self-development serves the needs of the newest service industries. It implies the transformation into a more flexible type of employee, one who excels at changing roles. Employees must be reliable but "sufficiently opportunistic" to switch their links depending on the situations that arise.[86] Organizational change requires "zero-drag" employees who are effortlessly adaptable[87] and who are capable of regard-ing a succession of differing projects as opportunities for self-development that will reveal more of their potential.[88]

Career experts often promise to liberate the individual. The constant drive for self-improvement often tends to have the reverse effect, however: it actually institutionalizes employees and makes them easier to control by encouraging them to identify with their employers' values. Identification with corporate values (e.g., competitiveness, innovation, going on a jour-ney, etc.) can mean that people view themselves as free agents when they are in fact bound all the more tightly to their corporate functions.

In *Das Schiff* the chief manipulator of these proceedings is Lovelace, an "Executive Search Consultant" (*DS* 172)—a polite euphemism for a headhunter. Lovelace is well aware that companies invest in personal coaching programs precisely because they want to retain their most prom-ising staff: "Hier werden Talente gefördert. . . . Die Konzerne versuchen High Potentials auf diese Weise an sich zu binden" (*DS* 199; Talents are promoted here. . . . Corporations do this in order to hold on to staff with high potential). In Samuel Richardson's *Clarissa* (1748), Lovelace is the Machiavellian libertine who specializes in the corruption of virtue. In *Das Schiff*, too, Lovelace is essentially a seducer. He flatters his clients by telling them, "Ich vermittle ausschließlich Topperformer!" (*DS* 235; I only act as an agent for top performers!). Lovelace is a big beast at the top of the human resources food chain. The narrative emphasizes his pronounced orality, observing his "Rachen" (*DS* 202; jaws) and the way he likes to suck on nuts and chocolate: "Schon als Schüler hat Lovelace Schokoladenrippen nicht zerkaut, sonder angelutscht" (*DS* 196; Even as a schoolboy Lovelace did not chew chocolate bars but sucked them). This orality is an obvious symbol for the killer instinct, much like Hermann Hagenström's turkey-and-lemon roll in *Buddenbrooks* or Macheath's egg-eating skills in the *Dreigroschenroman*. The way in which Lovelace seduces Pamela Smaart in *Das Schiff* is reminiscent of the way that Hagenström maneuvers Toni Buddenbrook into a kiss in *Buddenbrooks*. Lovelace engineers Smaart's invitation to Macau in order to seduce her (*DS* 272). He resembles a pimp; as Smaart reflects, "Neben einem Mann wie Lovelace wird man unwillkür-lich zum Accessoire degradiert" (*DS* 266; Next to a man like Lovelace, a person gets downgraded involuntarily into an accessory). He embodies a vision of the market in which people are downgraded into mere resources. This is the uncomfortable situation Pamela Smaart recognizes at the end of the novel. But this moment of insight does not lead to any real change. Instead, Smaart merely resolves "sich nicht unter Wert [zu] verkaufen" (*DS* 271; not to sell herself for less than her value). She will continue to sell herself on the condition that she gets a good price. It is not the fact that she has become a commodity that offends her, but merely the low price she was offered.

The Critique of Corporate Communication

Ironically, despite the great emphasis on communication, there is remarkably little dialogue in *Das Schiff*. The experts parrot their scientific knowledge in a bid to establish their professional credibility. Their priority is not to communicate but rather to project and maintain their professional *ethos*. Schönthaler's figures do not talk *to* each other but *at* each other. Communication in the novel is thereby often reduced to a series of ritualistic nostrums. Genuine communication implies reciprocity, listening, give-and-take. But there is little sense of give-and-take in *Das Schiff*. Perhaps this is a result of the dominant value of competition that all the characters seem to take for granted. Although they pay lip service to team spirit (*DS* 49, 246), they are, in fact, so determined to look out for No. 1 that the possibility of genuine cooperation seems remote. Even as they pretend to work together, they are busy scoring points off each other. Among the many different types of career consultant featured in *Das Schiff*, one figure is significantly absent: the trade union representative. This absence exemplifies the lack of solidarity in *Das Schiff*. The intense focus on "interpersonal," one-to-one communication conveniently rules out the possibility of collective bargaining. In the twenty-first-century workplace the decline in representative forms of consultation has been accompanied by a sharp increase in forms of communication that exclude collective bargaining, e.g., focus groups, improvement groups, appraisals, peer observations, and opinion surveys.[89] It is a clear case of divide and rule, as individual employees are more vulnerable when collective representation is sidelined. As a result, individual relationships in *Das Schiff* are regimented along such strictly professional lines that any spontaneous dialogue is unlikely. For example, Erik Jungholz knows very well that his conversations are not dialogues; they proceed according to a prearranged script: "Er kennt seinen Text" (*DS* 2; He knows his lines).

The only time in *Das Schiff* when a genuine dialogue seems to occur, it turns out to be a fake. This occurs when Pamela J. Smaart travels to Macau, known as "the Las Vegas of Asia," to attend a meeting of the Lac Léman Society, an elite transnational network loosely based on the neoliberal Mont Pelerin Society founded by Friedrich Hayek and Milton Friedman. In Macau, Smaart goes on an organized tour of the historic Old Town, where she meets a young woman named Liun Xiangsu. Liun claims to be a native of Szechuan Province and says that she feels like an outsider in Macau (*DS* 206). Smaart asks Liun about her career plans and starts to relax and enjoy herself:

> Smaart hat schon lange nicht mehr dieses Gefühl verspürt, so ungezwungen mit einem Menschen unterwegs zu sein, eine spontane Face-to-Face-Begegnung, vollkommen vorbehaltlos. . . . Normalerweise geht es immer um irgendetwas, sind Interessen zu

verfolgen oder Interessen zu wahren. Hier ist es anders, denkt Smaart. (*DS* 207)

[Smaart has not had this feeling for a long time, to be out and about with someone in such an informal way, a spontaneous face-to-face encounter, completely without reservations. . . . Normally there is always an agenda, there are interests to pursue or interests to protect. Here it is different, thinks Smaart.]

At this point, Smaart imagines she has escaped the business world that she normally inhabits, where communication is dominated by financial transactions. Here the narrator echoes Walter Benjamin's observation that modern conversations are dominated by the theme of money: "Die Freiheit des Gespräches geht verloren. . . . Unabwendbar drängt sich in jede gesellige Unterhaltung des Thema der Lebensverhältnisse, des Geldes" (The freedom of conversation is being lost. . . . The topic of the conditions of life, of money, intrudes itself sooner or later in every sociable exchange).[90] Such critiques can be traced back to the *Communist Manifesto*'s assertion that the bourgeoisie has reduced all relationships to "das nackte Interesse, die gefühllose 'bare Zahlung'" ("naked self-interest, callous 'cash payment'").[91] In spite of the exotic location in Macau, it soon becomes apparent that the usual capitalist rules apply. Liun Xiangsu takes Smaart to her uncle's casino, where Smaart gets drawn into a card game. Soon she is stripped of all her money and her Cartier wristwatch. The fantasy of a relationship undistorted by commercial interests turns out to be a mirage. Liun Xiangsu is not a naive girl after all, but a ruthless businesswoman, much like Smaart herself. Even a professional judge of character like Smaart has let herself be fooled.[92]

The inauthenticity of corporate communication is shown very clearly toward the end of *Das Schiff*. The human resources director, Dr. Frederick Quass, has just died in a hospital in Stuttgart as a result of head injuries received in a car crash (*DS* 260). The day after, Quass's wife, his children, and a couple of other relatives report to the hospital, where they are welcomed by a senior nurse and a "Diplom-Psychologin" (*DS* 260; certified psychologist). The senior nurse informs them that the psychologist can discuss any questions they may have; she is even trained as a child psychologist and as a "coach" (*DS* 260). As a new pilot project, the clinic can also provide the family information on a range of different funeral and burial options, if required (*DS* 261). First, however, the nurse asks them to fill out a feedback form:

Bevor Sie sich mit unserer Psychologin verständigen, bitte ich Sie, unseren Evaluationsbogen auszufüllen, den wir derzeit im Zuge einer breit angelegten Universitätsstudie erheben. . . . Uns hilft es, in Zukunft den Leidens- und Sterbeprozess für alle Beteiligten besser zu gestalten. In dem Sie uns sagen, wie Sie die Betreuung vor Ort empfunden haben, wie die Kommunikationsstrukturen aus Ihrer Sicht geregelt waren, . . . wie Sie den Leidens- und Sterbeprozess des Verschiedenen beurteilen und einiges Weitere. . . . Die Bewertungsskala reicht von 1 = schlecht bis 6 = sehr gut. (*DS* 261)

[Before you communicate with our psychologist, please could you fill out our evaluation form, for a survey we are carrying out as part of a large-scale academic study. . . . It will help us to shape the process of suffering and dying better in the future for all participants. Please tell us how you felt about the care received on site, how you thought the communication structures were organized, how you evaluate the suffering and dying process of the deceased, and some other details. . . . The evaluation scale ranges from 1 = bad to 6 = very good.]

This is beautifully observed. Even the process of dying and grieving is subjected to technocratic feedback questionnaires, designed to quantify levels of grief and suffering according to a six-point numerical scale. These feedback forms are not designed to be read by human beings but by computers. Despite the relentless focus on "communication structures," there is a sense here that ritualized, formalized feedback is replacing human interaction. What is sought is not qualitative depth of interaction but quantifiable data that can be easily digitized and subjected to computer analysis. It is very rare that an individual feedback form is taken seriously. Instead, the forms are typically fed into a computer and subjected to data mining, in which the frequency of key words and phrases is quantified. Incidentally, the technique of data mining also informs Franco Moretti's technique of "distant reading." A critique of Moretti's distant reading would go beyond the scope of this present study;[93] in both cases, though, large quantities of data are filtered according to statistical analysis, and individual particularities are ignored. Essentially, data mining operates like a giant sieve in which individual human narratives fall through the gaps. Even Moretti concedes that distant reading is a form of Faustian bargain. As he puts it, "What we really need is a little pact with the devil: we know how to read texts, now let's learn how *not* to read them."[94] In the service of positivist, numerically verifiable "outcomes," data mining is reductive: it degrades the unique specificity of every text, and it collapses complex narratives into the lowest common denominators.

Proposing a Toast: The Corporate Encomium

In the twenty-first century public speeches can be disseminated with greater ease than ever before by means of internet videos. Oratory still has enormous political and economic potential because it is a means to create consensus. Schönthaler has observed that the success of Apple owes much to Steve Jobs and his skill as a public speaker.[95] As *Das Schiff* draws to a

close, one of the high points is the speech given by the CEO of Pfeiffer
Beauty, Gröber, at the corporation's "Sommerprosit" (*DS* 246; summer
party). Gröber's status as a transnational entrepreneur is underlined by the
fact that he resides in Switzerland for tax purposes (*DS* 76). Gröber might
speak the language of teamwork and solidarity, but his tax avoidance tells
a different story. The summer party begins with a corporate gig by a rock
band, "Monkey Psychosis." The band performs a song with tailor-made
lyrics in praise of the corporation: "Wir Pushen die Benchmark / Ja, wir
sind PB!" (*DS* 244; We push the benchmark / Yes, we are PB!).
Simultaneously, young women appear—it is unclear whether they are students or models; in any case, they have presumably been hired to simulate
the atmosphere of a rock concert by pretending to be groupies, or perhaps,
to continue the sporting analogy, cheerleaders (*DS* 244). As soon as the
song ends, Gröber walks onto the balcony, holding a microphone. The
function of his speech seems simple: to thank the musicians and to mark
the beginning of the festivities. This is the epideictic (demonstrative)
rhetoric of eulogy and praise, which is "designed to forge a sense of identity and values around a set of ideal images."[96] The eulogy does not accommodate discussion and debate; instead, it invokes an imagined ideological
community. Thus, although the CEO's summer party speech avoids
political and economic references, it is a means to form consensus within
the company. It is a team-building exercise, an affirmation of allegiance to
the company and its values. In this type of situation there is no room for
dissent, only for assent.

Far from being a democratic exercise, the summer speech is an opportunity for the CEO to assert his authority over his colleagues. Even though
Gröber is a practiced speaker, he has a touch of nerves as he begins. His
opening gambit is "Hurrah!" (*DS* 244), which he immediately regrets; but
he has to press on, so he follows it up with "Monkey Psychosis" (*DS* 246).
Gröber moves swiftly from praising the teamwork of the band to praising
the teamwork of his coworkers. When he shouts, "Was für ein T-eeeam"
(*DS* 246; What a team), he clasps his index fingers together and points,
first at the band in the foyer and then in the direction of his colleagues. At
the same time, he performs a series of pirouettes (*DS* 246). These inclusive
gestures are simple but powerful; they suggest that the PB employees are
as well coordinated as a rock band, that they mesh together like musicians.
The music is not just a tribute to the employees' performance; it symbol-
izes their achievements. In this manner, the CEO flatters his audience,
suggesting that their jobs are the equivalent of "rock and roll." Corporate
rhetoric sometimes presents work itself as a form of play, as something
radically hedonistic or revolutionary, even alleging that work is "better
than sex."[97] "Do what you love" is the new unofficial work mantra in
many corporations.[98] Gröber is too skilled to make such statements explicitly; instead, he invites the audience to go along with the performance.

Despite the brevity of the CEO's speech, it draws on classical oratory insofar as he invokes a personal connection with every member of the audience. At one point he even calls them "meine Lieben" (*DS* 248; my dear friends). And he makes sure to thank every member of the workforce individually, paying tribute to "den persönlichen, professionellen Einsatz eines jeden Einzelnen" (*DS* 247; the personal, professional commitment of each and every individual). Roman orators would rhetorically fashion a version of their state in order to justify a particular course of action, and Gröber does the same in order to justify his own leadership.[99] He presents an ideal vision of the company's values, using the rule of three, producing a perfect tricolon: three substantives, each of two syllables, each one a trochee: "Wie ihr alle wisst . . . PB ist schon immer dem Besten, Wahren und Schönen verpflichtet!" (*DS* 247; As you all know, PB is always committed to the best, the true, and the beautiful!). He moves swiftly from the ideal to the practical announcement that the quarterly turnover has increased by 4.1 percent (*DS* 247). The implication is clear: ideals and personal commitment translate into increased sales. The CEO modulates his voice, sinking it by a musical third when expressing his regret for Frederick Quass's car accident (*DS* 247). He skillfully handles the moment of solemnity (a minute of silence for Quass) before returning to a mood of celebration.

The culmination of the speech confirms the importance of sport as a guiding metaphor for business in the early twenty-first century. The CEO declares that Erik Jungholz is the "Quartalssieg-eeer" (*DS* 248; the winner of this quarterly period). Now the scene resembles an Olympic ceremony in which the winning athlete receives a gold medal. Notice that at this corporate ceremony there are no silver and bronze medals: the winner takes it all. As "the employee of the quarter," Erik is symbolically crowned in front of his coworkers. Ironically, this top player will soon be poached by another company. He is in the process of transferring to a rival "team": Santor, a key player in cosmetic surgery and health tourism (*DS* 233). Erik tries to imprint the moment on his memory so that he can recall this positive feeling later (*DS* 249)—it could serve as a motivational factor in the future. He is already preparing mentally for his next professional contest. At the same time, he knows that he has to perform his acceptance of the award, and he uses his favorite rituals to help him, flexing and relaxing his muscles and throwing his head back to take in the crowd (*DS* 249). His hands raised, he turns in a circle and nods to his colleagues (*DS* 250). Champagne glasses are refilled, and then, gradually, the employees return to their desks. They are "beschwingt" (*DS* 250; buoyant), ready and willing to do their duty once again. As the noise subsides, there is no longer any need for an emotional display, and the CEO lapses into his usual professional persona, "jetzt schon wieder routiniert, ganz Herr seiner selbst" (*DS* 250; now already back in his slick routine, completely in control of himself). This is how the Erik Jungholz storyline concludes: the pseudo-Olympic ceremony is an affirmation of the corporate routine and its regime of athletic self-discipline. The players of the game are still bound by the rules, even if they do not believe in them.

The scene shows the continuing relevance of classical models of both oratory and athletics in the twenty-first century. Only the toughest and most disciplined athlete is to be acclaimed as the "winner." At the same time, the other employees are encouraged to emulate him. As the master of ceremonies, the CEO has the task of harnessing the audience's emotions. At one point, he lifts his gaze so that it encompasses the audience: "Wenn man den gesamten Raum kontrollieren will, muss man die Teilnehmer der letzten Reihe binden" (*DS* 247; If you want to control the entire room, then you have to bind the participants in the back row). The verbs are telling: "kontrollieren" (control) and "binden" (bind).[100] The employees are being given the symbolic equivalent of a pat on the back before they are sent back to work. It is like a general commending the troops, or a coach meeting with the players. In this way, the corporate award ceremony reveals the family resemblance among businesspeople, politicians, and the orators and athletes of classical civilization. Even so, something is missing from this game-playing model of social interaction: argumentation, which enables people to change the rules.[101] *Das Schiff* depicts a form of corporate rhetoric that lacks the essence of rhetoric: debate. It is smooth, but insipid.

Conclusion

BUSINESS RHETORIC HAS contemporary relevance: think of Donald Trump's *Trump: The Art of the Deal* (1987), cowritten with the journalist Tony Schwartz.[1] Trump's own career trajectory from real estate developer to TV show host to president of the United States exemplifies the many fluid interconnections among business, performance, and politics. Literary criticism can make a modest contribution to this complex interdisciplinary field. Focusing here on German-language novels and their depictions of economic activity, we have seen that rhetoric is central to business. The denials of rhetoric that we so often encounter here (Heinrich Mann's factory owner, Röggla's management consultants) are not to be taken at face value: such denials are a highly rhetorical move. The novels studied here alert readers that behind claims to be factual or impartial, there is always a political and/or economic agenda. The classical tradition of rhetoric, which still informs public relations, has often been sidelined, but these novels acknowledge the inevitability of rhetoric and the need to understand how it operates. As John Henderson points out, although Aristotle concedes that rhetoric involves manipulation, the ultimate aim of Aristotelian rhetoric is to attain the *logos* of reasoned debate. The teachers of rhetoric did not "wish away" the persuasive and performative aspects of oratory, but they "kept plugging the ethical into the performative."[2]

Many of the novels studied in this book contain set pieces in which the outcome depends upon the delivery of a public speech. In *Buddenbrooks* Consul Jean takes the wind out of his opponents' sails with a few well-aimed quips delivered in Plattdeutsch; Grünlich talks his way into getting his hands on Tony's dowry; and Hanno's lack of business talent is confirmed by his failure to recite a poem. In *Der Untertan* the protagonist achieves success as an orator precisely because he is so good at staying within his role. *Käsebier* contrasts two funeral orations, the authentic and the inauthentic. The *Dreigroschenroman* shows that noneconomic factors can have an important bearing on business, as Macheath persuades his workforce to accept their own pauperization. In *Malina* the narrator frustrates her interviewer because she refuses to remain in the rhetorical place he has assigned to her. In comparison, the dialogues between Ich and Malina are more meaningful because they stage a debate between opposing positions. In *Das Impressum* it is the relaxation of official discourse that matters. *Unsere Siemens-Welt* can be read as a sustained eulogy (*Festrede*) that doubles as a critique: by showing how the corporate mask slips, it reveals how the mask is constructed. *wir schlafen nicht* is composed of a series of interviews in which the management consultants rehearse their presentational skills. *Das Schiff* stages job interviews, commercial presentations, and award ceremonies in which keeping to the prearranged script is a condition of success. The point here is that oratory and rhetoric matter. The formulation of language, whether spoken or written, remains inseparable from the exercise of political and economic power.

Each of these novels displays a certain ambivalence toward rhetoric. They show how rhetoric is often used to facilitate exploitation, but they also show that rhetoric is an essential part of all communication. There are, of course, different types of rhetoric: for example, there is the kind that obscures injustice, and the kind that exposes it. The nine novels encourage readers to be aware of rhetorical manipulation but also to see that rhetoric can be potentially liberating if it points the way toward open, well-informed debate. In each novel, the reflection on rhetoric is connected with the choice of narrative technique. In *Buddenbrooks* irony and rhetorical questions leave the novel open to different interpretations. In *Der Untertan* authoritarian rhetoric is foregrounded in an attempt to inoculate readers against it. In *Käsebier* the narrative rehearses stereotypes associated with Neue Sachlichkeit, only to conclude by rejecting them and dropping the affectation of neutrality. In the *Dreigroschenroman* readers are given a crash course in manipulative tricks and how to detect them. *Malina* stages a tug of wills between two opposing forms of rhetoric: Malina's discourse of restraint and Ich's discourse of excess. The narrative of *Das Impressum* proceeds in fits and starts in an attempt to enlarge the available space of discourse. In *Unsere Siemens-Welt* the rhetoric of congratulation tips over into accusation. In *wir schlafen nicht* the use of reported speech alerts readers to the performative quality of management discourse. In *Das Schiff* the script is so polished that it almost conceals the absence of meaningful dialogue.

In many of the novels there is also a contrast between the rhetoric of cooperation and the underlying conflicts of interest it tries to conceal. Often, the characters' fates depend on their ability (or inability) to judge rhetoric. In *Buddenbrooks* Thomas mistakes the public image for the real thing. In *Der Untertan* Wolfgang Buck sees through the rhetoric, but he is unable to oppose it effectively. In *Käsebier* disaster ensues because the protagonists are unable to tell the difference between truth and falsehood. The same applies to the *Dreigroschenroman* when George Fewkoombey and Mary Swayer fall for the rhetoric of their employers and lose their lives. In *Malina* the narrator's debates with Malina about how to interpret her dreams become crucial. *Das Impressum* implies that the fate of the nation hinges on the SED's ability to tolerate more open, critical debate. In *Unsere Siemens-Welt* readers are challenged to decode the gap between the rhetoric of corporate social responsibility and actual business practices. In *wir schlafen nicht* the characters grope toward the possibility of a way out when they question the ideology in which they are trapped. In *Das Schiff* the careers of the main characters depend on whether or not they are able to keep to the script. These examples show that the ability to interpret and use language effectively is an essential skill, and not only in economic terms but for survival itself.

The Scottish poet Tom Leonard has been described as speaking "for the necessity 'not to be complicit' in a world that is saturated with sound bites, social inequality and corporate flannel."[3] For the social scientist Michael Billig, it is our lack of certainty about "reality" that gives our choices "their element of humanity."[4] When creative writers highlight the power of rhetoric, they do so in the hope of encouraging informed, enlightened discussion of the kind that is never conclusive because it always remains open to challenge. Instead of dismissing rhetoric or ignoring it, we need to become more literate about it. The process of literary criticism makes us more aware of how rhetoric works. The novels in this book challenge us to refine our interpretive skills and to make more informed decisions in the future, whether these are business decisions or other kinds. Studying literature can help us to reflect on how our values are constituted. In doing so, it points the way toward more reasoned forms of economic and political debate.

Notes

Introduction

Epigraph: Abbé d'Aubignac (François Hédelin), *La Pratique du théâtre* (Paris, 1657), 370; cited in Peter France, *Racine's Rhetoric* (Oxford: Oxford University Press, 1965), 2.

[1] For an overview, see Franziska Schößler, "Ökonomie," in *Literatur und Wissen: Ein interdisziplinäres Handbuch*, edited by Roland Borgards, Harald Niemeyer, Nicolas Pethes, and Yvonne Wübben (Stuttgart: Metzler, 2013), 101–5. On the modern period as a whole, see Enrik Lauer, *Literarischer Monetarismus: Studien zur Homologie von Sinn und Geld bei Goethe, Goux, Sohn-Rethell, Simmel und Luhmann* (St. Ingbert: Röhrig, 1994); Jochen Hörisch, *Kopf oder Zahl: Die Poesie des Geldes* (Frankfurt am Main: Suhrkamp, 1996); Joseph Vogl, *Das Gespenst des Kapitals* (Zurich: Diaphanes, 2010); Sandra Richter, *Mensch und Markt: Warum wir den Wettbewerb fürchten und ihn trotzdem brauchen* (Hamburg: Murmann, 2012). On the early modern period: Daniel Fulda, *Schau-Spiele des Geldes: Die Komödie und die Entstehung der Marktgesellschaft von Shakespeare bis Lessing* (Tübingen: Niemeyer, 2005). On the eighteenth century: Joseph Vogl, *Kalkül und Leidenschaft: Poetik des ökonomischen Menschen* (Zurich: Diaphanes, 2002); Thomas Wegmann, *Tauschverhältnisse: Zur Ökonomie des Literarischen und zum Ökonomischen in der Literatur von Gellert bis Goethe* (Würzburg: Königshausen & Neumann, 2002); Reinhard Saller, *Schöne Ökonomie: Die poetische Reflexion der Ökonomie in frühromantischer Literatur* (Würzburg: Königshausen & Neumann, 2007). On the nineteenth century: Christian Rakow, *Die Ökonomien des Realismus: Kulturpoetische Untersuchungen zur Literatur und Volkswirtschaftslehre 1850–1900* (Berlin: De Gruyter, 2013). On modernism: Bernd Blaschke, *Der homo oeconomicus und sein Kredit bei Musil, Joyce, Svevo, Unamuno und Celine* (Munich: Wilhelm Fink, 2004); Franziska Schößler, *Börsenfieber und Kaufrausch: Ökonomie, Judentum und Weiblichkeit bei Theodor Fontane, Heinrich Mann, Thomas Mann, Arthur Schnitzler und Émile Zola* (Bielefeld: Aisthesis, 2009). On contemporary fiction: Nadja Gernalzick, *Kredit und Kultur: Ökonomie- und Geldbegriff bei Jacques Derrida und in der amerikanischen Literaturtheorie der Postmoderne* (Heidelberg: Winter, 2002); Kremer, *Milieu und Performativität*; Sandra von der Horst, *Das Unternehmerbild in der deutschen Gegenwartsliteratur: Eine Analyse anhand der Romane "Der schwarze Grat" und "wenn wir sterben"* (Saarbrücken: VDM Verlag Dr. Müller, 2008); Susanne Heimburger,

Kapitalistischer Geist und literarische Kritik—Arbeitswelten in deutschsprachigen Gegenwartstexten (Munich: Text + Kritik, 2010).

2 Deirdre N. McCloskey, *The Rhetoric of Economics*, 2nd ed. (Madison: University of Wisconsin Press, 1998), xxi. The first edition (1985) was published under the author's birth name, Donald N. McCloskey.

3 Donald N. McCloskey, *Knowledge and Persuasion in Economics* (Cambridge: Cambridge University Press, 1994), xv. Editions published after 1995 bear the name Deirdre N. McCloskey.

4 Arjo Klamer, "The Third Way: A Cultural Economic Perspective," in *Economic Persuasions*, edited by Stephen Gudeman, Studies in Rhetoric and Culture 3 (New York: Berghahn, 2009), 183.

5 The first conference was published as Martha Woodmansee and Mark Osteen, eds., *The New Economic Criticism: Studies at the Intersection of Literature and Economics* (London: Routledge, 1999); papers from the second conference were published in the journal *New Literary History* 31, no. 2 (2000).

6 On the Bildungsroman, see Eva Ritthaler, *Ökonomische Bildung: Wirtschaft in deutschen Entwicklungsromanen von Goethe bis Heinrich Mann* (Würzburg: Königshausen & Neumann, 2017). On labor: André Lottmann, *Arbeitsverhältnisse: Der arbeitende Mensch in Goethes "Wilhelm Meister"-Romanen und in der Geschichte der politischen Ökonomie*, Epistemata Literaturwissenschaft 724 (Würzburg: Königshausen & Neumann, 2011); Susanna Brogi, Carolin Freier, Ulf Freier-Otten, and Katja Hartosch, eds., *Repräsentationen von Arbeit: Transdisziplinäre Analysen und künstlerische Produktion* (Bielefeld: Transcript, 2013). On the gift: Gisela Ecker, *"Giftige" Gaben: Über Tauschprozesse in der Literatur* (Munich: Wilhelm Fink, 2008). On inflation: Bernd Widdig, *Culture and Inflation in Weimar Germany* (Berkeley: University of California Press, 2001).

7 Pierre Bourdieu, *The Rules of Art: Genesis and Structure of the Literary Field*, translated by Susan Emanuel (Cambridge: Polity Press, 1996); Brigitte E. Jirku and Marion Schulz, eds., *Fiktionen und Realitäten: Schriftstellerinnen im deutschsprachigen Literaturbetrieb* (Frankfurt am Main: Peter Lang, 2013). The study of German literature in the context of the marketplace was pioneered by the Austrian-born critic Wilhelm Scherer (1841–86). See Rakow, *Die Ökonomien des Realismus*, 29–43.

8 Richard T. Gray, *Money Matters: Economics and the German Cultural Imagination, 1770–1850* (Seattle: University of Washington Press, 2008).

9 Cf. Kremer, *Milieu und Performativität*, 32–44. Kremer, however, neglects the affinities between Butler's work and classical rhetoric. On this topic, see Lynne Pearce, *The Rhetorics of Feminism: Readings in Contemporary Cultural Theory and the Popular Press* (New York: Routledge, 2004), 149–50.

10 McCloskey, *Knowledge and Persuasion*, 29.

11 McCloskey, 98, 167.

12 E.g., Alison Theaker, ed., *The Public Relations Handbook*, 3rd ed. (London: Routledge, 2008), 20; Owen Hargie, ed., *The Handbook of Communication Skills*, 3rd ed. (London: Routledge, 2006), 202–203.

¹³ S. Wolf and R. Baber, "Verkaufsrhetorik," in *Historisches Wörterbuch der Rhetorik*, edited by Gert Ueding, vol. 9: *St-Z* (Tübingen: Niemeyer, 2009), 1074–82.

¹⁴ Aristotle, *Rhetoric*, translated by W. Rhys Roberts (Oxford: Oxford University Press, 1924), 1.2.1355b25–26 (unpaginated). This translation is also available online, hosted by the Massachusetts Institute of Technology, http://classics.mit.edu/Aristotle/rhetoric.html.

¹⁵ Aristotle, 1.2.1356a.

¹⁶ Aristotle, 1.3.1358b6–7.

¹⁷ Aristotle, 1.3.1358b8–9.

¹⁸ Aristotle, *Politics* 125a, quoted in Melissa Lane, *Greek and Roman Political Ideas* (London: Penguin, 2014), 197.

¹⁹ Vogl, *Gespenst des Kapitals*, 116–20.

²⁰ Aristotle, *Rhetoric* 2.16.1391a13.

²¹ Aristotle, 1.4.1359b19–20.

²² Marcus Tullius Cicero, *De Officiis* (*The Offices*) 3.12–16, in *Cicero's Offices, Essays on Friendship and Old Age and Select Letters* (London: J. M. Dent; New York: E. P. Dutton, 1909), 133–41.

²³ Terry Eagleton, *Walter Benjamin or Towards a Revolutionary Criticism* (1981; New York: Verso, 2009), 101–2.

²⁴ Wilfried Barner, *Barockrhetorik: Untersuchungen zu ihren geschichtlichen Grundlagen* (Tübingen: Niemeyer, 1970), 89.

²⁵ Cicero, *De inventione* 1.1, translated by C. D. Yonge, http://www.classicpersuasion.org/pw/cicero/dnv1-1.htm (site discontinued).

²⁶ Quentin Skinner, *Reason and Rhetoric in the Philosophy of Hobbes* (Cambridge: Cambridge University Press, 1996), 3.

²⁷ Claude Adrien Helvétius, *De l'esprit* (1758), cited in Vogl, *Das Gespenst des Kapitals*, 36; translated by Joachim Redner and Robert Savage as *The Specter of Capital* (Stanford, CA: Stanford University Press, 2015), 21: "If the physical universe is subject to the laws of motion, the moral universe is no less subject to those of interest." Helvétius's theory was contradicted by his engagement for the freedom of speech, at a great personal cost. Cf. Jonathan Israel, *Democratic Enlightenment: Philosophy, Revolution and Human Rights 1750–1790* (Oxford: Oxford University Press, 2012), 668.

²⁸ Vogl, *Das Gespenst des Kapitals*, 44; *The Specter of Capital*, 22. For more discussion of the term *homo (o)economicus*, see Blaschke, *Der homo oeconomicus und sein Kredit*, 17–24.

²⁹ Kathy Eden, "Rhetoric," in *The Classical Tradition*, edited by Anthony Grafton, Glenn W. Most, and Salvatore Settis (Cambridge, MA: Harvard University Press, 2010), 830.

³⁰ Gert Ueding, *Moderne Rhetorik: Von der Aufklärung bis zur Gegenwart*, 2nd ed. (Munich: Beck, 2009), 79–82.

³¹ On this topic see Joachim Goth, *Nietzsche und die Rhetorik* (Tübingen: Niemeyer, 1970), and Sander L. Gilman, Carole Blair, and David J. Parent, eds.

and trans., *Friedrich Nietzsche on Rhetoric and Language* (New York: Oxford University Press, 1989).

[32] For a discussion of Sprachkritik and the *Sprachkrise* (language crisis), see Ritchie Robertson, "Modernism and the Self 1890–1924," in *Philosophy and German Literature, 1700–1990*, edited by Nicholas Saul (Cambridge: Cambridge University Press, 2002), 164–66; Dirk Göttsche, *Die Produktivität der Sprachkrise in der modernen Prosa* (Frankfurt am Main: Athenäum, 1987).

[33] Friedrich Nietzsche, *Kritische Gesamtausgabe der Werke*, 40 vols., edited by Giorgio Colli and Mazzino Montinari (Berlin: De Gruyter, 1967–91), 3.2:374.

[34] Katrin Kohl, "Die Rhetorik ist das Wesen der Philosophie Nietzsches (Hans Blumenberg). Klassische Tradition moderner Wirkung," in *Ecce Opus: Nietzsche-Revisionen im 20. Jahrhundert*, edited by Rüdiger Görner and Duncan Large (Göttingen: Vandenhoeck & Ruprecht, 2003), 211, 216. See also John Bender and David E. Wellbery, "Rhetoricality: On the Modernist Return of Rhetoric," in *The Ends of Rhetoric: History, Theory, Practice*, edited by John Bender and David E. Wellbery (Stanford, CA: Stanford University Press, 1990), 3–39.

[35] Nietzsche, *Kritische Gesamtausgabe der Werke*, 6.2:198 (*Jenseits von Gut und Böse*, § 247).

[36] Walter Benjamin, "Gehaltserhöhung?! Wo denken Sie hin!" in *Gesammelte Schriften*, 7 vols., edited by Rolf Tiedemann and Hermann Schweppenhäuser (Frankfurt am Main: Suhrkamp, 1972–99), 4.2:629–40. Broadcast March 26, 1931. I would like to thank Hussein Mitha for this reference.

[37] Ernst Bloch, "Kaufmanns-Latein im Ernst" (1928), in *Gesamtausgabe in 16 Bänden*, vol. 9: *Literarische Aufsätze* (Frankfurt am Main: Suhrkamp, 1977), 165–69.

[38] Kenneth Burke, "The Rhetoric of Hitler's 'Battle'" [1939], in *The Philosophy of Literary Form*, 3rd ed. (Berkeley: University of California Press, 1973), 204.

[39] Cf. Ueding, *Moderne Rhetorik*, 100–101.

[40] Marshall McLuhan, *The Mechanical Bride: Folklore of Industrial Man* (1951; London: Duckworth, 2011), 42.

[41] Erving Goffman, *The Presentation of Self in Everyday Life* (1959; London: Penguin, 1990); Goffman, *Stigma: Notes on the Management of Spoiled Identity* (1963; Harmondsworth, UK: Pelican, 1981).

[42] Goffman, *Presentation of Self*, 152.

[43] Goffman, 152.

[44] Goffman, 203–30.

[45] Chaim Perelman and Lucie Olbrechts-Tyteca, *The New Rhetoric: A Treatise on Argumentation*, translated by John Wilkinson and Purcell Weaver (Notre Dame, IN: University of Notre Dame Press, 1969).

[46] George Myerson, *Rhetoric, Reason and Society: Rationality as Dialogue* (London: Sage, 2004), 50.

[47] Hans Blumenberg, "Anthropologische Annäherung an die Aktualität der Rhetorik" [1971], in *Wirklichkeiten in denen wir leben: Aufsätze und eine Rede*

(Stuttgart: Reclam, 1981), 107; translated as "An Anthropological Approach to the Contemporary Significance of Rhetoric," in *After Philosophy: End or Transformation?*, edited by Kenneth Baynes, James Bohman, and Thomas McCarthy (Cambridge, MA: MIT Press, 1987), 432.

[48] Blumenberg, "Anthropologische Annäherung," 108; "Anthropological Approach," 433.

[49] Blumenberg, "Anthropologische Annäherung," 111; "Anthropological Approach," 435.

[50] Blumenberg, "Anthropologische Annäherung," 115–16; "Anthropological Approach," 439–40.

[51] Blumenberg, "Anthropologische Annäherung," 116; "Anthropological Approach," 440.

[52] Blumenberg, "Anthropologische Annäherung," 118; "Anthropological Approach," 442.

[53] Blumenberg, "Anthropologische Annäherung," 118; "Anthropological Approach," 442.

[54] Blumenberg, "Anthropologische Annäherung," 128–29; "Anthropological Approach," 451.

[55] Blumenberg, "Anthropologische Annäherung," 134; "Anthropological Approach," 455.

[56] For further discussion, see George Lakoff and Mark Johnson, *Metaphors We Live By* (Chicago: University of Chicago Press, 1980).

[57] Katrin Kohl, *Metapher* (Stuttgart: Metzler, 2007).

[58] Michael Billig, *Arguing and Thinking: A Rhetorical Approach to Social Psychology*, 2nd ed. (Cambridge: Cambridge University Press, 1996), 39–56.

[59] Billig, 46.

[60] Billig, 52–53.

[61] Billig, 148.

[62] Billig, 291–92.

[63] Ha-Joon Chang, *The Little Blue Book*, booklet inserted in *Economics: The User's Guide* (New York: Pelican, 2014).

[64] Ulrich Beck, *Was ist Globalisierung? Irrtümer des Globalismus—Antworten auf Globalisierung* (Frankfurt am Main: Suhrkamp, 1997), 232.

[65] Keith Tribe, *The Economy of the Word: Language, History, and Economics* (Oxford: Oxford University Press, 2015), 21–88.

[66] Tribe, 132.

[67] Tribe, 137.

[68] Rhetorical approaches to modern economics include Jerry Z. Muller, *The Mind and the Market: Capitalism in Modern European Thought* (New York: Knopf, 2002); Corinne Grenouillet and Catherine Vuillermot-Febvet, eds., *La langue du management et de l'économie à l'ère néolibérale: Formes sociales et littéraires* (Strasbourg: Presses universitaires de Strasbourg, 2015).

[69] For example, see Nicholas Wapshott, *Keynes—Hayek: The Clash That Defined Modern Economics* (New York: Norton, 2011).

[70] Friedrich A. Hayek, *Law, Legislation, and Liberty*, vol. 2: *The Mirage of Social Justice* (Chicago: University of Chicago Press, 1976), 56. Cf. also Muller, *Mind and the Market*, 371.

[71] Karl Polanyi, *The Great Transformation: The Political and Economic Origins of Our Time* (1944; Boston: Beacon Press, 2001), 71.

[72] Polanyi, 75.

[73] For a summary of Polanyi, see Wolfgang Streeck, *Re-Forming Capitalism: Institutional Changes in the German Political Economy* (Oxford: Oxford University Press, 2009), 246–52.

[74] James Arnt Aune, *Selling the Free Market: The Rhetoric of Economic Correctness* (New York: Guilford Press, 2001), xiv.

[75] Aune, *Selling the Free Market*, 10–11, 38–57.

[76] James Arnt Aune, *Rhetoric and Marxism* (Boulder, CO: Westview, 1994).

[77] Catherine Chaput and Joshua S. Hanan, "Theories of Economic Justice in the Rhetorical Tradition," in *Oxford Research Encyclopedia of Communication*, edited by Jon F. Nussbaum, online publication, November 2016, doi:10.1093/acrefore/9780190228613.013.148.

[78] Cf. Maiken Umbach, *German Cities and Bourgeois Modernism, 1890–1924* (Oxford: Oxford University Press, 2009), 147.

[79] Paul Betts, *The Authority of Everyday Objects: A Cultural History of West German Industrial Design* (Berkeley: University of California Press, 2004).

[80] Zafer Şenocak, *Deutschsein: Eine Aufklärungsschrift* (Hamburg: Körber-Stiftung, 2011), 60.

[81] According to Wikipedia, these were worth $1,283,000,000,000 in 2016: "List of Countries by Exports," https://en.wikipedia.org/wiki/List_of_countries_by_exports.

[82] Fraunhofer-Gesellschaft, https://www.fraunhofer.de/en/about-fraunhofer/profile-structure.html.

[83] Fraunhofer-Gesellschaft, https://www.fraunhofer.de/en/about-fraunhofer/profile-structure/facts-and-figures.html.

[84] On this point, see Sitta von Reden, ed., *Stiftungen zwischen Politik und Wirtschaft: Geschichte und Gegenwart im Dialog*, *Historische Zeitschrift*, Beiheft 66 (Berlin: De Gruyter Oldenbourg, 2015).

[85] The term "postindustrial society" was coined in 1969 by the French sociologist Alain Touraine: *La société post-industrielle: Naissance d'une société* (Paris: Denoël, 1969).

[86] For statistics on the German service sector, see "Statistiken zur Dienstleistungsbranche," accessed December 6, 2017, Statista, https://de.statista.com/themen/1434/dienstleistungsbranche/.

[87] Günter Minnerup, "Reflections on German History and Anglo-Saxon Liberalism," in *The Challenge of German Culture: Essays Presented to Wilfried van der Will*, edited by Michael Butler and Robert Evans (Basingstoke, UK: Palgrave, 2000), 178. For a recent biography of List, see Eugen Wendler, *Friedrich List (1789–1846): A Visionary Economist with Social Responsibility* (Berlin: Springer, 2014).

[88] Hans-Ulrich Wehler, *Deutsche Gesellschaftsgeschichte*, 5 vols. (Munich: Beck, 2003), 4:711.

[89] Werner Abelshauser, *Deutsche Wirtschaftsgeschichte: Von 1945 bis zur Gegenwart*, 2nd ed. (Munich: Beck, 2011), 30–43.

[90] Jeffrey R. Fear, *Organizing Control: August Thyssen and the Construction of German Corporate Management* (Cambridge, MA: Harvard University Press, 2005), 693.

[91] Fear argues that Dinkelbach's advocacy of Mitbestimmung was influenced by Catholic social thought, as evidenced in Dinkelbach's correspondence with the Catholic intellectual Peter Wilhelm Haurand, 692–93.

[92] For an analysis of Werner in the early drafts of Goethe's novel, see Johannes D. Kaminski, "Werner's Accounting Eye: Circulating Blood and Money in *Wilhelm Meisters theatralische Sendung*," *Publications of the English Goethe Society* 83, no. 1 (2014): 37–52.

[93] T. E. Carter, "Freytag's *Soll und Haben*: A Liberal National Manifesto as a Best-Seller," *German Life and Letters* 21 (1967/68): 320–29. More recently, see Florian Krobb, ed., *150 Jahre "Soll und Haben": Studien zu Gustav Freytags kontroversem Roman* (Würzburg: Königshausen & Neumann, 2005).

[94] Gustav Freytag, *Soll und Haben* (1855; Waltrop: Manuscriptum, 2002), 239. Unless otherwise stated, all English translations in this book are my own.

[95] Freytag, *Soll und Haben*, 240.

[96] Benedict Schofield, "Gustav Freytag's *Soll und Haben*: Politics, Aesthetics, and the Bestseller," in *The German Bestseller in the Late Nineteenth Century*, edited by Charlotte Woodford and Benedict Schofield (Rochester, NY: Camden House, 2012), 36.

[97] On Spielhagen's novel, see Rakow, *Ökonomien des Realismus*, 305–13, 451–55.

[98] On Raabe and globalization, see Dirk Göttsche and Florian Krobb, eds., *Wilhelm Raabe: Global Themes—International Perspectives* (London: Legenda, 2009).

[99] Ernest Schonfield, "Wirtschaftlicher Strukturwandel in Theodor Fontanes *Der Stechlin*," in *Theodor Fontane: Dichter des Übergangs*, edited by Patricia Howe, Fontaneana 10 (Würzburg: Königshausen & Neumann, 2013), 91–108.

[100] On technology in the literature of the Weimar Republic, see David Midgley, *Writing Weimar: Critical Realism in German Literature 1918–1933* (Oxford: Oxford University Press, 2000), 304–52.

[101] On K. A. Schenzinger, see Richter, *Mensch und Markt*, 132; Michael Minden, *Modern German Literature* (Cambridge: Polity, 2011), 156.

[102] See Wolfgang Emmerich, *Kleine Literaturgeschichte der DDR* (Berlin: Aufbau, 2000), 200–202.

[103] The standard work on fiction about the West German economic miracle is R. Hinton Thomas and Wilfried van der Will, *The German Novel and the Affluent Society* (Manchester, UK: Manchester University Press, 1968).

[104] Heinrich Böll, *Zum Tee bei Dr. Borsig: Hörspiele* (Munich: Deutscher Taschenbuch Verlag, 1973), 51.

[105] Ralph Glasser, *The New High Priesthood: The Social, Ethical and Political Implications of a Marketing-Orientated Society* (London: Macmillan, 1967).

[106] For a discussion of "the German model," see Streeck, *Re-Forming Capitalism*, 108–20.

[107] Rebecca Harding and William E. Paterson, *The Future of the German Economy: An End to the Miracle?* (Manchester, UK: Manchester University Press, 2000).

[108] Werner Meyer-Larsen, *Germany, Inc.: The New German Juggernaut and Its Challenge to World Business*, translated by Thomas Thornton (New York: Wiley, 2000).

[109] "Europe's Engine: Living with a Stronger Germany," *Economist*, March 13, 2010, 1–14.

[110] Florian Langenscheidt and Bernd Venohr, eds., *The Best of German Mittelstand: The World Market Leaders* (Cologne: DAAB Media, 2015).

[111] Barbara Weißenberger, interviewed by Georg Giersberg, "Der Betriebswirt: Englisch forschen und deutsch lehren," *Frankfurter Allgemeine Zeitung*, August 15, 2016, 18.

[112] Sandra Pott, "Wirtschaft in Literatur: Ökonomische Subjekte im Wirtschaftsroman der Gegenwart," *Kulturpoetik* 4, vol. 2 (2004): 205.

[113] Pott, 210.

[114] Philip Hobsbaum, *Essentials of Literary Criticism* (London: Thames and Hudson, 1983), 16–17.

[115] Other possible subjects would have been Franz Jung, *Die Eroberung der Maschinen* (1923), Willi Bredel, *Maschinenfabrik N&K* (1930), Erik Reger, *Union der festen Hand* (1931), Robert Musil, *Der Mann ohne Eigenschaften* (1930–42), Max Frisch, *Homo Faber* (1957), Martin Walser, *Ehen in Philippsburg* (1957), Günter Wallraff, *Wir brauchen dich* (*Industriereportagen*) (1966), Uwe Johnson, *Jahrestage* (1970–83), Urs Widmer, *Top Dogs* (1997), Ernst-Wilhelm Händler, *Wenn wir sterben* (2002), Ingo Schulze, *Neue Leben* (2005), Anne Weber, *Gold im Mund* (2005), Nora Bossong, *Gesellschaft mit beschränkter Haftung* (2012), Rainald Götz, *Johann Holtrop* (2012), Hans Magnus Enzensberger, *Immer das Geld!* (2015), and Ulrich Peltzer, *Das bessere Leben* (2015).

Chapter One

Epigraph: Thomas Mann, *Buddenbrooks: Verfall einer Familie*, Große kommentierte Frankfurter Ausgabe (GKFA), vol. 1.1, edited by Eckhard Heftrich (Frankfurt am Main: S. Fischer, 2002), 294; abbreviated as *B*. Thomas Mann, *Buddenbrooks: The Decline of a Family*, translated by John E. Woods (New York: Everyman's Library/Alfred A. Knopf, 1994), 262; abbreviated as *Bu*.

[1] For example, see Erich Heller, *Thomas Mann: The Ironic German* (Cambridge: Cambridge University Press, 1981), 27–67; Helmut Jendreiek, *Thomas Mann: Der demokratische Roman* (Düsseldorf: Bagel, 1977), 123–63.

[2] Cf. Michael Cowan, *Cult of the Will: Nervousness and German Modernity* (University Park: Penn State University Press, 2008), 41; Anna Kinder, *Geldströme: Ökonomie im Romanwerk Thomas Manns* (Berlin: De Gruyter, 2013), 53.

[3] For a survey of Fontane's influence on Thomas Mann, see Eckhard Heftrich, Helmuth Nürnberger, Thomas Sprecher, and Ruprecht Wimmer, eds., *Theodor Fontane und Thomas Mann: Die Vorträge des Internationalen Kolloquiums in Lübeck 1997*, Thomas-Mann-Studien, vol. 18 (Frankfurt am Main: Klostermann, 1998).

[4] Martin Swales, *Buddenbrooks: Family Life as the Mirror of Social Change* (Boston: Twayne, 1991).

[5] Elizabeth Boa, "*Buddenbrooks*: Bourgeois Patriarchy and Fin-de-siècle Eros," in *Thomas Mann*, edited by Michael Minden (London: Longman, 1995), 125–42.

[6] Sociohistorical studies of *Buddenbrooks* include Martin Ludwig, "Perspektive und Weltbild in Thomas Manns *Buddenbrooks*," in *Der deutsche Roman im 20. Jahrhundert: Analysen und Materialien zur Theorie und Soziologie des Romans*, vol. 1, edited by Manfred Brauneck (Bamberg: C. C. Buchner, 1976), 82–106; Jochen Vogt, *Thomas Mann: "Buddenbrooks"* (Munich: Wilhelm Fink, 1983); Hugh Ridley, *The Problematic Bourgeois: Twentieth-Century Criticism on Thomas Mann's "Buddenbrooks" and "The Magic Mountain"* (Columbia, SC: Camden House, 1994).

[7] On the unraveling of the Bürger/Künstler dichotomy in *Felix Krull*, see my previous monograph *Art and Its Uses in Thomas Mann's "Felix Krull"* (London: Maney/MHRA, 2008), 66–68, 77, 138–39.

[8] Thomas Mann, *Frühe Erzählungen 1893–1912*, Große kommentierte Frankfurter Ausgabe (GKFA), vol. 2.1, edited by Terence J. Reed (Frankfurt am Main: S. Fischer, 2004), 128.

[9] Stephen Joy, "Open Wide! An Oral Examination of Thomas Mann's Early Fiction," *German Life and Letters* 60, no. 4 (2007): 467.

[10] Jacob Burckhardt, *Die Kultur der Renaissance in Italien* (Berlin: Verlag von Th. Knaur Nachf., 1928), 138.

[11] Jakob Burckhardt, *Griechische Kulturgeschichte*, edited by Jakob Oeri, vol. 4 (Berlin: W. Spemann, 1902), 94.

[12] See, for example, Martin Travers, *Thomas Mann* (Basingstoke, UK: Macmillan, 1992), 26.

[13] Cf. Theodor Fontane, *Effi Briest* (Berlin: Insel, 2011), 291: "Jenes, wenn Sie wollen, uns tyrannisierende Gesellschafts-Etwas, das fragt nicht nach Charme und nicht nach Liebe und nicht nach Verjährung. Ich habe keine Wahl." translated by Hugh Rorrison and Helen Chambers as *Effi Briest* (London: Penguin, 2000), 173: "That, let's call it that social something which tyrannizes us, takes no account of charm, or love, or time limits. I've no choice. I must."

[14] Goffman, *Presentation of Self*, 22.

[15] Blumenberg, "Anthropologische Annäherung, 118–19; "Anthropological Approach," 441–43.

[16] Note the way that the political and the professional/economic spheres are coupled together in this phrase, suggesting that politics and economics go hand in hand.

[17] Thorstein Veblen, *The Theory of the Leisure Class: An Economic Theory of Institutions* (New York: Macmillan, 1899), 68–101.

[18] There is a parallel scene in Heinrich Mann's *Der Untertan*, in which Diederich Heßling meekly accepts his humiliation by an aristocrat.

[19] On the intellectual resonances between Mann and Weber, see Harvey Goldman, *Max Weber and Thomas Mann: Calling and Shaping of the Self* (Berkeley: University of California Press, 1988), and *Politics, Death, and the Devil: Self and Power in Max Weber and Thomas Mann* (Berkeley: University of California Press, 1992).

[20] Max Weber, *The Protestant Ethic and the Spirit of Capitalism,* translated by Talcott Parsons (London: Routledge, 2001), 25.

[21] Weber, 33.

[22] Weber, 120.

[23] Weber, 118.

[24] Weber, 119.

[25] Karl Marx and Friedrich Engels, *Manifesto of the Communist Party* (London: Lawrence & Wishart, 1983), 16.

[26] Franco Moretti, *The Bourgeois: Between History and Literature* (London: Verso, 2013), 101–8.

[27] This phrase comes from Mann's novella *Tonio Kröger* (1903).

[28] On the conflict between commercial interest and human feeling in *Buddenbrooks,* see T. J. Reed, *Thomas Mann: The Uses of Tradition,* 2nd ed. (Oxford: Oxford University Press, 1996), 66–67.

[29] Thomas Mann was interested in Machiavelli, who features as a character in Mann's drama *Fiorenza* (1905).

[30] Niccolò Machiavelli, *The Prince,* translated by George Bull (Harmondsworth, UK: Penguin, 1981), 100–101.

[31] Moretti, *The Bourgeois,* 184.

[32] Franco Moretti, "The Grey Area: Ibsen and the Spirit of Capitalism," *New Left Review* 61 (2010): 131.

[33] Moretti, *The Bourgeois,* 187. The term "creative destroyer" is, of course, a reference to Joseph Schumpeter's theory of creative destruction.

[34] The translation here is my own. Woods omits this phrase in his translation, converting it into an adverb: "He would . . . compulsively rearrange his writing utensils" (*Bu* 261).

[35] As Nicola von Bodman-Hensler puts it, "Mann establishes Johann's body in its refinement and vigour as the 'perfect form' of the bourgeois merchant": "Thomas Mann's Illness Mythologies in the Work of Philip Roth" (PhD thesis, King's College London, 2013), 43.

[36] Moretti, *The Bourgeois,* 168–74.

[37] Cf. Aristotle, *Rhetoric* 2.1.1377b.

[38] Cicero, *On the Ideal Orator* (*De Oratore*), translated by James M. May and Jakob Wisse (Oxford: Oxford University Press, 2001), 186 (= bk. 2, sec. 236).

[39] The sentence recalls Fontane's *Effi Briest*: "Man ist nicht bloß ein einzelner Mensch, man gehört einem Ganzen an" (290; "We're not just individuals, we're part of a larger whole," 173).

[40] The figure of Grünlich may also be informed by Mann's reading of Nietzsche, and particularly the late Nietzsche's critique of Richard Wagner as an unscrupulous manipulator of emotions. Both Mann and Nietzsche are ambivalent about classical rhetoric, recognizing its emotional force but also condemning it for its base intent and the crudity of its manipulations.

[41] Cicero, *Political Speeches*, translated by D. H. Berry (Oxford: Oxford University Press, 2006), 57 [*In Catilinam I*].

[42] Wilfried Barner, *Barockrhetorik*, 259.

[43] Cicero, *Political Speeches*, 173.

[44] Karl-Heinz Göttert, *Mythos Redemacht: Eine andere Geschichte der Rhetorik* (Frankfurt am Main: S. Fischer, 2015), 166.

[45] Cicero, *De Inventione* 2.14. On Cicero's practice of asking questions, see Billig, *Arguing and Thinking*, 145.

[46] Cicero's *In Catilinam I* may also be significant for Thomas Mann's development in another respect. At one point in the oration Cicero assumes the voice of Roma, the deity who embodies the city of Rome. For an entire paragraph he pretends to speak with Rome's voice. The speaker becomes the expression of his country's thoughts and aspirations. This anticipates Thomas Mann's development into a public figure with a claim to represent German culture.

[47] There is a similar scene "Der Bajazzo"; but, unlike Hanno, the Bajazzo will survive, and this is suggested by his skilled recital. Cf. Thomas Mann, *Frühe Erzählungen 1893–1912*, GKFA 2.1:126.

Chapter Two

Epigraph: Franz Kafka, *Das Schloß, in der Fassung der Handschrift*, edited by Malcom Pasley (Frankfurt am Main: Fischer, 1994), 85.

[1] Heinrich Mann, *Der Untertan*, edited by Peter-Paul Schneider, Studienausgabe in Einzelbänden (Frankfurt am Main: Fischer, 2001), 16 (abbreviated as *U*).

[2] Heinrich Mann, *The Loyal Subject*, edited by Helmut Peitsch, translated by Ernest Boyd and Daniel Theisen (New York: Continuum, 2006), 6 (abbreviated as *LS*).

[3] Martin Kohlrausch, "The Workings of Royal Celebrity: Wilhelm II as Media Emperor," in *Constructing Charisma: Celebrity, Fame, and Power in Nineteenth-Century Europe*, edited by Edward Berenson and Eva Giloi (New York: Berghahn, 2010), 55.

[4] Walther Rathenau, *Schriften und Reden*, edited by Hans Werner Richter (Frankfurt am Main: Fischer, 1964), 247.

⁵ Walther Rathenau, *Der Kaiser: Eine Betrachtung* (Berlin: S. Fischer, 1919), 30.

⁶ Martin Kohlrausch, *Der Monarch im Skandal: Die Logik der Massenmedien und die Transformation der wilhelminischen Monarchie* (Berlin: Akademie Verlag, 2005).

⁷ Cf. Alex Hall, "The Kaiser, the Wilhelmine State and Lèse-majesté," *German Life and Letters* 27, no. 2 (1974): 101–15.

⁸ Peter Sprengel, "Majestätsbeleidigung als Programm? Die frühe Moderne in opposition zum Wilhelminismus,'" in *Literatur im Kaiserreich: Studien zur Moderne* (Berlin: Erich Schmidt, 1993), 11.

⁹ Even Thomas Mann's *Königliche Hoheit* (1909; *Royal Highness*), which is much more sympathetic toward Wilhelm II, presents him as an artist and therefore as morally questionable.

¹⁰ Cf. Norman Domeier, *The Eulenburg Affair: A Cultural History of Politics in the German Empire*, translated by Deborah Lucas Schneider (Rochester, NY: Camden House, 2015).

¹¹ Sprengel, "Majestätsbeleidigung als Programm?" 43–44.

¹² Thomas Mann, *Betrachtungen eines Unpolitischen* (Frankfurt am Main: Fischer, 2002), 569. The word has legal implications: "grober Unfug" means "public nuisance," which was a crime punishable by a custodial sentence.

¹³ Werner Mahrholz, "Heinrich Manns 'Untertan': Bemerkungen über Talent und Menschlichkeit," in *Heinrich Mann: Texte zu seiner Wirkungsgeschichte in Deutschland*, edited by Renate Werner (Munich: Deutscher Taschenbuch Verlag, 1977), 102.

¹⁴ On this point, see Klaus Schröter, *Heinrich Mann: "Untertan"—"Zeitalter"—Wirkung. Drei Aufsätze* (Stuttgart: Metzler, 1971), 9–16.

¹⁵ Kurt Tucholsky, "Mit Rute und Peitsche durch Preußen-Deutschland," in *Heinrich Mann: Texte zu seiner Wirkungsgeschichte*, 113.

¹⁶ Schröter, *Heinrich Mann*, 32–36. Mann also compares the two novels in a letter to Félix Bertaux of October 10, 1922 (*U* 616). The parallel is significant because Mann saw Wilhelm II as "der Affe Napoleons" (Napoleon's ape); Heinrich Mann, *Essays*, 3 vols. (Berlin: Aufbau, 1954–61), 1:41.

¹⁷ Michael Nerlich, "Der Herrenmensch bei Jean-Paul Sartre und Heinrich Mann," *Akzente* 16 (1969): 460–79; Wolfgang Emmerich, *Heinrich Mann: "Der Untertan"* (Munich: Fink, 1980), 44–50; James Hawes, "Revanche and Radicalism: The Psychology of Power in *Der Prozess* and *Der Untertan*," *Oxford German Studies* 18–19 (1989–90): 119–31; Eberhard Lämmert, "Der Bürger und seine höheren Instanzen: Heinrich Mann, *Der Untertan*, und Franz Kafka, *Der Proceß*," in *Wer sind wir? Europäische Phänotypen im Roman des zwanzigsten Jahrhunderts*, edited by Eberhard Lämmert and Barbara Naumann (Munich: Fink, 1996), 41–59.

¹⁸ Werner Abelshauser, *Deutsche Wirtschaftsgeschichte*, 41.

¹⁹ Diederich's drinking partner in the student corporation is even called Delitzsch, after Hermann Schulze-Delitzsch (1808–83), one of the founders of the German cooperative movement.

[20] At the end of chapter 1, Diederich imagines German society as a gigantic corporation with the kaiser at its head (*U* 64). For an analysis of the hypnotic power that adheres to corporate institutions and bureaucracy, cf. Stefan Andriopoulos, *Possessed: Hypnotic Crimes, Corporate Fiction, and the Invention of Cinema* (Chicago: University of Chicago Press, 2008).

[21] Wehler, *Deutsche Gesellschaftsgeschichte*, 3:1238.

[22] Wehler, 3:1241.

[23] For the parallelism of events, cf. Peter-Paul Schneider's informative table in *U* 632–36.

[24] Hartmut Eggert, "Das persönliche Regiment: Zur Quellen- und Entstehungsgeschichte von Heinrich Manns 'Untertan,'" *Neophilologus* 55, no. 1 (1971): 298–316.

[25] Wilhelm Schröder, *Das persönliche Regiment: Reden und sonstige öffentliche Äusserungen Wilhelms II* (Munich: G. Birk, 1907).

[26] On the connection between the two texts, cf. also Helmut Arntzen, "Die Reden Wilhelms II. und Diederich Heßlings: Historisches Dokument und Heinrich Manns Romansatire," *literatur für leser* 3, no. 1 (1980): 1–14.

[27] Eggert, "Das persönliche Regiment," 302–3.

[28] Heinrich Mann's use of Schröder's book is confirmed by Peter Sprengel, "Majestätsbeleidigung als Programm?" 39–40.

[29] Schröder, *Das persönliche Regiment*, 3.

[30] Schröder, *Das persönliche Regiment*, 3.

[31] Schröder, *Das persönliche Regiment*, 12. This is one of the phrases that Diederich bellows together with Wolfgang Buck during their "duel of slogans" in chapter 5 (*U* 320).

[32] Schröder, *Das persönliche Regiment*, 96–97.

[33] Eggert, "Das persönliche Regiment," 310.

[34] Schröder, *Das persönliche Regiment*, 32. Schröder prints the phrase in boldface.

[35] Schröder, *Das persönliche Regiment*, 18.

[36] The use of ventriloquism is a feature of German modernism from Heinrich Heine onward. Cf. Anthony Phelan, *Reading Heinrich Heine* (Cambridge: Cambridge University Press, 2007).

[37] See also Diederich's rhetorical question, which is to be understood ironically by the reader: "Wer von uns hätte je aus seiner Gesinnung ein Geschäft gemacht?" (*U* 469; "Who among us has ever made money out of his loyalty?" *LS* 341). The English translation is inaccurate here: *Gesinnung* does not mean "loyalty" but "convictions" or "beliefs."

[38] Cf. Heinrich Mann, letter to Ludwig Ewers, October 31, 1906: "Sein Held soll der durchschnittliche Neudeutsche sein, einer, der den Berliner Geist in die Provinz trägt" (*U* 530; Its hero will be a typical new German who carries the Berlin spirit into the provinces).

[39] Willi Jasper, *Der Bruder: Heinrich Mann. Eine Biographie* (Munich: Hanser, 1992), 39.

[40] On Alberti, see Katherine Larson Roper, "Conrad Alberti's *Kampf ums Dasein*: The Writer in Imperial Berlin," *German Studies Review* 7, no. 1 (1984): 65–88.

[41] Conrad Alberti, "Cicero oder Darwin?" *Die Gesellschaft* 4, suppl. 4 (July 1888): 223.

[42] Conrad Alberti, ed., *Die Schule des Redners: Ein praktisches Handbuch der Beredsamkeit in Musterstücken* (Leipzig: Wigand, 1890).

[43] Cf. Roy Pascal, *From Naturalism to Expressionism: German Literature and Society 1880–1918* (New York: Basic Books, 1973), 96; Roper, "Conrad Alberti's *Kampf ums Dasein*," 76, 79–81.

[44] For Bismarck's denunciation of rhetoric, see Göttert, *Mythos Redemacht*, 236–39.

[45] Göttert, 201.

[46] Göttert, 61.

[47] Mary Beard, "The Acting Demagogue," *Times Literary Supplement Online*, October 10, 2016, http://www.the-tls.co.uk/articles/public/borrowed-eloquence/.

[48] The tension between Diederich and Wolfgang parallels the tension between Thomas and Christian Buddenbrook, as both Diederich and Thomas affect outrage at the suggestion that they are performing their roles.

[49] Aristotle, *Rhetoric* 1.2.1356a.

[50] Göttert, *Mythos Redemacht*, 136.

[51] This is an allusion to Bismarck, whose most important quality as an orator was said to be his *Sachlichkeit* (objectivity). Cf. Göttert, *Mythos Redemacht*, 204. This anticipates Tergit's critique of *Neue Sachlichkeit* (New Objectivity), discussed in chapter 3 of this book.

[52] Aristotle, *Rhetoric* 3.2.1404b.

[53] Earlier in the novel Diederich, too, is intoxicated by his own rhetoric: "In dem Schwindelgefühl, das seine starken Worte ihm erregt hatten" (*U* 107; "His strong words produced in him a kind of dizziness," *LS* 74).

[54] Michael Balfour, *The Kaiser and His Times* (Harmondsworth, UK: Penguin, 1975), 145.

[55] Wilhelm II declared this on June 16, 1898. Cf. Schröder, *Das persönliche Regiment*, 158.

[56] Kohlrausch, *Monarch im Skandal*, 66.

[57] Kohlrausch, "Workings of Royal Celebrity," 54.

[58] Wehler, *Deutsche Gesellschaftsgeschichte*, 3:368–76.

[59] For an overview, cf. Agnes Horvath, *Modernism and Charisma* (Basingstoke, UK: Palgrave Macmillan, 2013).

[60] Wehler, *Deutsche Gesellschaftsgeschichte*, 3:371.

[61] Reinhard Alter, *Die bereinigte Moderne: Heinrich Manns "Untertan" und politische Publizistik in der Kontinuität der deutschen Geschichte zwischen Kaiserreich und Drittem Reich* (Tübingen: Niemeyer, 1995), 52.

[62] Alter, *Die bereinigte Moderne*, 47. This term was also used by the British government during the miners' strike of 1984–85. Cf. Seumas Milne, *The Enemy Within: The Secret War against the Miners* (London: Verso, 2004).

[63] Helgard Mahrdt, *Öffentlichkeit, Gender und Moral: Von der Aufklärung zu Ingeborg Bachmann*, Palaestra 304 (Göttingen: Vandenhoeck & Ruprecht, 1998), 140.

[64] Wehler, *Deutsche Gesellschaftsgeschichte*, 3:1249.

[65] Burckhardt, *Kultur der Renaissance*, 162.

[66] Burckhardt, 165.

[67] Burckhardt, 164.

[68] Elizabeth Horodowich, *Language and Statecraft in Early Modern Venice* (Cambridge: Cambridge University Press, 2008), 131.

[69] "Opposition Research," Oxford Living Dictionaries, accessed November 30, 2017, https://en.oxforddictionaries.com/definition/opposition_research.

[70] One commentator called it "das Geschäft mit dem Rufmord" (the business of character assassination). Andrian Kreye, "Der Spuk geht jetzt erst los," *Süddeutsche Zeitung*, November 9, 2016, http://www.sueddeutsche.de/politik/us-wahl-der-spuk-geht-jetzt-erst-los-1.3241066.

[71] The use of sexual slander in *Der Untertan* may also be a contemporary allusion to the royal sex scandals that dogged the Wilhelmine period. Cf. Kohlrausch, *Monarch im Skandal*, esp. 156–301.

[72] Heinrich von Treitschke also led the intellectual charge against parliamentary liberalism. His five-volume *History of Germany in the Nineteenth Century* (1879–94) gave the Prussian monarchy sole credit for putting an end to *Kleinstaaterei* (patchwork of states) by unifying Germany in 1871. In this way, former liberals like Treitschke ensured that the idea of national unity was severed from the liberal idea of freedom.

[73] This split again in 1893, with Eugen Richter now leader of the Freisinninge Volkspartei (FVp, Free-Minded People's Party), which existed until 1910.

[74] Diederich is humiliated as follows: (1) in his audience with Wulckow, the dog is treated with more respect than he is; (2) he and his sisters are mocked as parvenus in the play *Die heimliche Gräfin* (The Secret Countess); (3) he is forced to sign the property deal on the morning of his wedding and arrives late for the ceremony; (4) he is thrown out by Lieutenant von Brietzen's servant.

[75] Cf. Jasper, *Der Bruder*, 233–34.

[76] Gordon A. Craig, *Germany 1866–1945* (Oxford: Oxford University Press, 1987), 266–68.

[77] Heinrich Mann, *Diktatur der Vernunft* (Berlin: Die Schmiede, 1923), 39. This passage was deleted when the essay was reprinted in 1929. Cf. Ernest Schonfield, "The Idea of European Unity in Heinrich Mann's Political Essays of the 1920s and Early 1930s," in *Europe in Crisis: Intellectuals and the European Idea, 1917–1957*, edited by Mark Hewitson and Matthew D'Auria (New York: Berghahn, 2012), 269.

[78] Jadassohn is a good example of what Theodor Lessing calls "Jewish self-hatred": *Der jüdische Selbsthaß* (Berlin: Jüdischer Verlag, 1930). For the connection between racism and cosmetic surgery, cf. Sander L. Gilman, *Creating Beauty to Cure the Soul: Race and Psychology in the Shaping of Aesthetic Surgery* (Durham, NC: Duke University Press, 1998).

[79] Alter, *Die bereinigte Moderne*, 54.

[80] On this point, see chapter 6 of John Phillip Short, *Magic Lantern Empire: Colonialism and Society in Germany* (Ithaca, NY: Cornell University Press, 2012).

[81] Abelshauser, *Deutsche Wirtschaftsgeschichte*, 34.

[82] For a history of the term, cf. Natascha Doll, *Recht, Politik und "Realpolitik" bei August Ludwig von Rochau (1810–1873): Ein wissenschaftsgeschichtlicher Beitrag zum Verhältnis von Politik und Recht im 19. Jahrhundert* (Frankfurt am Main: Klostermann, 2005). The concept was defined in 1853 by August Ludwig von Rochau, who wrote, "Daß *das Gesetz der Stärke* über das Staatsleben eine ähnliche Herrschaft ausübt wie *das Gesetz der Schwere* über die Körperwelt" (As the world of physical bodies is dominated by *the law of gravity*, so too is political life dominated by *the law of strength*): *Grundsätze der Realpolitik angewendet auf die staatlichen Zustände Deutschlands*, 2nd ed. (Stuttgart: Karl Göpel, 1859), 1.

[83] Max Weber, "Der Sinn der 'Wertfreiheit' der soziologischen und ökonomischen Wissenschaften" [1917], in *Gesammelte Aufsätze zur Wissenschaftslehre*, edited by Johannes Winckelmann (Tübingen: Mohr, 1988), 513.

[84] Quoted in Wolfgang J. Mommsen, *Max Weber and German Politics, 1880–1920*, translated by Michael S. Steinberg (Chicago: University of Chicago Press, 1984), 43.

[85] Wehler, *Deutsche Gesellschaftsgeschichte*, 3:1084. The sequel to *Der Untertan* is *Die Armen* (1917; *The Poor*). The novel describes Heßling's tyrannical regime over his workers, who live in miserable conditions.

Chapter Three

[1] References are to Gabriele Tergit, *Käsebier erobert den Kurfürstendamm*, edited by Nicole Henneberg (Frankfurt am Main: Schöffling, 2016; abbreviated as *Kb*).

[2] On the Sklarek scandal, see Stephan Malinowski, "Politische Skandale als Zerrspiegel der Demokratie: Die Fälle Barmat und Sklarek im Kalkül der Weimarer Rechten," *Jahrbuch für Antisemitismusforschung* 5 (1996): 46–64.

[3] Gabriele Tergit, "Moritz Rosenthal," *Die Weltbühne* 28, Erstes Halbjahr, 1932, 450–52.

[4] Wehler, *Deutsche Gesellschaftsgeschichte*, 4:298.

[5] Carl Sternheim, "Die Deutsche Revolution" [1918], in *Gesamtwerk*, 10 vols., edited by Wolfgang Emrich (Neuwied am Rhein: Luchterhand, 1966–76), 6:71.

[6] Sternheim, 6:76.

[7] Frächter's first name is spelled inconsistently. At the beginning of his career he is "Willi" (*Kb* 75). By the time he has taken over as director of the *Berliner Rundschau*, his name has changed to "Willy" (*Kb* 292).

[8] Dieter Wrobel, "Mediensatire wider die Entpolitisierung der Zeitung: Journalismuskritik in Romanen von Gabriele Tergit und Erich Kästner," in *"Laboratorium Vielseitigkeit": Zur Literatur der Weimarer Republik. Festschrift für*

Helga Karrenbrock zum 60. Geburtstag, edited by Petra Josting and Walter Fähnders (Bielefeld: Aisthesis, 2005), 270–71.

⁹ Wrobel, "Mediensatire," 271.

¹⁰ Cf. Corey Ross, *Media and the Making of Modern Germany: Mass Communications, Society, and Politics from the Empire to the Third Reich* (Oxford: Oxford University Press, 2008), 180.

¹¹ Wrobel, "Mediensatire," 278.

¹² Hans Wagener, *Gabriele Tergit: Gestohlene Jahre*, Schriften des Erich Maria Remarque-Archivs 28 (Göttingen: V & R unipress, 2013), 48.

¹³ Heinrich Mann, "Lachbühne in Berlin N," *Die Literarische Welt* 6, no. 1, January 3, 1930, 3; reprinted in Heinrich Mann, *Essays und Publizistik,* vol. 5: *1930 bis Februar 1933*, edited by Volker Riedel (Bielefeld: Aisthesis, 2009), 23–25.

¹⁴ Mann, *Essays und Publizistik,* 25.

¹⁵ Gabriele Tergit, *Etwas Seltenes überhaupt: Erinnerungen* (Frankfurt am Main: Ullstein, 1983), 78.

¹⁶ Fiona Sutton (née Littlejohn), "Models of Modernity: Readings of Selected Novels of the Late Weimar Republic" (PhD diss., University of Nottingham, 2001), 129, http://eprints.nottingham.ac.uk/12255/1/246931.pdf.

¹⁷ Andreas Huyssen, *Miniature Metropolis: Literature in an Age of Photography and Film* (Cambridge, MA: Harvard University Press, 2015), 10.

¹⁸ For an analysis of Tergit's feuilletons, see Frances Mossop, *Mapping Berlin: Representations of Space in the Weimar Feuilleton* (Oxford: Peter Lang, 2015), 117–51.

¹⁹ Christiane Schultze-Jena, "Roman und Reportage: Zum Zeitroman am Ende der Weimarer Republik, dargestellt an Gabriele Tergits Roman 'Käsebier erobert den Kurfürstendamm,'" Magisterarbeit, University of Hamburg, 1988–89; Petra Gute, "'Erfolg ist eine Sache der Suggestion': Lebenserfahrung im literarischen und publizistischen Werk Gabriele Tergits," Magisterarbeit, Free University of Berlin, 1992.

²⁰ Juliane Sucker, *"Sehnsucht nach dem Kurfürstendamm": Gabriele Tergit— Literatur und Journalismus in der Weimarer Republik und im Exil* (Würzburg: Königshausen & Neumann, 2015), 120–24.

²¹ Elizabeth Boa, "Urban Modernity and the Politics of Heimat: Gabriele Tergit's *Käsebier erobert den Kurfürstendamm*," *German Life and Letters*, forthcoming. I am grateful to Elizabeth Boa for allowing me to read her paper.

²² On this point, see Wrobel, "Mediensatire," 279–80, and Sucker, *Sehnsucht nach dem Kurfürstendamm*, 139n205.

²³ Wrobel, "Mediensatire," 282.

²⁴ For a detailed discussion of this term see Steve Plumb, *Neue Sachlichkeit: Unity and Diversity of an Art Movement* (Amsterdam: Rodopi, 2006).

²⁵ Sucker, *Sehnsucht nach dem Kurfürstendamm*, 126–30.

²⁶ Sucker, 129.

²⁷ Sucker, 128.

[28] Inge Stephan, "Stadt ohne Mythos: Gabriele Tergits Berlin-Roman *Käsebier erobert den Kurfürstendamm*," in *Neue Sachlichkeit im Roman: Neue Interpretationen zum Roman der Weimarer Republik*, edited by Sabina Becker and Christoph Weiß (Stuttgart: Metzler, 1995), 310.

[29] In Muriel Spark's novel *A Far Cry from Kensington* (London: Virago, 2009), the narrator gives similar advice to aspiring authors: "You are writing a letter to a friend, . . . and this is a dear and close friend, real—or better—invented in your mind like a fixation" (84).

[30] We shall return to this religious theme at the end of this chapter.

[31] Sucker, *Sehnsucht nach dem Kurfürstendamm*, 127.

[32] For a summary of the debate, see Dirk Kaesler, *Max Weber: An Introduction to His Life and Work*, translated by Philippa Hurd (Cambridge: Polity, 1988), 184–96. See also Manfred Schön, "Gustav Schmoller and Max Weber," in *Max Weber and His Contemporaries*, edited by Wolfgang J. Mommsen and Jürgen Osterhammel (London: Allen & Unwin, 1987), 59–70.

[33] Dirk Kaesler, *Max Weber: Preuße, Denker, Muttersohn. Eine Biographie* (Munich: Beck, 2014), 643–44.

[34] Wolfgang J. Mommsen, *The Age of Bureaucracy: Perspectives on the Political Sociology of Max Weber* (Oxford: Blackwell, 1974), 109. Ironically, the positions of the 1909 debate resembled a similar methodological debate of the 1880s between Schmoller and the Austrian economist Carl Menger, in which Schmoller argued that statistical data were more important than first principles. In the debate of 1909, Schmoller's position had changed so that it resembled that of his former rival, Menger. Cf. Erik Grimmer-Solem, *The Rise of Historical Economics and Social Reform in Germany 1864–1894* (Oxford: Oxford University Press, 2003), 248–64.

[35] Fiona Sutton, "Weimar's Forgotten Cassandra: The Writings of Gabriele Tergit in the Weimar Republic," in *German Novelists of the Weimar Republic: Intersections of Literature and Politics*, edited by Karl Leydecker (Rochester, NY: Camden House, 2006), 206.

[36] Sutton, "Models of Modernity," 142–43.

[37] Tergit, *Etwas Seltenes überhaupt*, 77.

[38] Cf. Oliver Nachtwey, *Die Abstiegsgesellschaft: Über das Aufbegehren in der regressiven Moderne* (Berlin: Suhrkamp, 2016), 113.

[39] Werner Hegemann, *Das steinerne Berlin: Geschichte der grössten Mietkasernenstadt der Welt* (Berlin: Kiepenhauer, 1930). Tergit's friendship with Hegemann is documented in *Etwas Seltenes überhaupt*, 30. For a discussion of architecture in *Käsebier*, see Ines Lauffer, *Poetik des Privatraums: Der architektonische Wohndiskurs in den Romanen der Neuen Sachlichkeit* (Bielefeld: Transcript, 2011), 83–112.

[40] For a discussion of Mietskasernen in Berlin from 1848 to 1900, see John B. Lyon, *Out of Place: German Realism, Displacement, and Modernity* (London: Bloomsbury, 2013), 40–71.

[41] Walter Benjamin, "Ein Jakobiner von heute: Zu Werner Hegemanns 'Das steinerne Berlin'" [1930], in *Gesammelte Schriften*, 3:263.

[42] Benjamin, 3:261.

[43] Ignaz Wrobel (i.e., Kurt Tucholsky), "Presse und Realität," *Die Weltbühne*, no. 41, October 13, 1921, 373.

[44] Ross, *Media and the Making*, 192.

[45] John Hartley, *Understanding News* (London: Routledge, 1990), 76–79, 126.

[46] Dieter Wrobel, "Mediensatire," 284.

[47] Erhard Schütz, *Romane der Weimarer Republik* (Munich: Fink, 1986), 156.

[48] For a discussion of Goebbels's early career as an Expressionist author, see David Barnett, "Joseph Goebbels: Expressionist Dramatist as Nazi Minister of Culture," *New Theatre Quarterly* 17, no. 2 (2001): 161–69.

[49] Quoted in Gabriele Tergit, *Käsebier erobert den Kurfürstendamm*, edited by Jens Brüning (Berlin: Das Neue Berlin, 2004), 266.

[50] Walter Benjamin, "Das Kunstwerk im Zeitalter seiner technischen Reproduzierbarkeit," in *Gesammelte Schriften*, 1.2:508.

[51] Sutton, "Models of Modernity," 140.

[52] Compare the biblical quotation "All is vanity and a striving after wind" (Eccles. 1:14).

[53] Boa, "Urban Modernity and the Politics of Heimat."

[54] This is a quotation from the Luther Bible, Rom. 3:23: "Sie sind allzumal Sünder."

[55] The fake piety of Frächter's oration resembles the sugary sentiment of the bishop's eulogy for the drowned sailors in Brecht's *Dreigroschenroman*, as will be discussed in the next chapter.

[56] In an interview in 1979, Tergit acknowledged her debt to the Bible, quoting from Exod. 23:2: "Ich habe von Jesaja gelernt: Folge nicht dem großen Haufen nach, richte dich nicht nach dem Urteil der Menge" (I learned from Isaiah: Do not follow the crowd in doing wrong, do not conform to the judgment of the crowd). Quoted in Wagener, *Gabriele Tergit: Gestohlene Jahre*, 12.

Chapter Four

Epigraph: Aristotle, *Rhetoric* 1.7.1365b.

[1] Bertolt Brecht, *Werke: Große kommentierte Berliner und Frankfurter Ausgabe*, edited by Werner Hecht, Jan Knopf, Werner Mittenzwei, and Klaus-Detlef Müller, 31 vols. (Berlin: Suhrkamp, 1989–98), 21:136 (abbreviated as *BFA*).

[2] David Bathrick, *The Powers of Speech: The Politics of Culture in the GDR* (Lincoln: University of Nebraska Press, 1995), 156–58.

[3] Benjamin, "Brechts Dreigroschenroman," in *Gesammelte Schriften*, 3:445–46.

[4] George Orwell, "Politics and the English Language," in *Why I Write* (London: Penguin, 2004), 120.

[5] Wolfgang Jeske, ed., *Brechts Romane* (Frankfurt am Main: Suhrkamp, 1984), 138–41.

[6] Ludger Claßen, *Satirisches Erzählen im 20. Jahrhundert: Heinrich Mann, Bertolt Brecht, Martin Walser, F. C. Delius* (Munich: Fink, 1985); Rolf J. Goebel, "Brechts

Dreigroschenroman und die Tradition des Kriminalromans," *Brecht-Jahrbuch* (1979): 67–81.

[7] Cornelie Ladd, "Fictions of Power, Powers of Fiction: Critical Representations of European Thought by Marx, Conrad and Brecht" (PhD diss., Columbia University, 1991).

[8] Ladd, "Fictions of Power," 223.

[9] Erdmut Wizisla, Helgrid Streidt, and Heidrun Loeper, *Die Bibliothek Bertolt Brechts: Ein kommentiertes Verzeichnis* (Frankfurt am Main: Suhrkamp, 2007), 297, 309.

[10] Laura Bradley, "Training the Audience: Brecht and the Art of Spectatorship," *Modern Language Review* 111, no. 4 (2016): 1029–48.

[11] Ladd, "Fictions of Power," 260.

[12] Bertolt Brecht, *Dreigroschenroman* (Frankfurt am Main: Suhrkamp, 1991), 326–27 (abbreviated as *D*).

[13] Aristotle, *Rhetoric* 1.2.1356a.

[14] Bertolt Brecht, *Tales from the Calendar*, translated by Yvonne Kapp (London: Methuen, 1961), 113.

[15] Göttert, *Mythos Redemacht*, 136.

[16] Bertolt Brecht, *Threepenny Novel*, translated by Desmond I. Vesey (Harmondsworth, UK: Penguin, 1961), 129 (abbreviated as *TN*).

[17] The Rothschild story comes from H. G. Wells, *BFA* 16:450.

[18] Brecht may also be referring to Lycurgus of Sparta, the legendary lawgiver; *BFA* 16:452.

[19] Burckhardt, *Griechische Kulturgeschichte*, 86.

[20] Burckhardt, 126–27.

[21] Ladd, "Fictions of Power," 250.

[22] Ladd, 259.

[23] Cicero, *On the Ideal Orator*, 132 (= bk. 2, sec. 30).

[24] This point forms the basis of a paper by Rikard Schönström, "Quotes as Commodities: The Use of Slogans in Bertolt Brecht's and Kurt Weill's *Mahagonny*," given on June 26, 2016, at the "Recycling Brecht Conference, 15th Symposium of the International Brecht Society," St. Hugh's College, University of Oxford.

[25] Cicero, *On the Ideal Orator*, 157 (= bk. 2, sec.130).

[26] Joy Connolly, "The Politics of Rhetorical Education," in *The Cambridge Companion to Ancient Rhetoric*, edited by Erik Gunderson (Cambridge: Cambridge University Press, 2009), 138.

[27] Bertolt Brecht, *Geschichten vom Herrn Keuner: Zürcher Fassung*, edited by Erdmut Wizisla (Frankfurt am Main: Suhrkamp, 2004), 65.

[28] Steve Giles, "Rewriting Brecht: *Die Dreigroschenoper* 1928–1931," *Literaturwissenschaftliches Jahrbuch* 30 (1989): 257.

[29] Tom Jeffrey, "Britain Needs More Democracy after the EU Referendum, Not Less," Huffington Post, June 27, 2016, http://www.huffingtonpost.co.uk/tom-jeffery/britain-needs-more-democr_b_10699898.html.

[30] Jeske, *Brechts Romane*, 138–41.

31 For a discussion of Hitler as an orator, see Göttert, *Mythos Redemacht*, 102–10.

32 Volker Ullrich, *Hitler: Ascent 1889–1939*, translated by Jefferson Chase (London: Bodley Head, 2016), 95.

33 One of Brecht's key sources for the novel was Fritz Kaufmann's *Erfolgreiche deutsche Wirtschaftsführer* (1931; Successful German Business Leaders). See Wizisla, Streidt, and Loeper, *Die Bibliothek Bertolt Brechts*, 415.

34 Craig, *Germany 1866–1945*, 508.

35 On Stinnes, see Widdig, *Culture and Inflation*, 135–59.

36 The phrase is from Rudyard Kipling, *The Light That Failed* (1891).

37 Wehler, *Deutsche Gesellschaftsgeschichte*, 3:1084.

38 Cf. Jeske, *Brechts Romane*, 138–41.

39 Radek's proposed policy, known as the "Schlageter line," raises uncomfortable questions about parallels between left-wing and right-wing extremism, and about the extent to which nationalism can compromise any political cause.

40 Burke, "Rhetoric of Hitler's 'Battle,'" 204.

41 Wizisla, Streidt, and Loeper, *Bibliothek Bertolt Brechts*, 334.

42 W. F. Haug, *Philosophieren mit Brecht und Gramsci* (Hamburg: Argument Verlag, 2006), 69–70, 75–77. Cf. also Helmut Fahrenbach, *Brecht zur Einführung* (Hamburg: Junius Verlag, 1986), 48.

43 Herbert Claas, *Die politische Ästhetik Bertolt Brechts vom Baal zum Caesar* (Frankfurt am Main: Suhrkamp, 1977), 51–54; Steve Giles, *Bertolt Brecht and Critical Theory: Marxism, Modernity and the Threepenny Lawsuit* (Bern: Peter Lang, 1997), 66–72.

44 Giles, *Brecht and Critical Theory*, 67.

45 Carl von Clausewitz, *Vom Kriege*, 3 vols. (Berlin 1832–34), 1:24.

46 For details of the 1922 Alfred Forke translation of Mê Ti owned by Brecht, see Wizisla, Streidt, and Loeper, *Bibliothek Bertolt Brechts*, 333–34. The new standard edition in English is Mo Zi, *The Book of Master Mo*, translated by Ian Johnston (London: Penguin, 2015).

47 The discussion of "volkstümlich" in "Katalog der Begriffe" may possibly refer to the "Realism debate" or "Expressionism debate" that took place between Ernst Bloch and Georg Lukács in 1938. If so, then this would date the fragment to 1938–40.

48 Bertolt Brecht, *Bertolt Brecht's Me-ti: Book of Interventions in the Flow of Things*, edited and translated by Anthony Tatlow (London: Bloomsbury, 2016), 78.

49 Brecht, *Bertolt Brecht's Me-ti*, 158.

50 Brecht, 77. This sentence could also be translated: "We construct lots of sentences, just as one chooses allies for the struggle."

51 Brecht, 52.

52 Wolfgang Streeck, *Gekaufte Zeit: Die vertagte Krise des demokratischen Kapitalismus. Frankfurter Adorno-Vorlesungen 2012* (Berlin: Suhrkamp, 2013), 97.

53 Friedrich A. Hayek, *The Constitution of Liberty* (1960; London: Routledge, 2006), 200.

[54] Hayek, 203.

[55] Hayek, 231.

[56] Craig, *Germany 1866–1945*, 438–39.

[57] Wehler, *Deutsche Gesellschaftsgeschichte*, 4:374.

[58] Stephen Parker, *Bertolt Brecht: A Literary Life* (London: Bloomsbury, 2014), 291.

[59] Friedrich Christian Delius, *Wir Unternehmer. Unsere Siemens-Welt. Einige Argumente zur Verteidigung der Gemüseesser. Satiren*. Werkausgabe in Einzelbänden (Reinbek bei Hamburg: Rowohlt, 2014), 180.

[60] Diarmuid Jeffreys, *Hell's Cartel: IG Farben and the Making of Hitler's War Machine* (London: Henry Holt, 2008).

[61] Robert K. Merton, "The Matthew Effect in Science," *Science* 159, no. 3810 (1968): 56–63.

[62] Wolfgang Streeck, "How Will Capitalism End?" *New Left Review* 87 (2014): 37. Cf. also Streeck, *Gekaufte Zeit*, 94.

[63] Adam Smith, *An Inquiry into the Nature and Causes of the Wealth of Nations* [1776], edited by Kathryn Sutherland (Oxford: Oxford University Press, 1993), bk. 4, chap. 2, 292.

[64] Streeck, *Gekaufte Zeit*, 97. Translated by Patrick Camiller as *Buying Time: The Delayed Crisis of Democratic Capitalism* (London: Verso, 2014), 62–63.

[65] Homer, *The Iliad*, translated by E. V. Rieu (London: Penguin, 2003), 51. Barbara Köhler also uses this Homeric simile in *Niemands Frau: Gesänge* (Frankfurt am Main: Suhrkamp, 2007), 61. I am grateful to Elena Theodorakopoulos for this reference.

[66] Cited in Jeske, *Brechts Romane*, 138.

[67] The word *Persönlichkeit* (personality) had great currency in the Wilhelmine period and was often used to describe Kaiser Wilhelm II. As we have seen, Heinrich Mann parodies this in *Der Untertan* (*U* 155).

[68] When Macheath becomes the director of the National Deposit Bank, he uses the same expression: "Vergessen Sie nicht . . . die Bank gehört einem Kind" (*USW* 283; "Don't forget . . . the bank belongs to a child," *TN* 263).

[69] Ladd, "Fictions of Power," 255.

[70] I have modified the translation here, because Vesey's translation changes the meaning of the original text. "Schwarzweißmalerei" does not mean "making black white and white black," it means representing something in black and white terms, using strong contrasts.

[71] Karl Marx and Friedrich Engels, *Manifest der kommunistischen Partei* (Berlin: Dietz, 1989), 76.

[72] Cf. Detlev Schöttker, *Bertolt Brechts Ästhetik des Naiven* (Stuttgart: Metzler, 1989), 293.

[73] Benjamin, *Gesammelte Schriften*, 3:446.

[74] Schöttker, *Bertolt Brechts Ästhetik*, 449.

[75] Cicero, *Pro Roscio Amerino*, section 84, accessed November 30, 2017, http://thelatinlibrary.com/cicero/sex.rosc.shtml.

Chapter Five

[1] *Epigraph*: Ingeborg Bachmann, *Kritische Schriften*, edited by Monika Albrecht and Dirk Göttsche (Munich: Piper, 2005), 299; abbreviated as *KS*. Ingeborg Bachmann. *Malina* (Frankfurt am Main: Suhrkamp, 1980), 356 (abbreviated as *M*). Translated by Philip Boehm as *Malina* (New York: Holmes & Meier, 1990), 225 (abbreviated as *Ma*).

[2] Georgina Paul, *Perspectives on Gender in Post-1945 German Literature* (Rochester, NY: Camden House, 2009), 72, 86–87.

[3] Sara Lennox, "The Feminist Reception of Ingeborg Bachmann," *Women in German Yearbook* 8 (1992): 105. Lennox's argument at this point draws on the work of Leslie Morris.

[4] Dirk Göttsche, "Research on Ingeborg Bachmann: Quo Vadis?" *Modern Language Review* 106, no. 2 (2011): 501.

[5] For a comparison between the two authors, see Imke Meyer, *Jenseits der Spiegel kein Land: Ich-Fiktionen in Texten von Franz Kafka und Ingeborg Bachmann* (Würzburg: Königshausen & Neumann, 2001).

[6] The arguments of Baackmann and Holschuh are summarized in Sara Lennox, "The Politics of Reading: A Half Century of Bachmann Reception," in *Literarische Wertung und Kanonbildung*, edited by Nicholas Saul and Ricarda Schmidt (Würzburg: Königshausen & Neumann, 2007), 159. Two recent examples of historicist reading are Sara Lennox, *Cemetery of the Murdered Daughters: Feminism, History, and Ingeborg Bachmann* (Amherst: University of Massachusetts Press, 2006), and Katya Krylova, *Walking through History: Topography and Identity in the Works of Ingeborg Bachmann and Thomas Bernhard* (Bern: Peter Lang, 2013).

[7] Ingeborg Bachmann, *Wir müssen wahre Sätze finden: Gespräche und Interviews*, edited by Christine Koschel and Inge von Weidenbaum (Munich: Piper, 1991), 90–91, abbreviated as *GuI*.

[8] For example, she chose never to publish her poem dedicated to the Italian Communist Party. See Arturo Larcati, "'Den eigenen Körper in den Kampf werfen': Zu Ingeborg Bachmanns Politik-Auffassung," *Germanisch-Romanische Monatsschrift* 54, no. 2 (2004): 215–34.

[9] Holger Gehle, "Ingeborg Bachmann und Martin Heidegger: Eine Skizze," in *Ingeborg Bachmann—Neue Beiträge zu ihrem Werk*, edited by Dirk Göttsche and Hubert Ohl (Würzburg: Königshausen & Neumann, 1993), 241–52. Gudrun Kohn-Waechter, "Das 'Problem der Post' in 'Malina' von Ingeborg Bachmann und Martin Heideggers 'Der Satz vom Grund,'" in *Die Frau im Dialog: Studien zu Theorie und Geschichte des Briefes*, edited by Anita Runge and Liselotte Steinbrügge (Stuttgart: Metzler, 1991), 225–42.

[10] Veronica O'Regan, "'Erfahrung nicht des Empirikers, sondern des Mystikers': A Re-Evaluation of Ingeborg Bachmann's Understanding of Wittgenstein and Its Application to *Simultan*," *Sprachkunst* 27 (1996): 47–65.

[11] Joachim Eberhardt, "Bachmann und Nietzsche," in *Über die Zeit schreiben: Literatur- und kulturwissenschaftliche Essays zu Ingeborg Bachmann*, edited by

Monika Albrecht and Dirk Göttsche, vol. 3 (Würzburg: Königshausen & Neumann, 2004), 135–55.

12 Sigrid Weigel, *Ingeborg Bachmann: Hinterlassenschaften unter Wahrung des Briefgeheimnisses* (Vienna: Zsolnay, 1999), 99–133.

13 Weigel, 528–30.

14 Áine McMurtry, *Crisis and Form in the Later Writing of Ingeborg Bachmann* (London: MHRA, 2012), 206–16.

15 McMurtry, 207.

16 Michael Minden, "Modernism's Struggle for the Soul: Rainer Maria Rilke's *Die Aufzeichnungen des Malte Laurids Brigge* and Ingeborg Bachmann's *Malina*," *German Life and Letters* 67, no. 3 (2014): 320–40.

17 Cf. Stephen D. Dowden, *Sympathy for the Abyss: A Study in the Novel of German Modernism. Kafka, Broch, Musil, and Thomas Mann* (Tübingen: Niemeyer, 1986).

18 Ingeborg Bachmann, *Die kritische Aufnahme der Existentialphilosophie Martin Heideggers* [1949], edited by Robert Pichl (Munich: Piper, 1985), 128. Cf. Joachim Eberhardt, *"Es gibt für mich keine Zitate": Intertextualität im dichterischen Werk Ingeborg Bachmanns* (Tübingen: Niemeyer, 2002), 98.

19 Ingeborg Bachmann, *Werke*, edited by Christine Koschel, Inge von Weidenbaum, and Clemens Münster, 4 vols. (Munich: Piper, 1993), 1:60.

20 Ingeborg Bachmann, *Darkness Spoken: The Collected Poems*, translated by Peter Filkins (Brookline, MA: Zephyr, 2006), 65.

21 Max Weber, "Wissenschaft als Beruf" [1919], in *Schriften 1894–1922*, edited by Dirk Kaesler (Stuttgart: Kröner, 2002), 500; translated as "The Vocation of Science," in *The Essential Weber: A Reader*, edited by Sam Whimster (London: Routledge, 2004), 281. The lecture was delivered in 1917.

22 Weber, "Wissenschaft als Beruf," 500; "Vocation of Science," 281.

23 Weber, "Wissenschaft als Beruf," 502.

24 Weber, "Vocation of Science," 282.

25 Joan W. Scott, "Experience," in *Feminists Theorize the Political*, edited by Judith Butler and Joan W. Scott (London: Routledge, 1992), 37. Cf. Stephanie Bird, "'What Matters Who's Speaking?': Identity, Experience, and Problems with Feminism in Ingeborg Bachmann's *Malina*," in *Gender and Politics in Austrian Fiction: Austrian Studies VII*, edited by Ritchie Robertson and Edward Timms (Edinburgh: Edinburgh University Press, 1996), 153.

26 Weber, "Wissenschaft als Beruf," 507; "Vocation of Science," 285.

27 Wolfgang Schluchter, *Paradoxes of Modernity: Culture and Conduct in the Theory of Max Weber*, translated by Neil Solomon (Stanford, CA: Stanford University Press, 1996), 15.

28 Weber, "Wissenschaft als Beruf," 510–11; "Vocation of Science," 287.

29 She does not believe in religion itself: "Es gibt keine Religion mehr" (Religion no longer exists). Ingeborg Bachmann, *"Todesarten"-Projekt: Kritische Ausgabe*, edited by Monika Albrecht and Dirk Göttsche, 4 vols. (Munich: Piper, 2005), 3.1:36 (abbreviated as *TP*).

[30] "Ivan will vielleicht nichts anderes als sein einfaches Leben" (*M* 336; "maybe Ivan doesn't want anything other than his simple life," *Ma* 211).

[31] Bird, "What Matters Who's Speaking?" 162.

[32] See the seventh chapter of Joseph A. Schumpeter's *Capitalism, Socialism and Democracy* (London: Routledge, 2010), 71–75.

[33] Max Weber, *Wirtschaft und Gesellschaft*, in *Gesamtausgabe*, vol. 1.23, edited by Knut Borchardt, Edith Hanke, and Wolfgang Schluchter (Tübingen: Mohr Siebeck, 2013), 199; translated as *Economy and Society*, vol. 1, edited by Guenther Roth and Claus Wittich (Berkeley: University of California Press, 1978), 44.

[34] Weber, "Wissenschaft als Beruf," 510.

[35] Weber, "Vocation of Science," 287.

[36] Georges Bataille, *The Accursed Share: An Essay on General Economy*, vol. 1: *Consumption*, translated by Robert Hurley (New York: Zone Books, 1967).

[37] The essay was written at some point between 1917 and 1920, and published posthumously in 1922.

[38] Max Weber, "Die drei reinen Typen der legitimen Herrschaft," in *Soziologie, universalgeschichtliche Analysen, Politik*, edited by Johannes Winckelmann (Stuttgart: Kröner, 1973), 159; translated as "The Three Types of Legitimate Rule," in *The Essential Weber: A Reader*, edited by Sam Whimster (London: Routledge, 2004), 138.

[39] Mommsen, *Max Weber and German Politics*, 422–23.

[40] Mommsen, 69.

[41] "Malina würde sagen, es heißt nicht Herr und Knecht. Es heißt: Knechte" (*TP* 3.1:426; Malina would say there are no masters and servants, only servants). He considers freedom, like peace, to be a mirage.

[42] Weber, *Wirtschaft und Gesellschaft*, in *Gesamtausgabe*, 1.23:192; *Economy and Society*, 1:38.

[43] Weber, *Wirtschaft und Gesellschaft*, in *Gesamtausgabe*, 1.23:193; *Economy and Society*, 1:39.

[44] Weber, *Wirtschaft und Gesellschaft*, in *Gesamtausgabe*, 1.23:196; *Economy and Society*, 1:42. N.b.: "Vergewaltigung" is usually translated as "rape."

[45] The interview, with Gerda Bödefeld, was first published on December 24, 1971. It is remarkable that Bachmann chose to communicate her concept of permanent warfare at Christmastime, precisely the time of year when there is supposed to be "peace on earth." On Bachmann's concept of permanent warfare, see also Jost Schneider, *Die Kompositionsmethode Ingeborg Bachmanns: Erzählstil und Engagement in "Das dreißigste Jahr," "Malina" und "Simultan"* (Bielefeld: Aisthesis, 1999), 55–63.

[46] Lennox, *Cemetery*, 298.

[47] Eberhardt, *"Es gibt für mich keine Zitate,"* 387. Unfortunately, this fact eluded the editors of the critical edition of the *Todesarten-Projekt*, who make no reference to this quotation from Marx.

[48] "Wie das Weib aus der Ehe in die allgemeine Prostitution, so tritt die ganze Welt des Reichtums, d.h. des gegenständlichen Wesens des Menschen, aus dem

Verhältnis der exklusiven Ehe mit dem Privateigentümer in das Verhältnis der universellen Prostitution der Gemeinschaft." Karl Marx, *Ökonomisch-Philosophische Manuskripte* [1844], commentary by Michael Quante (Frankfurt am Main: Suhrkamp, 2009), Third Manuscript, 114; translated as "Just as woman passes from marriage to general prostitution, so the entire world of wealth (that is, of man's objective substance) passes from the relationship of exclusive marriage with the owner of private property to a state of universal prostitution with the community. This type of communism—since it negates the personality of man in every sphere—is but the logical expression of private property, which is this negation." Karl Marx, *Economic & Philosophic Manuscripts of 1844*, Third Manuscript, "Private Property and Communism," accessed December 6, 2017, https://www.marxists.org/archive/marx/works/1844/manuscripts/comm. htm.

[49] On this point, cf. Hans Magnus Enzensberger, *Enzensbergers Panoptikum: Zwanzig Zehn-Minuten Essays* (Berlin: Suhrkamp, 2012), 12: "Es tut sich also, was die tatsächlichen wirtschaftlichen Praktiken der Spezies betrifft, ein riesiges Dunkelfeld auf" (As far as the actual economic practices of the human species are concerned, an enormous dark field opens up).

[50] Elaine Scarry, *The Body in Pain: The Making and Unmaking of the World* (1985; Oxford: Oxford University Press, 1987), 258.

[51] Scarry, 247–48.

[52] Scarry, 258.

[53] Lennox, *Cemetery*, 179.

[54] *TP* 1:253.

[55] Scarry, *Body in Pain*, 263.

[56] Scarry, 263.

[57] Scarry, 169.

[58] Scarry, 171.

[59] Scarry, 165.

[60] Göttsche, *Die Produktivität der Sprachkrise*, 208.

[61] Karen R. Achberger, "'Kunst als Veränderndes': Bachmann and Brecht," *Monatshefte* 83, no. 1 (1991): 11–12. Sara Lennox's otherwise authoritative survey of *Der gute Gott von Manhattan* leaves out this connection with Brecht: *Bachmann-Handbuch: Leben—Werk—Wirkung*, edited by Monika Albrecht and Dirk Göttsche (Stuttgart: Metzler, 2013), 92–96.

[62] Achberger, "Kunst als Veränderndes," 12–13.

[63] Achberger, 13. Achberger's reading accords with standard interpretations of Malina such as Dirk Göttsche's, who regards Ich as a kind of subsystem of the self, or "Rest-Ich," which, having lost its anchor in Ivan, becomes incapable of survival. Göttsche, *Die Produktivität der Sprachkrise*, 203.

[64] Bachmann, *Werke*, 2:158.

[65] This is the key to Christa Wolf's interpretation of Bachmann. "Die zumutbare Wahrheit. Prosa der Ingeborg Bachmann" [1966], in *Lesen und Schreiben* (Darmstadt: Luchterhand, 1972), 133. Translated as "Truth That Can Be Faced:

Ingeborg Bachmann's Prose," in *The Reader and the Writer* (Berlin/DDR: Seven Seas, 1977), 94.

[66] In the "Entwürfe" Bachmann is skeptical about communism, writing that it might be fulfilled if it could find "new human beings"; unfortunately, it only encounters "the old kind" of humans—although this does not invalidate it (*KS* 373). Elsewhere, she writes, "Der Kommunismus muß Luxus sein, oder er wird nicht sein" (*KS* 428; Communism must be luxury, or it will not exist).

[67] Wolfgang Iser, *Der Akt des Lesens: Theorie ästhetischer Wirkung* (Munich: Fink, 1976), 307–15; translated as *The Act of Reading: A Theory of Aesthetic Response* (Baltimore: Johns Hopkins University Press, 1978), 198–203.

[68] As Bachmann puts it in her first Frankfurt lecture: "Poesie wie Brot? Dieses Brot müßte zwischen den Zähnen knirschen und den Hunger wiedererwecken, ehe es ihn stillt." (*KS* 268; Poetry like bread? This bread would have to grind between the teeth and awaken hunger before it satisfies it.)

[69] Cf. Göttsche, *Produktivität der Sprachkrise*, 201.

[70] The phrase reappears in Ich's dialogue with Malina about her dreams: "Ich habe die Spuren verwischt" (*M* 216; "I covered up all the tracks," *Ma* 135).

[71] Cf. *GuI* 71; Eberhardt, *"Es gibt für mich keine Zitate,"* 332–34. This Flaubert quotation links hurting and making in much the same way that Elaine Scarry does.

[72] In a rejected draft, Ich's housekeeper Lina is presented as a herald of the revolution: "Trotzdem fühle ich die Revolution nur durch Lina auf mich zukommen, die hier bei uns Platz an der Sonne nicht findet" (*TP* 3.2:709; Despite this I can feel the Revolution approaching me through Lina, who cannot find her place in the sun with us). This recalls Lenin, who once argued that cooks should be trained in the work of government. V. I. Lenin, "Can the Bolsheviks Retain State Power?" in *Collected Works*, vol. 26: *September 1917–February 1918* (London: Lawrence & Wishart; Moscow: Progress Publishers, 1964), 113.

[73] Bertolt Brecht, *The Good Person of Szechwan*, translated by John Willett (London: Bloomsbury Methuen Drama, 2014), 82.

[74] The name "Malina" recalls the French word *malin*, suggesting that he is wily and cunning, especially when it comes to money.

[75] This is reminiscent of Shen Te's response to the homeless family who beg for shelter: "Sie sind ohne Obdach. / Sie sind ohne Freunde. / Sie brauchen jemand. / Wie könnte man da nein sagen?" (*BFA* 6:186; They have no shelter. They have no friends. They need someone. How could anyone say no?).

[76] From a Marxist perspective, too, such acts of charity are ineffectual, because what is required is fundamental structural change.

[77] Bachmann quotes Céline here: "Es gibt für den Armen zwei ausgezeichnete Methoden zu krepieren: entweder durch die vollständige Gleichgültigkeit des Nächsten im Frieden oder durch seinen Mordwahn im Krieg" (*KS* 292–93; For the poor there are two excellent ways to die: either through the complete indifference of their fellows in peacetime, or through their murderous madness in a war). There is another reference to Céline's novel *Journey to the End of the Night* at the beginning of *Malina* (*M* 23; *Ma* 11).

[78] Eberhardt, *"Es gibt für mich keine Zitate,"* 404–7.

[79] This is my own translation, since Philip Boehm's translation omits the repetition of the key word *indifference/indifferent* (*Ma* 214, 221). In Kant's original text the word *Gleichgültigkeit* (indifference) is italicized.

[80] Eberhardt, *"Es gibt für mich keine Zitate,"* 406–7.

[81] Maria Behre, "Nachforschungen in einem unerforschten Gebiet: Wissenschaftliches Lesen in Bachmanns 'Malina' als Drama der Introspektion," in *Über die Zeit schreiben*, 154.

[82] Immanuel Kant, *Kritik der reinen Vernunft*, in *Werkausgabe*, 12 vols., edited by Wilhelm Weischedel (Frankfurt am Main: Suhrkamp, 1974), 3:13.

[83] *Malina* contains forensic discourse in the analytical dialogue, and the charge of murder at the end of the novel opens up a forensic debate.

[84] Teresa Stratas, accompanying notes to compact disc of *Lotte Lenya Sings Kurt Weill's "The Seven Deadly Sins" ("Die sieben Todsünden")*, Sony Classical MHK 63222, 1997.

[85] Cf. Karen R. Achberger, "Der Fall Schönberg: Musik und Mythos in 'Malina,'" in *Ingeborg Bachmann: Text + Kritik*, edited by Heinz Ludwig Arnold (Munich: Text + Kritik, 1984), 122.

[86] *Malina* begins with Ivan taking possession of Ich; their relationship is a "Besitzübernahme" (*M* 28; "transfer of ownership," *Ma* 14), and it ends as the ownership of Ich is transferred from Ivan to Malina.

[87] Göttsche takes the view that Ich is incapable of existence. Göttsche, *Die Produktivität der Sprachkrise*, 206. Arguably, this overlooks Ich's interview with Herr Mühlbauer, which is a tour de force.

[88] Judith Butler, *Giving an Account of Oneself* (New York: Fordham University Press, 2005), 8.

[89] The fictional name of the newspaper in *Malina* might be an allusion to a pro-Nazi tabloid of the Weimar Republic, the *Berliner Nachtausgabe* (Berlin Evening Edition).

[90] Billig, *Arguing and Thinking*, 40.

[91] Billig, 71.

[92] Stephanie Bird, *Women Writers and National Identity: Bachmann, Duden, Özdamar* (Cambridge: Cambridge University Press, 2003), 92.

[93] Bird, "What Matters Who's Speaking?" 164.

[94] Billig, *Arguing and Thinking*, 280.

[95] Billig, 169.

Chapter Six

Epigraph: Cicero, *On the Ideal Orator*, 60 (= bk. 1, sec. 12).

[1] Cf. André Steiner, *The Plans That Failed: An Economic History of the GDR*, translated by Ewald Osers (New York: Berghahn, 2010), 105–39.

[2] Agnès Arp, *VEB, Vaters ehemaliger Betrieb: Privatunternehmer in der DDR* (Leipzig: Militzke, 2005); Peter Karl Becker and Sebastian Liebold, *Kleiner Markt*

im großen Plan: Drei Unternehmerinnen in der DDR (Markkleeberg: Sächsisches Wirtschaftsarchiv e.V. and Sax Verlag, 2015). The small family business is the subject of Erwin Strittmatter's epic trilogy *Der Laden* (1983, 1987, 1992; The Store).

[3] Ha-Joon Chang, *Economics: The User's Guide*, 60.

[4] Steiner, *The Plans That Failed*, 111.

[5] Mommsen, *Max Weber and German Politics*, 105.

[6] Mommsen, 105. This liberal critique of socialism goes back as far as the liberal leader Eugen Richter and his dystopian novel *Sozialdemokratische Zukunftsbilder: Frei nach Bebel* (1890; Scenes of a Social Democratic Future: Freely Adapted from Bebel).

[7] Mary Fulbrook, *Anatomy of a Dictatorship: Inside the GDR, 1949–1989* (Oxford: Oxford University Press, 1995), 44.

[8] Mary Fulbrook, *The People's State: East German Society from Hitler to Honecker* (New Haven, CT: Yale University Press, 2005), 12.

[9] Fulbrook, 236.

[10] Sara Jones, *Complicity, Censorship and Criticism: Negotiating Space in the GDR Literary Sphere* (Berlin: De Gruyter, 2011), 200.

[11] For an overview, see Thomas W. Goldstein, *Writing in Red: The East German Writers Union and the Role of Literary Intellectuals* (Rochester, NY: Camden House, 2017).

[12] Heiner Müller, *Krieg ohne Schlacht: Leben in zwei Diktaturen* (1992; Cologne: Kiepenheuer & Witsch, 2009), 172.

[13] Kant discusses his editorship of *Tua res* in his autobiography, *Abspann: Erinnerung an meine Gegenwart* (Berlin: Aufbau, 1991), 246–48.

[14] Jones, *Complicity, Censorship and Criticism*, 62–64. Kant's difficulties with GDR authorities in 1969 are also documented in Linde Salber, *Nicht ohne Utopie: Die wahre Geschichte des Hermann Kant. Biographie*, 2nd ed. (Ochsenfurt: Kulturmaschinen Verlag, 2015), 229–42.

[15] Reprinted in Hermann Kant, *Zu den Unterlagen: Publizistik 1957–1980* (Berlin: Aufbau, 1981), 286–90. *Das Impressum* itself comments that it is a capital error to entertain "gesamtdeutsche Illusionen" (*DI* 33; illusions about both Germanies).

[16] Reprinted in Kant, *Zu den Unterlagen*, 73–77.

[17] Jones, *Complicity, Censorship and Criticism*, 70.

[18] Jones, 40. Much has been made of Hermann Kant's conversations with the Stasi, but he is not the only author in this book who provided information to state censors. In 1912–13 Thomas Mann worked as an adviser to the Bavarian Commission of Censorship. Similarly to Kant, Mann's role on this commission was ambivalent. Ritchie Robertson interprets Mann's activity as an attempt to mediate between authorities and avant-garde authors: "Savonarola in Munich: A Reappraisal of Thomas Mann's *Fiorenza*," *Publications of the English Goethe Society* 74, no. 1 (2005): 57.

[19] Jones, *Complicity, Censorship and Criticism*, 93.

[20] Emmerich, *Kleine Literaturgeschichte der DDR*, 204. Jones, *Complicity, Censorship and Criticism*, 93.

[21] I am grateful to my colleague Joseph Russo for this reference.

[22] Jones, *Complicity, Censorship and Criticism*, 40.

[23] Eugene Garver, *Machiavelli and the History of Prudence* (Madison: University of Wisconsin Press, 1987), 100–105.

[24] Hermann Kant, *Das Impressum* (Berlin: Rütten & Loening, 1975), 177; abbreviated *DI*.

[25] The name *Neue Berliner Rundschau* recalls the *Deutsche Rundschau*, Germany's oldest political review, founded in 1874 by Julius Rodenberg.

[26] Bathrick, *The Powers of Speech*, 15–17.

[27] Simone Barck, Martina Langermann, and Siegfried Lokatis, *"Jedes Buch ein Abenteuer": Zensur-System und literarische Öffentlichkeiten in der DDR bis Ende der sechziger Jahre* (Berlin: Akademie Verlag, 1997), 418.

[28] Jones, *Complicity, Censorship and Criticism*, 203. Cf. Wolfgang Bialas, *Vom unfreien Schweben zum freien Fall: Ostdeutsche Intellektuelle im gesellschaftlichen Umbruch* (Frankfurt am Main: Fischer, 1996), 203–4.

[29] Jones, *Complicity, Censorship and Criticism*, 80.

[30] Bertolt Brecht, *Mother Courage and Her Children*, translated by John Willett (London: Methuen, 1983), 46.

[31] On this point, see Martin Diewald, "'Kollektiv,' 'Vitamin B' oder 'Nische'? Persönliche Netzwerke in der DDR," in *Kollektiv und Eigensinn: Lebensverläufe in der DDR und danach*, edited by Johannes Huinink and Karl Ulrich Mayer (Berlin: Akademie Verlag, 1995), 223–60.

[32] Hermann Kant, "Der dritte Nagel," in *Der dritte Nagel: Erzählungen* (Berlin: Rütten & Loening, 1981), 65–102.

[33] Hermann Kähler, "Impressum—Impressionen," *Sinn und Form*, 24, no. 4 (1972): 876.

[34] For example, E. W. Herd states that "Kant uses his gift for anecdote to talk his way out of the problems his novels claim to be dealing with." "Narrative Technique in Two Novels by Hermann Kant," in *"Erfahrung und Überlieferung": Festschrift for C. P. Magill*, edited by Hinrich Siefken and Alan Robinson (Cardiff: University of Wales Press, 1974), 195.

[35] Fritz J. Roethlisberger, "The Foreman: Master and Victim of Double Talk," *Harvard Business Review* 23, no. 3 (1945): 285–86.

[36] Jones, *Complicity, Censorship and Criticism*, 80.

[37] Wolfgang Engler, *Die Ostdeutschen: Kunde von einem verlorenen Land* (Berlin: Aufbau, 1999), 118.

[38] Jones, *Complicity, Censorship and Criticism*, 88–89.

[39] Cf. Jones, *Complicity, Censorship and Criticism*, 63, and Konrad Franke, "'Deine Darstellung ist uns wesensfremd': Romane der 60er Jahre in den Mühlen der DDR-Zensur," in *Literaturentwicklungsprozesse: Die Zensur der Literatur in der DDR*, edited by Ernest Wichner and Herbert Wiesner (Frankfurt am Main: Suhrkamp, 1993), 101–27.

[40] For a general analysis of this event, see Richard Millington, *State, Society and Memories of the Uprising of 17 June 1953 in the GDR* (New York: Palgrave Macmillan, 2014).

[41] Garver, *Machiavelli*, 100.

[42] Jones, *Complicity, Censorship and Criticism*, 90. Kant does this, for example, in chapter 12, when he depicts a Soviet major who is a great aficionado of the Prussian General von Moltke, thus invoking Soviet authority in order to challenge the GDR's dismissive attitude to Prussian history.

[43] Cicero writes that the orator must "have his finger on the pulse of every class, every age group, every social rank": *On the Ideal Orator*, 112 (= bk. 1, sec. 223).

[44] Brecht makes a similar point in his poem "Grabschrift für Gorki" (Epitaph for Gorky), when he calls Maxim Gorky "Der Lehrer des Volkes / Der vom Volk gelernt hat" (*BFA* 12:60; The people's teacher / Who learned from the people).

[45] Cf. Anton Semyonovich Makarenko, *Problems of Soviet School Education* (Moscow: Progress, 1965).

[46] Cf. Christopher Young, "East versus West: Olympic Sport as a German Cold War Phenomenon," in *Divided, but Not Disconnected: German Experiences of the Cold War*, edited by Tobias Hochscherf, Christoph Laucht, and Andrew Plowman (New York: Berghahn, 2010), 148–62.

[47] Mary Fulbrook once told me in conversation that her research into GDR bureaucracy was excellent training for her role as dean of the Faculty of Social and Historical Sciences at University College London.

Chapter Seven

[1] On documentary literature, see Nikolaus Miller, *Prolegomena zu einer Poetik der Dokumentarliteratur*, Münchner germanistische Beiträge 30 (Munich: Fink, 1982).

[2] On corporate bureaucracy and modernity, see Andriopoulos, *Possessed*.

[3] Günter Wallraff, *"Wir brauchen dich": Als Arbeiter in deutschen Industriebetrieben* (Munich: Rütten & Loening, 1966); Günter Wallraff and Jens Hagen, *Was wollt ihr denn, ihr lebt ja noch: Chronik einer Industrieansiedlung* (Reinbek bei Hamburg: Rowohlt, 1973); Bernt Engelmann and Günter Wallraff, *Ihr da oben—wir da unten* (Cologne: Kiepenheuer & Witsch, 1973).

[4] Jost Hermand, "Unser aller Zukunft? Mathias Schebens *Konzern 2003*," *Basis: Jahrbuch für deutsche Gegenwartsliteratur* 10 (1980): 7–35.

[5] Friedrich Christian Delius, *Wir Unternehmer: Unsere Siemens-Welt. Einige Argumente zur Verteidigung der Gemüseesser. Satiren*, Werkausgabe in Einzelbänden (Reinbek bei Hamburg: Rowohlt, 2014), 157 (abbreviated as *USW*).

[6] "Zwar schreibt das neue Gesetz . . . die Möglichkeit der Einsichtnahme in den Personalakten vor—aber wir werden uns noch einige Modifikationen einfallen lassen, damit wenigstens die Diskretion bei dem wichtigen Teil der Führungsakten erhalten bleibt" (*USW* 308; The new law may provide the opportunity to view one's personnel file—but we will come up with a few modifications in order to ensure that discretion is preserved, at least as far as the most important sections of the management files are concerned.)

[7] Max Weber, *Wirtschaft und Gesellschaft*, in *Gesamtausgabe*, vol. 1.22,4 (Tübingen: Mohr Siebeck, 2005), 157; *Economy and Society*, 2:956.

[8] Weber, *Wirtschaft und* Gesellschaft, in *Gesamtausgabe*, 1.22,4:158–59; *Economy and Society*, 2:957–58. David Graeber also cites Weber on this point: *The Utopia of Rules: On Technology, Stupidity, and the Secret Joys of Bureaucracy* (Brooklyn, NY: Melville House, 2015), 12.

[9] Weber, *Wirtschaft und Gesellschaft*, in *Gesamtausgabe*, 1.22,4:185–86; *Economy and Society*, 2:973–74.

[10] Weber, *Wirtschaft und Gesellschaft*, in *Gesamtausgabe*, 1.22,4:160: "Für den spezifischen Charakter der modernen Amtstreue ist entscheidend, daß sie . . . einem unpersönlichen *sachlichen Zweck* gilt. Hinter diesem sachlichen Zweck pflegen natürlich, ihn ideologisch verklärend, . . . 'Kulturwertideen': 'Staat,' 'Kirche,' 'Gemeinde,' 'Partei,' 'Betrieb' zu stehen"; *Economy and Society*, 2:959: "It is decisive for the modern loyalty to an office that . . . it is devoted to *impersonal* and *functional* purposes. These purposes, of course, frequently gain an ideological halo from cultural values such as state, church, community, party or enterprise."

[11] Friedrich Christian Delius, *Ein Held der inneren Sicherheit* [1981], in *Deutscher Herbst: Drei Romane* (Reinbek bei Hamburg: Rowohlt, 2012), 37.

[12] Keith Bullivant, *Realism Today: Aspects of the Contemporary West German Novel* (Leamington Spa, UK: Berg, 1987), 130. Cf. Lothar Baier, "Wie Macht wirkt: Friedrich Christian Delius' erster Roman: 'Ein Held der inneren Sicherheit,'" *Die Zeit*, April 24, 1981, http://www.zeit.de/1981/18/wie-macht-wirkt/komplettansicht.

[13] Cf. Julian Preece, *Baader-Meinhof and the Novel: Narratives of the Nation/Fantasies of the Revolution, 1970–2010* (New York: Palgrave Macmillan, 2012), 53–54.

[14] According to H. V. Perlmutter's classification of transnationals, Siemens is an "ethnocentric transnational" because company policy is largely set and put into practice from Siemens headquarters in Munich. Cf. Anthony Giddens, *Sociology* (Cambridge: Polity, 1989), 535.

[15] Bernard Dieterle, "Ein Dokument der Dokumentarliteratur: Paratextuelle Überlegungen zu Delius' Festschrift," in *F. C. Delius: Studien über sein literarisches Werk*, edited by Manfred Durzak and Hartmut Steinecke (Tübingen: Stauffenberg, 1997), 34.

[16] Occasionally, *Wir Unternehmer* also contains brief factual commentary in italics, provided by Karl-Heinz Stanzik, in order to serve as a corrective to some of the wilder claims made by the speakers.

[17] Cf. *USW* 15: "Binsenwahrheiten, die Berufung auf das, was nun einmal so sei, die die Aufforderung zum Verzicht auf Reflexion einschließen" (Truisms: by invoking that which is obvious, these truisms invite the audience to suspend their reflective faculties).

[18] Cicero, *On the Ideal Orator*, 157 [= bk. 2, secs. 130–31].

[19] Aristotle, *Rhetoric* 2.21.1395b1–3. The discussion of commonplaces continues in 1395b30–1396b19.

20 For a discussion of commonplaces, see Billig, *Arguing and Thinking*, 228–37.

21 Cf. Gregor Gysi, *Worte des Vorsitzenden Gregor Gysi*, edited by Hanno Harnisch and Olaf Miemiec (Berlin: Eulenspiegel, 2015), 90: "'Verantwortlich' im Sinne der herrschenden Ideologie bedeutet: Sei hier unkritisch, mach einfach mit" ("Being responsible" according to the dominant ideology means: Don't be critical, just play ball).

22 Karl Kraus, "Die Sprache" [December 1932], in *Die Sprache* (Frankfurt am Main: Suhrkamp, 1987), 373.

23 Gerwin Marahrens, "Über die sprachliche Struktur und Genesis der Aphorismen von Karl Kraus," in *Karl Kraus: Diener der Sprache, Meister des Ethos*, edited by Joseph P. Strelka (Tübingen: Francke, 1990), 81.

24 Marianne Jørgensen and Louise Phillips, *Discourse Analysis as Theory and Method* (London: Sage, 2002), 125.

25 Cf. John Hesk, "Types of Oratory," in Gunderson, *Cambridge Companion to Ancient Rhetoric*, 157.

26 Hesk, 157.

27 Billig, *Arguing and Thinking*, 119.

28 Dieterle, "Dokument der Dokumentarliteratur," 38.

29 Wilfried Feldenkirchen, *Siemens: Von der Werkstatt zum Weltunternehmen* [1997], 2nd ed. (Munich: Piper, 2003); translated by Richard A. Michell as *Siemens: From Workshop to Global Player* (Munich: Piper, 2000).

30 Wilfried Feldenkirchen, *Siemens 1918–1945* (Munich: Piper, 1995); translated by Tom Rattray and John Taylor as *Siemens 1918–1945* (Columbus: Ohio State University Press, 1999). Quotations in the text are from the English version.

31 Dieter Maurer, "Siemens-Projektleiter stirbt bei Fahrt mit Elektro-Oldtimer," *Badische Zeitung*, June 21, 2010, http://www.badische-zeitung.de/titisee-neustadt/feldkirchen-stirbt-bei-fahrt-mit-elektro-oldtimer--32483811.html.

32 Feldenkirchen, *Siemens 1918–1945*, 8.

33 Hans Domizlaff, *Die Gewinnung des öffentlichen Vertrauens: Ein Lehrbuch der Markentechnik* [1939], 7th ed. (Hamburg: Marketing Journal Gesellschaft für angewandtes Marketing mbH, 2005).

34 Domizlaff, *Die Gewinnung*, 10.

35 Domizlaff, 11.

36 Another moment reminiscent of *Buddenbrooks* in Delius's work is in *Wir Unternehmer*, when Albrecht Pickert refers to Max Weber's theory of innerworldly asceticism: "[die] asketische Grundhaltung des Unternehmers" (*USW* 80; the entrepreneur's fundamental attitude of asceticism).

37 Feldenkirchen, *Siemens 1918–1945*, 142.

38 Feldenkirchen, *Siemens 1918–1945*, 362; Feldenkirchen, *Siemens: Von der Werkstatt*, 399. The three main companies were amalgamated to form Siemens AG in 1966.

39 Cf. Hans Domizlaff, *Nachdenkliche Wanderschaft: Autobiographische Fragmente* (1950; Zurich: Criterion, 1992), 565.

40 Hans Domizlaff, *Der Sozialisierungstod: Aufruf zur Verteidigung des Produktiven Unternehmertums* (Berlin: Lektorat für Buch, Bühne, Film, 1949).

[41] Hans Domizlaff, *Die Seele des Staates: Regelbuch der Elite* (Hamburg: Self-pub. [Hans Dulk], [1957]).

[42] Feldenkirchen, *Siemens 1918–1945*, 5.

[43] S. Jonathan Wiesen, *West German Industry and the Challenge of the Nazi Past, 1945–1955* (Chapel Hill: University of North Carolina Press, 2001).

[44] Wiesen, *West German Industry*, 22–24. On forced labor see also Feldenkirchen, *Siemens 1918–1945*, 130–38, 164–74; and Carola Sachse, "Zwangsarbeit jüdischer und nichtjüdischer Frauen und Männer bei der Firma Siemens 1940 bis 1945," *Internationale wissenschaftliche Korrespondenz zur Geschichte der deutschen Arbeiterbewegung* 27 (1991): 1–12. In addition, a Communist newspaper published an article alleging that Siemens built and installed the gas chambers at Auschwitz; this claim has never been proved: "Krupp an KZ Auschwitz beteiligt: Siemens lieferte die Vergassungsanlage" (Krupp participated in Auschwitz; Siemens supplied the gas chambers), *Deutsche Volkszeitung*, August 5, 1945. Cf. Wiesen, *West German Industry*, 45. This claim was reproduced by Delius in the first edition of *Unsere Siemens-Welt* but excised from subsequent editions.

[45] Max Stein, "Report on the Employment of Slave Work by the Siemens Concern during World War II," Office of the Conference on Jewish Material Claims against Germany, Frankfurt am Main; cited in Wiesen, *West German Industry*, 25.

[46] For details of the dispute, see Benjamin B. Ferencz, *Less than Slaves: Jewish Forced Labor and the Quest for Compensation* [1979], 2nd ed. (Bloomington: Indiana University Press 2002); in German, *Lohn des Grauens: Die verweigerte Entschädigung für jüdische Zwangsarbeiter. Ein Kapitel deutscher Nachkriegsgeschichte* (Frankfurt am Main: Campus, 1986).

[47] Betts, *Authority of Everyday Objects*, 244.

[48] Wiesen, *West German Industry*, 30–31.

[49] Wiesen, 39.

[50] Feldenkirchen, *Siemens 1918–1945*, 174.

[51] Feldenkirchen, 581–82, 82n157.

[52] Feldenkirchen, 582n160.

[53] Feldenkirchen, 174. Most of the conflicts between Siemens and "those in power" occurred over the implementation of programs by the Deutsche Arbeitsfront (DAF, German Labor Front), as will be discussed in the next section.

[54] Feldenkirchen, *Siemens 1918–1945*, 582n161.

[55] This is similar to Friedrich A. Hayek's critique of totalitarian states in *The Road to Serfdom* (1944), which is based on the damage they do to the economy, since he defines individual freedom primarily in terms of economic freedom.

[56] Even the loyal Feldenkirchen concludes: "The company's decision to use forced labor was made primarily on the grounds of cost and technical efficiency. . . . Other criteria—of an ethical nature, for example—were not taken into consideration." *Siemens 1918–1945*, 364.

[57] Carola Sachse, *Siemens, der Nationalsozialismus und die moderne Familie: Eine Untersuchung zur sozialen Rationalisierung in Deutschland im 20. Jahrhundert* (Hamburg: Rasch und Röhring, 1990).

[58] Sachse, *Siemens, der Nationalsozialismus,* 246.

[59] Joan Campbell, *Joy in Work, German Work: The National Debate, 1800–1945* (Princeton, NJ: Princeton University Press, 1989), 101.

[60] J. Ronald Shearer, "Talking about Efficiency: Politics and the Industrial Rationalization Movement in the Weimar Republic," *Central European History* 28, no. 4 (1995): 487.

[61] Sachse, *Siemens, der Nationalsozialismus,* 128.

[62] Campbell, *Joy in Work,* 157.

[63] Sachse, *Siemens, der Nationalsozialismus,* 246.

[64] Sachse, 27. Sexist company policies are also discussed in Delius's text (*USW* 290–91).

[65] Peter Reichel, *Der schöne Schein des Dritten Reiches: Faszination und Gewalt des Faschismus* (Munich: Hanser, 1991), 235.

[66] Campbell, *Joy in Work,* 334; Wehler, *Deutsche Gesellschaftsgeschichte,* 3:734. Delius also alludes to the superficiality of similar renovation programs in the postwar context: "Trotzdem bleiben wir bemüht, . . . durch einen freundlichen, farbenfrohe Anstrich der Arbeitsräume die tägliche Arbeit wesentlich zu erleichtern" (*USW* 291; Even so we remain committed to making daily work much easier by making work areas bright, friendly, and colorful).

[67] Betts, *Authority of Everyday Objects,* 37–39.

[68] Betts, 40.

[69] Sachse, *Siemens, der Nationalsozialismus,* 89.

[70] Sachse, 90–91, 245.

[71] Sachse, 237.

[72] Sachse, 249.

[73] Sachse, 249.

[74] Sachse, 251.

[75] On the management of the slave labor program, see Michael Thad Allen, "The Banality of Evil Reconsidered: SS Mid-Level Managers of Extermination through Work," *Central European History* 30, no. 2 (1997): 253–94.

[76] There is a similar logic at work when another member of the board, Franz Heinrich Ulrich, states that what counts in business is not consideration for people but consideration for "die harten Gegebenheiten des Geschäfts" (*USW* 267; the harsh circumstances of business).

[77] The partnership between Siemens and Westinghouse concerned both nuclear power stations (pressurized water reactors [PWRs]) and nonnuclear power stations (Combined Cycle Gas Turbine plants [CCGTs]). Cf. Feldenkirchen, *Siemens: Von der Werkstatt,* 332–33. After the Westinghouse corporation went bankrupt in the 1990s, Siemens acquired its nonnuclear Power Generation Business Unit based in Orlando, Florida, in 1998. The nuclear wing of Westinghouse was acquired by British Nuclear Fuels, which later sold it to Toshiba in 2006.

[78] Friedrich Christian Delius, *Konservativ in 30 Tagen: Ein Hand- und Wörterbuch Frankfurter Allgemeinplätze* (Reinbek bei Hamburg: Rowohlt, 1988), 178.

[79] Delius, 182–83.

80 Delius, 185.

81 Deborah Cowen, *The Deadly Life of Logistics: Mapping Violence in Global Trade* (Minneapolis: University of Minnesota Press, 2014), 4.

82 On corporations as political actors, see Colin Crouch, *The Strange Non-Death of Neoliberalism* (Cambridge: Polity Press, 2011).

83 Delius's text claims that the patent law was passed in 1876, but it was actually passed on May 25, 1877. It led to the establishment of the Kaiserliches Patentamt (Imperial Patent Office), which started to operate in Berlin on July 1, 1877.

84 Quintus Tullius Cicero, *How to Win an Election: An Ancient Guide for Modern Politicians*, translated by Philip Freeman (Princeton, NJ: Princeton University Press, 2012), 29.

85 Crouch, *The Strange Non-Death*, 47.

86 Joseph Vogl, *Der Souveränitätseffekt* (Zurich: Diaphanes, 2015), 221.

87 Crouch, *The Strange Non-Death*, 90.

88 "Nennen wir ausnahmsweise einmal das unschöne Wort—Monopole" (*USW* 160; Just this once let us use that unpleasant word—monopoly).

89 European Commission Press Release IP/09/1432, Brussels, October 7, 2009, http://europa.eu/rapid/press-release_IP-09-1432_en.htm?locale=en.

90 General Court of the European Union Press Release No 15/11, Luxembourg, March 3, 2011, http://europa.eu/rapid/press-release_CJE-11-15_en.htm.

91 Eric Lichtblau and Carter Dougherty, "Siemens to Pay $1.34 Billion in Fines," *New York Times*, December 15, 2008, http://www.nytimes.com/2008/12/16/business/worldbusiness/16siemens.html?_r=2&hp=&pagewanted=print. For details of the US fines, see the forthcoming history of Siemens since 1981 by Hartmut Berghoff and Cornelia Rauh. N.b: This study is not independent; it has been officially commissioned by Siemens itself.

92 Wassilis Aswestopoulos, "Griechischer Staatsanwalt klagt Siemens-Vorstände an," *Focus Online Money*, November 27, 2014, http://www.focus.de/finanzen/boerse/aktien/2368-seiten-anklageschrift-griechischer-staatsanwalt-klagt-siemens-vorstaende-an_id_4305617.html.

Chapter Eight

Epigraph: Kathrin Röggla, *wir schlafen nicht* (Frankfurt am Main: S. Fischer, 2004), 52 (abbreviated as *wsn*); translated by Rebecca Thomas as *We Never Sleep*, Studies in Austrian Literature, Culture and Thought (Riverside, CA: Ariadne Press, 2009), 46 (abbreviated as *WNS*).

1 Janina Kugel, "Das Eckbüro hat ausgedient," interview by Sven Astheimer, *Frankfurter Allgemeine Zeitung*, November 14–15, 2015, C1.

2 Kugel, C1.

3 Kathrin Röggla, *besser wäre: keine. Essays und Theater* (Frankfurt am Main: S. Fischer, 2013), 212.

4 Graeber, *Utopia of Rules*, 17.

[5] Graeber, 17.

[6] Graeber, 20.

[7] Ulrich Beck, *Risikogesellschaft: Auf dem Weg in eine andere Moderne* (Frankfurt am Main: Suhrkamp, 1986); translated by Mark Ritter as *Risk Society: Towards a New Modernity* (Thousand Oaks, CA: Sage, 1992), 143. In West Germany, the first big step toward deregulation was taken by the Beschäftigungsförderungsgesetz (Employment Promotion Act) of April 26, 1985, which exempted newly established small enterprises from the obligation to prepare a social plan when laying off workers.

[8] Karin Krauthausen, "'ob das jetzt das interview sei?': Das konjunktivische Interview in Kathrin Rögglas Roman *wir schlafen nicht*" (lecture, University of Nantes, June 12, 2004), http://www.kathrin-roeggla.de/text/karin-krauthausen-ob-das-jetzt-das-interview-sei. See also Herta Luise Ott, who considers the extent to which Röggla's text is implicated in the phenomena it critiques: "*Nous ne dormons pas*: critique idéologique à travers une critique des langages chez Kathrin Röggla," *Germanica* 39 (2006): 57–74.

[9] Kremer, *Milieu und Performativität*; Anke S. Biendarra, "Prekäre neue Arbeitswelt. Narrative der New Economy," in *Das erste Jahrzehnt: Narrative und Poetiken des 21. Jahrhunderts*, edited by Julia Schöll and Johanna Bohley (Würzburg: Königshausen & Neumann, 2012), 69–82.

[10] David Clarke, "The Capitalist Uncanny in Kathrin Röggla's *wir schlafen nicht*: Ghosts in the Machine," *Angermion* 4 (2011): 147–63; Elaine Martin, "New Economy Zombies: Kathrin Röggla's *wir schlafen nicht*," in *Transitions: Emerging Women Writers in German-Language Literature*, German Monitor 76, edited by Valerie Hefernan and Gillian Pye (New York: Rodopi, 2013), 131–48.

[11] Anna Katharina Schaffner, "'Catastrophe Sociology' and the Metaphors We Live By: On Kathrin Röggla's *wir schlafen nicht*," *Modern Language Review* 112, no. 1 (2017): 211–12.

[12] Schumpeter, *Capitalism, Socialism and Democracy*, 71–75.

[13] Röggla, *besser wäre: keine*, 214. Cf. Naomi Klein, *The Shock Doctrine: The Rise of Disaster Capitalism* (New York: Picador, 2008). See also Philip Mirowski, *Never Let a Serious Crisis Go to Waste: How Neoliberalism Survived the Financial Meltdown* (New York: Verso, 2013).

[14] Röggla, *besser wäre: keine*, 211. Cf. Karl E. Weick and Kathleen M. Sutcliffe, *Managing the Unexpected: Sustained Performance in a Complex World*, 3rd ed. (Hoboken, NJ: Wiley, 2015).

[15] Röggla, *besser wäre: keine*, 211.

[16] Jonathan Crary, *24/7: Late Capitalism and the Ends of Sleep* (London: Verso, 2013).

[17] McKinsey also features in Rolf Hochhuth's play *McKinsey kommt* (2004; McKinsey Is Coming). Although the company does not appear directly in the play, the title phrase invokes the firings that are being planned.

[18] Duff McDonald, *The Firm: The Story of McKinsey and Its Secret Influence on American Business* (New York: Simon & Schuster, 2013), 83.

[19] For example, two of the greatest orators in modern British history, Edmund Burke and Winston Churchill, emerged at times of political crisis.

[20] Graeber, *Utopia of Rules*, 21.

[21] On this point see Ott, "*Nous ne dormons pas*," 57–74, and Röggla, *besser wäre: keine*, 326.

[22] Röggla, *besser wäre: keine*, 319.

[23] Kathrin Röggla in conversation with Susanna Brogi and Katja Hartosch, "'Manage dich selbst oder stirb': Die Autorin Kathrin Röggla im Gespräch," in *Repräsentationen von Arbeit: Transdisziplinäre Analysen und künstlerische Produktion*, edited by Susanna Brogi, Carolin Freier, Ulf Freier-Otten, and Katja Hartosch (Bielefeld: Transcript, 2013), 491–92. On this point see also Schaffner, "Catastrophe Sociology," 212.

[24] Röggla, *besser wäre: keine*, 320.

[25] Aristotle, *Rhetoric* 1.2.1356a.

[26] Röggla, *besser wäre: keine*, 115.

[27] Later, the online editor goes into more detail: "was hätten sie sich denn gedacht? daß man ungestraft von tausend kick-off meetings sprechen könne. . . . wie lange könne man ungestraft von dienstleistungsgesellschaft sprechen und davon ausgehen, daß man ungeschoren davonkomme, wenn man ständig die rede von dienstleistungs- und wissensgesellschaft im mund führe? . . . daß man ungestraft menschliche stimmen nachmachen könne, als wäre nichts" (*wsn* 189; "what had they thought? that they could keep getting away with talking about thousands of *kick-off meetings*? . . . how long could they keep getting away with talking about a service economy and assume that they would get off unscathed when they constantly talked about a service economy and a knowledge society? . . . that you could get away with imitating human voices as if it were nothing," *WNS* 166–67).

[28] Wolfgang Streeck, *Gekaufte Zeit: Die vertagte Krise des demokratischen Kapitalismus*. Frankfurter Adorno-Vorlesungen 2012 (Berlin: Suhrkamp, 2013), 13.

[29] Oliver Stallwood, Interview with Moray MacLennan, *Metro*, Wednesday, February 14, 2018, 28.

[30] The British equivalent would be the seductive slogan "Keep Calm and Carry On." For an analysis of this term, see Owen Hatherley, *The Ministry of Nostalgia: Consuming Austerity* (London: Verso, 2017).

[31] Röggla, *besser wäre: keine*, 324.

[32] Michel Foucault, *On the Government of the Living: Lectures at the Collège de France, 1979–1980*, translated by Graham Burchell (New York: Palgrave Macmillan, 2014), 17.

[33] Röggla, *besser wäre: keine*, 327.

[34] Foucault, *On the Government of the Living*, 232.

[35] Krauthausen, "ob das jetzt das interview sei?"

[36] In a similar vein, Miya Tokumitsu has shown that the rhetoric of "doing what you love" is often used as a justification for poor working conditions: "In the Name

of Love," *Jacobin Magazine*, January 12, 2014, https://www.jacobinmag.com/2014/01/in-the-name-of-love/.

[37] Röggla, *besser wäre: keine*, 321.

[38] Röggla, 323. Röggla also uses the term "Topüberzeuger" (top persuaders), 319.

[39] Aristotle, *Rhetoric* 1.2.1356a.

[40] Röggla, *besser wäre: keine*, 323. The phrase "Fakten, Fakten, Fakten" is a quotation from the German publicist Helmut Markwort, who was the editor of *Focus* magazine from 1993 to 2010 and has worked as a top manager for Hubert Burda Media, a global media company.

[41] Roethlisberger, "The Foreman," 284.

[42] On this point see Schaffner, "Catastrophe Sociology," 218.

[43] Cf. Catherine Steel, *Cicero, Rhetoric, and Empire* (Oxford: Oxford University Press, 2001), 13.

[44] For a study of the rhetorical use of anecdotes in modern British politics, see Judi Atkins and Alan Finlayson, "'. . . A 40-Year-Old Black Man Made the Point to Me': Everyday Knowledge and the Performance of Leadership in Contemporary British Politics," *Political Studies* 61, no. 1 (2013): 161–77.

[45] Marcus Fabius Quintilianus (Quintilian), *Institutes of Oratory; or, Education of an Orator*, translated by John Selby Watson (London: George Bell and Sons, 1891), bk. 3, ch. 5, sec.7. On this point see Arlene Victoria Holmes Henderson, "A Defence of Classical Rhetoric in Scotland's Curriculum for Excellence" (EdD thesis, University of Glasgow 2013), 62–63.

[46] On voice disorders see Lutz-Christian Anders, "Stimm-, Sprechstörungen," in *Historisches Wörterbuch der Rhetorik*, vol. 9: *St-Z*, edited by Gert Ueding (Tübingen: Niemeyer, 2009), 99–108.

[47] Another text that explores the link between oratory and hypnosis is Thomas Mann's *Mario und der Zauberer* (1930; *Mario and the Magician*).

[48] Marcus Tullius Cicero, *On the Ideal Orator*, 112 [= bk. 1, sec. 223].

[49] Roethlisberger, "The Foreman," 285–86.

[50] Roethlisberger, 294–95.

[51] Röggla, *besser wäre: keine*, 319–20.

[52] Röggla, 323.

[53] Henderson, "Defence of Classical Rhetoric," 63.

[54] This is a quotation from Robert Burns's poem "To a Louse, On Seeing One on a Lady's Bonnet at Church" (1786). The original Scots phrase is: "To see oursels as ithers see us!."

[55] George Mead argues that "all mental activity" involves the ability to take "the role of another." Cited in Billig, *Arguing and Thinking*, 142.

[56] Compare Cicero's point that the orator must be steeped in the "traditions, the character and the inclinations of his fellow citizens": *On the Ideal Orator*, 157 [= bk. 2, sec. 130].

[57] As Roethlisberger puts it, the manager "is painfully tutored to focus his attention upward to his immediate superiors and the logics of evaluation they represent": "The Foreman," 288.

[58] Röggla, *besser wäre: keine*, 311.

[59] Blumenberg, "Anthropologische Annäherung," 117; "An Anthropological Approach," 441.

Chapter Nine

Epigraph: Philipp Schönthaler, *Das Schiff das singend zieht auf seiner Bahn* (Berlin: Matthes & Seitz, 2013), 6 (abbreviated as *DS*).

[1] I am grateful to Daniel Steuer for this insight, and for his comments on a draft version of this chapter.

2 See Nancy Etcoff, *Survival of the Prettiest: The Science of Beauty* (New York: Doubleday, 1999).

[3] Philipp Schönthaler, *Negative Poetik: Die Figur des Erzählers bei Thomas Bernhard, W. G. Sebald und Imre Kertész* (Bielefeld: transcript, 2011).

[4] Philipp Schönthaler, *Nach oben ist das Leben offen* (Berlin: Matthes & Seitz, 2012), 4–25.

[5] Cf. Eckhard Heftrich, "Der Totentanz in Thomas Manns Roman *Der Zauberberg*," in *Tanz und Tod in Kunst und Literatur*, edited by Franz Link (Berlin: Duncker & Humblot, 1993), 335–50.

[6] Thomas E. Schmidt, "Der eigene Körper als Feind," *Die Zeit*, January 23, 2014, 47.

[7] Abbé d'Aubignac, *La Pratique du théâtre*, 370; cited in France, *Racine's Rhetoric*, 2.

[8] The figure of the corporate athlete also appears in John von Düffel's novel *Ego* (2001). See Kremer, *Milieu und Performativität*, 94–113.

[9] The phrase occurs in Alexander Thomas and Mona Scheuermeyer, *Beruflich in Kanada: Trainingsprogramm für Manager, Fach- und Führungskräfte* (Göttingen: Vandenhoeck & Ruprecht, 2006), 10.

[10] Alexander Thomas, "Interkulturalität und Unternehmen," in *Orte der Diversität: Formate, Arrangements und Inszenierungen*, edited by Cristina Allemann-Ghionda and Wolf-Dietrich Bukow (Wiesbaden: VS Verlag, 2011), 227.

[11] Erik Gunderson, "The Rhetoric of Rhetorical Theory," in Gunderson, *Cambridge Companion to Ancient Rhetoric*, 119.

[12] Philipp Schönthaler, *Porträt des Managers als junger Autor: Zum Verhältnis von Wirtschaft und Literatur. Eine Handreichung* (Berlin: Matthes & Seitz, 2016), 29.

[13] Schönthaler, 144.

[14] Jakob Burckhardt, *Griechische Kulturgeschichte*, 94–95.

[15] Cicero, *On the Ideal Orator*, 286 [= bk. 3, sec. 200].

[16] Cf. Wolfgang Schönpflug, "Rieffert, Johann Baptist," in *Deutschsprachige Psychologinnen und Psychologen 1933–45*, edited by Uwe Wolfradt, Elfriede Billmann-Mahecha, and Armin Stock (Wiesbaden: Springer Fachmedien, 2015), 368–70.

[17] Cf. J. B. Rieffert, "Psychotechnik im Heere," *Bericht über den 7. Kongress für experimentelle Psychologie in Marburg 1921*, edited by Karl Bühler (Jena, 1922),

79–96; J. B. Rieffert, *Pragmatische Bewußtseinstheorie auf experimenteller Grundlage* (Leipzig: Akademische Verlagsgesellschaft, 1929).

[18] For an overview of Wehrmacht psychology, see Ulfried Geuter, *The Professionalization of Psychology in Nazi Germany*, translated by Richard J. Holmes (Cambridge: Cambridge University Press, 1992), 125–62.

[19] Martin Kusch, review of *Gestalt Psychology in German Culture, 1890–1967: Holism and the Quest for Objectivity*, by Mitchell G. Ash, *British Journal for the History of Science*, 29, no. 4 (1996), 485.

[20] Cf. Joachim Riedl, "Labor Auschwitz," *Die Zeit*, September 27, 1985, http://www.zeit.de/1985/40/labor-auschwitz/komplettansicht.

[21] Schönpflug, "Rieffert, Johann Baptist," 369.

[22] J. B. Rieffert and J. W. Dunlap, *Tests for Selection of Personnel in German Industry*, U.S. Naval Technical Mission in Europe, Report no. 300–45, Publ. no. 22933 (1945).

[23] Zygmunt Bauman, *Wasted Lives: Modernity and Its Outcasts* (Cambridge: Polity, 2004), 5.

[24] Karl Marx, *Ökonomisch-Philosophische Manuskripte*, Third Manuscript, 141.

[25] This structure is reminiscent of Elfriede Jelinek's novel *Die Liebhaberinnen* (1975; *Women as Lovers*), which contrasts the fortunes of two women: Brigitte, the "good" example, and Paula, the "bad" example.

[26] Chris Anderson, *TED Talks: The Official TED Guide to Public Speaking* (Boston: Houghton Mifflin Harcourt, 2016), xi. Cf. also Kirstin Schmidt, "Sieben Erfolgsfaktoren für die perfekte Rede," *Wirtschaftswoche*, February 24, 2017, http://www.wiwo.de/erfolg/coach/optimierung/rhetorik-sieben-erfolgsfaktoren-fuer-die-perfekte-rede/19367322-all.html.

[27] Anderson, *TED Talks*, 146. Anderson's guide to public speaking scrupulously avoids mentioning Aristotle and Cicero by name—a surprising omission, given his Oxford education. In any case, Anderson's key categories of "delivery" and "connection with the audience" are central themes for both Aristotle and Cicero. Other examples include Gerald M. Phillips, *Communication Incompetencies: A Theory of Training Oral Performance Behavior* (Carbondale: Southern Illinois University Press, 1991), and Peter Thompson, *Persuading Aristotle: A Masterclass in the Timeless Act of Strategic Persuasion in Business* (London: Kogan Page, 1999).

[28] Aristotle, *Rhetoric* 1.2.1355b25–26. Cf. Stefan Kammhuber, "Interkulturelle Rhetorik," in *Handbuch Interkulturelle Kommunikation und Kooperation*, vol. 1: *Grundlagen und Praxisfelder*, edited by Alexander Thomas, Eva-Ulrike Kinast, and Sylvia Schroll-Machl (Göttingen: Vandenhoeck & Ruprecht, 2003), 274.

[29] Kammhuber, "Interkulturelle Rhetorik," 275.

[30] Aristotle, *Rhetoric* 1.9.1367b.

[31] Kammhuber, "Interkulturelle Rhetorik," 285.

[32] Klaus Antoni, "Interkulturelle Kommunikation—Brücke des Verstehens oder globalisierter Zynismus?" in *Ware Mensch—Die Ökonomisierung der Welt*, edited by Heinz-Dieter Assmann, Frank Baasner, and Jürgen Werthheimer, Schriftenreihe Wertewelten 4 (Baden-Baden: Nomos, 2014), 199.

[33] Catherine Steel, "Divisions of Speech," in Gunderson, *Cambridge Companion to Ancient Rhetoric*, 80.

[34] Moritz Freiherr Knigge, *Spielregeln: Wie wir miteinander umgehen sollten* (Cologne: Lübbe, 2004); Brigitte Nagiller, *Klasse mit Knigge: Stilsicher in allen Lebenslagen* (Frankfurt am Main: Wirtschaftsverlag Carl Ueberreuter, 2003).

[35] Chris Warhurst and Dennis Nickson, *Looking Good, Sounding Right: Style Counselling in the New Economy* (London: Industrial Society, 2001), 9.

[36] Cf. Chris Warhurst and Dennis Nickson, "'Who's Got the Look?' Emotional, Aesthetic and Sexualized Labour in Interactive Services," *Gender, Work and Organization* 16, no. 3 (2009): 385–404. On July 11–12, 2016, the University of Sheffield hosted an international conference on the theme of Aesthetic Labor, organized by Seán Williams (Sheffield), Giselinde Kuipers (Amsterdam), and Victoria Robinson (York).

[37] Aristotle, *Rhetoric* 3.1.1403b–1404a.

[38] James Porter, "Rhetoric, Aesthetics and the Voice," in Gunderson, *Cambridge Companion to Ancient Rhetoric*, 96.

[39] Cicero, *On the Ideal Orator*, 92 [= bk. 1, sec. 156].

[40] Cicero, *On the Ideal Orator*, 236 [= bk. 3, sec. 44]. Cicero says that when Gaius Gracchus was making a speech, he employed a man to stand behind him with a flute and sound a note if his voice was too loud or too quiet—an ancient version of a modern autocue (295) [= bk. 3, sec. 225].

[41] *Neue Deutsche Biographie*, vol. 9: *Hess-Hüttig* (Berlin: Duncker & Humblot, 1972), 62.

[42] Lakoff and Johnson, *Metaphors We Live By*. On this point, see also Schaffner, "'Catastrophe Sociology,'" 215–16.

[43] Alessandro Archangeli, "Sports," in Grafton, Most, and Settis, *The Classical Tradition*, 905–6.

[44] Jim Loehr and Tony Schwartz, "The Making of a Corporate Athlete," *Harvard Business Review* 79, no. 1 (2001): 120–28 (122).

[45] Loehr and Schwartz, 122.

[46] Loehr and Schwartz, 123.

[47] Loehr and Schwartz, 128.

[48] Peter Kelly, Steven Allender, and Derek Colquhoun, "New Work Ethics? The Corporate Athlete's *Back End Index* and Organizational Performance," *Organization* 14, no. 2 (2007): 267–85 (276).

[49] Kelly, Allender, and Colquhoun, 279.

[50] Schönthaler, *Nach oben ist das Leben offen*, 29.

[51] Torbjörn Vestberg, Roland Gustafson, Liselotte Maurex, Martin Ingvar, and Predrag Petrovic, "Executive Functions Predict the Success of Top-Soccer Players," *Public Library of Science (PLOS) One* 7, no. 4 (2012), http://journals.plos.org/plosone/article?id=10.1371/journal.pone.0034731.

[52] In Schönthaler's short stories, characters perform tai chi-style movements or Feldenkrais exercise therapy: *Nach oben ist das Leben offen*, 18–19, 27–30.

[53] Loehr and Schwartz, "Making of a Corporate Athlete," 123.

54 Loehr and Schwartz regard positive thinking as essential for the corporate athlete: 124–25.

55 Loehr and Schwartz, 125.

56 Compare Richard Sennett, *The Corrosion of Character: The Personal Consequences of Work in the New Capitalism* (New York: Norton, 1998), 99: "The modern work ethic . . . requires such 'soft skills' as being a good listener and being cooperative."

57 Ilka Piepgras, "Du bist, was du denkst," *Zeit-Magazin* no. 22, May 19, 2016, 18.

58 Peter Kelly, *The Self as Enterprise: Foucault and the Spirit of 21st Century Capitalism* (Burlington, VT: Gower Publishing, 2013), 155.

59 Kelly, 155.

60 Nachtwey, *Die Abstiegsgesellschaft*, 113.

61 Nachtwey, 114.

62 Nachtwey, 109.

63 On the misuses of the state education system, see Katharina Rutschky, ed., *Schwarze Pädagogik: Quellen zur Naturgeschichte der bürgerlichen Erziehung* (Frankfurt am Main: Ullstein, 1987).

64 On the connections between sport and totalitarian regimes, see the films of Leni Riefenstahl and Elfriede Jelinek's *Ein Sportstück* (1998; *Sports Play*). This connection is also expressed polemically by the Austrian author Stefanie Sargnagel, who writes, "Erfolg ist wie joggen—was für Nazis" (Success is like jogging—something for Nazis): *Binge Living: Callcenter-Monologe* (2013; Vienna: Redelsteiner Dahimène Edition, 2015), 164.

65 Philipp Schönthaler, "Die Theorie ins Spiel bringen," in Jean Baudrillard, *Das radikale Denken*, translated by Riek Walther (Berlin: Matthes & Seitz, 2013), 40.

66 Schönthaler, 41.

67 In fact, Marx regards existence itself as a form of social activity: *Ökonomisch-Philosophische Manuskripte*, 119: "Mein *eignes* Dasein *ist* gesellschaftliche Thätigkeit" (My *own* existence *is* a social activity). Italics in the original.

68 For Baudrillard, culture itself is a "Zauberwerk" (work of magic). See Schönthaler, "Die Theorie ins Spiel bringen," 46, 48–49.

69 Schönthaler, "Die Theorie ins Spiel bringen," 43–44.

70 I am grateful to Philip Schlesinger for providing this insight: "The Creative Economy: Invention of a Global Orthodoxy," *Innovation: The European Journal of Social Science Research* 30, no. 1 (2017): 73–90.

71 Entrepreneurs today are even counseled to adopt anarchic guerrilla tactics as a positive business model. See Jay Conrad Levinson, *Guerilla Marketing: Easy and Inexpensive Strategies for Making Big Profits from Your Small Business*, 4th ed. (Boston: Houghton Mifflin, 2007).

72 Billig, *Arguing and Thinking*, 40.

73 Billig, 52–53.

74 Schönthaler, "Die Theorie ins Spiel bringen," 42.

75 Schönthaler, 54.

76 Foucault, *On the Government of the Living*, 233.

77 Foucault, 234.

78 At the beginning of his essay "Beantwortung der Frage: Was ist Aufklärung?" (1784; Answering the Question: What Is Enlightenment?), Kant writes, "Habe ich ein Buch, das für mich Verstand hat, einen Seelsorger, der für mich Gewissen hat, einen Arzt, der für mich die Diät beurteilt, u.s.w., so brauche ich mich ja nicht selbst zu bemühen. Ich habe nicht nötig zu denken, wenn ich nur bezahlen kann; andere werden das verdrießliche Geschäft schon für mich übernehmen" (If I have a book that thinks for me, a pastor who acts as my conscience, a physician who prescribes my diet, and so on, then I have no need to exert myself. I have no need to think, if only I can pay; others will take care of that disagreeable business for me). *Was ist Aufklärung? Aufsätze zur Geschichte und Philosophie* (Göttingen: Vandenhoeck & Ruprecht, 1994), 55.

79 "Wer kann da heute noch sagen, dass sein Zorn wirklich sein Zorn ist, wo ihm so viele Leute dreinreden und es besser verstehen als er?!" ("Who can say nowadays that his anger is really his own anger when so many people talk about it and claim to know more than he does?"). Robert Musil, *Der Mann ohne Eigenschaften*, edited by Adolf Frisé, 2 vols. (Hamburg: Rowohlt, 1987), 1:150; translated by Sophie Wilkins and Burton Pike as *The Man without Qualities* (London: Picador, 1997), 158.

80 Vogl, *Das Gespenst des Kapitals*, 136; *The Specter of Capital*, 99.

81 Wanda Vrasti, "Working in Prenzlau," *New Left Review* 101 (2016): 60.

82 Vrasti, 61.

83 Vrasti, 55.

84 Vrasti, 53.

85 Vrasti, 55.

86 Luc Boltanski and Ève Chiapello, *The New Spirit of Capitalism*, translated by Gregory Elliott (London: Verso, 2005), 462.

87 Kelly, *The Self as Enterprise*, 156.

88 Boltanski and Chiapello, *New Spirit of Capitalism*, 462.

89 Cf. David Lapido and Frank Wilkinson, "More Pressure, Less Protection," in *Job Insecurity and Work Intensification*, edited by Brendan Burchell, David Lapido, and Frank Wilkinson (London: Routledge, 2002), 27.

90 Benjamin, "Einbahnstraße," in *Gesammelte Schriften*, 4.1:98.

91 Marx and Engels, *Manifest der kommunistischen Partei*, 14; translated as *The Communist Manifesto* (London: Lawrence & Wishart, 1983), 16.

92 The character's name "Liun Xiangsu" is itself a giveaway; it resembles the French word for "leech" (*sangsue*). But as a human resources consultant, Smaart, too, is a parasite.

93 A brilliant critique of Moretti's distant reading was provided by one of my former students, Geronimo Sarmiento Cruz, in an outstanding Masters essay: "The Commodification of Alterity: Against Moretti's Method of Distant Reading" (University College London, 2013).

94 Franco Moretti, *Distant Reading* (New York: Verso, 2013), 48.

95 Schönthaler, *Porträt des Managers*, 18–26.

[96] Hesk, "Types of Oratory," 157.

[97] Kelly, *The Self as Enterprise*, 96.

[98] Tokumitsu, "In the Name of Love."

[99] John Dugan, "Rhetoric and the Roman Republic," in Gunderson, *Cambridge Companion to Ancient Rhetoric*, 180.

[100] Modern corporations aim to "tell stories that draw people in." The goal is "die anderen an sich zu binden" (to ensure binding loyalty). Schönthaler, *Porträt des Managers*, 29.

[101] Billig, *Arguing and Thinking*, 40.

Conclusion

[1] Donald J. Trump with Tony Schwartz, *Trump: The Art of the Deal* (New York: Random House, 1987). See also George H. Ross, *Trump-Style Negotiation: Powerful Strategies and Tactics for Mastering Every Deal* (Hoboken, NJ: Wiley, 2006).

[2] John Henderson, "The Runaround: A Volume Retrospect on Ancient Rhetorics," in Gunderson, *Cambridge Companion to Ancient Rhetoric*, 290.

[3] Roderick Watson, cited on cover blurb for Bertolt Brecht, *Mother Courage and Her Children*, translated by Tom Leonard (Middlesbrough, UK: Smokestack Books, 2014).

[4] Billig, *Arguing and Thinking*, 286.

Bibliography

Primary Texts

Bachmann, Ingeborg. *Darkness Spoken: The Collected Poems.* Translated by Peter Filkins. Brookline, MA: Zephyr, 2006.

———. *Die kritische Aufnahme der Existentialphilosophie Martin Heideggers* [1949]. Edited by Robert Pichl. Munich: Piper, 1985.

———. *Kritische Schriften.* Edited by Monika Albrecht and Dirk Göttsche. Munich: Piper, 2005 (abbreviated as *KS*).

———. *Malina.* Frankfurt am Main: Suhrkamp, 1980 (abbreviated as *M*). Translated by Philip Boehm as *Malina.* New York: Holmes & Meier, 1990 (abbreviated as *Ma*).

———. *"Todesarten"-Projekt: Kritische Ausgabe.* Edited by Monika Albrecht and Dirk Göttsche. 4 vols. Munich: Piper, 2005 (abbreviated as *TP*).

———. *Werke.* Edited by Christine Koschel, Inge von Weidenbaum, and Clemens Münster. 4 vols. Munich: Piper, 1993.

———. *Wir müssen wahre Sätze finden: Gespräche und Interviews.* Edited by Christine Koschel and Inge von Weidenbaum. Munich: Piper, 1991 (abbreviated as *GuI*).

Brecht, Bertolt. *Bertolt Brecht's Me-ti: Book of Interventions in the Flow of Things.* Edited and translated by Anthony Tatlow. London: Bloomsbury, 2016.

———. *Dreigroschenroman.* Frankfurt am Main: Suhrkamp, 1991 (abbreviated as *D*). Translated by Desmond I. Vesey as *Threepenny Novel.* Harmondsworth, UK: Penguin, 1961 (abbreviated as *TN*).

———. *Geschichten vom Herrn Keuner. Zürcher Fassung.* Edited by Erdmut Wizisla. Frankfurt am Main: Suhrkamp, 2004.

———. *The Good Person of Szechwan.* Translated by John Willett. London: Bloomsbury Methuen Drama, 2014.

———. *Mother Courage and Her Children.* Translated by Tom Leonard. Middlesbrough, UK: Smokestack Books, 2014.

———. *Tales from the Calendar.* Translated by Yvonne Kapp. London: Methuen, 1961.

————. *Werke: Große kommentierte Berliner und Frankfurter Ausgabe.* Edited by Werner Hecht, Jan Knopf, Werner Mittenzwei, and Klaus-Detlef Müller. 31 vols. Berlin: Suhrkamp, 1989–98 (abbreviated as *BFA*).

Delius, Friedrich Christian. *Abspann: Erinnerung an meine Gegenwart.* Berlin: Aufbau, 1991.

————. *Deutscher Herbst: Drei Romane.* Reinbek bei Hamburg: Rowohlt, 2012.

————. *Konservativ in 30 Tagen: Ein Hand- und Wörterbuch Frankfurter Allgemeinplätze.* Reinbek bei Hamburg: Rowohlt, 1988.

————. *Wir Unternehmer: Unsere Siemens-Welt. Einige Argumente zur Verteidigung der Gemüseesser. Satiren.* Werkausgabe in Einzelbänden. Reinbek bei Hamburg: Rowohlt, 2014 (abbreviated as *USW*).

Kant, Hermann. *Der dritte Nagel: Erzählungen.* Berlin: Rütten & Loening, 1981.

————. *Das Impressum* [1972]. Berlin: Rütten & Loening, 1975 (abbreviated as *DI*).

————. *Zu den Unterlagen: Publizistik 1957–1980.* Berlin: Aufbau, 1981.

Mann, Heinrich. *Essays.* 3 vols. Berlin: Aufbau, 1954–61.

————. *Essays und Publizistik,* vol. 5: *1930 bis Februar 1933.* Bielefeld: Aisthesis, 2009.

————. *Der Untertan.* Edited by Peter-Paul Schneider. Studienausgabe in Einzelbänden. Frankfurt am Main: Fischer, 2001 (abbreviated as *U*). Translated by Ernest Boyd and Daniel Theisen as *The Loyal Subject.* Edited by Helmut Peitsch. New York: Continuum, 2006 (abbreviated as *LS*).

Mann, Thomas. *Betrachtungen eines Unpolitischen.* Frankfurt am Main: Fischer, 2002.

————. *Buddenbrooks: Verfall einer Familie.* Große kommentierte Frankfurter Ausgabe, vol. 1.1. Edited by Eckhard Heftrich. Frankfurt am Main: S. Fischer, 2002 (abbreviated as *B*). Translated by John E. Woods as *Buddenbrooks: The Decline of a Family.* New York: Everyman's Library/ Alfred A. Knopf, 1994 (abbreviated as *Bu*).

Röggla, Kathrin. *besser wäre: keine. Essays und Theater.* Frankfurt am Main: S. Fischer, 2013.

————. *wir schlafen nicht.* Frankfurt am Main: Fischer, 2004 (abbreviated as *wsn*). Translated by Rebecca Thomas as *We Never Sleep.* Studies in Austrian Literature, Culture and Thought. Riverside, CA: Ariadne Press, 2009 (abbreviated as *WNS*).

Röggla, Kathrin, Susanna Brogi, and Katja Hartosch. "'Manage dich selbst oder stirb.' Die Autorin Kathrin Röggla im Gespräch." In *Repräsentationen von Arbeit: Transdisziplinäre Analysen und künstlerische Produktion,* edited by Susanna Brogi, Carolin Freier, Ulf Freier-Otten, and Katja Hartosch, 491–501. Bielefeld: Transcript, 2013.

Schönthaler, Philipp. *Nach oben ist das Leben offen.* Berlin: Matthes & Seitz, 2012.

———. *Negative Poetik: Die Figur des Erzählers bei Thomas Bernhard, W. G. Sebald und Imre Kertész.* Bielefeld: Transcript, 2011.

———. *Porträt des Managers als junger Autor: Zum Verhältnis von Wirtschaft und Literatur. Eine Handreichung.* Berlin: Matthes & Seitz, 2016.

———. *Das Schiff das singend zieht auf seiner Bahn.* Berlin: Matthes & Seitz, 2013 (abbreviated as *DS*).

———. "Die Theorie ins Spiel bringen." In Jean Baudrillard, *Das radikale Denken*, translated by Riek Walther, 27–62. Berlin: Matthes & Seitz, 2013.

Tergit, Gabriele. *Etwas Seltenes überhaupt: Erinnerungen.* Frankfurt am Main: Ullstein, 1983.

———. *Käsebier erobert den Kurfürstendamm.* Edited by Nicole Henneberg. Frankfurt am Main: Schöffling, 2016 (abbreviated as *Kb*).

Other Primary Texts

Alberti, Conrad. "Cicero oder Darwin?" *Die Gesellschaft* 4, suppl. 4 (July 1888): 223.

———, ed., *Die Schule des Redners: Ein praktisches Handbuch der Beredsamkeit in Musterstücken.* Leipzig: Wigand, 1890.

Aristotle. *Rhetoric.* Translated by W. Rhys Roberts. Oxford: Oxford University Press, 1924.

Aubignac, Abbé François Hédelin d'. *La Pratique du théâtre.* Paris, 1657.

Benjamin, Walter. *Gesammelte Schriften.* Edited by Rolf Tiedemann and Hermann Schweppenhäuser. 7 vols. Frankfurt am Main: Suhrkamp, 1972–99.

Bloch, Ernst. *Gesamtausgabe in 16 Bänden.* Frankfurt am Main: Suhrkamp, 1977.

Böll, Heinrich. *Zum Tee bei Dr. Borsig: Hörspiele.* Munich: Deutscher Taschenbuch Verlag, 1973.

Burckhardt, Jacob. *Griechische Kulturgeschichte.* Edited by Jakob Oeri. 4 vols. Berlin: W. Spemann, 1898–1902.

———. *Die Kultur der Renaissance in Italien.* Berlin: Verlag von Th. Knaur, 1928.

Cicero, Marcus Tullius. *Cicero's Offices, Essays on Friendship and Old Age and Select Letters.* London: J. M. Dent; New York: E. P. Dutton, 1909.

———. *De inventione* 1.1, translated by C. D. Yonge. http://www.classicpersuasion.org/pw/cicero/dnv1-1.htm. Site discontinued.

————. *On the Ideal Orator* (*De Oratore*). Translated by James M. May and Jakob Wisse. Oxford: Oxford University Press, 2001.

————. *Political Speeches*. Translated by D. H. Berry. Oxford: Oxford University Press, 2006.

————. *Pro Roscio Amerino*, section 84. Accessed November 30, 2017. http://thelatinlibrary.com/cicero/sex.rosc.shtml.

Cicero, Quintus Tullius. *How to Win an Election: An Ancient Guide for Modern Politicians*. Translated by Philip Freeman. Princeton, NJ: Princeton University Press, 2012.

Clausewitz, Carl von. *Vom Kriege*. 3 vols. Berlin, 1832–34.

Domizlaff, Hans. *Die Gewinnung des öffentlichen Vertrauens: Ein Lehrbuch der Markentechnik* [1939]. 7th ed. Hamburg: Marketing Journal Gesellschaft für angewandtes Marketing mbH, 2005.

————. *Nachdenkliche Wanderschaft: Autobiographische Fragmente* [1950]. Zurich: Criterion, 1992.

————. *Die Seele des Staates: Regelbuch der Elite*. Hamburg: Self-published [Hans Dulk], [1957].

————. *Der Sozialisierungstod: Aufruf zur Verteidigung des Produktiven Unternehmertums*. Berlin: Lektorat für Buch, Bühne, Film, 1949.

Enzensberger, Hans Magnus. *Enzensbergers Panoptikum: Zwanzig Zehn-Minuten Essays*. Berlin: Suhrkamp, 2012.

Fontane, Theodor. *Effi Briest* [1895]. Berlin: Insel, 2011. Translated by Hugh Rorrison and Helen Chambers as *Effi Briest*. London: Penguin, 2000.

Foucault, Michel. *On the Government of the Living: Lectures at the Collège de France, 1979–1980*. Translated by Graham Burchell. New York: Palgrave Macmillan, 2014.

Freytag, Gustav. *Soll und Haben* [1855]. Waltrop: Manuscriptum, 2002.

Gysi, Gregor. *Worte des Vorsitzenden Gregor Gysi*. Edited by Hanno Harnisch and Olaf Miemiec. Berlin: Eulenspiegel, 2015.

Hayek, Friedrich A. *The Constitution of Liberty* [1960]. London: Routledge, 2006.

————. *Law, Legislation, and Liberty*. 3 vols. Chicago: University of Chicago Press, 1973–79.

————. *The Road to Serfdom* (London: Routledge, 1944)

Hegemann, Werner. *Das steinerne Berlin: Geschichte der grössten Mietkasernenstadt der Welt*. Berlin: Kiepenhauer, 1930.

Homer, *The Iliad*. Translated by E. V. Rieu. London: Penguin, 2003.

Jelinek, Elfriede. *Ein Sportstück*. Reinbek bei Hamburg: Rowohlt, 1998. Translated by Penny Black as *Sports Play*. London: Oberon Books, 2012.

Kafka, Franz. *Das Schloß, in der Fassung der Handschrift*. Edited by Malcom Pasley. Frankfurt am Main: Fischer, 1994.

Kant, Immanuel. *Was ist Aufklärung? Aufsätze zur Geschichte und Philosophie.* Göttingen: Vandenhoeck & Ruprecht, 1994.

———. *Werkausgabe.* Edited by Wilhelm Weischedel. 12 vols. Frankfurt am Main: Suhrkamp, 1974.

Köhler, Barbara. *Niemands Frau: Gesänge.* Frankfurt am Main: Suhrkamp, 2007.

Kraus, Karl. *Die Sprache.* Frankfurt am Main: Suhrkamp, 1987.

Lenin, V. I. "Can the Bolsheviks Retain State Power?" In *Collected Works,* vol. 26: *September 1917–February 1918,* 87–136. London: Lawrence & Wishart; Moscow: Progress Publishers, 1964.

Lessing, Theodor. *Der jüdische Selbsthaß.* Berlin: Jüdischer Verlag, 1930.

Machiavelli, Niccolò. *The Prince.* Translated by George Bull. Harmondsworth, UK: Penguin, 1981.

Marx, Karl. *Ökonomisch-Philosophische Manuskripte* [1844]. Commentary by Michael Quante. Frankfurt am Main: Suhrkamp, 2009. Translated as *Economic & Philosophic Manuscripts of 1844.* Accessed December 6, 2017. https://www.marxists.org/archive/marx/works/1844/manuscripts/comm.htm.

Marx, Karl, and Friedrich Engels. *Manifest der kommunistischen Partei.* Berlin: Dietz, 1989. Translated as *Manifesto of the Communist Party.* London: Lawrence & Wishart, 1983.

Mo Zi. *The Book of Master Mo.* Translated by Ian Johnston. London: Penguin, 2015.

Müller, Heiner. *Krieg ohne Schlacht: Leben in zwei Diktaturen* [1992]. Cologne: Kiepenheuer & Witsch, 2009.

Musil, Robert. *Der Mann ohne Eigenschaften.* Edited by Adolf Frisé. 2 vols. Hamburg: Rowohlt, 1987. Translated by Sophie Wilkins and Burton Pike as *The Man without Qualities.* London: Picador, 1997.

Nietzsche, Friedrich. *Kritische Gesamtausgabe der Werke.* Edited by Giorgio Colli and Mazzino Montinari. 40 vols. Berlin: De Gruyter, 1967–.

Orwell, George. "Politics and the English Language." In *Why I Write,* 102–20. London: Penguin, 2004.

Polanyi, Karl. *The Great Transformation: The Political and Economic Origins of Our Time* [1944]. Boston: Beacon Press, 2001.

Quintilianus, Marcus Fabius (Quintilian). *Institutes of Oratory; or, Education of an Orator.* Translated by John Selby Watson. London: George Bell and Sons, 1891.

Rathenau, Walther. *Der Kaiser: Eine Betrachtung.* Berlin: S. Fischer, 1919.

———. *Schriften und Reden.* Edited by Hans Werner Richter. Frankfurt am Main: Fischer, 1964.

Rieffert, J. B. *Pragmatische Bewußtseinstheorie auf experimenteller Grundlage.* Leipzig: Akademische Verlagsgesellschaft, 1929.

————. "Psychotechnik im Heere." In *Bericht über den 7. Kongress für experimentelle Psychologie in Marburg 1921*, edited by Karl Bühler, 79–96. Jena, 1922.

Rieffert, J. B., and J. W. Dunlap. *Tests for Selection of Personnel in German Industry*, U.S. Naval Technical Mission in Europe, Report no. 300–345, Publ. no. 22933, 1945. Sargnagel, Stefanie. *Binge Living: Callcenter-Monologe* [2013]. Vienna: Redelsteiner Dahimène Edition, 2015.

Schröder, Wilhelm. *Das persönliche Regiment: Reden und sonstige öffentliche Äusserungen Wilhelms II*. Munich: G. Birk, 1907.

Schumpeter, Joseph A. *Capitalism, Socialism and Democracy* [1943]. London: Routledge, 2010.

Şenocak, Zafer. *Deutschsein: Eine Aufklärungsschrift*. Hamburg: Körber-Stiftung, 2011.

Smith, Adam. *An Inquiry into the Nature and Causes of the Wealth of Nations* [1776]. Edited by Kathryn Sutherland. Oxford: Oxford University Press, 1993.

Spark, Muriel. *A Far Cry from Kensington*. London: Virago, 2009.

Sternheim, Carl. *Gesamtwerk*. 10 vols. Edited by Wolfgang Emrich. Neuwied am Rhein: Luchterhand, 1966–76.

Trump, Donald J., with Tony Schwartz. *Trump: The Art of the Deal*. New York: Random House, 1987.

Veblen, Thorstein. *The Theory of the Leisure Class: An Economic Theory of Institutions*. New York: Macmillan, 1899.

Weber, Max. "Die drei reinen Typen der legitimen Herrschaft." In *Soziologie, universalgeschichtliche Analysen, Politik*, edited by Johannes Winckelmann, 151–66. Stuttgart: Kröner, 1973. Translated as "The Three Types of Legitimate Rule." In Whimster, *The Essential Weber*, 133–45.

————. *The Essential Weber: A Reader*. Edited by Sam Whimster. London: Routledge, 2004.

————. *The Protestant Ethic and the Spirit of Capitalism*. Translated by Talcott Parsons. London: Routledge, 2001.

————. "Der Sinn der 'Wertfreiheit' der soziologischen und ökonomischen Wissenschaften" [1917]. In *Gesammelte Aufsätze zur Wissenschaftslehre*, edited by Johannes Winckelmann, 489–540. Tübingen: Mohr, 1988.

————. "Wissenschaft als Beruf" [1919]. In *Schriften 1894–1922*, edited by Dirk Kaesler, 474–511. Stuttgart: Kröner, 2002. Translated as "The Vocation of Science." In Whimster, *The Essential Weber*, 270–87.

————. *Wirtschaft und Gesellschaft*. In *Gesamtausgabe*. Vol. 1.22 (parts 1–5) and vol. 1.23. Edited by Knut Borchardt, Edith Hanke, and Wolfgang Schluchter. Tübingen: Mohr Siebeck, 1999–2013. Translated as *Economy and Society*, edited by Guenther Roth and Claus Wittich. 2 vols. Berkeley: University of California Press, 1978.

Secondary Sources

Abelshauser, Werner. *Deutsche Wirtschaftsgeschichte: Von 1945 bis zur Gegenwart.* 2nd ed. Munich: Beck, 2011.

Achberger, Karen R. "Der Fall Schönberg. Musik und Mythos in 'Malina.'" In *Ingeborg Bachmann: Text + Kritik,* edited by Heinz Ludwig Arnold, 120–31. Munich: Text + Kritik, 1984.

———. "'Kunst als Veränderndes': Bachmann and Brecht." *Monatshefte* 83, no. 1 (1991): 7–16.

Albrecht, Monika, and Dirk Göttsche, eds. *Bachmann-Handbuch: Leben—Werk—Wirkung.* Stuttgart: Metzler, 2013.

Allen, Michael Thad. "The Banality of Evil Reconsidered: SS Mid-Level Managers of Extermination through Work." *Central European History* 30, no. 2 (1997): 253–94.

Alter, Reinhard. *Die bereinigte Moderne: Heinrich Manns "Untertan" und politische Publizistik in der Kontinuität der deutschen Geschichte zwischen Kaiserreich und Drittem Reich.* Tübingen: Niemeyer, 1995.

Anders, Lutz-Christian. "Stimm-, Sprechstörungen." In Ueding, *Historisches Wörterbuch der Rhetorik,* vol. 9: *St-Z,* 99–108.

Anderson, Chris. *TED Talks: The Official TED Guide to Public Speaking.* Boston: Houghton Mifflin Harcourt, 2016.

Andriopoulos, Stefan. *Possessed: Hypnotic Crimes, Corporate Fiction, and the Invention of Cinema.* Chicago: University of Chicago Press, 2008.

Antoni, Klaus. "Interkulturelle Kommunikation—Brücke des Verstehens oder globalisierter Zynismus?" In *Ware Mensch—Die Ökonomisierung der Welt,* edited by Heinz-Dieter Assmann, Frank Baasner, and Jürgen Werthheimer, 189–201. Schriftenreihe Wertewelten 4. Baden-Baden: Nomos, 2014.

Archangeli, Alessandro. "Sports." In Grafton, Most, and Settis, *The Classical Tradition,* 905–6.

Arntzen, Helmut. "Die Reden Wilhelms II. und Diederich Heßlings: Historisches Dokument und Heinrich Manns Romansatire." *literatur für leser* (1980): 1–14.

Arp, Agnès. *VEB, Vaters ehemaliger Betrieb: Privatunternehmer in der DDR.* Leipzig: Militzke, 2005.

Aswestopoulos, Wassilis. "Griechischer Staatsanwalt klagt Siemens-Vorstände an." *Focus Online Money,* November 27, 2014. http://www.focus.de/finanzen/boerse/aktien/2368-seiten-anklageschrift-griechischer-staatsanwalt-klagt-siemens-vorstaende-an_id_4305617.html.

Atkins, Judi, and Alan Finlayson. "'. . . A 40-Year-Old Black Man Made the Point to Me': Everyday Knowledge and the Performance of Leadership in Contemporary British Politics." *Political Studies* 61, no. 1 (2013): 161–77.

Aune, James Arnt. *Rhetoric and Marxism*. Boulder, CO: Westview, 1994.

———. *Selling the Free Market: The Rhetoric of Economic Correctness*. New York: Guilford Press, 2001.

Baier, Lothar. "Wie Macht wirkt: Friedrich Christian Delius' erster Roman: 'Ein Held der inneren Sicherheit.'" *Die Zeit*, April 24, 1981. http://www.zeit.de/1981/18/wie-macht-wirkt/komplettansicht.

Balfour, Michael. *The Kaiser and His Times*. Harmondsworth, UK: Penguin, 1975.

Barck, Simone, Martina Langermann, and Siegfried Lokatis. *"Jedes Buch ein Abenteuer": Zensur-System und literarische Öffentlichkeiten in der DDR bis Ende der sechziger Jahre*. Berlin: Akademie Verlag, 1997.

Barner, Wilfried. *Barockrhetorik: Untersuchungen zu ihren geschichtlichen Grundlagen*. Tübingen: Niemeyer, 1970.

Barnett, David. "Joseph Goebbels: Expressionist Dramatist as Nazi Minister of Culture." *New Theatre Quarterly* 17, no. 2 (2001): 161–69.

Bataille, Georges. *The Accursed Share: An Essay on General Economy*. Vol. 1: *Consumption*. Translated by Robert Hurley. New York: Zone Books, 1967.

Bathrick, David. *The Powers of Speech: The Politics of Culture in the GDR*. Lincoln: University of Nebraska Press, 1995.

Bauman, Zygmunt. *Wasted Lives: Modernity and Its Outcasts*. Cambridge: Polity, 2004.

Beard, Mary. "The Acting Demagogue." *Times Literary Supplement Online*, October 10, 2016. http://www.the-tls.co.uk/articles/public/borrowed-eloquence/.

Beck, Ulrich. *Risikogesellschaft: Auf dem Weg in eine andere Moderne*. Frankfurt am Main: Suhrkamp, 1986. Translated by Mark Ritter as *Risk Society: Towards a New Modernity*. Thousand Oaks, CA: Sage, 1992.

———. *Was ist Globalisierung? Irrtümer des Globalismus—Antworten auf Globalisierung*. Frankfurt am Main: Suhrkamp, 1997.

Becker, Peter Karl, and Sebastian Liebold. *Kleiner Markt im großen Plan: Drei Unternehmerinnen in der DDR*. Markkleeberg: Sächsisches Wirtschaftsarchiv e.V. and Sax Verlag, 2015.

Behre, Maria. "Nachforschungen in einem unerforschten Gebiet: Wissenschaftliches Lesen in Bachmanns 'Malina' als Drama der Introspektion." In *Über die Zeit schreiben: Literatur- und kulturwissenschaftliche Essays zu Ingeborg Bachmann*, edited by Monika Albrecht and Dirk Göttsche, vol. 1, 137–57. Würzburg: Königshausen & Neumann, 1998.

Bender, John, and David E. Wellbery, eds. *The Ends of Rhetoric: History, Theory, Practice*. Stanford, CA: Stanford University Press, 1990.

Betts, Paul. *The Authority of Everyday Objects: A Cultural History of West German Industrial Design*. Berkeley: University of California Press, 2004.

Bialas, Wolfgang. *Vom unfreien Schweben zum freien Fall: Ostdeutsche Intellektuelle im gesellschaftlichen Umbruch.* Frankfurt am Main: Fischer, 1996.

Biendarra, Anke S. "Prekäre neue Arbeitswelt. Narrative der New Economy." In *Das erste Jahrzehnt: Narrative und Poetiken des 21. Jahrhunderts,* edited by Julia Schöll and Johanna Bohley, 69–82. Würzburg: Königshausen & Neumann, 2012.

Billig, Michael. *Arguing and Thinking: A Rhetorical Approach to Social Psychology* [1987]. 2nd ed. Cambridge: Cambridge University Press, 1996.

Bird, Stephanie. "'What Matters Who's Speaking?': Identity, Experience, and Problems with Feminism in Ingeborg Bachmann's *Malina*." In *Gender and Politics in Austrian Fiction,* edited by Ritchie Robertson and Edward Timms, 150–65. Austrian Studies 7. Edinburgh: Edinburgh University Press, 1996.

———. *Women Writers and National Identity: Bachmann, Duden, Özdamar.* Cambridge: Cambridge University Press, 2003.

Blaschke, Bernd. *Der homo oeconomicus und sein Kredit bei Musil, Joyce, Svevo, Unamuno und Celine.* Munich: Wilhelm Fink, 2004.

Blumenberg, Hans. "Anthropologische Annäherung an die Aktualität der Rhetorik" [1971]. In *Wirklichkeiten in denen wir leben: Aufsätze und eine Rede,* 104–36. Stuttgart: Reclam, 1981. Translated as "An Anthropological Approach to the Contemporary Significance of Rhetoric." In *After Philosophy: End or Transformation?* edited by Kenneth Baynes, James Bohman, and Thomas McCarthy, 429–58. Cambridge, MA: MIT Press, 1987.

Boa, Elizabeth. "*Buddenbrooks*: Bourgeois Patriarchy and Fin-de-Siècle Eros." In *Thomas Mann,* edited by Michael Minden, 125–42. London: Longman, 1995.

———. "Urban Modernity and the Politics of Heimat: Gabriele Tergit's *Käsebier erobert den Kurfürstendamm*." *German Life and Letters* (forthcoming).

Bodman-Hensler, Nicola von. "Thomas Mann's Illness Mythologies in the Work of Philip Roth." PhD diss., King's College London, 2013.

Boltanski, Luc, and Ève Chiapello. *The New Spirit of Capitalism.* Translated by Gregory Elliott. London: Verso, 2005.

Bourdieu, Pierre. *The Rules of Art: Genesis and Structure of the Literary Field.* Translated by Susan Emanuel. Cambridge: Polity, 1996.

Bradley, Laura. "Training the Audience: Brecht and the Art of Spectatorship." *Modern Language Review* 111, no. 4 (2016): 1029–48.

Brogi, Susanne, Carolin Freier, Ulf Freier-Otten, and Katja Hartosch, eds. *Repräsentationen von Arbeit: Transdisziplinäre Analysen und künstlerische Produktion.* Bielefeld: Transcript, 2013.

Bullivant, Keith. *Realism Today: Aspects of the Contemporary West German Novel.* Leamington Spa, UK: Berg, 1987.

Burke, Kenneth. "The Rhetoric of Hitler's 'Battle'" [1939]. In *The Philosophy of Literary Form*, 191–220. Berkeley: University of California Press, 1973.

Butler, Judith. *Giving an Account of Oneself.* New York: Fordham University Press, 2005.

Campbell, Joan. *Joy in Work, German Work: The National Debate, 1800–1945.* Princeton, NJ: Princeton University Press, 1989.

Carter, T. E. "Freytag's *Soll und Haben*: A Liberal National Manifesto as a Best-Seller." *German Life and Letters* 21 (1967/68): 320–29.

Chang, Ha-Joon. *Economics: The User's Guide.* New York: Pelican, 2014.

Chaput, Catherine, and Joshua S. Hanan. "Theories of Economic Justice in the Rhetorical Tradition." In *Oxford Research Encyclopedia of Communication*, edited by Jon F. Nussbaum. Online publication, November 2016, doi:10.1093/acrefore/9780190228613.013.148.

Claas, Herbert. *Die politische Ästhetik Bertolt Brechts vom Baal zum Caesar.* Frankfurt am Main: Suhrkamp, 1977.

Clarke, David. "The Capitalist Uncanny in Kathrin Röggla's *wir schlafen nicht*: Ghosts in the Machine." *Angermion* 4 (2011): 147–63.

Claßen, Ludger. *Satirisches Erzählen im 20. Jahrhundert: Heinrich Mann, Bertolt Brecht, Martin Walser, F. C. Delius.* Munich: Fink, 1985.

Connolly, Joy. "The Politics of Rhetorical Education." In Gunderson, *Cambridge Companion to Ancient Rhetoric*, 126–41.

Cowan, Michael. *Cult of the Will: Nervousness and German Modernity.* University Park: Penn State University Press, 2008.

Cowen, Deborah. *The Deadly Life of Logistics: Mapping Violence in Global Trade.* Minneapolis: University of Minnesota Press, 2014.

Craig, Gordon A. *Germany 1866–1945.* Oxford: Oxford University Press, 1987.

Crary, Jonathan. *24/7: Late Capitalism and the Ends of Sleep.* London: Verso, 2013.

Crouch, Colin. *The Strange Non-Death of Neoliberalism.* Cambridge: Polity Press, 2011.

Cruz, Geronimo Sarmiento. "The Commodification of Alterity: Against Moretti's Method of Distant Reading." MA essay, University College London, 2013.

Dieterle, Bernard. "Ein Dokument der Dokumentarliteratur: Paratextuelle Überlegungen zu Delius' Festschrift." In *F. C. Delius: Studien über sein literarisches Werk*, edited by Manfred Durzak and Hartmut Steinecke, 33–47. Tübingen: Stauffenberg, 1997.

Diewald, Martin. "'Kollektiv,' 'Vitamin B' oder 'Nische'? Persönliche Netzwerke in der DDR." In *Kollektiv und Eigensinn: Lebensverläufe in der DDR und danach*, edited by Johannes Huinink and Karl Ulrich Mayer, 223–60. Berlin: Akademie Verlag, 1995.

Doll, Natascha. *Recht, Politik und "Realpolitik" bei August Ludwig von Rochau (1810–1873): Ein wissenschaftsgeschichtlicher Beitrag zum Verhältnis von Politik und Recht im 19. Jahrhundert*. Frankfurt am Main: Klostermann, 2005.

Domeier, Norman. *The Eulenburg Affair: A Cultural History of Politics in the German Empire*. Translated by Deborah Lucas Schneider. Rochester, NY: Camden House, 2015.

Dowden, Stephen D. *Sympathy for the Abyss: A Study in the Novel of German Modernism. Kafka, Broch, Musil, and Thomas Mann*. Tübingen: Niemeyer, 1986.

Dugan, John. "Rhetoric and the Roman Republic." In Gunderson, *Cambridge Companion to Ancient Rhetoric*, 178–93.

Eagleton, Terry. *Walter Benjamin, or Towards a Revolutionary Criticism* [1981]. New York: Verso, 2009.

Eberhardt, Joachim. "Bachmann und Nietzsche." In *Über die Zeit schreiben: Literatur- und kulturwissenschaftliche Essays zu Ingeborg Bachmann*, edited by Monika Albrecht and Dirk Göttsche, vol. 3, 135–55. Würzburg: Königshausen & Neumann, 2004.

———. *"Es gibt für mich keine Zitate": Intertextualität im dichterischen Werk Ingeborg Bachmanns*. Tübingen: Niemeyer, 2002.

Ecker, Gisela. *"Giftige" Gaben: Über Tauschprozesse in der Literatur*. Munich: Wilhelm Fink, 2008.

Eden, Kathy. "Rhetoric." In Grafton, Most, and Settis, *The Classical Tradition*, 826–30.

Eggert, Hartmut. "Das persönliche Regiment: Zur Quellen- und Entstehungsgeschichte von Heinrich Manns 'Untertan.'" *Neophilologus* 55, no. 1 (1971): 298–316.

Emmerich, Wolfgang. *Heinrich Mann: "Der Untertan."* Munich: Fink, 1980.

———. *Kleine Literaturgeschichte der DDR*. Berlin: Aufbau, 2000.

Engelmann, Bernt, and Günter Wallraff. *Ihr da oben—wir da unten*. Cologne: Kiepenheuer & Witsch, 1973.

Engler, Wolfgang. *Die Ostdeutschen: Kunde von einem verlorenen Land*. Berlin: Aufbau, 1999.

Etcoff, Nancy. *Survival of the Prettiest: The Science of Beauty*. New York: Doubleday, 1999.

European Commission. Press Release IP/09/1432, Brussels, October 7, 2009. http://europa.eu/rapid/press-release_IP-09-1432_en.htm?locale=en.

"Europe's Engine: Living with a Stronger Germany." *Economist*, March 13, 2010, 1–14.

Fahrenbach, Helmut. *Brecht zur Einführung*. Hamburg: Junius Verlag, 1986.

Fear, Jeffrey R. *Organizing Control: August Thyssen and the Construction of German Corporate Management*. Cambridge, MA: Harvard University Press, 2005.

Feldenkirchen, Wilfried. *Siemens 1918–1945*. Munich: Piper, 1995. Translated by Tom Rattray and John Taylor as *Siemens 1918–1945*. Columbus: Ohio State University Press, 1999.

———. *Siemens: Von der Werkstatt zum Weltunternehmen* [1997]. 2nd ed. Munich: Piper, 2003. Translated by Richard A. Michell as *Siemens: From Workshop to Global Player*. Munich: Piper, 2000.

Ferencz, Benjamin B. *Less than Slaves: Jewish Forced Labor and the Quest for Compensation*. 2nd ed. Bloomington: Indiana University Press 2002.

France, Peter. *Racine's Rhetoric*. Oxford: Oxford University Press, 1965.

Franke, Konrad. "'Deine Darstellung ist uns wesensfremd': Romane der 60er Jahre in den Mühlen der DDR-Zensur." In *Literaturentwicklungsprozesse: Die Zensur der Literatur in der DDR*, edited by Ernest Wichner and Herbert Wiesner, 101–27. Frankfurt am Main: Suhrkamp, 1993.

Fraunhofer-Gesellschaft. https://www.fraunhofer.de/en.html. Accessed February 22, 2018.

Fulbrook, Mary. *Anatomy of a Dictatorship: Inside the GDR, 1949–1989*. Oxford: Oxford University Press, 1995.

———. *The People's State: East German Society from Hitler to Honecker*. New Haven, CT: Yale University Press, 2005.

Fulda, Daniel. *Schau-Spiele des Geldes: Die Komödie und die Entstehung der Marktgesellschaft von Shakespeare bis Lessing*. Tübingen: Niemeyer, 2005.

Garver, Eugene. *Machiavelli and the History of Prudence*. Madison: University of Wisconsin Press, 1987.

Gehle, Holger. "Ingeborg Bachmann und Martin Heidegger: Eine Skizze." In *Ingeborg Bachmann—Neue Beiträge zu ihrem Werk*, edited by Dirk Göttsche and Hubert Ohl, 241–52. Würzburg: Königshausen & Neumann, 1993.

General Court of the European Union. Press Release No 15/11, Luxembourg, March 3, 2011. http://europa.eu/rapid/press-release_CJE-11-15_en.htm.

Gernalzick, Nadja. *Kredit und Kultur: Ökonomie- und Geldbegriff bei Jacques Derrida und in der amerikanischen Literaturtheorie der Postmoderne*. Heidelberg: Winter, 2002.

Geuter, Ulfried. *The Professionalization of Psychology in Nazi Germany*. Translated by Richard J. Holmes. Cambridge: Cambridge University Press, 1992.

Giddens, Anthony. *Sociology*. Cambridge: Polity, 1989.

Giles, Steve. *Bertolt Brecht and Critical Theory: Marxism, Modernity and the Threepenny Lawsuit.* Bern: Peter Lang, 1997.

———. "Rewriting Brecht: *Die Dreigroschenoper* 1928–1931." *Literaturwissenschaftliches Jahrbuch* 30 (1989): 249–79.

Gilman, Sander L. *Creating Beauty to Cure the Soul: Race and Psychology in the Shaping of Aesthetic Surgery.* Durham, NC: Duke University Press, 1998.

Gilman, Sander L., Carole Blair, and David J. Parent, eds. *Friedrich Nietzsche on Rhetoric and Language.* New York: Oxford University Press, 1989.

Glasser, Ralph. *The New High Priesthood: The Social, Ethical and Political Implications of a Marketing-Orientated Society.* London: Macmillan, 1967.

Goebel, Rolf J. "Brechts *Dreigroschenroman* und die Tradition des Kriminalromans." *Brecht-Jahrbuch* (1979): 67–81.

Goffman, Erving. *The Presentation of Self in Everyday Life* [1959]. London: Penguin, 1990.

———. *Stigma: Notes on the Management of Spoiled Identity* [1963]. Harmondsworth, UK: Pelican, 1981.

Goldman, Harvey. *Max Weber and Thomas Mann: Calling and Shaping of the Self.* Berkeley: University of California Press, 1988.

———. *Politics, Death, and the Devil: Self and Power in Max Weber and Thomas Mann.* Berkeley: University of California Press, 1992.

Goldstein, Thomas W. *Writing in Red: The East German Writers Union and the Role of Literary Intellectuals.* Rochester, NY: Camden House, 2017.

Goth, Joachim. *Nietzsche und die Rhetorik.* Tübingen: Niemeyer, 1970.

Göttert, Karl-Heinz. *Mythos Redemacht: Eine andere Geschichte der Rhetorik.* Frankfurt am Main: S. Fischer, 2015.

Göttsche, Dirk. *Die Produktivität der Sprachkrise in der modernen Prosa.* Frankfurt am Main: Athenäum, 1987.

———. "Research on Ingeborg Bachmann: Quo Vadis?" *Modern Language Review* 106, no. 2 (2011): 495–501.

Göttsche, Dirk, and Florian Krobb, eds. *Wilhelm Raabe: Global Themes—International Perspectives.* London: Legenda, 2009.

Graeber, David. *The Utopia of Rules: On Technology, Stupidity, and the Secret Joys of Bureaucracy.* Brooklyn, NY: Melville House, 2015.

Grafton, Anthony, Glenn W. Most, and Salvatore Settis, eds. *The Classical Tradition.* Cambridge, MA: Harvard University Press, 2010.

Gray, Richard T. *Money Matters: Economics and the German Cultural Imagination, 1770–1850.* Seattle: University of Washington Press, 2008.

Grenouillet, Corinne, and Catherine Vuillermot-Febvet, eds. *La langue du management et de l'économie à l'ère néolibérale: Formes sociales et littéraires.* Strasbourg: Presses universitaires de Strasbourg, 2015.

Grimmer-Solem, Erik. *The Rise of Historical Economics and Social Reform in Germany 1864–1894.* Oxford: Oxford University Press, 2003.

Gunderson, Erik, ed. *The Cambridge Companion to Ancient Rhetoric.* Cambridge: Cambridge University Press, 2009.

———. "The Rhetoric of Rhetorical Theory." In Gunderson, *Cambridge Companion to Ancient Rhetoric,* 109–25.

Gute, Petra. "'Erfolg ist eine Sache der Suggestion': Lebenserfahrung im literarischen und publizistischen Werk Gabriele Tergits." Magisterarbeit, Freie Universität Berlin, 1992.

Hall, Alex. "The Kaiser, the Wilhelmine State and Lèse-majesté." *German Life and Letters* 27, no. 2 (1974): 101–15.

Harding, Rebecca, and William E. Paterson. *The Future of the German Economy: An End to the Miracle?* Manchester, UK: Manchester University Press, 2000.

Hargie, Owen, ed. *The Handbook of Communication Skills.* 3rd ed. London: Routledge, 2006.

Hartley, John. *Understanding News.* London: Routledge, 1990.

Hatherley, Owen. *The Ministry of Nostalgia: Consuming Austerity.* London: Verso, 2017.

Haug, W. F. *Philosophieren mit Brecht und Gramsci.* Hamburg: Argument Verlag, 2006.

Hawes, James. "Revanche and Radicalism: The Psychology of Power in *Der Prozess* and *Der Untertan.*" *Oxford German Studies* 18–19 (1989–90): 119–31.

Heftrich, Eckhard. "Der Totentanz in Thomas Manns Roman *Der Zauberberg.*" In *Tanz und Tod in Kunst und Literatur,* edited by Franz Link, 335–50. Berlin: Duncker & Humblot, 1993.

Heftrich, Eckhard, Helmuth Nürnberger, Thomas Sprecher, and Ruprecht Wimmer, eds. *Theodor Fontane und Thomas Mann: Die Vorträge des Internationalen Kolloquiums in Lübeck 1997,* Thomas-Mann-Studien, vol. 18. Frankfurt am Main: Klostermann, 1998.

Heimburger, Susanne. *Kapitalistischer Geist und literarische Kritik— Arbeitswelten in deutschsprachigen Gegenwartstexten.* Munich: Text + Kritik, 2010.

Heller, Erich. *Thomas Mann: The Ironic German.* Cambridge: Cambridge University Press, 1981.

Henderson, Arlene Victoria Holmes. "A Defence of Classical Rhetoric in Scotland's Curriculum for Excellence." EdD thesis, University of Glasgow, 2013.

Henderson, John. "The Runaround: A Volume Retrospect on Ancient Rhetorics." In Gunderson, *Cambridge Companion to Ancient Rhetoric,* 278–90.

Herd, E. W. "Narrative Technique in Two Novels by Hermann Kant." In *"Erfahrung und Überlieferung": Festschrift for C. P. Magill.* Edited by Hinrich Siefken and Alan Robinson, 185–96. Cardiff: University of Wales Press, 1974.

Hermand, Jost. "Unser aller Zukunft? Mathias Schebens *Konzern 2003.*" *Basis: Jahrbuch für deutsche Gegenwartsliteratur* 10 (1980): 7–35.

Hesk, John. "Types of Oratory." In Gunderson, *Cambridge Companion to Ancient Rhetoric*, 145–61.

"Hey, Julius." In *Neue Deutsche Biographie*, vol. 9: *Hess-Hüttig*, 62. Berlin: Duncker & Humblot, 1972.

Hobsbaum, Philip. *Essentials of Literary Criticism.* London: Thames and Hudson, 1983.

Hörisch, Jochen. *Kopf oder Zahl: Die Poesie des Geldes.* Frankfurt am Main: Suhrkamp, 1996.

Horodowich, Elizabeth. *Language and Statecraft in Early Modern Venice.* Cambridge: Cambridge University Press, 2008.

Horst, Sandra von der. *Das Unternehmerbild in der deutschen Gegenwartsliteratur: Eine Analyse anhand der Romane "Der schwarze Grat" und "wenn wir sterben."* Saarbrücken: VDM Verlag Dr. Müller, 2008.

Horvath, Agnes. *Modernism and Charisma.* Basingstoke: Palgrave Macmillan, 2013.

Huyssen, Andreas. *Miniature Metropolis: Literature in an Age of Photography and Film.* Cambridge, MA: Harvard University Press, 2015.

Iser, Wolfgang. *Der Akt des Lesens: Theorie ästhetischer Wirkung.* Munich: Fink, 1976. Translated as *The Act of Reading: A Theory of Aesthetic Response.* Baltimore: Johns Hopkins University Press, 1978.

Israel, Jonathan. *Democratic Enlightenment: Philosophy, Revolution and Human Rights 1750–1790.* Oxford: Oxford University Press, 2012.

Jasper, Willi. *Der Bruder: Heinrich Mann. Eine Biographie.* Munich: Hanser, 1992.

Jeffrey, Tom. "Britain Needs More Democracy after the EU Referendum, Not Less." Huffington Post, June 27, 2016. http://www.huffingtonpost.co.uk/tom-jeffery/britain-needs-more-democr_b_10699898.html.

Jeffreys, Diarmuid. *Hell's Cartel: IG Farben and the Making of Hitler's War Machine.* London: Henry Holt, 2008.

Jendreiek, Helmut. *Thomas Mann: Der demokratische Roman.* Düsseldorf: Bagel, 1977.

Jeske, Wolfgang, ed. *Brechts Romane.* Frankfurt am Main: Suhrkamp, 1984.

Jirku, Brigitte E., and Marion Schulz, eds. *Fiktionen und Realitäten: Schriftstellerinnen im deutschsprachigen Literaturbetrieb.* Frankfurt am Main: Peter Lang, 2013.

Jones, Sara. *Complicity, Censorship and Criticism: Negotiating Space in the GDR Literary Sphere.* Berlin: De Gruyter, 2011.

Jørgensen, Marianne, and Louise Phillips. *Discourse Analysis as Theory and Method.* London: Sage, 2002.

Joy, Stephen. "Open Wide! An Oral Examination of Thomas Mann's Early Fiction." *German Life and Letters* 60, no. 4 (2007): 467–80.

Kähler, Hermann. "Impressum—Impressionen." *Sinn und Form,* 24, no. 4 (1972): 866–77.

Käsler, Dirk. *Max Weber: An Introduction to His Life and Work.* Translated by Philippa Hurd. Cambridge: Polity, 1988.

———. *Max Weber: Preuße, Denker, Muttersohn; Eine Biographie.* Munich: Beck, 2014.

Kaminski, Johannes D. "Werner's Accounting Eye: Circulating Blood and Money in *Wilhelm Meisters theatralische Sendung.*" *Publications of the English Goethe Society* 83, no. 1 (2014): 37–52.

Kammhuber, Stefan. "Interkulturelle Rhetorik." In *Handbuch Interkulturelle Kommunikation und Kooperation,* vol. 1: *Grundlagen und Praxisfelder,* edited by Alexander Thomas, Eva-Ulrike Kinast, and Sylvia Schroll-Machl, 274–86. Göttingen: Vandenhoeck & Ruprecht, 2003.

Kelly, Peter. *The Self as Enterprise: Foucault and the Spirit of 21st Century Capitalism.* Burlington, VT: Gower, 2013.

Kelly, Peter, Steven Allender, and Derek Colquhoun. "New Work Ethics? The Corporate Athlete's *Back End Index* and Organizational Performance." *Organization* 14, no. 2 (2007): 267–85.

Kinder, Anna. *Geldströme: Ökonomie im Romanwerk Thomas Manns.* Berlin: De Gruyter, 2013.

Klamer, Arjo. "The Third Way: A Cultural Economic Perspective." In *Economic Persuasions,* edited by Stephen Gudeman, 176–200. Studies in Rhetoric and Culture 3. New York: Berghahn, 2009.

Klein, Naomi. *The Shock Doctrine: The Rise of Disaster Capitalism.* New York: Picador, 2008.

Knigge, Moritz Freiherr. *Spielregeln: Wie wir miteinander umgehen sollten.* Cologne: Lübbe, 2004.

Kohl, Katrin. *Metapher.* Stuttgart: Metzler, 2007.

———. "Die Rhetorik ist das Wesen der Philosophie Nietzsches (Hans Blumenberg): Klassische Tradition moderner Wirkung." In *Ecce Opus: Nietzsche-Revisionen im 20. Jahrhundert,* edited by Rüdiger Görner and Duncan Large, 205–25. Göttingen: Vandenhoeck & Ruprecht, 2003.

Kohlrausch, Martin. *Der Monarch im Skandal: Die Logik der Massenmedien und die Transformation der wilhelminischen Monarchie.* Berlin: Akademie Verlag, 2005.

————. "The Workings of Royal Celebrity: Wilhelm II as Media Emperor." In *Constructing Charisma: Celebrity, Fame, and Power in Nineteenth-Century Europe*, edited by Edward Berenson and Eva Giloi, 52–66. New York: Berghahn, 2010.

Kohn-Waechter, Gudrun. "Das 'Problem der Post' in 'Malina' von Ingeborg Bachmann und Martin Heideggers 'Der Satz vom Grund.'" In *Die Frau im Dialog: Studien zu Theorie und Geschichte des Briefes*, edited by Anita Runge and Liselotte Steinbrügge, 225–42. Stuttgart: Metzler, 1991.

Krauthausen, Karin. "'ob das jetzt das interview sei?': Das konjunktivische Interview in Kathrin Rögglas Roman *wir schlafen nicht*." Lecture, University of Nantes, June 12, 2004. http://www.kathrin-roeggla.de/text/karin-krauthausen-ob-das-jetzt-das-interview-sei.

Kremer, Christian. *Milieu und Performativität: Deutsche Gegenwartsprosa von John von Düffel, Georg M. Oswald und Kathrin Röggla.* Marburg: Tectum, 2008.

Kreye, Andrian, "Der Spuk geht jetzt erst los." *Süddeutsche Zeitung*, November 9, 2016. http://www.sueddeutsche.de/politik/us-wahl-der-spuk-geht-jetzt-erst-los-1.3241066.

Krobb, Florian, ed. *150 Jahre Soll und Haben: Studien zu Gustav Freytags kontroversem Roman.* Würzburg: Königshausen und Neumann, 2005.

"Krupp an KZ Auschwitz beteiligt: Siemens lieferte die Vergassungsanlage." *Deutsche Volkszeitung*, August 5, 1945.

Krylova, Katya. *Walking through History: Topography and Identity in the Works of Ingeborg Bachmann and Thomas Bernhard.* Bern: Peter Lang, 2013.

Kugel, Janina. "Das Eckbüro hat ausgedient." Interview by Sven Astheimer. *Frankfurter Allgemeine Zeitung*, November 14–15, 2015, C1.

Kusch, Martin. Review of *Gestalt Psychology in German Culture, 1890–1967: Holism and the Quest for Objectivity*, by Mitchell G. Ash. *British Journal for the History of Science*, 29, no. 4 (1996), 483–86.

Ladd, Cornelie. "Fictions of Power, Powers of Fiction: Critical Representations of European Thought by Marx, Conrad and Brecht." PhD diss., Columbia University, 1991.

Lakoff, George, and Mark Johnson. *Metaphors We Live By.* Chicago: University of Chicago Press, 1980.

Lämmert, Eberhard. "Der Bürger und seine höheren Instanzen: Heinrich Mann, *Der Untertan*, und Franz Kafka, *Der Proceß*." In *Wer sind wir? Europäische Phänotypen im Roman des zwanzigsten Jahrhunderts*, edited by Eberhard Lämmert and Barbara Naumann, 41–59. Munich: Fink, 1996.

Lane, Melissa. *Greek and Roman Political Ideas.* London: Penguin, 2014.

Langenscheidt, Florian, and Bernd Venohr, eds. *The Best of German Mittelstand: The World Market Leaders.* Cologne: DAAB Media, 2015.

Lapido, David, and Frank Wilkinson. "More Pressure, Less Protection." In *Job Insecurity and Work Intensification*, edited by Brendan Burchell, David Lapido, and Frank Wilkinson, 8–38. London: Routledge, 2002.

Larcati, Arturo. "'Den eigenen Körper in den Kampf werfen': Zu Ingeborg Bachmanns Politik-Auffassung." *Germanisch-Romanische Monatsschrift* 54, no. 2 (2004): 215–34.

Lauer, Enrik. *Literarischer Monetarismus: Studien zur Homologie von Sinn und Geld bei Goethe, Goux, Sohn-Rethell, Simmel und Luhmann.* St. Ingbert: Röhrig, 1994.

Lauffer, Ines. *Poetik des Privatraums: Der architektonische Wohndiskurs in den Romanen der Neuen Sachlichkeit.* Bielefeld: Transcript, 2011.

Lennox, Sara. *Bachmann-Handbuch: Leben—Werk—Wirkung.* Edited by Monika Albrecht and Dirk Göttsche. Stuttgart: Metzler, 2013.

———. *Cemetery of the Murdered Daughters: Feminism, History, and Ingeborg Bachmann.* Amherst: University of Massachusetts Press, 2006.

———. "The Feminist Reception of Ingeborg Bachmann." *Women in German Yearbook* 8 (1992): 73–111.

———. "The Politics of Reading: A Half Century of Bachmann Reception." In *Literarische Wertung und Kanonbildung*, edited by Nicholas Saul and Ricarda Schmidt, 151–62. Würzburg: Königshausen & Neumann, 2007.

Levinson, Jay Conrad. *Guerilla Marketing: Easy and Inexpensive Strategies for Making Big Profits from Your Small Business.* 4th ed. Boston: Houghton Mifflin, 2007.

Lichtblau, Eric, and Carter Dougherty. "Siemens to Pay $1.34 Billion in Fines." *New York Times*, December 15, 2008. http://www.nytimes.com/2008/12/16/business/worldbusiness/16siemens.html?_r=2&hp=&pagewanted=print.

Loehr, Jim, and Tony Schwartz. "The Making of a Corporate Athlete." *Harvard Business Review* 79, no. 1 (2001): 120–28.

Lottmann, André. *Arbeitsverhältnisse: Der arbeitende Mensch in Goethes "Wilhelm Meister"-Romanen und in der Geschichte der Politischen Ökonomie.* Epistemata Literaturwissenschaft 724. Würzburg: Königshausen & Neumann, 2011.

Ludwig, Martin. "Perspektive und Weltbild in Thomas Manns *Buddenbrooks*." In *Der deutsche Roman im 20. Jahrhundert: Analysen und Materialen zur Theorie und Soziologie des Romans*, vol. 1, edited by Manfred Brauneck, 82–106. Bamberg: C. C. Buchner, 1976.

Lyon, John B., *Out of Place: German Realism, Displacement, and Modernity.* London: Bloomsbury, 2013.

Mahrdt, Helgard. *Öffentlichkeit, Gender und Moral: Von der Aufklärung zu Ingeborg Bachmann.* Palaestra 304. Göttingen: Vandenhoeck & Ruprecht, 1998.

Mahrholz, Werner. "Heinrich Manns 'Untertan': Bemerkungen über Talent und Menschlichkeit." In Werner, *Heinrich Mann: Texte zu seiner Wirkungsgeschichte*, 101–3.

Makarenko, Anton Semyonovich. *Problems of Soviet School Education*. Moscow: Progress, 1965.

Malinowski, Stephan. "Politische Skandale als Zerrspiegel der Demokratie: Die Fälle Barmat und Sklarek im Kalkül der Weimarer Rechten." *Jahrbuch für Antisemitismusforschung* 5 (1996): 46–64.

Marahrens, Gerwin. "Über die sprachliche Struktur und Genesis der Aphorismen von Karl Kraus." In *Karl Kraus: Diener der Sprache, Meister des Ethos*, edited by Joseph P. Strelka, 49–86. Tübingen: Francke, 1990.

Martin, Elaine. "New Economy Zombies: Kathrin Röggla's *wir schlafen nicht*." In *Transitions: Emerging Women Writers in German-Language Literature*, edited by Valerie Hefernan and Gillian Pye, 131–48. German Monitor 76. New York: Rodopi, 2013.

Maurer, Dieter. "Siemens-Projektleiter stirbt bei Fahrt mit Elektro-Oldtimer," *Badische Zeitung*, June 21, 2010. http://www.badische-zeitung.de/titisee-neustadt/feldkirchen-stirbt-bei-fahrt-mit-elektro-oldtimer--32483811.html.

McCloskey, Deirdre N. *Knowledge and Persuasion in Economics*. Cambridge: Cambridge University Press, 1994.

McCloskey, Donald N. *The Rhetoric of Economics* [1985]. 2nd ed. Madison: University of Wisconsin Press, 1998.

McDonald, Duff. *The Firm: The Story of McKinsey and Its Secret Influence on American Business*. New York: Simon & Schuster, 2013.

McLuhan, Marshall. *The Mechanical Bride: Folklore of Industrial Man* [1951]. London: Duckworth, 2011.

McMurtry, Áine. *Crisis and Form in the Later Writing of Ingeborg Bachmann*. London: MHRA, 2012.

Merton, Robert K. "The Matthew Effect in Science." *Science* 159, no. 3810 (1968): 56–63.

Meyer, Imke. *Jenseits der Spiegel kein Land: Ich-Fiktionen in Texten von Franz Kafka und Ingeborg Bachmann*. Würzburg: Königshausen & Neumann, 2001.

Meyer-Larsen, Werner. *Germany, Inc.: The New German Juggernaut and Its Challenge to World Business*. Translated by Thomas Thornton. New York: Wiley, 2000.

Midgley, David. *Writing Weimar: Critical Realism in German Literature 1918–1933*. Oxford: Oxford University Press, 2000.

Miller, Nikolaus. *Prolegomena zu einer Poetik der Dokumentarliteratur*. Münchner germanistische Beiträge 30. Munich: Fink, 1982.

Millington, Richard. *State, Society and Memories of the Uprising of 17 June 1953 in the GDR.* New York: Palgrave Macmillan, 2014.

Milne, Seumas. *The Enemy Within: The Secret War against the Miners.* London: Verso, 2004.

Minden, Michael. *Modern German Literature.* Cambridge: Polity, 2011.

———. "Modernism's Struggle for the Soul: Rainer Maria Rilke's *Die Aufzeichnungen des Malte Laurids Brigge* and Ingeborg Bachmann's *Malina.*" *German Life and Letters* 67, no. 3 (2014): 320–40.

Minnerup, Günter. "Reflections on German History and Anglo-Saxon Liberalism." In *The Challenge of German Culture: Essays Presented to Wilfried van der Will,* edited by Michael Butler and Robert Evans, 175–86. Basingstoke: Palgrave, 2000.

Mirowski, Philip. *Never Let a Serious Crisis Go to Waste: How Neoliberalism Survived the Financial Meltdown.* New York: Verso, 2013.

Mommsen, Wolfgang J. *The Age of Bureaucracy: Perspectives on the Political Sociology of Max Weber.* Oxford: Blackwell, 1974.

———. *Max Weber and German Politics, 1880–1920.* Translated by Michael S. Steinberg. Chicago: Chicago University Press, 1984.

Moretti, Franco. *The Bourgeois: Between History and Literature.* London: Verso, 2013.

———. "The Grey Area: Ibsen and the Spirit of Capitalism." *New Left Review* 61 (2010): 117–33.

Mossop, Frances. *Mapping Berlin: Representations of Space in the Weimar Feuilleton.* Oxford: Peter Lang, 2015.

Muller, Jerry Z. *The Mind and the Market: Capitalism in Modern European Thought.* New York: Knopf, 2002.

Myerson, George. *Rhetoric, Reason and Society: Rationality as Dialogue.* London: Sage, 2004.

Nachtwey, Oliver. *Die Abstiegsgesellschaft: Über das Aufbegehren in der regressiven Moderne.* Berlin: Suhrkamp, 2016.

Nagiller, Brigitte. *Klasse mit Knigge: Stilsicher in allen Lebenslagen.* Frankfurt am Main: Wirtschaftsverlag Carl Ueberreuter, 2003.

Nerlich, Michael. "Der Herrenmensch bei Jean-Paul Sartre und Heinrich Mann." *Akzente* 16 (1969): 460–79.

O'Regan, Veronica. "'Erfahrung nicht des Empirikers, sondern des Mystikers': A Re-Evaluation of Ingeborg Bachmann's Understanding of Wittgenstein and its Application to *Simultan.*" *Sprachkunst* 27 (1996): 47–65.

Ott, Herta Luise. "*Nous ne dormons pas:* Critique idéologique à travers une critique des langages chez Kathrin Röggla." *Germanica* 39 (2006): 57–74.

Oxford Living Dictionaries. "Opposition Research." Accessed November 30, 2017. https://en.oxforddictionaries.com/definition/opposition_research.

Parker, Stephen. *Bertolt Brecht: A Literary Life.* London: Bloomsbury, 2014.

Pascal, Roy. *From Naturalism to Expressionism: German Literature and Society 1880–1918.* New York: Basic Books, 1973.

Paul, Georgina. *Perspectives on Gender in Post-1945 German Literature.* Rochester, NY: Camden House, 2009.

Pearce, Lynne. *The Rhetorics of Feminism: Readings in Contemporary Cultural Theory and the Popular Press.* New York: Routledge, 2004.

Perelman, Chaim, and Lucie Olbrechts-Tyteca. *The New Rhetoric: A Treatise on Argumentation.* Translated by John Wilkinson and Purcell Weaver. Notre Dame, IN: University of Notre Dame Press, 1969.

Phelan, Anthony. *Reading Heinrich Heine.* Cambridge: Cambridge University Press, 2007.

Phillips, Gerald M. *Communication Incompetencies: A Theory of Training Oral Performance Behavior.* Carbondale: Southern Illinois University Press, 1991.

Piepgras, Ilka. "Du bist, was du denkst." *Zeit-Magazin* no. 22, May 19, 2016, 14–23.

Plumb, Steve. *Neue Sachlichkeit: Unity and Diversity of an Art Movement.* Amsterdam: Rodopi, 2006.

Porter, James. "Rhetoric, Aesthetics and the Voice." In Gunderson, *Cambridge Companion to Ancient Rhetoric*, 92–108.

Pott, Sandra. "Wirtschaft in Literatur: Ökonomische Subjekte im Wirtschaftsroman der Gegenwart," *KulturPoetik* 4, no. 2 (2004): 202–17.

Preece, Julian. *Baader-Meinhof and the Novel: Narratives of the Nation/ Fantasies of the Revolution, 1970–2010.* New York: Palgrave Macmillan, 2012.

Rakow, Christian. *Die Ökonomien des Realismus: Kulturpoetische Untersuchungen zur Literatur und Volkswirtschaftslehre 1850–1900.* Berlin: De Gruyter, 2013.

Reden, Sitta von, ed. *Stiftungen zwischen Politik und Wirtschaft: Geschichte und Gegenwart im Dialog. Historische Zeitschrift.* Beiheft 66. Berlin: De Gruyter Oldenbourg, 2015.

Reed, T. J. *Thomas Mann: The Uses of Tradition.* 2nd ed. Oxford: Oxford University Press, 1996.

Reichel, Peter. *Der schöne Schein des Dritten Reiches: Faszination und Gewalt des Faschismus.* Munich: Hanser, 1991.

Richter, Sandra. *Mensch und Markt: Warum wir den Wettbewerb fürchten und ihn trotzdem brauchen.* Hamburg: Murmann, 2012.

Ridley, Hugh. *The Problematic Bourgeois: Twentieth-Century Criticism on Thomas Mann's "Buddenbrooks" and "The Magic Mountain."* Columbia, SC: Camden House, 1994.

Riedl, Joachim. "Labor Auschwitz." *Die Zeit*, September 27, 1985. http://www.zeit.de/1985/40/labor-auschwitz/komplettansicht.

Ritthaler, Eva. *Ökonomische Bildung: Wirtschaft in deutschen Entwicklungsromanen von Goethe bis Heinrich Mann*. Würzburg: Königshausen & Neumann, 2017.

Robertson, Ritchie. "Modernism and the Self 1890–1924." In *Philosophy and German Literature, 1700–1990*, edited by Nicholas Saul, 150–96. Cambridge: Cambridge University Press, 2002.

———. "Savonarola in Munich: A Reappraisal of Thomas Mann's *Fiorenza*." *Publications of the English Goethe Society* 74, no. 1 (2005): 51–66.

Rochau, August Ludwig von. *Grundsätze der Realpolitik angewendet auf die staatlichen Zustände Deutschlands*. 2nd ed. Stuttgart: Karl Göpel, 1859.

Roethlisberger, Fritz J. "The Foreman: Master and Victim of Double Talk." *Harvard Business Review* 23, no. 3 (1945): 283–98.

Roper, Katherine Larson. "Conrad Alberti's *Kampf ums Dasein*: The Writer in Imperial Berlin." *German Studies Review* 7, no. 1 (1984): 65–88.

Ross, Corey. *Media and the Making of Modern Germany: Mass Communications, Society, and Politics from the Empire to the Third Reich*. Oxford: Oxford University Press, 2008.

Ross, George H. *Trump-Style Negotiation: Powerful Strategies and Tactics for Mastering Every Deal*. Hoboken, NJ: Wiley, 2006.

Rutschky, Katharina, ed. *Schwarze Pädagogik: Quellen zur Naturgeschichte der bürgerlichen Erziehung*. Frankfurt am Main: Ullstein, 1987.

Sachse, Carola. *Siemens, der Nationalsozialismus und die moderne Familie: Eine Untersuchung zur sozialen Rationalisierung in Deutschland im 20. Jahrhundert*. Hamburg: Rasch und Röhring, 1990.

———. "Zwangsarbeit jüdischer und nichtjüdischer Frauen und Männer bei der Firma Siemens 1940 bis 1945." *Internationale wissenschaftliche Korrespondenz zur Geschichte der deutschen Arbeiterbewegung* 27 (1991): 1–12.

Salber, Linde. *Nicht ohne Utopie: Die wahre Geschichte des Hermann Kant. Biographie*. 2nd ed. Ochsenfurt: Kulturmaschinen Verlag, 2015.

Saller, Reinhard. *Schöne Ökonomie: Die poetische Reflexion der Ökonomie in frühromantischer Literatur*. Würzburg: Königshausen & Neumann, 2007.

Scarry, Elaine. *The Body in Pain: The Making and Unmaking of the World* [1985]. Oxford: Oxford University Press, 1987.

Schaffner, Anna Katharina. "'Catastrophe Sociology' and the Metaphors We Live By: On Kathrin Röggla's *wir schlafen nicht*." *Modern Language Review* 112, no. 1 (2017): 205–22.

Schlesinger, Philip. "The Creative Economy: Invention of a Global Orthodoxy." *Innovation: The European Journal of Social Science Research* 30, no. 1 (2017): 73–90.

Schluchter, Wolfgang. *Paradoxes of Modernity: Culture and Conduct in the Theory of Max Weber*. Translated by Neil Solomon. Stanford, CA: Stanford University Press, 1996.

Schmidt, Kirstin. "Sieben Erfolgsfaktoren für die perfekte Rede." *Wirtschaftswoche*, February 24, 2017. http://www.wiwo.de/erfolg/coach/optimierung/rhetorik-sieben-erfolgsfaktoren-fuer-die-perfekte-rede/19367322-all.html.

Schmidt, Thomas E. "Der eigene Körper als Feind." *Die Zeit*, January 23, 2014, 47.

Schneider, Jost. *Die Kompositionsmethode Ingeborg Bachmanns: Erzählstil und Engagement in "Das dreißigste Jahr," "Malina" und "Simultan."* Bielefeld: Aisthesis, 1999.

Schofield, Benedict. "Gustav Freytag's *Soll und Haben*: Politics, Aesthetics, and the Bestseller." In Woodford and Schofield, *The German Bestseller in the Late Nineteenth Century*, 20–38.

Schön, Manfred. "Gustav Schmoller and Max Weber." In *Max Weber and His Contemporaries*, edited by Wolfgang J. Mommsen and Jürgen Osterhammel, 59–70. London: Allen & Unwin, 1987.

Schonfield, Ernest. *Art and Its Uses in Thomas Mann's "Felix Krull."* London: Maney/MHRA, 2008.

———. "*Buddenbrooks* as Bestseller." In Woodford and Schofield, *The German Bestseller in the Late Nineteenth Century*, 94–112.

———. "The Idea of European Unity in Heinrich Mann's Political Essays of the 1920s and Early 1930s." In *Europe in Crisis: Intellectuals and the European Idea, 1917–1957*, edited by Mark Hewitson and Matthew D'Auria, 257–70. New York: Berghahn, 2012.

———. "Wirtschaftlicher Strukturwandel in Theodor Fontanes *Der Stechlin*." In *Theodor Fontane: Dichter des Übergangs*, edited by Patricia Howe, 91–108. Würzburg: Königshausen & Neumann, 2013.

Schönpflug, Wolfgang. "Rieffert, Johann Baptist." In *Deutschsprachige Psychologinnen und Psychologen 1933–45*, edited by Uwe Wolfradt, Elfriede Billmann-Mahecha, and Armin Stock, 368–70. Wiesbaden: Springer Fachmedien, 2015.

Schönström, Rikard. "Quotes as Commodities: The Use of Slogans in Bertolt Brecht's and Kurt Weill's *Mahagonny*." Lecture given on June 26, 2016, at the "Recycling Brecht Conference, 15th Symposium of the International Brecht Society," St. Hugh's College, University of Oxford.

Schößler, Franziska. *Börsenfieber und Kaufrausch: Ökonomie, Judentum und Weiblichkeit bei Theodor Fontane, Heinrich Mann, Thomas Mann, Arthur Schnitzler und Émile Zola*. Bielefeld: Aisthesis, 2009.

———. "Ökonomie." In *Literatur und Wissen: Ein interdisziplinäres Handbuch*, edited by Roland Borgards, Harald Niemeyer, Nicolas Pethes, and Yvonne Wübben, 101–5. Stuttgart: Metzler, 2013.

Schöttker, Detlev. *Bertolt Brechts Ästhetik des Naiven*. Stuttgart: Metzler, 1989.

Schröter, Klaus. *Heinrich Mann: "Untertan"—"Zeitalter"—Wirkung: Drei Aufsätze*. Stuttgart: Metzler, 1971.

Schultze-Jena, Christiane. "Roman und Reportage: Zum Zeitroman am Ende der Weimarer Republik, dargestellt an Gabriele Tergits Roman 'Käsebier erobert den Kurfürstendamm.'" Magisterarbeit, Universität Hamburg, 1988–89.

Schütz, Erhard. *Romane der Weimarer Republik*. Munich: Fink, 1986.

Scott, Joan W. "Experience." In *Feminists Theorize the Political*. Edited by Judith Butler and Joan W. Scott, 22–40. London: Routledge, 1992.

Sennett, Richard. *The Corrosion of Character: The Personal Consequences of Work in the New Capitalism*. New York: Norton, 1998.

Shearer, J. Ronald. "Talking about Efficiency: Politics and the Industrial Rationalization Movement in the Weimar Republic." *Central European History* 28, no. 4 (1995): 483–506.

Short, John Phillip. *Magic Lantern Empire: Colonialism and Society in Germany*. Ithaca, NY: Cornell University Press, 2012.

Skinner, Quentin. *Reason and Rhetoric in the Philosophy of Hobbes*. Cambridge: Cambridge University Press, 1996.

Sprengel, Peter. *Literatur im Kaiserreich: Studien zur Moderne*. Berlin: Erich Schmidt, 1993.

Stallwood, Oliver. Interview with Moray MacLennan. *Metro*, Wednesday, February 14, 2018, 28.

Statista. "Statistiken zur Dienstleistungsbranche." Acessed December 6, 2017. https://de.statista.com/themen/1434/dienstleistungsbranche/. Acessed December 6, 2017.

Steel, Catherine. *Cicero, Rhetoric, and Empire*. Oxford: Oxford University Press, 2001.

———. "Divisions of Speech." In Gunderson, *Cambridge Companion to Ancient Rhetoric*, 77–91.

Stein, Max. "Report on the Employment of Slave Work by the Siemens Concern during World War II." Office of the Conference on Jewish Material Claims against Germany, Frankfurt am Main. Cited in Wiesen, *West German Industry*, 25.

Steiner, André. *The Plans That Failed: An Economic History of the GDR*. Translated by Ewald Osers. New York: Berghahn, 2010.

Stephan, Inge. "Stadt ohne Mythos: Gabriele Tergits Berlin-Roman *Käsebier erobert den Kurfürstendamm*." In *Neue Sachlichkeit im Roman: Neue Interpretationen zum Roman der Weimarer Republik*, edited by Sabina Becker and Christoph Weiß, 291–313. Stuttgart: Metzler, 1995.

Sternheim, Carl. "Die Deutsche Revolution" [1918]. In *Gesamtwerk*, 10 vols., edited by Wolfgang Emrich, 6:71–86. Neuwied am Rhein: Luchterhand, 1966–76.

Stratas, Teresa. Notes to CD of *Lotte Lenya Sings Kurt Weill's "The Seven Deadly Sins" ("Die sieben Todsünden")*. Sony Classical MHK 63222, 1997.

Streeck, Wolfgang. *Gekaufte Zeit: Die vertagte Krise des demokratischen Kapitalismus. Frankfurter Adorno-Vorlesungen 2012*. Berlin: Suhrkamp, 2013. Translated by Patrick Camiller as *Buying Time: The Delayed Crisis of Democratic Capitalism*. London: Verso, 2014.

———. "How Will Capitalism End?" *New Left Review* 87 (2014): 35–64.

———. *Re-Forming Capitalism: Institutional Changes in the German Political Economy*. Oxford: Oxford University Press, 2009.

Sucker, Juliane. *"Sehnsucht nach dem Kurfürstendamm": Gabriele Tergit— Literatur und Journalismus in der Weimarer Republik und im Exil*. Würzburg: Königshausen & Neumann, 2015.

Sutton, Fiona (née Littlejohn). "Models of Modernity: Readings of Selected Novels of the Late Weimar Republic." PhD diss., University of Nottingham, 2001.

———. "Weimar's Forgotten Cassandra: The Writings of Gabriele Tergit in the Weimar Republic." In *German Novelists of the Weimar Republic: Intersections of Literature and Politics*, edited by Karl Leydecker, 193–209. Rochester, NY: Camden House, 2006.

Swales, Martin. *Buddenbrooks: Family Life as the Mirror of Social Change*. Boston: Twayne, 1991.

Theaker, Alison, ed. *The Public Relations Handbook*. 3rd ed. London: Routledge, 2008.

Thomas, Alexander. "Interkulturalität und Unternehmen." In *Orte der Diversität: Formate, Arrangements und Inszenierungen*, edited by Cristina Allemann-Ghionda and Wolf-Dietrich Bukow, 221–40. Wiesbaden: VS Verlag, 2011.

Thomas, Alexander, and Mona Scheuermeyer. *Beruflich in Kanada: Trainingsprogramm für Manager, Fach- und Führungskräfte*. Göttingen: Vandenhoeck & Ruprecht, 2006.

Thomas, R. Hinton, and Wilfried van der Will. *The German Novel and the Affluent Society*. Manchester, UK: Manchester University Press, 1968.

Thompson, Peter. *Persuading Aristotle: A Masterclass in the Timeless Act of Strategic Persuasion in Business*. London: Kogan Page, 1999.

Tokumitsu, Miya. "In the Name of Love." *Jacobin Magazine*, January 12, 2014: https://www.jacobinmag.com/2014/01/in-the-name-of-love/.

Touraine, Alain. *La société post-industrielle: Naissance d'une société.* Paris: Denoël, 1969.

Travers, Martin. *Thomas Mann.* Basingstoke: Macmillan, 1992.

Tribe, Keith. *The Economy of the Word: Language, History, and Economics.* Oxford: Oxford University Press, 2015.

Tucholsky, Kurt. "Mit Rute und Peitsche durch Preußen-Deutschland." In Werner, *Heinrich Mann: Texte zu seiner Wirkungsgeschichte*, 108–13.

———. [Ignaz Wrobel, pseud.]. "Presse und Realität." *Die Weltbühne*, no. 41, October 13, 1921, 373.

Ueding, Gert, ed. *Historisches Wörterbuch der Rhetorik.* 12 vols. Tübingen: Niemeyer, 1992–2015.

———. *Moderne Rhetorik: Von der Aufklärung bis zur Gegenwart.* 2nd ed. Munich: Beck, 2009.

Ullrich, Volker. *Hitler: Ascent 1889–1939.* Translated by Jefferson Chase. London: Bodley Head, 2016.

Umbach, Maiken. *German Cities and Bourgeois Modernism, 1890–1924.* Oxford: Oxford University Press, 2009.

Vestberg, Torbjörn, Roland Gustafson, Liselotte Maurex, Martin Ingvar, and Predrag Petrovic. "Executive Functions Predict the Success of Top-Soccer Players." *Public Library of Science (PLOS) One* 7, no. 4 (2012). http://journals.plos.org/plosone/article?id=10.1371/journal.pone.0034731.

Vogl, Joseph. *Das Gespenst des Kapitals.* Zurich: Diaphanes, 2010. Translated by Joachim Redner and Robert Savage as *The Specter of Capital.* Stanford, CA: Stanford University Press, 2015.

———. *Kalkül und Leidenschaft: Poetik des ökonomischen Menschen.* Zurich: Diaphanes, 2002.

———. *Der Souveränitätseffekt.* Zurich: Diaphanes, 2015.

Vogt, Jochen. *Thomas Mann: "Buddenbrooks."* Munich: Wilhelm Fink, 1983.

Vrasti, Wanda. "Working in Prenzlau." *New Left Review* 101 (2016): 49–61.

Wagener, Hans. *Gabriele Tergit: Gestohlene Jahre.* Schriften des Erich Maria Remarque-Archivs 28. Göttingen: V & R unipress, 2013.

Wallraff, Günter. *"Wir brauchen dich": Als Arbeiter in deutschen Industriebetrieben.* Munich: Rütten & Loening, 1966.

Wallraff, Günter, and Jens Hagen. *Was wollt ihr denn, ihr lebt ja noch: Chronik einer Industrieansiedlung.* Reinbek bei Hamburg: Rowohlt, 1973.

Wapshott, Nicholas. *Keynes—Hayek: The Clash That Defined Modern Economics.* New York: Norton, 2011.

Warhurst, Chris, and Dennis Nickson. *Looking Good, Sounding Right: Style Counselling in the New Economy.* London: The Industrial Society, 2001.

———. "'Who's Got the Look?' Emotional, Aesthetic and Sexualized Labour in Interactive Services." *Gender, Work and Organization* 16, no. 3 (2009): 385–404.

Wegmann, Thomas. *Tauschverhältnisse: Zur Ökonomie des Literarischen und zum Ökonomischen in der Literatur von Gellert bis Goethe.* Würzburg: Königshausen & Neumann, 2002.

Wehler, Hans-Ulrich. *Deutsche Gesellschaftsgeschichte.* 5 vols. Munich: Beck, 2003.

Weick, Karl E., and Kathleen M. Sutcliffe. *Managing the Unexpected: Sustained Performance in a Complex World.* 3rd ed. Hoboken, NJ: Wiley, 2015.

Weigel, Sigrid. *Ingeborg Bachmann: Hinterlassenschaften unter Wahrung des Briefgeheimnisses.* Vienna: Zsolnay, 1999.

Weißenberger, Barbara, interviewed by Georg Giersberg. "Der Betriebswirt: Englisch forschen und deutsch lehren." *Frankfurter Allgemeine Zeitung,* August 15, 2016, 18.

Wendler, Eugen. *Friedrich List (1789–1846): A Visionary Economist with Social Responsibility.* Berlin: Springer, 2014.

Werner, Renate, ed. *Heinrich Mann: Texte zu seiner Wirkungsgeschichte in Deutschland.* Munich: Deutscher Taschenbuch Verlag, 1977.

Widdig, Bernd. *Culture and Inflation in Weimar Germany.* Berkeley: University of California Press, 2001.

Wiesen, S. Jonathan. *West German Industry and the Challenge of the Nazi Past, 1945–1955.* Chapel Hill: University of North Carolina Press, 2001.

Wikipedia. "List of Countries by Exports." Last modified on February 16, 2018. https://en.wikipedia.org/wiki/List_of_countries_by_exports.

Wizisla, Erdmut, Helgrid Streidt, and Heidrun Loeper, *Die Bibliothek Bertolt Brechts: Ein kommentiertes Verzeichnis.* Frankfurt am Main: Suhrkamp, 2007.

Wolf, Christa. "Die zumutbare Wahrheit: Prosa der Ingeborg Bachmann" [1966]. In *Lesen und Schreiben,* 121–34. Darmstadt: Luchterhand, 1972. Translated as "Truth That Can Be Faced: Ingeborg Bachmann's Prose." In *The Reader and the Writer,* 83–96. Berlin/DDR: Seven Seas, 1977.

Wolf, S., and R. Baber. "Verkaufsrhetorik." In Ueding, *Historisches Wörterbuch der Rhetorik,* vol. 9: *St-Z,* 1074–82.

Woodford, Charlotte, and Benedict Schofield, eds. *The German Bestseller in the Late Nineteenth Century.* Rochester, NY: Camden House, 2012.

Woodmansee, Martha, and Mark Osteen, eds. *The New Economic Criticism: Studies at the Intersection of Literature and Economics.* New York: Routledge, 1999.

Wrobel, Dieter. "Mediensatire wider die Entpolitisierung der Zeitung. Journalismuskritik in Romanen von Gabriele Tergit und Erich Kästner." In *"Laboratorium Vielseitigkeit": Zur Literatur der Weimarer Republik. Festschrift für Helga Karrenbrock zum 60. Geburtstag*, edited by Petra Josting and Walter Fähnders, 267–86. Bielefeld: Aisthesis, 2005.

Young, Christopher. "East versus West: Olympic Sport as a German Cold War Phenomenon." In *Divided, but Not Disconnected: German Experiences of the Cold War*, edited by Tobias Hochscherf, Christoph Laucht, and Andrew Plowman, 148–62. New York: Berghahn, 2010.

Index

Abelshauser, Werner, 12, 205n89, 210n18, 214n81
accountants, 6
accounting, 205n92
Achberger, Karen R., 111, 224nn61–63, 226n85
administration, 154, 158, 159
administrators, 3, 57, 127, 166
Adorno, Theodor W., 99
advertising, 6, 14, 61, 68, 72, 73, 83, 133, 140–42, 159, 160, 161, 172
aesthetic labor, 179, 240n36
aesthetics, 4, 39, 67, 73, 98, 99, 112, 145
agency, 11
agon, 22, 173, 185. *See also* competition
Alberti, Conrad, 46, 212nn40–43
alienation, 109, 154
alienation effect. *See* *Verfremdungseffekt*
Allen, Michael Thad, 233n75
Allies, 12, 90, 143
Alter, Reinhard, 212n61
alter ego, 80, 89, 98, 101, 113
Althusser, Louis, 7
ambition, 44, 45, 46, 54, 63, 131, 142, 146, 181
America, United States of: American market, 15; authorities, 152; business, 134, 235n18; export economy, 11; public opinion, 82; teaching of rhetoric, 5; US Navy, 175; variety of capitalism, 159
Anders, Lutz-Christian, 237n46
Andersen, Hans Christian, 68, 159
Anderson, Chris, 177, 239nn26–27
Andriopoulos, Stefan, 211n20, 229n2

anecdotes, 123–24, 125, 126–27, 164, 228n34, 237n44
anti-Semitism, 6, 54, 71, 85, 144
Antoni, Klaus, 177, 239n32
appearances, 17, 20, 22–23, 27, 38, 39, 63, 170, 179
Apple, 191
appropriation, 109
Aretino, Pietro, 51
argument, 3, 6, 7–8, 35, 49, 80, 81, 85, 167, 170, 185; central argument of this book, 81, 122; to change the rules, 8; essence of rhetoric, 185; *ethos* takes precedence, 162–63; how human thought proceeds, 8; invention of, 37; in *Malina*, 118–19; neoliberal, 89; noneconomic, 6, 17, 87; open-ended, 18; planning, 126; store of, 84, 136, 148–49; training, 165; weighing them up, 16. *See also* debate; *logos*
aristocracy, 12, 25, 42, 53, 70, 81, 106, 142, 208n18
Aristotle, 2–3, 6, 7, 18, 21, 48–49, 64, 78, 80, 136–37, 162, 163, 177–78, 179, 195, 239n27
arms dealing, 105, 148
arms race, 147–49
Arntzen, Helmut, 211n26
Arp, Agnès, 120, 226n2
artists, 13, 21–22, 25, 36, 39, 46, 60, 67, 99, 207n7, 210n9
asceticism, 22, 26, 164, 181, 231n36
assessment, 18, 165, 174–76
assessment center, 18, 172, 174–76
Athens, 81, 89, 152
athletes, 18, 172, 174, 176, 181–84, 193, 194, 238n8, 240nn44–49, 241n54

Cicero, Marcus Tullius, works by:
Catilinarian orations, 35–37,
209n41, 209n46; *De inventione* (*On
Invention*), 4, 209n45; *De Officiis*
(*The Offices*), 201n22; *De Oratore*
(*On the Ideal Orator*), 35, 83, 84,
120, 166, 174, 180, 209n38,
229n43, 237n56, 238n15, 240n40;
Pro Roscio Amerino (*On Behalf of
Roscius of Ameria*), 220n75
Cicero, Quintus Tullius, 150, 234n84
circumlocution, 18, 125–26
citizens, 21, 23, 36, 44, 84, 121, 124,
237n56. *See also Bürger*
citizenship, 139
Claas, Herbert, 87, 219n43
Clarke, David, 154, 235n10
class, 4, 13, 24, 38, 40, 42, 57, 58,
59, 60, 67, 69, 83, 89, 124, 145,
166, 183, 184, 208n17, 229n43
class struggle, 67, 73, 121, 128
Claßen, Ludger, 217n6
classical rhetoric, 1–7, 17, 18, 20,
21–22, 27, 34–38, 46–47, 56,
79–81, 84–86, 88, 89, 92, 122,
124, 130, 136, 139, 154, 157–58,
161–62, 165, 166–68, 173–74,
177, 179–80, 187, 193, 194, 195,
200n9, 201n29, 209n40
Classicism, 119
Clausewitz, Carl von, 88, 219n45
clichés, 66, 78, 84, 85, 89, 100, 117,
118
coaches, 172, 179, 180–83, 186–88,
190, 194
coercion, 106, 180
cognition, 8, 87, 105, 112, 182
coins, 116, 117
Cold War, 14, 15, 133, 229n46
collective bargaining, 154, 189
comedy, 35, 60
commerce, 12, 21, 22, 25, 55, 116.
See also business
commodity, 10, 72, 108, 110, 115,
188, 218n24
commonplaces, 18, 48, 84–85, 122,
124, 132, 136–37, 230n19,
231n20

communication, 2–3, 8, 21, 92–93,
124, 125, 127, 153, 154, 159, 162,
164, 165, 166, 168, 170, 172–74,
176–80, 183, 185, 189–91, 196,
200n12, 204n77, 215n10, 239n27–
28
communicative rationality, 7. *See also*
argument
communism, 10, 28, 60, 86, 96–97,
144, 190, 225n66
compensation, 54, 143, 232n46
competence, 162, 165, 167, 177, 187
competing spheres, 101
competition, 12, 22, 58, 69, 106, 107,
131, 154, 173, 184–87, 189. See
also *agon*; *Wettbewerb*
competitiveness, 22, 44, 120, 154,
181, 185, 188
competitors, 33, 59, 68, 94–95, 96,
156
complicity, 122, 143–46, 197,
227n10, 227n18
computers, 191
concentration camps, 143, 146. *See
also* Auschwitz; Ravensbrück;
Sachsenhausen
confession, 75
connections (between art and
commerce), 22, 142
connections (between business,
politics, and creative language), 1, 2,
81, 122, 195
connections (between language and
power), 78, 196
connections (personal/business), 42,
58, 59, 62, 91, 141, 150, 156, 164,
228n31
Connolly, Joy, 218n26
Conrad, Joseph, 218n7
conscience, 27–28, 32, 67, 75, 100,
242n78
consensus, 2, 7, 8, 55, 191, 192
conservatism, 47, 66, 136, 145
conservatives, 37, 41, 42, 55, 66, 136
construction industry, 6, 59, 68, 70,
71, 72
construction of identity, 6, 43, 82,
209n3

value systems, 100, 101, 122
value-judgment dispute, 66
values (corporate), 186, 188, 192, 193
values (moral), 1, 2, 7, 17, 36, 48, 58, 60, 62, 63, 65, 66, 67, 74, 101, 102, 104, 115, 122, 124, 130, 137, 139, 163, 177, 197, 230n10
Vanderbilt, Cornelius, 86
Veblen, Thorstein, 24, 208n17
Verfremdungseffekt, 113
Vergangenheitsbewältigung, 144
Vestberg, Torbjörn, 240n51
Vienna, 13, 66, 100, 107, 112, 114, 116, 117
Vienna Circle, 87–88
Vietnam War, 99
violence, 67, 93, 100, 102, 106, 108, 176, 234n81
vir bonus, 48, 80
vocal delivery. *See* delivery
vocation, 26, 101, 103
Vogl, Joseph, 3, 186, 199n1, 201nn27–28, 234n86
Vogt, Jochen, 207n6
voice, 6, 18, 45, 92, 105, 109, 111, 116, 150, 165–66, 179–80, 193, 236n27, 240n38, 240n40
voice disorders, 237n46
voice loss, 116, 165–66. *See also* speech impediments
Volkseigene Betriebe (VEBs, Publicly Owned Operations), 120, 226n2
Vollmar, Georg, 53
Vorwärts, 122
Vrasti, Wanda, 187, 242nn81–85

Wagener, Hans, 215n12, 217n56
Wagner, Richard, 38, 180, 209n40
Wall Street Crash, 57, 60
Wallraff, Günter, 133, 206n115
Walser, Martin, 206n115
Wander, Maxie, 133
Wapshott, Nicholas, 203n69
war, 3, 14, 15, 37, 54, 74, 83, 88, 90, 99, 100–103, 106, 112, 121, 127, 133, 134, 139, 143–44, 146–49, 151, 156–57, 163, 173

Warhurst, Chris, 240n35–36
Weber, Anne, 206n115
Weber, Max, 17, 22, 25–27, 50, 55, 66–67, 99, 100–102, 104–6, 117, 120, 134, 164, 181, 208n19, 216n32–34
Weber, Max, works by: "Die drei reinen Typen der legitimen Herrschaft" ("The Three Types of Legitimate Rule"), 50, 105, 223n38; *Die protestantische Ethik* (*The Protestant Ethic*), 22, 25–27, 164, 181, 208n20–24, 231n36; "Der Sinn der 'Wertfreiheit'" ("The Meaning of Freedom from Value Judgment"), 214n83; *Wirtschaft und Gesellschaft* (*Economy and Society*), 104, 106, 134, 223n33, 223nn42–44, 230n7, 230nn9–10; "Wissenschaft als Beruf" ("The Vocation of Science"), 101–2, 104, 222nn21–24, 222n26, 222n28
Wegmann, Thomas, 199n1
Wehler, Hans-Ulrich, 42, 51, 205n88, 211n21
Weick, Karl E., 235n14
Weigel, Sigrid, 99, 222n12
Weimar Republic, 74, 76, 90, 145, 175
Weiss, Peter, 133
Weißenberger, Barbara, 206n111
Wendler, Eugen, 204n87
Werkbund, 11, 145
Werner, Renate, 210n13
Wertarbeit (quality work), 11, 68
West Germany. *See* Federal Republic of Germany
Westinghouse Corporation, 148, 233n77
Wettbewerb (competition), 99, 199n1. *See also* competition
Widdig, Bernd, 200n6, 219n35
Widmer, Urs, 206n115
Wiesen, Jonathan S., 143, 232nn43–45
Wilhelm I, 49, 52
Wilhelm II, 17, 40–43, 46, 49, 50, 209n3, 210n7–9, 210n16, 220n67